THE PRINCIPLES OF S

CW00457240

The Principles of Social Evolution

C. R. HALLPIKE

CLARENDON PRESS · OXFORD

1988

Oxford University Press, Walton Street, Oxford OX2 6DP
Oxford New York Toronto
Delhi Bombay Calcutta Madras Karachi
Petaling Jaya Singapore Hong Kong Tokyo
Nairobi Dar es Salaam Cape Town
Melbourne Auckland
and associated companies in
Berlin Ibadan

Oxford is a trade mark of Oxford University Press

Published in the United States
by Oxford University Press, New York

First published 1986
First issued in paperback 1988

British Library Cataloguing in Publication Data
Hallpike, C.R. (Christopher Robert)
The principles of social evolution
1. Society. Evolution
I. Title
303.4'4
ISBN 0–19–827596–X

Library of Congress Cataloging in Publication Data
Hallpike, C.R. (Christopher Robert)
The principles of social evolution / C.R. Hallpike.
p. cm.
Bibliography: p.
Includes index.
1. Social evolution. I. Title.
[GN360.H35 1988] 573.2—dc 19 88–9903
ISBN 0–19–827596–X (pbk.)

Printed in Great Britain
at the University Printing House, Oxford
by David Stanford
Printer to the University

Preface

THIS book is in some ways a development of conclusions reached in my previous works on the Konso and the Tauade, and on primitive thought. During field work among the Konso of Ethiopia I became sceptical of the functionalist belief that the institutions of primitive society fitted together like the parts of a watch, each performing some vital task for the good of society as a whole. Their elaborate age-grading system, in particular, was quite unnecessary from a functional point of view, and it was obvious that the Konso could have organized themselves in many other ways, all of which would have allowed them to survive quite adequately in their particular environment and to have enjoyed an orderly pattern of social life. The fact that the Borana Galla (to whom the Konso are closely related historically) had essentially similar social institutions, religious beliefs, and cultural values to those of the Konso, despite a totally different, exclusively pastoral economy, also suggested that, for primitive society at least, the existence of common historical origins was likely to have much greater predictive value about their culture as a whole than any specific features of the environment and local adaptations to it. In particular, I proposed (1972: 164–5, 329–32) that societies were organized in terms of certain general principles which could give them coherency over very long periods of time despite extensive change.

Later experience of the Tauade of Papua also led me to doubt the common assumption that societies must be well adapted to their physical environments. Here was a people with rich resources, and endowed in particular with vast areas of land, who yet in pre-colonial times had one of the highest levels of violent conflict in the world. Their major interest was in raising large herds of pigs which devastated their gardens and produced innumerable quarrels and even homicides, and which were then slaughtered in such quantities that the meat was thrown to the dogs. Enormous labour was spent in erecting imposing villages for these feasts, but after only a few months these villages and their great men's houses were abandoned to decay. Large areas of barren grassland had been produced by unnecessary burning, and it was their traditional practice to keep rotting corpses in their hamlets. No doubt, the Tauade had survived to be studied, but their major institutions and practices seemed to have had very little to do with this fact! It also became clear that the basic principles of Tauade society were typical of New Guinea as a whole, and were systematically different from those of many African societies.

My book *The Foundations of Primitive Thought* showed that it is possible to place some of the major aspects of thought in an evolutionary sequence by applying the conclusions of Piaget and other developmental psychologists to ethnographic data. But while psychology is highly relevant to collective representations, we cannot use it to explain the evolution of social systems, which have their own properties that are independent of the thought processes of individuals. The present work should therefore be construed as parallel or complementary to that on primitive thought, and as a further demonstration of the essential contribution that an evolutionary perspective makes to anthropology. Some of the more general ideas from my study of primitive thought do appear, however, in the present book, particularly the very important idea that the frequency and survival of a trait may be explained by the undemanding nature of the environment and the relative ease of producing it, rather than by its superior adaptive efficiency. I have also found that Piaget's conception of development as a process by which the organism accommodates to the environment, but also assimilates its experience of the environment according to its own structural forms, is applicable, *mutatis mutandis*, to social evolution as well as to cognitive development.

Some of my fellow anthropologists, such as Professor Beidelman (1981), have chided me for not referring to moral values in *The Foundations of Primitive Thought*. I fear that I must again disappoint them on this occasion. The evolution of morals is so difficult a problem that it requires a volume to itself, but now that I have produced an account of social as well as cognitive evolution, I hope that it will be possible to combine the conclusions of these two books in a future work on the development of moral ideas.

C.R.H.
Ancaster
Ontario
August 1985

Acknowledgements

I SHOULD first like to thank the Warden and Fellows of Robinson College, Cambridge, for electing me to a Bye Fellowship which allowed me to spend the Michaelmas and Easter Terms of 1984–5 in their congenial and stimulating company during the completion of this book. While in Cambridge, Dr Joseph Needham kindly allowed me to use the facilities of the East Asian History of Science Library, where I benefited greatly by many discussions with Mr Kenneth Robinson, and especially from his comments on the Chinese section of Chapter VI and the use of some of his unpublished material. I am particularly grateful to Professor Derk Bodde, Professor Emeritus of Chinese Studies in the University of Pennsylvania, for allowing me to read and to quote extensively from his unpublished monograph on Chinese civilization. I should like to make it clear, however, that I alone am responsible for the conclusions drawn from it. Professor Bodde also greatly assisted me by many general and specific comments on Chapter VI, especially the section on China. I am also most grateful to Dr Paul Baxter for allowing me to quote from his unpublished Doctoral thesis on the Borana, and for his comments on my discussion of the Borana in Chapter IV. Professor Rodney Needham and Dr Martin Brett read the whole of the first draft, and made numerous criticisms and suggestions that were of the greatest value in my subsequent revisions. The book would not be the same without their help. Professor P. D. M. Macdonald, of the Department of Mathematics and Statistics, McMaster University, generously gave me many hours of instruction in the statistical analysis of the cross-cultural data in Chapter IV, for which I am extremely grateful. I should also like to thank Dean Peter George, of the Faculty of Social Sciences, McMaster University, for giving me unlimited access to the word-processing facilities of the Faculty, and the staff of the word-processing centre for their very efficient production of the many drafts of the type-script. I am also obliged to the Editors of the *Journal of Social and Biological Structures* and of *The Behavioral and Brain Sciences* for permission to use portions of articles that were originally published in their journals. Finally, I am glad of this opportunity for thanking my wife for her support and encouragement during the five years spent in writing this book, and for her assistance in reading the proofs.

Contents

It may be we are more likely to discover the secret of adaptation and evolution by seeking for it in ourselves than outside human society among animals and plants.

A. M. Hocart

I

Introduction

1. A challenge evaded

ANYONE acquainted with the facts of history, anthropology, and archaeology knows that the organization of human society has changed profoundly in the few thousand years since hunting and gathering were replaced by the domestication of crops and animals. Outstanding among these changes is the vast increase in the size of societies, from the few dozens of hunter-gatherer bands to the hundreds of millions of some modern states. Evidently, the co-ordination of such enormous numbers of persons is likely to require different principles of organization from those which suffice for tiny societies, principles so different and so novel in their structural forms that we are justified in talking not just of social change, but of evolution.

The emergence of the state and of the institutions of centralized government (the most significant of all social innovations) has been accompanied by a general growth in social inequality and stratification, by an ever greater division and specialization of labour, and by a tendency to differentiate functions that once were mingled together—religious and secular authority, or the legislative, judicial, and executive branches of the modern European state, for example. Kinship and other types of ascriptive relationship have ceased to be central organizing principles of society, and there has been what Maine (1861) described as a development from Status to Contract:

Starting, as from one terminus of history, from a condition of society in which all the relations of Persons are summed up in the relations of Family, we seem to have steadily moved towards a phase of social order in which all these relations arise from the free agreement of Individuals. (Maine 1931: 140)

Durkheim envisaged society as evolving from the primitive state of 'mechanical solidarity' to the 'organic solidarity' characterized most completely in modern industrial society. By 'mechanical solidarity' he meant a social order based on a number of homogeneous units, such as clans, that are undifferentiated in function and lack any hierarchical organization, and have an extremely low division of labour. In this type of society there is great uniformity of beliefs and sentiments such that the moral, mental, and social life of the individual is absorbed into the collective whole, and hence there is the lack of any differentiation between the religious and the social. The development of organic solidarity is associated with an increased division of labour and involves a differentiation of social functions, co-ordinated by centralized authority, so that social relations become more individualistic, wider in range, and dependent on occupation rather than attributes of birth. This process accompanies the increase of societal size and density. (Durkheim's two types of solidarity are a development of Tönnies's (1887) distinction between *Gemeinschaft* and *Gesellschaft*.[1])

Membership of a particular culture has ceased to be the necessary basis of a person's religious practice and belief, which have increasingly become a matter of private confession, and the rise of the world religions has been marked by an increased emphasis on general ethical and credal principles at the expense of outward observances, especially those centred on the body.

We also know that these evolutionary developments in society and culture as a whole have been associated with major changes in economy and in settlement pattern, from shifting hamlets to urbanization and the growth of large cities; the rise of professional armies and the use of warfare for political conquest rather than raiding and vengeance; the increase of production for surplus and exchange rather than for consumption alone; the growth of trade and coined money; writing; and the development of ever more potent technologies that have successively harnessed the power of animals, of wind and water, and finally the physico-chemical processes of steam, electricity, and nuclear power. While objections of detail can be raised to all these characterizations of the

[1] The *Gemeinschaft*, 'community', is essentially the small, face-to-face, intimate grouping typical of rural, folk societies dominated by custom and kinship and embracing the whole life of the individual. *Gesellschaft*, 'society', is the opposite, and typified by the impersonal and contractual, large-scale, bureaucratic, and commercial relations of the modern centralized state. The development from mechanical to organic solidarity and *Gemeinschaft* to *Gesellschaft* also involves a general development from 'ascribed' to 'achieved' status, and from 'particularistic' to 'universalistic' criteria of group membership (to use Parsonian terminology).

major changes from primitive society to modern states, as to all such necessarily broad generalizations, there is a good deal of truth in the overall picture which they present.

In view of these extremely obvious facts one might expect that the problem of explaining them would be of central theoretical interest to modern social anthropology, which has traditionally been concerned with the study of primitive society and early states, but this is not the case. Introductory textbooks certainly refer to evolutionary theory, but this is usually presented as a somewhat obsessive preoccupation of Victorian scholarship which, at best, laid the foundations of really valuable modern anthropological theory, such as functionalism (I. M. Lewis 1976: 36–46), and which, at worst, was wild speculation, 'crude over-simplifications of events which can never be known in detail', 'fanciful and sometimes absurd inventions' (Beattie 1964: 7). Some early evolutionary schemes, such as McLennan's (1865) proposed sequence in the evolution of marriage from promiscuity to matriliny, polyandry, and exogamy; from these to patriliny, the levirate, and endogamy; and finally to monogamy and polygyny, are doubtless open to such charges. So, also, is Freud's theory of the primal horde, where

There is only a violent, jealous father who keeps all the females for himself, and drives away the growing sons . . . One day the expelled brothers joined forces, slew and ate the father, and thus put an end to the father horde. Together they dared and accomplished what would have remained impossible for them singly. Perhaps some advance in culture, like the use of a new weapon, had given them the feeling of superiority. Of course these cannibalistic savages ate their victim. This violent primal father had surely been the envied and feared model for each of the brothers. Now they accomplished their identification with him by devouring him and each acquired a part of his strength. The totem feast, which is perhaps mankind's first celebration, would be the repetition and commemoration of this memorable criminal act with which so many things began, social organization, moral restrictions, and religion. (Freud 1938: 141—2, first published 1913).

Such evolutionary speculations were not only fantastic but often ethnocentric, as Kroeber observes:

In these schemes we of our land and day stood at the summit of the ascent. Whatever seemed most different from our customs was therefore reckoned as earliest, and other phenomena were disposed wherever they would best contribute to the straight evenness of the climb upward. The relative occurrences of phenomena in time and space were disregarded in favour of their logical fitting into a plan. It was argued that since we hold to definitely monogamous marriage, the beginnings of the human sexual union probably lay in the opposite condition of indiscriminate promiscuity. Since we accord precedence to descent from the father, and generally know him, early society must have reckoned descent from the mother and no one knew his own father. We abhor incest; therefore the most primitive men normally married their sisters. (Kroeber 1948: 6)

But while many or most of the substantive propositions of the early evolutionists are now rightly rejected, this does not explain why the subject of evolution is now of little interest to social anthropologists; nor, of course, do these easy victories over the Victorian evolutionists do anything to discredit the idea of social evolution itself. Bad theories can be replaced by better theories, and fresh hypotheses can be formulated and tested against new evidence, if the will is there to do it. This, after all, is the normal procedure of science. The current indifference or even hostility to evolutionary concepts has therefore to be explained in terms of contemporary theory, and not by the failure of the pioneers alone.

It is often asserted that evolutionism was opposed by structural-functionalist theory, but this is far from true. Spencer's evolutionary theories are based on a thoroughgoing organic and functionalist philosophy and, as we have seen, the equally functionalist Durkheim held a strongly evolutionist view of society. Radcliffe-Brown, too, generally approved of Spencer's evolutionary theories, and rejected only 'pseudo-historical speculations' (Radcliffe-Brown 1952: 7–9), and there is in fact a very close logical connection between functionalism and evolutionism:

We have seen that both the evolutionists and the structural-functionalists propose that a set of social variables are interrelated. Furthermore, these are, for the most part, the selfsame variables. Both, for example, propose that size, specialization, social organization, economic structure, amount of trade, and the like are associated. Their difference, then, rests in the diachronic approach of the evolutionists versus the synchronic view of the structural-functionalists. But how different are these approaches? If, as the evolutionists propose, one 'stage' of society follows another, the elements at any given level must change together into those typical of the next level. Hence, these elements are interdependent, and the functionalists are correct. And if, on the other hand, certain elements in a culture or society imply others, as the structural-functionalists would have us believe, then any change must involve the transformation from one functionally interrelated set to another. This implies an ordered series of types of society and, therefore, the evolutionists are right. Each of these schemes, then, implies the other; the structural-functionalists stress pattern, and the evolutionists stress change, but they are both talking about the same thing: a set of socio-cultural variables which vary together–an interrelated set of cultural characteristics. (L. C. Freeman 1968: 195. See also Diener *et al.* 1980.)

The writings of the British structural-functionalists, in particular, are filled with evolutionary statements, of which I shall quote a small sample here:

As political organization develops there is an increasing differentiation whereby certain persons–chiefs, kings, judges, military commanders, etc.– have special roles in the social life . . . In Africa it is often hardly possible to separate, even in thought, political office from ritual or religious office. (Radcliffe-Brown 1940: xxi)

Gluckman writes of Lozi law:

Free 'contractual' relations between persons not already united by social position existed, but were proportionately few and unimportant in Lozi life. In this respect a study of Lozi law, as of law in most simple societies, validates Maine's most widely accepted generalization, 'that the movement of [the] progressive societies has hitherto been a movement *from Status to Contract*': i.e. that early law is dominantly the law of status, and as Maine puts it elsewhere, 'the separation of the Law of Persons [from that] of Things has no meaning in the infancy of law [. . .] the rules belonging to the two departments are inextricably [mingled] together, and . . . the distinctions of the later jurists are appropriate only to the later jurisprudence' (Maine 1931: 214–15). We may add that the major part of the Law of Obligation is also 'inextricably mixed together' with the Law of Persons and the Law of Things . . . (Gluckman 1973: 28)

Fortes and Evans-Pritchard, in *African Political Systems*, set up an essentially evolutionary scale of political development (even though they avoid the actual word 'evolution'):

It seems probable to us that three types of political system can be distinguished. Firstly, there are those very small societies in which even the largest political unit embraces a group of people all of whom are united to one another by ties of kinship, so that political relations are coterminous with kinship relations and the political structure and kinship organization are completely fused. Secondly, there are societies in which a lineage structure is the framework of the political system, there being a precise co-ordination between the two, so that they are consistent with each other, though each remains distinct and autonomous in its sphere. Thirdly, there are societies in which an administrative organization is the framework of the political structure.

The numerical and territorial range of a political system would vary according to the type to which it belongs. A kinship system would seem to be incapable of uniting such large numbers of persons into a single organization for defence and the settlement of disputes by arbitration as a lineage system and a lineage system incapable of uniting such numbers as an administrative system. (Fortes and Evans Pritchard 1940: 6 7)

As Goody has summed up the matter: ' . . . despite the many and often justified criticisms of the application of evolutionary doctrine to social facts, only a real flat-earther would now regard the overall history of political systems as static, cyclical, regressive, indeed as anything other than a process of elaboration' (Goody 1971: 20).

Structural-functionalism as such was not, therefore, inherently hostile to evolutionary theorizing, even if in practice its adherents were indifferent to history and were more interested in explaining stability than change. Paradoxically, those anthropologists who advocated a historical approach to the understanding of society, Evans-Pritchard and Boas in particular, were much less sympathetic to general theories of social evolution than were Radcliffe-Brown or Durkheim. So Evans-Pritchard, who could say that without knowing something of its history, 'we view a society in false perspective, two-dimensionally' (Evans-Pritchard 1961: 6), and who quoted with approval Dumont's remark that 'history is the movement by which a society reveals itself as what it is (Dumont 1957: 21)' (Evans-Pritchard 1961: 12), was strongly opposed to any theory of social evolution because he doubted that there were any laws of society at all:

Would it therefore be temerarious . . . to ask ourselves if we should not question the basic assumption which has for so long been taken for granted, that there are any sociological laws of the kind sought; whether social facts, besides being remarkably complex, are not so totally different from those studied by the inorganic and organic sciences that neither the comparative method nor any other is likely to lead to the formulation of generalizations comparable to the laws of those sciences? (Evans-Pritchard 1963: 26–7)

History, therefore, can enlarge our understanding of particular societies, but there is little or no prospect of any comparative generalizations about the histories of different societies that might constitute a theory of social evolution. As is well known, Boas and some of his followers took this particularism to such a degree that they found it more or less impossible to give coherent accounts even of individual societies. So Murdock notes that 'Despite Boas' "five-foot shelf" of monographs on the Kwakiutl, this tribe falls into the quartile of those whose social structure and related practices are least adequately described among the 250 covered in the present study' (Murdock 1949: xiv, n. 5). Lowie, a disciple of Boas, concludes his massive *Primitive Society* with the notorious passage:

To that planless hodgepodge, that thing of shreds and patches called civilization, its historian can no longer yield superstitious reverence. He will realize better than others the obstacles to infusing design into the amorphous product . . . (Lowie 1921: 428)

Obviously, if one regards societies as nothing but jumbles of bits and pieces brought together by the contingencies of history and cultural diffusion, theories of social evolution are indeed a complete waste of time. Relativism, not functionalism, is the enemy of evolutionism. Opposition to the idea of social evolution has probably been fortified by the belief that the notion of social laws is in conflict with our experience of free will. As Evans-Pritchard says,

That there are limiting principles in social organization no one would deny, but within those limits there is nothing inevitable about human institutions. Men have continuous choice in the direction of their affairs, and if a decision is found to be disadvantageous it is not beyond their wit to make a second to correct the first. To deny this is not only to ignore the rôle of values and sentiments but also to deny that of reason in social life. (Evans-Pritchard 1963: 27)

Leslie White, of course, took the opposite view, that all social life and its evolution was totally deterministic and that free will was an illusion, but both he and Evans-Pritchard seem to have shared the assumption that the existence of laws of social evolution, if proved, would be directly relevant to the issue of free will versus determinism.

The simple answer to claims that societies are nothing but amorphous heaps of bits and pieces, or enormously variable, or governed by the unpredictable free wills of individuals, is that if these were true there would be none of those regularities in social change of the kind that we describe as evolutionary. But since such regularities do exist, it is therefore likely that some general principles of social evolution also exist, whether or not we call them 'laws'.

Other anthropologists, such as Nadel, seem to feel that the whole question of social evolution is just too big to handle:

> The truth of the matter is that evolution belongs to those all-embracing concepts which, though inescapable, are too remote from the concrete problems of empirical enquiry to be much use in solving them. We need the concept of evolution, as it were, to satisfy our philosophical conscience; but the 'laws' of evolution are of too huge a scale to help us in understanding the behaviour of the Toms, Dicks and Harrys among societies and cultures, which after all is our main concern. Perhaps, indeed, there are no particular 'laws' of evolution but only one 'law'–or postulate, if you like–that there *is* evolution. (Nadel 1951: 106)

One would make two replies to this: the first is that, like everyone else, anthropologists are guided by vague generalities of a theoretical type in all their work, however empirical, and they will certainly have *some* assumptions about social evolution. One cannot therefore simply avoid theorizing altogether: the only alternatives are to try to make one's theoretical assumptions clear, coherent, and logical, or to sink back into that warm bath of comforting evasions supplied by academic fashion.[2] The second reply is that, as we shall see, it is actually possible to discuss the

---

[2] In the recent opinion of Professor Kuper, at least, the theoretical confusion of contemporary social anthropology is something on which we can all congratulate ourselves. General theory, or 'grand' theory, as he prefers to call it, is apparently like some kind of cosmology, a matter of faith: 'One can spend one's time arguing about essentially theological world-views and occasionally using bits and pieces of ethnographic information to illustrate them, or, on the contrary, one can begin with empirical observations and attempt to relate them to each other' (Kuper 1983: 202). One of his examples of 'grand' theory is the following statement by Marx: 'It is not the consciousness of men that determines their existence, but, on the contrary, their social existence that determines their consciousness.' This is a perfectly comprehensible opinion about the relation between social institutions and individual thought processes, and is also testable, as I showed, for example, in Chapters II and III of my *Foundations of Primitive Thought*. The more general the proposition, the harder it is, no doubt, to select those facts and arguments that are most apt to substantiate or weaken it, but Kuper's attitude to theory seems to rest on a much more eccentric epistemology than this: 'Grand theory is about 'reality', and reality cannot be known through observational techniques, and cannot be reconstituted. One may believe that it has a material location (in the mode of production or in the structure of the brain), but this must remain a matter of faith. Where anthropologists try to reconstruct theories of reality they end up merely illustrating them' (ibid., 204). Whatever all this may mean, Kuper has no doubt that anthropology is somehow progressing: 'We progress through the refinement of methods and models, through (above all) comparison; and the proof of our progress is that we can explain more' (ibid., 204). Just how we decide that one method, model, or use of comparative material is more 'progressive' or 'explains more' than another remains, of course, wholly obscure.

principles of social evolution with considerably more precision than
sceptics such as Nadel believe possible.

One can therefore heartily agree with Maurice Bloch when he
refers to 'this largely negative and vague theoretical attitude of
modern Western anthropologists' towards social evolution (Bloch
1983: 65), and to their 'extraordinary theoretical cowardice' (ibid.,
121):

When we look at the work of these Western anthropologists who would be
most horrified to be labelled evolutionist, we find that their work
continually implies unexamined evolutionary assumptions. The assumption
of evolution exists in the very terms they use, as for example when they talk
of primitives, or pre-literate societies, or of simple societies. This
unexamined evolutionism is also evident when Western anthropologists try
to generalize from their findings. For example, when Fortes states that
descent groups are broken down when states evolve, he is obviously making
an evolutionary statement. Western anthropology is peppered with such
examples. This means that the non-evolutionism of many Western
anthropologists appears to Soviet anthropologists as either laziness or
dishonesty. (Ibid., 120–1)

The curious spectacle of anthropologists who know quite well
that primitive societies are very different from modern industrial
states, yet refuse to discuss social evolution, forces one to the
conclusion that their indifference to the idea not only has very
feeble theoretical foundations (as we have seen), but has also been
strongly influenced by a growing moralistic embarrassment at the
very idea of grading societies on what has commonly been regarded
not just as a scale of increasing complexity, but as a scale of moral
progress.[3] While there would still, perhaps, be general agreement

---

[3] Lord John Russell (1823: vii–x), for example, describes four stages in the
evolution of civil government: the state of savage life; the state of imperfect
government, 'when men are in some degree settled, when property is established;
but the force of government is yet too weak to afford adequate protection to those
who acknowledge its authority'; the state of order without liberty, typified by China,
Persia, India, the provinces of the Roman Empire, and most of contemporary
Europe; and, finally, 'the union of liberty with order' (liberty without order being
essentially the second stage). 'The union of liberty with order, then, is the last stage
of civilization and the perfection of civil society.' There is, of course, absolutely no
reason to suppose that because a particular order of society may be morally
desirable, there must be an inevitable evolutionary tendency to produce it and, as
Lowie said, the very nature of the morally best society is itself a matter of endless
dispute. It is obviously essential, therefore, for moral judgements to be rigorously
excluded from all explanations of social evolution. Some of the Victorian
evolutionists were quite clear that primitive society could in some respects be morally

that human technology has evolved in an objectively progressive way, there would now be very much less agreement that society itself had become better in an ethical sense. More than sixty years ago Lowie expressed the problem as follows:

Tools are contrivances for defiinite practical purposes; if these are accomplished more expeditiously and efficiently by one set of tools, then that set is better. Hence it is a purely objective judgement that metal axes are superior to those of stone . . . But in the sphere of social life there is no objective criterion for grading cultural phenomena. The foremost philosophers are not agreed as to the ultimate ideals to be sought through social existence . . . Democracy has become a slogan of modern times, but it has also roused the impassioned protests of men of genius and of reactionary biologists . . . It is not obvious that obligatory monogamy is in an absolute sense the most preferable form of marriage . . . Of course it is true that social organizations differ in complexity, but that difference fails to provide a criterion of progress. (Lowie 1921; 424–6)

The obvious fallacy here is the supposition that social institutions, unlike tools, can *only* be compared on the basis of morality, and not of efficiency or power or morphological type. Yet it is quite clear that the arts of government and warfare, to take two obvious examples, have undergone a development in sheer efficiency quite as marked as that of technology, whatever our personal opinions on the morality of warfare and the state. And Lowie concedes, of course, that social organization has also become more complex. The claim that society has evolved does not, therefore, imply that the individuals or institutions in societies still in more primitive forms of this development are morally inferior to those of. advanced, modern industrial states–in many cases the reverse may be true. But this long-standing confusion between social evolution and moral progress was increased by the confusion betwen cultural and biological inheritance. So the influence of Darwinism and the belief that culture was the expression of racial characteristics led to the view that social evolution was essentially a struggle between higher and lower races which would lead to the extinction or at least the subjugation of the more primitive. This idea of a sequence of races, in the course of which the lower races were replaced by higher, newer races–as the Neanderthal was by the Cro-Magnon–

superior to civilized society: see, for example, Spencer 1893: II.233–9 and Tylor 1871: I.25–8. There was also an important degenerationist tradition which held that primitive society had been pure and noble, and that social evolution had been accompanied by increasing moral corruption through greed, class conflict, and governmental oppression. Taoism and Marxism are well-known examples of this ancient tradition.

passed into the intellectual orthodoxy of the decades before the Second World War (e.g. Keith 1925: 41), and, as is well known, the pages of *Mein Kampf* are filled with references to the nobility of the struggle between races, and the justification by natural law of the subjugation and extinction of the 'inferior' by the 'superior'. While never accepted by anthropologists, these associations of 'primitive' with, more or less, 'subhuman' have lingered on in the popular mind. So, in response to the accusation by some educated Papua New Guineans that anthropology is demeaning to their people because it deals with 'primitive' societies, Professor Strathern asks:

. . . is the category of 'primitive' at all necessary to anthropology? I think not, in that anthropology does not have to be intrinsically concerned with some hypothetical category of this sort. That does not exclude a legitimate interest in problems of historical evolution of social systems, or a concern, say, with differences between societies with and without literate modes of communication. It is the evaluative (pejorative) dimension of the term primitive which is so unscientific and damaging. It may in fact blind us to the very first principle[4] of a true anthropology: serious respect for other cultures *prior* to any secondary 'judgements' on them. (Strathern 1983: 5)

Since the term 'primitive' was used by every major anthropologist until recent years with no pejorative implications, to refer primarily to societies lacking centralized government and writing, it is difficult to avoid the conclusion that its present odium (and that of evolution) derives from the ethos of the post-colonial world[5] and the relativistic, egalitarian mentality of the age. It has certainly not been discredited by more careful scholarship and more incisive thinking, but is merely politically unfashionable.[6] This being so, the search for euphemistic alternatives, such as 'simple', 'pre-literate', 'tribal' or whatever, is ultimately pointless, for it is not really the words themselves which give offence but their connotation of inequality. So the apparently innocuous word 'tribal' must be avoided in Africa: 'It has come to be used by people who consider

---

[4] Might one suggest that the *very* first principle of a true anthropology should be respect for the truth?

[5] Not surprisingly, the contemporary interest in problems of modernization in newly independent nations has done little to stimulate an interest in evolutionary theory: 'We are dismayed that most anthropological literature dealing with culture change and acculturation generally ignores evolutionary theory in both biology and anthropology . . . (Alland and McCay 1973: 143). But for exceptions to this generalization see the papers in Berringer, Blanksten, and Mack 1965.

[6] For further discussion of why academics especially have been hostile to evolutionism see in particular Campbell 1965: 23–6.

that they are civilized, as a way of describing societies which they do not regard as civilized, and so it is very naturally thought to be an offensive word by educated members of the peoples who are called tribes' (Mair 1962: 14). Similarly, Canadian Indians have recently objected to the description of their traditional religion as 'pagan', but as scientists we cannot allow our researches to be dictated by political fashion and by popular misconceptions about human society and its evolution. To repeat, the concept of 'primitive' when used scientifically in the study of social evolution has no connotation of racial or moral inferiority, and as I have said on a previous occasion there is no other term which is semantically equivalent (Hallpike 1979: vi). In a recent book Professor Leach, however, seems determined to perpetuate these confusions:

It is virtually dogma among social anthropologists of my sort that cultural otherness does not carry with it any necessary hierarchy of superiority/ inferiority which can be appropriately labelled by such terms as 'primitive', 'backward', 'underdeveloped', 'childish', 'ignorant', 'simple', 'primeval', 'pre-literate', or whatever. My interest in the others arises because they are other, not because they are inferior. (Leach 1982: 123–4)

When the concepts of 'pre-literate', 'simple', and 'primitive' are equated with 'backward', 'childish', 'ignorant', and 'inferior', and an intellectual fascination with the origin of things is regarded as a debased desire to gloat over the underprivileged, there is a powerful inducement to take the final step and deny that there is any such thing as primitive society at all:

In my own view there is no significant discontinuity in terms of either structure or form between 'modern' societies and 'primitive' societies. The social anthropologist can find what he is looking for in either . . . is it possible to formulate a useful stereotype of what this notional entity 'a primitive society' or 'a savage (wild) society' is like? The answer is: No! (Ibid., 141)[7]

[7] Goddard (1965), in a paper that owes much to Lévi-Strauss's discussion of the concept of 'primitive' (1963: 101–19), claims that there are no primitive societies at all. But by 'primitive' he means: showing no evidence of any historical change at all (ibid., 261); having no complex social institutions (ibid., 260); and being entirely ordered on the basis of kinship; thus '. . . there is good prima facie evidence that all apparent cases of true primitiveness would turn out, under scrutiny, to be instances of pseudo-primitiveness. That is to say, no existing society is fully grounded in kinship, so none are truly primitive' (ibid., 274). It is obvious that all societies have undergone some social change in the course of their existence, that many primitive societies have elaborate institutions, and that we always find principles of social order in addition of kinship—gender, residence, and relative age, for example. This

It might be wondered what evidence Leach produces to justify this bizarre claim. On pp. 142–5 he considers three 'useless stereotypes' of primitive societies: that they are 'homogeneous', 'segmented' (organized into kin groups), and 'mythopoeic'. His brief discussion of these (highly over-simplified) stereotypes is confused, and irrelevant to the point at issue, and he makes no attempt whatever to confront the overwhelming evidence on all the other aspects of primitive societies that distinguish them from industrial states. All reason and evidence seem to have been overwhelmed by moral fervour.

This denial of social evolution, and even of the very concept of 'primitive society', must in the end deprive social anthropology of any distinctive subject of study at all. For if there is no genuine difference between primitive and modern societies and the essence of social anthropology is merely the study of cultural variations– even those confined to small, face-to-face groups–the social anthropology of the future seems destined to become again what it once was: nothing more than a collection of oddities about exotic peoples, only now the quaint and curious anecdotes are likely to be about tourists in the Pacific, football hooligans in England, homosexual bars in California, street-hawkers in Hong Kong, hippy communes, and any other subcultures whose customs are surprising to middle-class academia.

Fortunately, however, social evolution is much too important a subject just to disappear because it is unfashionable. While it is largely ignored in the major journals and textbooks, a surprisingly large literature has been quietly accumulating in specialist areas of anthropology and on the periphery of the subject.[8] American scholars have been especially prominent, and one thinks of White's *Evolution of Culture* (1959), Steward's *Theory of Culture Change* (1955), Sahlins's and Service's *Evolution and Culture* (1960), Service's *Primitive Social Organization* (1971) and *Origins of the State and Civilization* (1975), Otterbein's *Evolution of War* (1970), Fried's *Evolution of Political Society* (1967), and many other

does not mean that pre-state societies do not have many important characteristics in common, however. But what conceivable purpose is served by setting up an unworkable definition of 'primitive', and then showing that no society conforms to it?

[8] For a summary of some major themes in anthropological theories of social evolution see Dole 1973, and for a more extensive historical treatment of these ideas see Stocking 1968, 1974.

publications referred to in the References. The origins of the state, in particular, have stimulated much evolutionary interest, most recently, for example, Claessen and Skalnik, (eds.) *the Early State* (1978*a*) and *The Study of the State* (1982), and Haas, *The Evolution of the Prehistoric State* (1982). Archaeology, from the very nature of the subject, has not neglected evolution to the same extent as did social anthropology, and in recent years, since Childe (1951), the issue has been the centre of considerable debate, e.g. Renfrew (ed.) *The Explanation of Culture Change* (1973), and Renfrew and Cooke (eds.) *Transformations* (1979). Marxism, of course, has an inherent interest in social evolution, and French Marxists especially have been attempting to apply the basic categories of historical materialism to primitive society. (See Maurice Bloch, *Marxism and Anthropology* (1983), for a convenient general summary, and Bloch 1975, Friedman and Rowlands (eds.) 1977*a*, Seddon 1978, and Terray 1972 for detailed papers.) Finally, since Huxley's paper of 1956, comparing cultural and biological evolution, which had some influence on Sahlins's and Service's *Evolution and Culture* (1960), there has been an increasing number of publications from biologists and biologically minded anthropologists, trying in one way or another to apply Darwinism to social evolution. The rise of socio-biology, in particular, has prompted many publications, such as Lumsden's and Wilson's *Genes, Mind, and Culture* (1981), and Alexander's *Darwinism and Human Affairs* (1979), as well as many others to which reference will be made in Chapter II. The economist Kenneth Boulding (1970, 1978, 1983) has also attempted to explain social evolution in Darwinian terms, and in general one may conclude that, far from having died out with Herbert Spencer, as some social anthropologists might like to believe, evolutionary biology has never been more vigorously applied to social evolution than at present.

Nor is it possible to maintain that social evolution can be treated as just one among a number of specialist concerns, like symbolism or economic anthropology. Social anthropology is nothing if not comparative, but we cannot compare societies on the basis of their resemblances and differences alone. The Nuer have neither writing nor centralized government, whereas the Ancient Egyptians had both, but it is evidently futile to conclude that the two societies are simply different in these respects, since it is obvious that these differences are not just expressions of cultural preference, but also involve different levels of evolutionary development. Unless, therefore, we can distinguish between cultural variation (cognatic versus lineal descent, for example) and differences in evolutionary development, the whole comparative enterprise becomes hopelessly confused.

2. The problem defined

The idea of evolution is much more specific than that of mere change. Evolution implies change in a certain direction, and also denotes a process of unrolling or opening out of something wrapped up (a scroll or bud, for example), and hence, by extension, 'the process of evolving, developing, or working out in detail, what is implicitly or potentially contained in an idea or principle', and 'the development or growth, according to its *inherent tendencies*, of anything that may be compared to a living organism (e.g. of a political constitution, science, language, etc.)'; it also applies to 'the rise or origination of anything by *natural* development, as distinguished from its production by a specific act; "growing" as opposed to "being made" '. (All quotations are from the *Oxford English Dictionary*; my italics.) We are not of course the prisoners of dictionaries: most neo-Darwinian biologists, for example, would deny that biological evolution must have any inherent directional tendency, and while the social scientist might be readier to accept the directionality of social evolution, he would certainly distinguish this from historical inevitability of a kind analogous to the growth of an organism.

Despite these qualifications, however, I shall argue that social evolution is indeed directional, without being deterministic, inevitable, or purposeful, and that it can also be regarded, in certain ways, as a process by which latent potential is realized. It is also, quite clearly, a process involving increased elaboration of structural forms, and for all these reasons we are therefore entitled to talk of social evolution, and not merely of social change.

In some cases, certain institutional or technological forms must precede others, and provide an essential basis for the later forms: thus pictorial scripts must precede alphabets; hunting and gathering must precede agriculture; uncentralized modes of political authority must precede centralized government; and barter must precede the use of money. But we must avoid the temptation of supposing that this is true of all social phenomena, since there are many institutions which cannot be arranged in any developmental sequence: it was the failure to recognize this which vitiated many of the early evolutionary schemes. The great accumulation of ethnographic knowledge in the last eighty years or so has shown us that such institutions as matriliny, patriliny, and cognation; exogamy and endogamy; the levirate and marriage by capture; polygyny, polyandry, and monogamy; or systems of kinship terminology, for example, are all found in a wide variety of combinations that display no developmental features (see especially Murdock 1949: 184–259).

There are, on the other hand, some modes of social order, such as the distinction between sacred and secular authority, or certain types of belief, such as that in a Supreme Being, whose essential features seem able to persist *unchanged* throughout radical alterations in other aspects of social organization and religion.

The study of social evolution must therefore take account of these essential facts from the outset, just as it must recognize that evolutionary development has been extremely uneven in different parts of the world. This is particularly obvious in technology and in forms of government so that the state, for example, has only emerged spontaneously in a minority of societies, while industrialism was first created in one small area of the world alone.

But we observed at the beginning of this book that there are certain features of society which do show a very obvious evolutionary development, such as the dramatic increase in social size, in stratification and inequality, in the division of labour, and in the centralization of political authority. This process has been accompanied by a decline in the importance of such ascriptive principles as kinship in the organization of society, the change in the nature of warfare from raiding and vengeance to political conquest, and a variety of economic changes such as the development of agriculture and the use of metal and more potent sources of energy, the rise of towns and cities, and the development of trade, money, and writing. In so far as these changes seem to be interrelated, to have clear directional properties, and to occur independently in many areas of the world, it is legitimate to ask if there are certain general principles by which such a process can be explained. This question suggests itself with particular force when we consider the independent emergence of so complex an institution as the state (in the sense of the centralization of political authority with the monopoly of armed force) at various times and places.

Our aim, then, is to explain these directional properties of social change, and it will be highly instructive to give particular attention to the evolution of the state, for two reasons. In the first place, the emergence of the state is closely related to those other aspects of social evolution we have just noted, and secondly, any valid theory of social evolution should be able to explain the development of complex institutions as well as general tendencies. It must be emphasized, however, that this book is about the nature of social evolution, not the origins of the state. The discussion of the state is nothing more than an example, or test case, of a general theory, and to suppose otherwise would entirely misconstrue the aims of the book.

The origin of the state and of 'civil government' is one of the oldest philosophical problems, and raises in the clearest form one of the central issues of this book: to what extent can the evolutionary process be attributed to the conscious purposes of man? Various classical thinkers tried to demonstrate that the origin of law and government was in the rational and purposeful reaction of men to the evils of anarchy. So, according to Lucretius, after men attained language and culture, kings founded cities for protection and safety; they distributed riches according to merit, but with the discovery of gold, the basis of envy and vanity, kings were slain and

things came to the uttermost dregs of confusion, when each man for himself sought dominion and exaltation. Then there were some who taught them to create magistrates, and established law, that they might be willing to obey statutes. For mankind, tired of living in violence, was fainting from its feuds, so they were readier of their own will to submit to statutes and strict rules of law. (*De Rerum Natura*, Bk. V, lines 1136–50)

Similarly, for Hume, government originated as a rational response to the anarchy generated by selfishness:

The same self-love, therefore, which renders men so incommodious to each other, taking a new and more convenient direction, produces the rules of justice, and is the *first* motive of their observance. But when men have observ'd, that tho' the rules of justice be sufficient to maintain any society, yet 'tis impossible for them, of themselves, to observe those rules, in large and polish'd societies; they establish government, as a new invention to attain their ends, and preserve the old, or procure new advantages, by a more strict execution of justice. (Hume 1888: 543)

And although Rousseau (in his *Discourse on the Origins of Social Inequality*) suggested that the rich had instigated government for the sinister motive of better protecting their own property, he was in no doubt that government was consciously introduced by general consent for the benefit of all.[9]

These theories are quite correct on two major issues. First, they recognize the essential interdependence between conflict[10] and co-operation which Darwinian theories of social evolution, with their exclusively competitive bias, are incapable either of recognizing or explaining. Secondly, they stress the benefits that government confers on the people as a whole, a truism which has been obscured by the obsession of Marxists, in particular, with the purely exploitative and oppressive aspects of the state. These, of course, are only too obvious in all periods of history, including the present, but no theory of social evolution can ignore the equally important fact that, as we shall see in Chapter V, centralized government could never have come into existence unless the exercise of authority had seemed to confer important benefits on the people who maintained it. (Hume also recognized, as did Plato and Aristotle, the relationship between type of government and the size of society.)

As actual explanations of a social process, however, these theories of the purposeful establishment of the state are manifestly inadequate. While specific institutions and customs can certainly be introduced or modified by the conscious decisions of individual people to attain certain goals, it is quite implausible to suppose that men ever sat down and consciously planned the essential features of the state. In all societies the average person finds it difficult to understand how his own society actually works, and when leaders or those with influence desire to bring about social change, we know

[9] The belief that the state was a conscious invention seems to have survived longer than one might suppose: ' . . . the early American sociologist Lester F. Ward saw the state as "the result of an extraordinary exercise of the rational . . . faculty" which seemed to him so exceptional that "it must have been the emanation of a single brain or a few concerting minds" . . . (*Dynamic Sociology* (1883) 2.224)' (Carneiro 1970*b*: 738 n. 2).

[10] As Dahrendorf has observed, '[Marx] tended to believe that the only way in which social conflicts could produce structural changes was by revolutionary upheavals. But despite such errors he did discover the formative force of conflicting social groups or classes. (Note. Like all discoveries, it is not, strictly speaking, original. It would not be difficult to find, throughout the history of pre-Marxian philosophy from Heraclitus to Hegel, numerous thinkers who regarded 'conflict as the father of all things'.)' (Dahrendorf 1959: 125).

from recent historical experience in particular that the planning of such social change is always apt to confound the most intelligent reformers. The larger the aim, the greater must be the influence of the contingent and the unforeseen, and the harder it will be to secure the compliance of the people. More generally, it can be argued that the very aims of such reformers or innovators are themselves the product of that society which they are seeking to change, since no individual can place himself entirely outside the traditions in which he has been brought up, so that the changes he wishes to bring about must themselves express the underlying and implicit assumptions of his culture. It is even more implausible to suppose that those general evolutionary tendencies which we have already summarized in this chapter could have been co-ordinated by the conscious intention of individuals.

Human mental capacities have, of course, been central to the evolution of society, since they mediate all experience, and it is only through thought that we can define our natural and social environment and the problems of controlling it, but we cannot realistically regard social evolution or such institutions as the state as the result of conscious purpose, which can only operate within a restricted range, and on a short-term basis. How, then, are we to explain the very evident facts of social evolution once we have rejected explanations based on purpose?

In the evolutionary theories of the nineteenth and twentieth centuries at least four main themes predominate. One of the oldest debates is between those who ascribe the development of societies to their internal properties, to certain laws of growth (an 'endogenist' theory), and those who maintain that external factors are primarily responsible (an 'exogenist' theory). Secondly, there is the opposition between structuralism and atomism; structuralism emphasizes the irreducible properties of wholes which cannot be explained by the properties of the parts, while atomistic theories believe that it is possible to understand structured wholes as aggregates of some kind of basic unit or 'building block'. Thirdly, there is the long-standing opposition between Idealists and Materialists; and fourthly, there are deterministic theories of evolution, as opposed to theories that assume the predominant importance of random, stochastic processes. These themes can be combined in a variety of ways.

Not surprisingly, the explanation of social phenomena since the nineteenth century has drawn heavily on biological models. So we observed in the previous section that there is a strong connection between functionalism and evolution. According to this view, ultimately derived from Spencer, societies are functionally integrated systems, in the manner of organisms, so that innovations appear and survive because they meet the functional requirements of society as a whole, and the direction of the evolutionary process thus resembles in some ways the growth and maturation of the individual organism. It is therefore assumed that every institution and custom exists because it makes some essential contribution to the well-being of the society in its struggle for survival in the natural environment and with other societies, and that this struggle for survival will also lead to new and more efficient institutions and inventions. (We should note, however, that while there is an inherent tendency for endogenist theories also to be functionalist theories, this association is not logically necessary. Structures may have other origins than the functional needs of a system.) In endogenist theories the environment is primarily important as the inducer of change *within* the social system: 'According to the endogenous paradigm, external factors are only stimuli; the theoretical interest is centred upon the system's reaction, upon the repercussions for this or that element within it' (Smith 1973: 150).

A second type of biological model, which is significantly different from that of functionalism, is that of Darwinism,[11] which has been widely employed in recent years to explain social evolution (though anticipations of this go back at least to Keller 1915). Essentially, the Darwinian model envisages a population of organisms (or genes in a gene pool), in which some variant forms, whether of gene or organism, are better adapted to the environment than competing forms, thus allowing organisms possessing a more adaptive trait to leave more offspring than those without such a trait, or, allowing genes of one type to spread in the gene pool at the expense of genes of a competing type. Similarly, societies can be represented not as structures but as populations of traits, such as modes of descent, types of residence, forms of political authority and dispute settlement, and so on. There is variation among these traits, and

[11] By 'Darwinism' I should be taken to mean 'neo-Darwinism', the modern synthesis of the classical Darwinian theory of natural selection with Mendelian heredity and population genetics (Abercrombie *et al.* 1973: 191; Huxley 1974; Mayr 1980). The term 'neo-Darwinism' is clumsy, however, and will therefore be used sparingly throughout this book.

some variations will be better adapted to the social (or natural) environment than others, and so will eventually displace the less well-adapted forms. Because culture is transmitted from person to person it follows that there will be errors and innovations in this transmission analogous to mutation in sexual reproduction, and it is not therefore necessary to invoke either structure or purpose: the only requirements are variation and selection. The direction of social evolution, like its biological counterpart, is thus the result of the selective influence of the environment. Following Rindos (1984) I shall refer to this theory as 'cultural selectionism'.

There is clearly much that is plausible in such an explanation of social evolution.[12] We are familiar with many types of institution and invention that have appeared at certain times and places and either displaced existing and competing forms, or else failed to survive. One of the great advantages of this Darwinian approach is that it avoids the problem of explaining just how it is that societies can produce those institutions that are functionally necessary for them, by treating the emergence of novelty simply as a random process that is bound to occur in the transmission of culture from person to person and from generation to generation. And if it is possible for such a theory to explain the development of all the marvellous intricacies of animals and plants, surely it should be relatively easy to apply it to the much cruder systems of human society? Darwinism is therefore a good example of an exogenist, atomistic theory in which the environment plays the role of the selective agency, and is therefore responsible for any directional features of the evolutionary process.

The materialist tradition also stresses the enormous importance of the environment and the technological responses to the problems

[12] Indeed, so simple and powerful does the theory of natural selection appear that one encounters it in areas of scholarship seemingly far removed from biology and anthropology. As D. T. Campbell has pointed out, for example, Popper's theory of knowledge has an essentially Darwinian character, and he quotes the following passage from the *Logic of Scientific Discovery*: 'According to my proposal, what characterizes the empirical method is its manner of exposing to falsification, in every conceivable way, the system to be tested. Its aim is not to save the lives of untenable systems but, on the contrary, to select the one which is by comparison the fittest, by exposing them all to the fiercest struggle for survival.' (Quoted in Campbell 1974: 415.) Similarly the distinguished historian and theorist of art, Professor E. H. Gombrich, writes ' . . we have learned from Darwin that all evolution can be seen in terms of survival of the fittest and a good case can always be made out for applying this approach also to the history of civilization' (Gombrich 1982: 217), and see, in particular, the paragraph following this quotation.

it presents, but this type of theory need *not* assume random variation (any more than did Lamarckism, for example), and also cuts across the endogenist/exogenist distinction. On materialist assumptions one aspect of society, the mode of production and reproduction (commonly referred to as the 'infrastructure'), occupies a key position with regard to the rest of society, whose institutions and beliefs it determines either directly (e.g. Leslie White and Marvin Harris), or ultimately and indirectly (e.g. Marx), Theories such as Marxism that stress the importance of the interaction between different aspects of society (such as the infrastructure and the superstructure) in giving direction to evolution, are more endogenist in type than those of 'vulgar materialism', which regard social institutions as being directly affected by environmental conditions, particularly through the harnessing of energy (White 1959, R. N. Adams 1975). Some materialists may ascribe great importance to selection, e.g. Harris 1971: 152; 1984: 130–3; R. N. Adams 1981.

The four basic themes can therefore be combined in a number of ways, but for our purposes we may regard functionalism, cultural selectionism and materialism as the three most important types of evolutionary theory.

In all these types of theory there are certain common assumptions, notably the importance attributed to adaptation and competition. Indeed, the general idea that culture is inherently adaptive, and that institutions exist primarily because they are useful or functional, is extremely widespread among anthropologists, whether or not they have any clear ideas about evolution. The concept of adaptation will therefore occupy a central position in this book, and we shall see that far from being simple and self-evident (as it is assumed to be in Sahlins and Service 1960: 45–68, for example) it dissolves under analysis into one of the most elusive concepts in social theory. In particular, we shall find good reasons to question the accepted belief that if institutions are common and enduring, this must be because they are adaptive. Alternative explanations will be proposed, and we shall give particular attention to the origins of innovation. It will become clear that the very nature of an environmental 'problem' is much more obscure than materialists suppose, and depends to a considerable extent on cultural definitions of the environment. This brings us to a second common assumption of these three theories: that ideas and systems of belief are mere reflections or epiphenomena of the more 'basic' features of society, especially those concerned with physical survival. This assumption will be examined in Section 2 of Chapter III and in Chapter VI, from which it will become clear that it is highly over-simplified. To recognize the fundamental importance of thought does not, however, commit one to an Idealist type of theory.

While my aim is to explain social evolution without giving adaptation a central position, and therefore by denying the claims of materialism, it must be emphasized that the relations between society and the natural environment will be treated as of the first importance; in my view, however, the environment and man's technological interaction with it are opportunistic rather than deterministic, so that the environment can be regarded as opening up possibilities for human exploitation, rather than as imposing certain solutions, or acting as the prime selective agency in a Darwinian manner.

I shall also advance the view that both the selectionist and the functionalist types of theory are radically mistaken, and that while societies cannot be treated as mere populations of traits, they are not functional systems either; or, more precisely, that they become increasingly functional in the course of evolution, with the state marking a watershed in this process. It might be supposed that by denying both selectionism and functionalism I have left myself no other ground to stand on. In fact, I shall show that it is possible to provide an account of the directional features of social evolution by examining the structural properties of certain common institutions, and the ways in which they can combine together and mutually reinforce one another. To this extent, the old idea of evolution as the manifestation of latent potential is therefore correct, though for reasons quite unconnected with any kind of analogy between society and organism.

In conclusion, then, I shall propose an endogenist theory of evolution, but one which is not a functionalist theory, and in the course of our enquiry the concepts of adaptation, function, competition, variation, and selection will be of fundamental importance. The theory defended will also be of a structuralist type, and in Chapter VI we shall see how it is possible for societies to maintain certain core principles more or less indefinitely despite major evolutionary changes. For it must not be forgotten that continuity over change is also an essential feature of social evolution, and no theory which fails to take account of this can be adequate to the facts.

3. Social structure, causality, and the individual

In the previous section I referred to the concept of 'structure', and claimed to be presenting a theory of social evolution that was, among other things, 'structuralist'. The inherent obscurities in the term require clarification (on a previous occasion I have said that it has generated more dense metaphysical smoke than any other concept in our discipline (Hallpike 1972: 330)), especially since it has important implications for the debate between materialism and idealism, and between individualism and holism.

As J. A. Barnes has said, 'We probably have to resign ourselves to living with confusion about what is meant by structuralism' (Barnes 1983: xi), but the concept in recent years has unfortunately acquired a somewhat modish reputation in anthropology through the work of Lévi-Strauss, from which I should like to disassociate myself. Of course, if we take 'structure' to mean something like 'the idea of the mutual relations of the constituent parts or elements of a whole as defining its peculiar nature or character' (*Shorter Oxford English Dictionary*), then all science is concerned with elucidating the structure of different aspects of nature and society.

But it would be idle to deny that when, for example, systems theorists or sociological functionalists talk of the distinctive properties of structures, of wholes being more than the sum of their parts, and of the impossibility of understanding a part in isolation from the whole, they do have in mind a particular concept of structure, of a kind that is often referred to as 'holistic'. This concept of structure is obviously highly relevant in the case of 'goal-seeking' entities such as organisms, or of purposefully designed machines, or of social systems.

Biological and sociological conceptions of structure will therefore share certain important assumptions about wholes,[13] so that in

---

[13] The philosopher D. C. Phillips (1977) has attempted to deny that the essential or defining properties of parts can be changed by their membership of a whole (the theory of Internal Relations), because in this case knowledge either of parts or whole would be impossible. In so far as he is referring to societies or artefacts at one point in time he is obviously correct: the parts of an engine retain their essential characteristics when the engine is dismantled, and we can establish the essential properties of the parts of an organism or the institutions of a society independently of

biology one finds an important tradition arguing, on structural principles, against genetic reductionism (e.g. D'Arcy Thompson 1917, von Bertalanffy 1971, Webster and Goodwin 1982), as well as a current orthodoxy in favour of it (an extreme position being Dawkins 1978); and a somewhat analogous division of opinion exists in the social sciences between functionalists and individualists, though the balance of opinion in this case is more in favour of holism. These common assumptions and debates are obviously produced by the 'organic' properties shared by social and biological systems, but the differences between these systems, and hence between their respective 'structuralisms', are just as important as the similarities.

According to Piaget, ' . . . the notion of structure is comprised of three key ideas: the idea of wholeness, the idea of transformation, and the idea of self-regulation' (Piaget 1971: 5), which is essentially the same as von Bertalanffy's notion of 'system'. Both Piaget and von Bertalanffy, however, were professionally concerned with the development and adaptation which are characteristic of organisms in relation to their environments, and there is every reason to be cautious in applying their essentially biological conception of structure or system to society, and this is particularly true of the idea of 'self-regulation'. While there are good empirical reasons for treating organisms as efficient, functional, self-regulating systems, there is very much less reason for regarding societies in the same light because they are composed of separate, conscious individuals who are linked by information exchanges and not by bonds of an essentially physical nature. They are thus inherently less stable than organisms, for which metamorphosis beyond certain rigid limits results only in death. Functional efficiency and self-regulation must not therefore be assumed in the case of social systems.

'Structure' will also have special implications for the building of social systems because these are systems of ideas, of meaning. In this respect societies have a number of very important structural

our knowledge of the whole, even though we cannot dismantle either. But when we consider these systems as processes in time, his argument is plainly false, because the essential properties of the parts may well have become changed by their previous interaction with one another in the context of the whole, and may even have been brought into existence as a result of the nature of the whole. Whether or not these interactions have been governed by conscious planning (as in the design of an engine), or by purely systemic processes (an organism), or by a combination of both (a society), is beside the point, which is that in the development of organic and social systems over time, the essential properties of the parts will be altered by the development of the whole.

characteristics: it is very easy to understand the persistence of form over change in content, and all systems of rules, categories, values, and goals easily develop hierarchical forms from the general to the particular. Again, the distinction between core and periphery, the compatibility and incompatibility of organizational and ideological principles, and structural elaboration along different pathways, are all aspects of structure that are particularly relevant to societies as systems of ideas.

On the other hand, the structured properties of societies must not lead us into a characteristic error of some structural-functionalists, who suppose that societies have needs and interests of their own, distinct from those of their individual members. Here I entirely agree with Popper, Agassi, and others who recognize that social systems have properties that cannot be reduced to those of psychology, and that individual actions can have unintended social consequences, but say

. . . 'wholes' do exist (though, of course, not in the same sense in which people exist), but they have no (distinct) interests. These 'wholes' are social groups as well as social institutions — in the widest sense of the word, and covering a wide variety, from customs and constitutions, and from neighbourhoods to states. An institution may have aims and interests only when people *give it an aim*, or act in accord with what *they consider should be its interest*: a society or an institution cannot have aims and interests of its own. (Agassi 1960: 247)

Having emphasized the importance of structure, it is time to revert to the question of causality, and to the importance of individuals in social systems. In this connection the most essential point to bear in mind is that social *structures* cannot be *efficient causes*. It is therefore necessary to recognize that societies have two aspects that are analytically (though not practically) distinct: the structural and the causal. So, we may examine the structural potentials of particular institutions, such as monarchy, or age-grouping, or unilineal descent groups, and so on, yet such structures are not causes because institutions, ideas, values, and even technology cannot by themselves actually *do* anything. In a society the only efficient causes are individual human beings and their artefacts, which bring about the transformation of these various structures. On the other hand, while individuals have the powers of choice, of reason, and of creative imagination because they have brains, they are not absolutely autonomous in these respects. That is, what they do and why they do it are not only the expression of their private motivations, understandings, purposes, and so on, but are also expressions of the institutions, categories, rules, beliefs, and values of the particular society into which the individuals composing it have been socialized, which they did not create as individuals, and which will outlast them. (I discuss the relation between individual thought processes and collective representations at length in Chapter II of *The Foundations of Primitive Thought*.) Structures, therefore, rather like a landscape, are a set of potentialities for movement, facilitating some kinds, impeding others, and prohibiting still others, but never actually compelling movement in any direction. But while these institutions and cultural forms, these structures, cannot do anything because they only exist in the minds and customary activities of real individual people, they certainly possess structural properties that are as objective as those of the material world, and it can easily be shown that some institutions will not fit with others, or can be elaborated in certain directions and not in others. In the same way, belief and value systems have a structure which will be more compatible with some institutions and modes of social behaviour than others, and will develop in some directions more easily than in others. Likewise, certain innovations will not work because they are incompatible with the basic principles of these structures.

Societies are therefore fundamentally unlike organisms because (a) they are systems of ideas, of meaning, and of information flow, as opposed to the material connections within physical organisms, and (b) they are composed of autonomous individuals who may try to use the social system for their own ends, not necessarily for the good of some superorganic entity, 'the society'. The apparent necessity of choosing between the interests of the individual and the interests of society as 'the' explanation of social behaviour and social institutions is thus a false dilemma: 'societies' do not have interests or needs or goals, since these are attributes only of living organisms, but it is still perfectly possible to explain certain aspects of society in terms of the structural principles on which the society is organized and by which, therefore, the actions and thoughts of individuals are affected. Nor need we assume that, because society is composed of individuals often trying to maximize their self-interest, they will necessarily succeed in doing so; or on the other hand that the results of their actions will automatically be functional or adaptive for the society as a whole. Certain features of society, such as the feud, can be explained in terms of the working of systems without any assumptions that the features in question are intended by specific individuals at all, or even functionally valuable.

The fault of various brands of determinism (materialist, idealist, or structural functionalist) is to attribute powers of efficient causality to structures, instead of to individuals. The opposite error, of treating efficient causes as if they could of themselves generate social structures, is committed by naive individualists, such as some psychologists and socio-biologists, who suppose that it is possible to deduce the structure of society from the simple aggregation of individual motives and actions alone.

Social structures are therefore brought into relation with the world by the thoughts and actions of individuals so that there is, on the one hand, a process of accommodation to reality, and on the other the assimilation of that reality to the particular structures of society and its belief system. While in one way social evolution can be regarded as a development of the structural potential of different societies, structures do not develop by themselves, but only by the ways in which the participating individuals interact with one another and with the physical world.

II

Darwinism and Social Evolution

1. Introduction

THE idea that societies have developed according to some regular principles was current long before it was supposed that biological species could ever change. Aristotle, Lucretius, Ibn-Khaldun, Vico, Hume, Hegel, Comte, and Marx all developed theories of social evolution independently of any contribution from biology, many of whose evolutionary concepts have in fact been derived from social prototypes—'competition', 'adaptation', 'selection', 'fitness', 'progress', and so on. I stress the pre-Darwinian origins of theories of social evolution because the overweening claims of sociobiology may have persuaded some that social evolution can properly be studied only in a Darwinian context, with natural selection as the basic explanatory concept.

The idea of social evolution long antedates that of the evolution of species simply because we have, since the beginning of civilization, known vastly more about the history and working of society than about the physical organisms around us. It is too easy to forget that Darwinism is a theory designed to escape as far as possible from the limitations of serious ignorance: we have never observed one species turning into another, and the fossil record, far from being replete with intermediate types, seems strikingly deficient in them (see Stanley 1981); we know relatively little about the ways in which genes interact with one another; and we know even less about the ways in which genes regulate the epigenetic process.

By contrast, in the case of society we have a great deal of evidence on how societies of one type have changed into those of another; we have ample knowledge of the modes of interaction of individuals, and of how socialization occurs, and we also know a great deal about the interaction of ideology and social action, the effects of technological innovation, and so on. The problem for the social scientist is that the wealth of data is almost too great and that the object of his study, society, is a higher-order type of system than those studied by biologists, since it is in a sense an 'organism' of organisms. Thus to apply biological conceptions to social evolution is to try to explain the better known in terms of the lesser known (cf. Ginsberg 1956), rather as though someone were to investigate a society by studying the footprints of its members instead of by observing the actual people and their activities. No doubt the science of Footprintology would stimulate prodigies of explanatory ingenuity and give rise to an impressive body of statistical mathematics, supported by the claim that 'We have here in the footprint the basic unit of social interaction, which can be measured empirically', but no rational person would actually prefer this mode of investigation if it were possible instead to observe the people who made the footprints.

Since societies and organisms share some basic properties of open systems it is, of course, possible to discern some general resemblances between social and biological evolution. This 'Grand Design' approach is typified by Huxley's definition of evolution in general as '. . . a self-maintaining, self-transforming, and self-transcending process, directional in time and therefore irreversible, which in its course generates ever fresh novelty, greater variety, more complex organization, higher levels of awareness, and increasingly conscious mental activity' (Huxley 1956: 3). He notes in the same paper that the evolutionary process involves increasing divergence with increased specialization of organisms as they adapt to particular habitats, but also general progress in physiological efficiency such as in speed of neural impulses, improved sensory apparatus and homeostatic mechanisms, etc. He also notes that evolutionary advance occurs through a succession of dominant types which themselves diverge through 'adaptive radiation' leading to an ultimate stabilization as the possibilities of adaptive development in any organic design are exhausted, and that in the succession of dominant types the new successful group almost always originates from relatively unspecialized members of previous groups. (W. Bray 1973 also lists a number of resemblances between social and biological evolution.)

Sahlins and Service, in their *Evolution and Culture* (1960), were greatly influenced by Huxley's paper, and proposed a distinction between specific evolution, characterized by the increasing divergence and adaptive specialization of particular societies, and general evolution, characterized by a progressive, stage-like, increase in organizational complexity. Their 'Law of Cultural

Dominance' is closely patterned on Huxley's observations on the succession of dominant types, and their 'Law of Evolutionary Potential' follows directly from Huxley's statement that new dominant types emerge from those types that have relatively generalized rather than highly specialized adaptive characteristics. At this point it is important to note that while some of these resemblances between biological and social evolution are valid they are not unique to the organic and cultural realms since something like them is also to be found in the course of *inorganic* evolution, as Herbert Spencer, for example, pointed out in great detail.[1] Thus assuming the validity of the 'Big Bang' theory, the evolution of the physical universe began with an undifferentiated 'quark soup', followed by the synthesis of hydrogen and helium, the emergence of galaxies (of a number of different types), the condensation of stars and the formation of the remaining elements, and the appearance of what might be called an inorganic 'dominant type'—the star with planets. Some of these planets were capable of forming atmospheres and this in turn resulted in meteorological and geological processes of great complexity. Stars, in addition, are known to have 'life' cycles, because they can harness energy in the form of thermo-nuclear reactions. It is not straining language too far to say that the same evolutionary laws of progression from homogeneity to heterogeneity, of simple to complex forms of organization, and local specialization of form, as well as general 'progress' are to be found in the course of inorganic as in organic evolution. But few[2] would claim that the *mechanisms* of this process could be remotely comparable to those of biological and cultural evolution.

My point is that these Grand Design overviews of evolution in general are merely descriptive and have no explanatory force. They suggest that a problem exists and therefore have some value, but they give us no clue to its possible solutions which, in view of the enormous differences between the inorganic, the organic, and the cultural, are likely to be very different in each case. Are anthropologists, for example, greatly helped by the claim that if they saw their subject '. . . in the conceptual framework of combined divergence, stabilization, extinction, and advance, they would reach a truer and more satisfying picture of cultural evolution

[1] See below, Chapter III, Section 1a.
[2] As an example see D. T. Campbell 1974: 420.

than those produced by historians and sociologists like Spengler, Sorokin or Toynbee' (Huxley 1956: 24)? Huxley's reference to divergence, stabilization, extinction, and advance is really nothing more than a list of the implications of *change*. If a set of entities 'changes' even in location and motion this involves the possibility that not all may change in the same way, or as fast as, others ('divergence'); that some types of entity may go on changing while others cease to change ('stabilization'); and that some may disappear altogether ('extinction') while others become relatively commoner ('have greater fitness'). 'Advance' is the only item in Huxley's list that is not implied by 'change', and this item is also highly controversial both among biologists and among social scientists.

The object of this chapter is therefore to show that it is impossible to apply Darwinian principles to the evolution of human society because they are inherently of the wrong type to be applied to socio-cultural systems. At this point it is important to remember the distinction between a truly Darwinian explanation of social evolution and that of a Spencerian, functionalist type. The second tradition emphasizes the structural, organic properties of social evolution, while the Darwinian model emphasizes the notion of society as a population of traits, and evolution as the result of changes in their relative frequency over time through variation and selection. A genuinely Darwinian, or cultural selectionist, account of social evolution, which will concern us in this chapter, is relatively new (as Rindos 1984, Toulmin 1981, D. T. Campbell 1965, 1974, D. Freeman 1974, Alland 1972, Blute 1979, Ruyle 1973, and others have pointed out).

I shall not, however, be much concerned with possible relations between social evolution and human biology, although in general terms, of course, human behaviour and abilities are obviously the result of the genetic constitution of the species. So, I would certainly accept that males are, on average, genetically disposed to be more physically aggressive than females, and that this has an essential bearing on warfare; or, that dancing is naturally agreeable to most human beings, and that this is an important factor in explaining its more or less universal occurrence. But there is no evidence that social change in historical times or differences between societies in specific institutions or aspects of culture can be shown to have a significant genetic basis. Indeed, the extremely rapid rates of social change that are possible, or the ability of people to acquire elaborate skills such as writing despite the fact that their entire ancestry has been non-literate, seem good evidence that social evolution is minimally related to biological evolution. The real interest of neo-Darwinism for the purposes of this book lies in the possibility that its theoretical concepts can be extended to social evolution, not in the exaggerated and often fanciful claims of some sociobiologists about the genetic basis of social behaviour and institutions.

2. Society and organism

Let us first remind ourselves of the basic resemblances and differences between societies and organisms:

(*a*) *Resemblances between societies and organisms*:
  (i) The institutions of societies are interrelated in a manner analogous to the organs of the body, and preserve their continuity despite changes of individual membership, just as individual cells are renewed in organs.
  (ii) There is a specialization of organic function analogous to the social division of labour.
  (iii) In both cases self-maintenance and feedback processes occur.
  (iv) There are adaptive responses to the physical environment.
  (v) In organisms we find the transmission of matter, energy, and information analogous to trade, communication, etc., in societies.

(*b*) *Societies are unlike organisms in the following respects*:
  (i) They are not physical entities at all, since their individual members are linked by information bonds, not by those of a purely physical nature.
  (ii) Societies are not clearly bounded, e.g. two societies may be distinct politically, but not culturally or religiously.
  (iii) Societies do not reproduce, so that cultural transmission from generation to generation is indistinguishable from general processes of self-maintenance.
  (iv) Societies are capable of metamorphosis to a degree only found in organic phylogeny.
  (v) The individual members of a society, unlike cells, are capable of acting with purpose and foresight, and of learning from experience.

   (vi) Structure and function are far less closely related in
        societies than in organisms.
(*c*) *Societies resemble species, not organisms, in that*:
        (i) Species, like societies, do not reproduce.
        (ii) Both have phylogenies and metamorphosis.
        (iii) Both are composed of competing individuals.

Unlike species, however, societies are organized systems, whereas
species are simply collections of individual organisms.

It is obvious that all the *resemblances* are those in which societies
and organisms share properties of *organization* and *structure*:
specialization and continuity of function, self-maintenance and
homeostatic processes, transmission of information and energy,
and adaptive responses to the physical environment. In so far as
organisms and societies share certain properties it has long been
found illuminating to employ organic analogies when discussing
society, so that institution = organ, cell = individual, centralized
government = the brain, communication = the nervous system,
and so on. Spencer, Durkheim, Radcliffe-Brown, and Talcott
Parsons are well known theorists in this tradition which, as we have
already noted, is rather different from true Darwinism, which is
what concerns us here.

So, if we are to apply the theory of natural selection at any more
specific level than that of Grand Design theorizing, it is necessary to
adapt our social theory to those transformational features of
organisms which are the basis of Darwinism. These are, that
organisms reproduce; that they do so by transmission of numerous
particles of hereditary information (genes); that, in consequence,
there is variation between organisms; and that there is competition
between organisms, and in a sense between genes, expressed in a
differential rate of reproduction which is a function of adaptive
success. In this model there are four crucial elements: a distinction
between organism and environment (something which adapts, and
something else in relation to which adaptation occurs); reproduction and self-maintenance as distinct processes; a unit of
selection (the organism or the gene); and a structureless, purely
quantitative concept of 'fitness',[3] which is defined in terms of
reproductive success.

---

[3] It is important to note that the concept of fitness has two related but distinct
definitions; the first, traditional, one is sometimes referred to as 'engineering
fitness'—stronger limbs, more acute eyesight, and so on. The second is quantitative,

But as soon as we try to apply this model of evolution to society fundamental difficulties occur, which derive from the various ways in which societies are quite *unlike* organisms. Thus as Huxley clearly recognized, a society '. . . is at one and the same time both soma and germ-plasm, both a mechanism of maintenance and a mechanism of reproduction or transmission' (Huxley 1956: 9). This is because societies are primarily information systems and not held together by physical linkages as in the case of organisms and are thus immortal. As Buckley expresses it:

The evolution of levels leading up to the sociocultural system shows greater and greater dependence on indirect, arbitrary, or symbolic communication linkage of components and less and less on substantive and energy linkages, until at the sociocultural level the system is linked almost entirely by conventionalized information exchange, with *process* overshadowing any rigid substantial structure such as is found at organismic levels. (Buckley 1967: 50)

The existence of a specific mechanism of heredity is a consequence of organic mortality, and therefore cannot be relevant to systems whose continuity is not dependent on vital processes of a biological type. To put the matter succinctly, we can say that while biological systems have two distinct developmental processes, phylogeny and ontogeny, in social systems these are one and the same. It therefore follows that biologists who apply a statistical, 'gene-pool' model to social systems, and try to estimate the 'fitness' of some social trait by its relative frequency, are guilty of the same sort of absurdity as a sociologist who supposed that retinal cells have less fitness than muscle cells because there are fewer of them. This fundamental misunderstanding of the nature of social systems and their evolution pervades almost all the attempts to explain it in Darwinian terms.

I shall therefore show that such basic Darwinian concepts as the

and refers to the relative reproductive success of organisms with a certain trait: the greater the prevalence of organisms with this trait in the total population, the greater the fitness of the organism in question is said to be. For reservations on the value of the second conception of fitness, see e.g. Waddington 1967: 12–13, and Huxley 1974: 584ff. So Mary Williams also points out that the circularity of " 'What will survive?' 'The fittest.' 'What are the fittest?' 'Those that survive' " is given plausibility by the purely quantitative definition of fitness. Such a definition ignores the equally essential postulate of Darwinism that 'fitness is a property of the relationship between the organism and the environment' (Williams 1973: 90). I therefore agree with her contention that the concept of natural selection is not inherently circular, even though (as we shall have occasion to observe later) it may very easily become so in unreflecting use. For a more general defence of the logical coherence of Darwinism see Caplan 1979.

unit of selection, fitness, adaptation, competition, and mutation are irrelevant to social evolution, in so far as they are given a distinctively biological meaning. 1. Darwinian theory is essentially a theory of differential *reproduction*. But for societies, unlike organisms, reproduction and self-maintenance are one and the same thing, so that there can be no 'basic unit' of social reproduction comparable to the gene, nor, as we shall see, are there any 'basic units' of socio-cultural systems at all. There are thus no *units* of selection.

2. The concept of biological 'fitness' is purely statistical and so can be applied only to structureless agglomerations like gene pools or species. When we are analysing structures, especially those of a non-reproducing kind, however, the differential frequencies of the various components at any point in time tells us nothing of any value about how such structures work, or what their transformations are likely to be in the future.

3. The concept of biological 'adaptation' rests on the distinction between organism and environment, such that the design of the organism accommodates itself to the environment, which *is not itself changed* by this adaptation. But in the case of social systems, (*a*) these are not clearly bounded in the manner of organisms, and (*b*) as far as both inter- and intra-societal relations are concerned there is no analogue for that 'environment' which is itself unchanged by adaptation. Instead of a one-way process of 'adaptation', then, we have a continuous process of *mutual adjustment*.

4. Darwinian theory, whether applied at the level of the individual organism or of the gene, is essentially *competitive*, since it is concerned with the differential rates of survival and reproduction of organisms and genes. Social systems have competition, to be sure, but it is only part of that process of mutual adjustment in which the various elements of social systems also facilitate one another's operation, or *co-operate*.

5. It follows from the foregoing that there is no significant resemblance between the *mutation*, the basic source of variation in the Darwinian scheme of things, and social *invention*, which is purposeful, responsive, and can be diffused. Whereas biological variation can be treated as random, social variation is the product of particular societies and cultural traditions, and therefore far from random.

3. The search for the 'basic building blocks' of culture

Cultural selectionism is therefore inherently atomistic, since it perceives socio-cultural systems as composed of some kind of cultural unit or building block. Indeed it is a commonplace that understanding any form of behaviour or aspect of reality involves its resolution into its component parts—this is, after all, the basic meaning of 'analysis'.

It is necessary, however, to distinguish between 'components' and 'units'. Components are usually bounded, and they can combine with other components while retaining their identity but cannot be split up or disintegrated without losing it. In this sense automobiles, for example, have components—glass, electric motors, upholstered seats, nuts and bolts, pistons, gearwheels, and so on—but these are all *generically heterogeneous*, and many of them not even distinctive of automobiles. Units, however, are not simply components, but also have a fundamental *generic similarity*. Obvious examples are atoms, molecules, phonemes, musical notes, genes, letters of an alphabet, and so on. While there are different kinds of atoms or genes, every atom and every gene nevertheless shares certain common properties with all atoms and all genes such that we can say that this is, or is not, an atom or a gene. In some branches of study units like these are often basic to the nature of the phenomena in question: physics, chemistry, linguistics, and so on. Other branches of study, however, such as electronics, engineering, or Newtonian mechanics, have basic processes but no basic units at all, except certain purely conventional units of measurement, which are not the same thing. Whether or not a particular type of phenomenon can usefully be described as having basic units is not therefore something that can be decided a priori but is a matter of empirical determination.

In the case of biology it is clear that the basic unit of composition is the cell and that the unit of replication, of heredity, is the gene. But even here, let it be noted, we have already distinguished between two types of unit, one of which is relevant when we consider the structure and function of an organism, and the other when we consider the inheritance of that structure.

When we come to society these problems are enormously increased. The most obvious candidate for the status of basic unit, or basic building block, is 'the individual', and it is certainly incontestable that without any individual members no society can exist at all. It is also true that individuals are the efficient causes of social interaction: institutions, customs, beliefs, and so on cannot of themselves do anything, but equally, the individual members of society are not causally autonomous. That is, what they do and why they do it are the expression of the institutions, beliefs, and values of the particular society into which the individuals composing it have been socialized, which they did not create as individuals, and which will outlast them. In addition, institutions and social relations are structured by rules and categories and so have organizational properties that are distinct from the actions and disposition of individuals. In this sense to say that individuals are the basic units of society is to confuse composition with organization. Social organization is obviously the organization of human beings, rather than of bees, or of inorganic molecules, but the principles and components of that organization—segmentary lineages, hierarchies of authority, roles and statuses—are not individuals, they are the categories, rules and values by which those individuals are organized.

Some sociobiologists, such as Alexander (1979) and Durham (1976b) have attempted to show that a wide variety of social institutions, from kinship, marriage, and priestly celibacy to warfare and the emergence of the state, can be explained on the assumption that individuals pursue strategies of maximizing their 'inclusive fitness' (the proportion of their genes in the gene pool). We shall examine this theory in some detail later in this chapter in the section dealing with the Darwinian failure to explain co-operation. Since, however, we have already discussed the basic fallacies of naive individualism in the previous chapter, there is no need to reiterate that analysis here. Sociobiologists who attempt to apply the concept of inclusive fitness to human society rely, in short, on obsolete notions of naive individualism long since refuted in the social sciences.

It may be possible to say that particular subsystems of a society have basic units: so, the units of a kinship system are 'roles' of a certain type; the units of an economic system are units of currency; the units of music are notes; the units of a traffic design system are vehicles; the units of a game of chess are the moves of each player; and the units of a book for the indexer are the pages, and so on, but clearly these units are not people and, equally clearly, they can only be treated as units within the particular subsystem to which they

belong. Certain subsystems may have individuals as their units—
the unit of the demographer's 'population' is clearly 'the
individual', as is the unit of 'admittances to public amusement
parks'—but taking social systems in general, it is fallacious to
suppose that they are composed of any one kind of unit, or that they
are simply the sum of notes, moves, individuals, vehicles, pages,
etc. The units of the various subsystems, in so far as they are units at
all, only make sense in the organizational context of the particular
subsystems to which each belongs; to ignore these subsystems
makes as much gibberish out of the organization of society as to
ignore syntax would make gibberish out of language.

Nevertheless, we can obviously distinguish between societies in
terms of a large number of different traits or characteristics—lineal
versus cognatic descent, centralized or acephalous government,
forms of marital residence, features of technology, and so on. It
might therefore be supposed that each 'society' (however we define
this) is the sum of a number of traits, that some combinations of
traits are more adaptive than others, and that the particular
combinations of traits characterizing those societies that have
survived to be studied have thereby proved their adaptive value
(e.g. Murdock 1960: 247–8, Otterbein 1970; Netting 1974*b*, etc.).
The hypothesis would be that a process of cultural selection has
eliminated maladaptive combinations of traits by a process of trial
and error, especially over the 10,000 years or so since the
introduction of agriculture and the domestication of animals,
during which variation has reached its highest level.

According to Harris, '. . . the most successful innovations are
those that tend to increase population size, population density, and
per capita energy production. The reason for this is that, in the long
run, larger and more powerful sociocultural systems tend to replace
or absorb smaller and less powerful sociocultural systems.' (Harris
1971: 152). Harris also envisages a trial-and-error process at the
individual level: 'individuals regularly accept innovations that seem
to offer them more security, greater reproductive efficiency, and
higher energy yields for lower energy inputs. Yet it cannot be
denied that the ultimate test of any innovation is the crunch of
competing systems and differential survival and reproduction. But
that crunch may sometimes be delayed for hundreds of years' (ibid.,
152). We must obviously assume, according to this theory, that not
all new traits are automatically beneficial and that, in the words of

another anthropologist, '. . . among the social and technological alternatives available, those that negatively affect the viability of the population adopting them would either be eliminated over time or cause the extinction of that population' (Netting 1974*b*: 485).

But while the theory that cultural selection operates primarily on variations in discrete traits and trait combinations may seem plausible when we consider traits one at a time, it runs immediately into one of the basic obstacles confronting any atomistic theory when it tries to explain the generation of organized wholes: this is the gigantic numbers of possible combinations of 'atoms' (traits) that are involved in anything like a human society, since we must remember that any trait can have a number of different forms. (We are bound, of course, to consider *combinations* of traits, since traits may enhance or nullify one another's effectiveness.) So even a minimally adequate trait list for any society would consist of a large number of variables, each with a number of variant forms. *The Outline of Culture Materials* (Murdock *et al.* 1961) lists 571 basic traits such as 'weapons', 'kinship terminology', 'marital residence', 'ethnobotany', 'legal norms', and 'child care', (under 71 gross categories, nos. 18 to 88). Each basic trait has a number of different possible forms, and I give those for 'marital residence' (Column 16, *Ethnographic Atlas*, Murdock 1967) as an example. For this trait there are at least the following variants: avunculocal, ambilocal, optionally uxorilocal or avunculocal, optionally patrilocal (or virilocal) or avunculocal, matrilocal, neolocal, duolocal, patrilocal, uxorilocal, and virilocal. Let us assume, however, that the average society merely has a quarter of these 571 basic traits, or 143, and that there are on average 10 variant forms of each trait (certainly a gross underestimate). It would follow that the number of possible combinations of trait variants would be 10^{143}. (While this kind of precision is obviously for the sake of illustration only, it is likely that a rough estimate of possible trait combinations for primitive societies and early states would be a two figure number raised to a three figure power.)

The Darwinian model solves this problem of gigantic numbers of possible trait combinations by relying on the existence of millions or billions of individual organisms, evolving over millions of generations. But the application of this model to social evolution immediately encounters the problems that social differentiation of any importance can only have occurred after the domestication of plants and animals, no more than about 10,000 years ago (and a good deal less for most societies); that the total number of societies, however we define 'society', has only been a few thousand over this period; and that these societies have not appeared and disappeared with a frequency remotely comparable to a population of living organisms. It does not seem likely, therefore, that the 'crunch of competing systems' would have had time to do much in the way of selection. So, if we perform another somewhat fanciful calculation, and assume that over the last 10,000 years as many as 10,000 societies have each tried out one new trait combination per year (a wildly excessive estimate of the rate of social change) this would still only give us 100 million, or 10^8 trait combinations, an inconceivably tiny fraction of the total possible ($1/10^{135}$, to be exact). But if there has only been time for societies to test this minute fraction of trait combinations, the possibility of similar *complexes* of traits, such as divine kingship plus polytheism plus bureaucracy, arising in different parts of the world quite independently of one another would be inconceivably small.

D. T. Campbell (1974: 421–2) prefers the concept of 'blind' to 'random' variation, on the grounds that modern notions of mathematical randomness are not required in their full rigour. He proposes three essential criteria for blind variation: (1) that the variations shall be independent of environmental conditions; (2) that a correct solution may occur at any point in the trial sequence; and (3) that there is no process of learning from an incorrect trial, of the kind that would allow the agent to infer anything from the 'direction of error' of the previous trial(s). This revision of randomness does not seem to me, however, to resolve the central issue, namely, that the number of possible trait combinations is astronomically large, and to account for the speed and direction of social evolution by a relatively small number of societies one therefore has to suppose an impossibly high level of variation, together with extreme selective pressure.

If social evolution were really the result of a random shuffling of myriads of little traits, we should also expect the process to be one of gradual, almost imperceptible change, but an obvious feature of human history is the extreme *rapidity* with which major changes often occur—the rise of the Greek city states 800–500 BC, the appearance of Bronze Age Shang culture in China *c*.1800 BC, of the Renaissance, and of the industrialization of Britain 1750–1850. The

same phenomenon is also observable in the arts and sciences.
(It should also be noted that at this point in the argument we are
ignoring the problem of selection, yet without an effective process
of selection mere random variation leads nowhere. In the next
chapter it will become clear that adaptive explanations of many
social traits encounter even more serious difficulties than variation.
D. T. Campbell (1965: 23–6), for example, concedes that the application of a variation-and-retention model to social evolution
encounters severe difficulties in specifying how any process of social
selection could work.)

It might be objected that not all traits are of equal importance,
and that many are dependent on only a few; this is obviously much
more realistic, but necessarily implies that social traits are part of a
structure and therefore concedes the essential point in my
argument. (Cultural materialists in particular are likely to adopt this
line of argument, which we shall examine in detail in Chapter IV.) It
may well be true, therefore, that certain traits, such as military or
commercial efficiency, provide a significant competitive advantage,
but once it is conceded that these traits are only components of a
wider social structure, their emergence cannot, therefore, be
assumed to be the result of *random* variation at all, since it will be
the result of a complicated developmental process.

Major social change also necessarily involves simultaneous
changes in a wide variety of traits, an extremely improbable
occurrence if we supposed that selection only operated on single
traits. (This, of course, is also a major problem in Darwinian
accounts of biological evolution.) We can illustrate this by
considering the typical characteristics of the African state, which
tend to be imposed *en bloc* whenever the basic conditions for the
emergence of centralized government are right.

Murdock (1959: 37–9) notes the following typical characteristics
of African monarchical states, under the following headings: (1)
monarchical absolutism; (2) eminent domain; (3) divine kingship
and ritual isolation of the king; (4) insignia of office, especially
drums and stools; (5) royal capitals, with each new king founding a
new capital or residence; (6) an elaborate court with many specialized functionaries; (7) detailed protocol emphasizing prostration
before the king; (8) royal harems; (9) the Queen Mother, Queen
Consort, and Queen Sister (or two of the three) having exceptional
prestige; (10) a territorial bureaucracy; (11) ministers of state almost

always acting as provincial governors; (12) a proliferation of titles; (13) governors and high officials usually chosen from social categories ineligible to succeed to the throne; (14) succession to the throne almost never automatic; (15) anarchic interregnums; (16) human sacrifice at a king's funeral. Not all these features are necessarily present in every state, and many if not all can be found individually outside Africa, but this specific combination of traits seems to be particularly African. Some of these features are functionally associated in fairly obvious ways, while others are linked in a more arbitrary way, but what is so striking is the tendency for the whole 'design type' of African monarchy to diffuse wholesale:

However geographically remote and however dissimilar the other aspects of culture, political forms seem everywhere to conform to a single fundamental pattern. Nor does the size of a state seem to make any essential difference. Even a petty paramount chief who has subjugated a few neighboring communities and destroyed the preexisting primitive democracy seems invariably to institute, in so far as he can on a small scale, the forms prevailing in larger states in the vicinity or even at some distance. It is almost as though all of Africa south of the Sahara were permeated, as it were, by a mental blueprint of a despotic political structure, transmitted from generation to generation as a part of traditional verbal culture, and always available to be transmuted into reality whenever some individual arises with the imagination, enterprise, strength, and luck to establish, with the aid of his kinsmen, an authoritarian regime over people residing beyond the limits of his local community. (Murdock 1959: 37)

The general profile of social evolution both cross-culturally and historically is therefore quite incompatible with the notion that selection operates at the level of the individual trait. Political, economic, religious, and technological similarities in unrelated cultures that have appeared within a few hundred years of one another, rapid change, and simultaneous shifts in many variables are well attested facts of social evolution that can only be explained on the obvious assumption that societies are not just heaps of bits and pieces but integrated systems, and that it is often the *higher* levels of socio-cultural systems that induce lower level changes.

The cultural-selectionist approach to social evolution has tried to find the basic unit of culture by postulating the existence of 'social genes'. We are asked to believe that societies are composed of tiny self-replicating particles—the 'memory image' (Blum 1963), the 'idea' (Boulding 1970), the 'instruction' (Cloak 1975), the 'meme' (Dawkins 1978), the 'concept' (Hill 1978), and the 'culturgen' (Lumsden and Wilson 1981)—which, like the gene, are units of information competing for survival. Thus Boulding claims that

> In social systems the gene is the image or the idea in the mind of man, ideas such as the plans recorded in the blueprint that create a building or an automobile, the idea or the image of the future that creates a new enterprise, the proposal of marriage that creates a new family, the image of a new kind of life in the teaching that creates a new religion. The parallel with the gene is exact. The essential structure of both consists in information, information which in a favourable environment is capable of creating a teleological process to produce the appropriate phenotype. (Boulding 1970: 21–2)

While both genes and ideas convey information, the parallel between them is scarcely 'exact', as we shall see.

F. T. Cloak has tried to work out the same idea more rigorously, regarding the competing units of biological and cultural evolution as the 'instruction'. His theory is very close to that of Dawkins's 'selfish gene' and has been well summarized by Barkow:

> For Cloak, the basic unit of both biological and cultural evolution is the 'instruction'. The 'message' a gene carries is an instruction. But cultures are also composed of molecular traits consisting of instructions. Both biological and cultural evolution involve nothing but the differential propagation of instructions: soma and society are merely an instruction's way to make more instructions. They [soma and society] are epiphenomena. Evolution is not about the survival of the individual carrier of an instruction or about his culture; it is about instructions competing with each other to increase their (respective) frequencies. (Barkow 1978: 11)

Cloak's theory certainly overcomes the inherent vagueness of the gene = idea formulation, but by the radical assumption that culture is acquired as a series of discrete particles:

> On the basis of various natural experiments and observations, I believe that culture is acquired in tiny, unrelated snippets, which are specific interneural instructions culturally transmitted from generation to generation. These 'corpuscles of culture' are transmitted and acquired with fidelity and ease because the organisms in question are phylogenetically adapted for transmitting and acquiring cultural corpuscles, an adaptation that has required at least 2 million years, and perhaps 40 million, of intense 'selection pressure'. (Cloak 1975: 167–8)

Consistently with his notion of the 'bit-by-bit' acquisition of culture, Cloak supposes that the instructions of which our culture is composed have no hierarchical ordering among themselves: 'The notion of an evolving set of simple cultural instructions implies that there is no more *intrinsic* order among those instructions than there is among the genes of a chromosome' (ibid., 175).

In very similar fashion Dawkins proposes that the essential property of the gene is that it is a particle of replication, and argues that replication (and cultural selection) in human society is achieved by cultural transmission or imitation in the form of particles—the 'memes':

Examples of memes are tunes, ideas, catch-phrases, clothes, fashions, ways of making pots or of building arches. Just as genes propagate themselves in the gene pool by leaping from body to body via sperms or eggs, so memes propagate themselves in the meme pool by leaping from brain to brain via a process which, in the broad sense, can be called imitation. (Dawkins 1978: 206)

More recently, Lumsden and Wilson have proposed the 'culturgen' as the basic unit of culture:

A culturgen is a relatively homogeneous set of artifacts, behaviours, or mentifacts (mental constructs having little or no direct correspondence with reality) that either share without exception one or more attribute states selected for their functional importance or at least share a consistently recurrent range of such attribute states within a given polythetic set. (Lumsden and Wilson 1981: 27)

This definition is so vague and all-encompassing that a culturgen could be any discriminable aspect of thought or behaviour whatsoever. It is as though the 'thing' were to be proposed as the basic unit of physics. While the definition includes the requirement that a culturgen have 'functional importance', we cannot say that something has functional importance until we can first define what that something is.

In the first place, let us inject a note of reality into these deliberations by remembering that none of these authors can provide a shred of evidence that culturgens, memes, or instructions actually exist as units in any independent sense at all, since they can produce no criteria for identifying them or for distinguishing them from other such units, unlike genes, atoms, and molecules.

Secondly, if the concept of 'information' is to be used in a social context it is not enough to propose the existence of units of information: there also has to be some organized context in which these units of information make sense, and are structured in terms of levels of generality, of specialization, and of sequence, in particular. So, if we are baking a cake, we have to mix the ingredients before we put them in the oven, not after; the instructions for baking a cake have to be kept entirely separate from starting a car, and whether we bake a cake or start our car depends on higher level priorities for allocating our time. The absence of any such structural concepts inevitably reduces the examples of memes and culturgens to ridiculous laundry lists of odds and ends—Dawkins's tunes, catch-phrases, and ways of making pots, and Lumsden's and Wilson's food items, colour classifications, 6000 attributes of camels among Arabs, and the ten-second-slow-downs by drivers which cause traffic jams. Just as there can be no information without structure, the notion of the 'social gene' is even more vulnerable than the social trait to the problem of gigantic numbers. The idea of society being divided into 143 basic traits each with 10 variants caused insuperable problems, but if socio-cultural systems were further fragmented into memes or culturgens the numbers involved would pass entirely into the realms of fantasy. Moreover, if our social environment were composed of structureless myriads of tiny culturgens, it would be impossible for any individual ever to acquire culture at all. To take an obvious example, we know that language is not acquired only in the form of isolated 'memes' (words in a lexicon, or should it be morphemes, phonemes, or letters of the alphabet?), but that we order these sounds and words by a limited number of general rules and categories, so that we can utter and comprehend statements that we have never encountered before. All learning involves the construction of hierarchies of rules and categories, and the application of these rules and categories in the appropriate contexts. And if individuals could not acquire culture obviously no communication or indeed any social life at all would be possible.

In fact, such theories of basic units of culture do not rest on any evidence, or on any sociological theory at all, but are simply proposed because if one is trying to explain culture on the basis of a neo-Darwinian theory of natural selection, it is highly inconvenient *not* to have a 'unit' like the meme or culturgen, quantifications of which can be treated as continuously variable over time like the gene.

4. Inheritance and variation

(*a*) *Societies as systems of inheritance*[4]

The 'population' model not only assumes that societies can be regarded as a population of discrete entities, but requires that the process of cultural transmission be equated with the biological transmission of genetic characteristics. So, if each culture is a population of 'those aspects of thought, speech, behaviour and artefacts which can be learned and transmitted', then

The feature common to all the above 'cultural entities' is that they are capable of being transmitted culturally from one individual to another. Transmission may imply copying error (or imitation); copying carries with it the chance of error. Thus we have in cultural transmission the analogs to reproduction and mutation in biological entities. Ideas, languages, values, behavior, and technologies, when transmitted, undergo 'reproduction', and when there is a difference between the subsequently transmitted version of the original entity, and the original entity itself, 'mutation' has occurred. (Cavalli-Sforza and Feldman 1981: 10)

In the analysis of systems it is clearly essential to distinguish between reproduction and self-maintenance (a process in which there is *also* continuity and variation). In the case of organisms these are quite distinct processes, whereas for societies they are one and the same: individual organisms maintain themselves during their lifetime but, being mortal, can only perpetuate their 'design type' by producing actual replicas of themselves (with variations) by reproduction. A society, however, can perpetuate its design type indefinitely, because it is not a physical structure at all, but a set of ideas, rules, categories, and so on in the minds of the individuals who sustain it. If, then, one wishes to apply biological analogies to societal continuity and change, this can only be done in terms of the *shared* properties of organisms: in this case, self-maintenance. But to say that the England of today is a 'reproduction' (with variations) of the England of last year is as gross an abuse of the whole concept of reproduction by the biologist as would be the assertion by the sociologist that an old man is a reproduction of his boyhood self (with variations), because all the cells in his body have been renewed several times over. He is not a reproduction, but the same man who has changed over the years. Replication certainly exists in

---

[4] I am grateful to Professor P. J. Richerson for correcting some errors in an earlier draft of this subsection.

all societies, as when a standard type of artefact is made again and again, or when a rumour is repeated from person to person, but this kind of replication is only one of numerous kinds of social activity: it is certainly not the essence of all social continuity. So, observing a rule, for example, is not a *reproduction* of the rule (as when many copies of a parliamentary statute are printed), but is simply the continued existence of the rule.

The fact that societies do not reproduce but maintain themselves with differing degrees of continuity also means that the variation-and-selection model of evolution, plausible enough for physical organisms in their natural environment, cannot be applied to social systems.

(b) Mutation and invention

In certain respects the resemblances between mutation and invention are obvious: both are temporally and spatially localized in origin; both may give competitive advantages to their possessors; and both may spread and displace competing types. The real problem in trying to assimilate mutations and inventions into a single evolutionary model lies in the requirement that variation must be blind. For according to neo-Darwinian theory mutations (in which I include recombination—see Mayr 1980: 22–4) occur at random, in a manner not under the control of the organism or its genes, and not as a response to environmental conditions, and, if such a mutation is of adaptive advantage to the organism it will allow the organism to leave more offspring than those organisms without the mutation in question. How does this model apply to social innovation? According to Cavalli-Sforza:

The equivalent of a mutant, in sociocultural evolution, is a new *idea*. If it turns out to be acceptable and advantageous, it will spread easily. If not, it is likely to be forgotten . . . There are close parallels between mutation and the process giving origin to new ideas, *invention*. Both phenomena are in the nature of rare, discrete changes, which occur almost randomly, but may recur. (Cavalli-Sforza 1971: 536)

Indeed, the basic logic of random variation plus environmental selection is so simple that it can be applied to psychology and sociology. Thus B. F. Skinner (1981) has proposed that there is a fundamental similarity between biological selection, individual learning, and the process of social evolution: all involve 'selection by consequences', operating respectively at the levels of genetic mutation, individual behaviour, and social practices. For Skinner, of course, 'creativity' presents no more difficulty than mutation does for the biologist—it is simply a randomizing process:

> The creative mind has never been without its problems, as the classical discussion in Plato's *Meno* suggests. It was an insoluble problem for stimulus-response psychology because if behaviour were nothing but responses to stimuli, the stimuli might be novel but not the behaviour. Operant conditioning solves the problem more or less as natural selection solved a similar problem in evolutionary theory. As accidental traits, arising from mutations, are selected by their contribution to survival, so accidental variations in behaviour are selected by their reinforcing consequences . . . creative thinking is largely concerned with the production of 'mutations'. Explicit ways of making it more likely that original behavior will occur by introducing 'mutations' are familiar to writers, artists, composers, mathematicians, scientists, and inventors. Either the setting or the topography of behavior may be deliberately varied. The painter varies his colors, brushes, and surfaces to produce new textures and forms. The composer generates new rhythms, scales, melodies, and harmonic sequences, sometimes through the systematic permutation of older forms, possibly with the help of mathematical or mechanical devices.[5] The mathematician explores the results of changing a set of axioms. The results may be reinforcing in the sense that they are beautiful or, in most of mathematics and in science and invention, successful. (Skinner 1974: 113–15)

Social evolution, too, proceeds in a similar way:

> The process presumably begins at the level of the individual. A better way of making a tool, growing food, or teaching a child is reinforced by its consequences—the tool, the food, or a useful helper, respectively. A culture evolves when practices originating in this way contribute to the success of the practicing group in solving its problems. It is the effect on the

---

[5] Professor Skinner's theory of creative thought irresistibly recalls that of another Professor, from Swift's Academy of Lagado, who had constructed a large frame in which were many wooden blocks on each of whose faces a word was written. These blocks were mounted on rods connected to handles at the side of the frame: 'The Professor then desired me to observe, for he was going to set his Engine at work. The Pupils at his Command took each of them hold of an Iron Handle, whereof there were Forty fixed round the edges of the frame; and giving them a sudden Turn, the whole Disposition of the Words was entirely changed. He then commanded Six and Thirty of the Lads to read the several Lines softly as they appeared upon the Frame; and where they found three or four Words together that might make Part of a Sentence, they dictated to the four remaining Boys who were Scribes . . . the Professor shewed me several Volumes in large Folio already collected, of broken Sentences, which he intended to piece together; and out of those rich Materials to give the World a compleat Body of all Arts and Sciences.' (Swift, *Gulliver's Travels*, (Nonesuch Edition), pp. 179–80.)

group, not the reinforcing consequences for individual members, which is responsible for the evolution of the culture. (Skinner 1981: 502)

Not surprisingly, this view of evolution tells us nothing whatever about the *origins* of social change, or the lack of it:

Why do people continue to do things in the same way for many years, and why do groups of people continue to observe old practices for centuries? The answers are presumably the same: either new variations (new forms of behavior or new practices) have not appeared or those which have appeared have not been selected by the prevailing contingencies (of reinforcement or of the survival of the group). At all three levels [biological, behavioural, and social] a sudden, possibly extensive, change is explained as due to new variations selected by prevailing contingencies or to new contingencies. (Ibid., 502)

No doubt, the military supremacy of large centralized states with professional armies over small, uncentralized tribal societies, or the supersession of stone tools by metal tools are clear instances of 'selection by consequences', but the reasons for the victory of large centralized states and metal tools are perfectly obvious. The real problem is to explain how and why centralized states and metal tools originated in the first place, and it is therefore sheer mystification to treat innovation as 'random variation', since the sources of novelty are just as important as the success or failure of novelty.

Skinner has replied to this criticism (first made in Hallpike 1984*b*: 489), 'I can easily compose a scenario in which the smelting and use of metals came into existence through entirely accidental contingencies, and I do not think the account would be mystification' (Skinner 1984: 505). The 'mystification' of which I accuse the selectionists lies in their belief that social variation is blind, and that we cannot therefore explain it as the outcome of human thought and action operating within particular social circumstances. On this point, Skinner and other selectionists are unfortunately the victims of a confusion, which is that merely because there is an obvious contingent or accidental element in social innovation, it can therefore be treated as *random*, or simply as blind, by Campbell's definition. In this Darwinian scheme of things the whole point of treating variation as blind is to avoid the problem of orthogenesis,[6]

---

[6] Defined as a 'steady trend of evolution in a given direction over a prolonged period of time, affecting related groups of organisms, due to the working out of inherent trends within the inherited material. It is not generally accepted that

or inherent directional properties in evolution. The neo-Darwinian model therefore requires that *new* variation shall not be a response to, or affected by, any state of the environment, or influenced by any learning from previous successes or failures. For if this kind of feedback process occurs, then variation may be a function of the *internal* organization of the source of that variation, whether the source is an organism, a society, or some kind of learning machine. In other words, orthogenesis would reappear. And once this was possible, the organization of variation might have an importance equal to or greater than selection in explaining those evolutionary or developmental processes we are trying to understand.

But in the case of social systems we have noted that individuals are not causally autonomous, since what they do and believe is itself a product of their culture and social organization. Thus social variation and social selection are not distinct at all—as they must be to satisfy Darwinian requirements—but only different aspects of one and the same system. This is a very different state of affairs from variation in organisms, which is selected by a quite *distinct* environment.

No one would deny, therefore, that there are 'accidental contingencies' in all social innovation, but this is quite compatible with the claim that social variation is very strongly affected by existing features of social organization and general cultural traditions. (Leslie White and Marvin Harris, indeed, go so far as to claim that every invention is more or less inevitably determined by circumstances.) To this extent orthogenesis is theoretically quite possible for societies, and the understanding of the origins of innovation is therefore a legitimate and indeed a fundamental problem.

A good example is the invention of gunpowder and cannon in China, which shows clearly that the sequence of variations involved was the result of certain distinctive aspects of Chinese society and culture, which crucially influenced the thoughts and actions of those individuals concerned in the development of gunpowder. The example of gunpowder also illustrates very well that is is highly misleading to represent social innovation as some kind of atomistic

orthogenesis is the proper explanation of the many known instances of persistent evolutionary trends' (Abercrombie *et al.* 1973: 204). In Huxley's view, 'Most biologists . . . look askance at orthogenesis, in its strict sense, as implying an inevitable grinding out of results predetermined by some internal germinal clockwork. This is too much akin to vitalism and mysticism for their liking: it removes evolution out of the field of analysable phenomena . . . ' (Huxley 1974: 465). We shall consider this question in more detail in Chapter III.

'event', akin to the mutation of a gene. In reality, it is typically a *combinatorial* process that involves the mutual interaction of a variety of existing artefacts, ideas, and cultural traditions. These propositions are clearly demonstrated by Joseph Needham's account of the origins of gunpowder and firearms in China: 'The beginnings of the gunpowder story take us back to those wilder shores of religion and liturgy which involved the 'smoking out' of undesirable things in general. The burning of incense was only part of a much wider complex in Chinese custom, fumigation as such (*hsün*)' (Needham 1980: 39). This was used for a wide variety of hygienic and insecticidal purposes such as annual house cleaning, at least as early as the seventh century BC, and later in removing infestations of bookworms from scholars' libraries.

Not only in peace, moreover, but also in war, the ancient Chinese were great smoke producers. Toxic smokes and smoke-screens generated by pumps and furnaces for siege warfare occur in the military sections of the *Mo Tzu* book (fourth century BC), especially as part of the techniques of sapping and mining; for this purpose mustard and other dried vegetable material containing irritant volatile oils were used. (Ibid., 39)

Chinese warfare as a whole also

illustrates a cardinal feature of Chinese technology and science, the belief in action at a distance. In the history of naval warfare, for instance, one can show that the projectile mentality dominated over ramming or boarding, with its close-contact combat. Smokes, perfumes, hallucinogens, incendiaries, flames and ultimately the use of the propellent force of gunpowder itself, form part of one consistent tendency discernible throughout Chinese culture from the earliest times to the transmission of the bombard, gun and cannon to the rest of the world about AD 1300. (Ibid., 39)

Yet a further essential element in the discovery of gunpowder was provided by the Chinese alchemical tradition and its investigations of elixirs. Saltpetre (*hsiao shih*) was also used as a flux at least as early as the second century BC, and by the seventh century AD the combination of saltpetre, sulphur, and carbon was known to produce a deflagrating[7] compound. The first military uses of this 'fire chemical' or 'fire drug' (*huo yao*) were in bamboo tubes, in the tenth century, to produce the fire-lance: 'The gunpowder which it contained was emphatically not a high-nitrate brisant explosive mixture, but more like a rocket composition, as in a 'Roman

---

[7] That is, involving rapid burning rather than an explosion.

candle', deflagrating violently and shooting forth powerful flames, not going off suddenly with a mighty bang' (ibid., 40). Once the basic gunpowder formula was being used for military purposes and confined in a tube (initially of bamboo, and also of thick paper), subsequent development was rapid. Projectiles were included in the larger versions of the fire-lances, the 'eruptors', and

Lastly there appeared the metal-barrel firearm characterized by two other basic features: the use of high-nitrate gunpowder, and the total occlusion of the muzzle (or front orifice) by a projectile such as a bullet or cannon-ball, so that the gunpowder exerted its full propellent effect. This type of firearm may be described as the 'true' gun or cannon, and if, as we believe, it appeared in early Yuan times, about 1290, its development had taken just about three and a half centuries since the first of the fire-lance flame throwers. (Ibid., 40)

Incense and fumigation, chemical smoke in warfare, 'action at a distance', alchemy, bamboo tubing, fire-lances, and metal casting, are a disparate collection of cultural traits which nevertheless had the clear developmental potential, when combined within the same society, of leading eventually to the emergence of cannon. To be sure there were accidental discoveries in this process, as Needham records, but it is also quite reasonable to claim that the special characteristics of Chinese society led to this innovation before it occurred in any other society, and to claim that many other societies would never have independently discovered gunpowder and fire-arms at all because they lacked the special features of the Chinese tradition. We shall see that an essentially similar kind of explanation can also be provided for the development of the state.

Treating the emergence of significant novelty as a mere random event certainly has a seductive appeal: it excuses us from difficult investigations of the structural properties of social systems, and it also makes it a great deal easier to produce mathematical models of innovation. But it achieves these 'advantages' at the expense of abandoning any understanding of the origins of novelty, which is of fundamental importance in social evolution.

Some cultural selectionists concede, however, that human invention is indeed very different from biological mutation precisely because inventions are *not* random. How, then, can these two contrasting types of innovation be assimilated into the same Darwinian model? Cavalli-Sforza and Feldman address the problem as follows:

. . . it is important to emphasize the distinction between *mutation* in the biological and in the cultural processes. In the former, mutation is typically an error in the copy, which as a result is not identical to the master, or it is a chemical change in the master to be copied. In both cases *randomness* seems to be the rule. On the other hand, in the cultural process, the change is not necessarily a copying error, but can often be directed innovation, that is, innovation with a purpose, and might therefore appear to be nonrandom. *This would be a crucial issue only if there were a high chance that a cultural innovation could be truly adaptive as a consequence of being purposeful* [*my emphasis*]. All evidence points to this being impossible in biology: biological 'innovation' by mutation is apparently truly random. If cultural innovations are not truly random, but are designed to solve specific problems, they may increase the rate of the corresponding adaptation in evolution over that expected for a truly random process. We might speculate, however, that whatever the good faith and insight of the proponents of innovations of any kind, the chance that the innovations will prove truly adaptive in the long run is not 100%, so that many innovations, however purposeful and intelligent they may seem to their proponents and first adopters, may not turn out to be highly adaptive, at least on a long term basis. Because of this, and because some cultural mutation is simply copy error, a significant proportion of new cultural mutations might be truly random without any semblance of adaptiveness. (Cavalli-Sforza and Feldman 1981: 65–6)

In the first place, while we would all agree that the chance of every cultural innovation being adaptive in the long run is less than 100 per cent, this is a very long way indeed from establishing that their chances of being adaptive are truly random. Secondly, by treating invention as similar to mutation because in both cases their consequences are only, allegedly, randomly related to adaptiveness, the biologists have here quite lost sight of the elementary fact that while organic mutations do not normally change the physical environment of the organism, social innovations very definitely can change their social environment: printing, the steam engine, and universal suffrage are obvious examples. While the early stages of all human endeavours are liable to be superseded by more efficient forms, they nevertheless lay the foundations for the later stages. Merely because particular innovations such as mounted knights in armour or sailing ships are later superseded, we do not therefore have a justification for equating these with adaptive failures in the world of organic life. The disasters and miscalculations of history may also be put to profitable use by later generations. We shall return to this question in more detail below, Section 5*a*; but for the present we may simply note that the unpredictability of future adaptiveness cannot restore that element of randomness which is essential to the selectionist position.

In the case of social evolution, therefore, we cannot operate on the basis of that neat separation between variation and selection that is possible in the case of organic evolution. While social innovations are initially produced by individuals, individuals do not innovate in a vacuum, or in some entirely private or idiosyncratic world of their own, but as members of a particular society at a particular period of history.

(c) *Frequency and Fitness*

The spread of a successful invention is held to be analogous to the spread of a successful trait in a population or a gene in a gene pool because both are instances of increased 'fitness'. So Cavalli-Sforza writes: 'If we take the word 'airplane' it is clear why it has an increasing fitness and has come in common usage, and undergone a rapid evolution' (Cavalli-Sforza 1971: 539). Here, too, the analogy is superficial and misleading. Social systems are structured phenomena, whereas biological populations or gene pools are not. The significance of the adaptive mutation is that it facilitates reproduction by organisms possessing it relative to those that do not, and hence 'fitness' must be defined in purely quantitative terms as the frequency of one gene or trait relative to competing genes or traits. But in a structured system the quantitative measure of fitness applied by biologists to the structureless gene pool or population is analytically quite valueless. What, for example, does it contribute to our knowledge of English or of anything else to say that 'and' and 'but' have a greater fitness than 'adaptive' and 'selection'? Or, if we agree that the 'note' as a sound of definite and acceptable pitch is the unit of music, and if we suppose for the sake of argument that in different periods of Western music certain notes have been commoner than others, in what way would the studies of musicologists be illuminated by this knowledge? Obviously the relative frequency of notes is not the result of some rudimentary competition of the notes among themselves, but of the working of higher-order principles—scales, the technology of musical instruments, theories of harmony, the composer's style—and itself can have no explanatory value at all. The relative frequency of notes, or of words like 'airplane', are simply epiphenomena of other and more basic social processes.

In social terms something may be common because it is useful and rare because it is useless; or its frequency may be a function of its degree of specialization; or because it is common it may have no value; or it may be rare because it is difficult to attain and common because it is easy; or it may be rare because, in a hierarchical organization, the topmost positions are necessarily less numerous than the lower positions. Generals are much rarer than privates, but what would it mean to say that they had less 'fitness'? At this point it is worth emphasizing again that *if* common evolution can be expressed as change in the relative frequency of things, but this does not prove the marvellous power and versatility of Darwinism: it is simply part of the definition of change itself!

Similarly, while in the gene pool or population frequency is likely to be closely related to the longevity of the gene or trait this is by no means the case in ordered systems. So monarchy, with only one living representative at any one time, may outlast whole classes—such as monks or samurai—because of the importance in the structure of the monarchical institution. Micrometers are very rare by comparison with ordinary rulers, but the significance of micrometers in the technological structure guarantees their survival. Thus the degree of spread of an invention may be quite irrelevant to any measure of its success. If 'fitness' means anything in a social context it is 'power to induce further change in the system', or 'power to control the continuing operation of the system', hence the importance of kings and computers, whatever their 'relative frequency'.

5. Competition and co-operation

Co-operation and competition are clearly of central importance both in social and biological evolution, but the differences between societies and organisms necessarily involve us in great analytical problems when we try to compare co-operation and competition in these two types of system. In the case of organisms, the relations between their component parts are clearly of a basically co-operative nature, whereas the relations between organisms are not only co-operative (as in the case of social insects, or the protection of the young by their parents), but may also be highly competitive. The Darwinian paradigm, in particular, assumes this as the norm, to such an extent that the explanation of any co-operation between non-kin becomes a major difficulty.[8] Hence the continuing debate between those biologists who maintain that selection can only work in the interests of the individual organism and its close relatives, and those who believe that it is also possible for behaviour which benefits the group to be selected for. (We shall consider this in detail in subsection (*b*) below.) Since societies are composed of individual organisms, this fairly clear separation between co-operation (intraorganic), and competition (inter-organic) simply does not exist: the members of society not only compete against each other but also co-operate and, in the same way, we shall see that the artefacts of culture not only compete with one another (ball-point and fountain pens, for example), but can also be said to facilitate one another's operation (paper and ink, for example).

These difficulties are compounded by those who try to interpret social systems according to the cultural-selectionist model: by this interpretation societies themselves become nothing more than populations of competing individuals, or of competing cultural traits, or both, and the obviously co-operative aspects of society now become as problematic and difficult to explain as the co-operation between different organisms. Worse still, cultural selectionism tends to a complete confusion between organism and environment, since selection itself is now no longer an independent variable operating from outside society but becomes an integral aspect of its internal working, a dependent variable in fact. It would seem that the very essence of the concept of selection is that what does the selecting should not itself be directly affected by what it selects. If, as in society, everything to some extent can potentially affect everything else, there is absolutely no point in retaining the concept of selection at all: mutual selection is nothing more than mutual interaction.

(a) Competition between and within societies

Let us now examine the problems created by the simple assumption that societies are like organisms and compete against one another in such a way that only the best adapted survive: ' . . . an analogy might be drawn here between a living organism and a sociocultural system, both of which must struggle against environmental forces

---

[8] The Darwinian emphasis on competition was a major problem for the Victorians who wished to apply it to social evolution. See, for example, Drummond 1897, and Kidd 1894.

and against their fellow organisms' (Newcomb 1950: 37) and 'As societies compete, the less well adapted tend to fall by the wayside, leaving outstanding those best able to withstand the competition' (Carneiro 1970*a*: xii).

The idea that societies are analogous to competing organisms encounters a major problem in the very nature of societies. This is that societies are not clearly bounded, in the manner of organisms. When we talk of 'a society' we normally have in mind a political unit, yet obviously there are many other societal bonds that do not conform to political boundaries: culture, religion, political ideology, language, economics, and technology, to name only the most obvious. Thus, whether we treat Western Europe as a single society, but politically fragmented, or as a collection of discrete societies depends very much on our analytical point of view. Competition, in short, may exist politically in very different forms from economic or religious competition, within the same geographical area.

Many empires have risen in the course of world history, but they have also fallen, in many cases leaving more or less intact the local cultures that they have temporarily absorbed at the political level. Military superiority has often been accompanied by cultural inferiority, and the conquerors in arms have on many occasions been subdued by the arts of their victims—the Magyars by Western European Christendom, the Galla by Amharic culture, the Mongols by the Chinese, Arabs by Persian, Romans by Greek, and so on. The political map of Europe has been redrawn many times: Roman, Carolingian, Angevin, Spanish, Austrian, Napoleonic, Hitlerian, and lately the Common Market; the religious map has changed to a lesser extent, the cultural still less, and the linguistic least of all.

In short, the notion of clearly bounded, tightly knit entities, 'societies', that compete with one another to the point of annihilation of their neighbours, is highly unrealistic when we consider world history as a whole. Rather, we find 'competition' at many different levels, and the competing units at any one level may not correspond with the 'units' at other levels.

While it is obviously true that such social traits as centralized government and professional armies give societies possessing them an advantage over those that do not, these traits have arisen independently in many different parts of the world, or have been spread by diffusion. We do *not* find that a few societies have been victorious over the rest, which have been eliminated by the victor, and that the only societies now existing are the victorious ones and their descendants.

Thus the diffusion of culture by a variety of means (conquest, voluntary imitation, trade, migration, etc.) overlies the distribution of political groups and their interrelationships. Indeed, it is very important to note that even in so far as it is true to represent societies as competing entities, the edge of competition is for the most part effectively blunted by diffusion, since competitors can learn from one another without paying the extreme penalty of extinction, unlike organic evolution in which diffusion has no place at all. In this sense the co-operation between societies has, throughout history, been just as important as the competition between them.

It is possible, of course, to say that any designated 'society' is equivalent to 'organism', and that all neighbouring societies correspond to 'environment', but when societies interact with one another *all* are necessarily changed to some extent by this process of interaction, and in such conditions it is simply misleading to use the organism/environment analogy since, as we have already noted, this presupposes that the environment is *unchanged* by the 'adaptation' of the organism. When we are trying to explain intersocietal relations it is therefore more accurate to think in terms of mutual adjustment by subsystems of a larger system.

This point becomes even more obvious when we consider intrasocietal processes, and indeed we find that the organism/environment analogy is applied more often to the component parts of societies such as competing business firms or products than to societies as wholes. It is these commercial analogies in particular which have lent plausibility to the use of the biological theory of natural selection in explaining social evolution, since it is evidently supposed that we can treat a society simply as the sum of competing entities of this kind. (It was probably the importance of commerce in Victorian Britain that helped convince those of Darwin's contemporaries who were not biologists of the basic truth of his theory.)[9]

[9] Russell remarks that 'From the historical point of view, what is interesting is Darwin's extension to the whole of life of the economics that characterized the philosophical radicals. The motive force of evolution, according to him, is a kind of biological economics in a world of free competition. It was Malthus's doctrine of

In the entirely structureless world of Darwinian theory[10] where every form of organization is seen as merely the sum of a number of traits or elements, the basic explanatory device is to invite us to consider some entities—let it be ball-point and fountain pens—which compete against each other in a particular environment, and as a result of this competition one or other becomes quantitatively dominant, usually because of superior adaptive qualities, and so increases its 'fitness'. But this kind of superficial analogy-mongering simply will not do.

In the first place, what is the unit of selection in the case of social systems? Products like the ball-point pen were invented by individuals, their production financed by another group of individuals (the shareholders), and they are manufactured by companies; companies not only compete with one another in their products but also co-operate by hiring other companies such as advertisers, business efficiency experts, subsidiary component manufacturers, etc., while companies also exist within nation states, which can compete with one another by improving the conditions of trade for their own companies by protective tariffs, more efficient commercial law, etc., but also have an interest in preserving the system of world trade by co-operation. Thus nation states are not the ultimate level of competition, since they are themselves linked in a wide system of international trade that constitutes a total economic system.

Once, therefore, we place a phenomenon such as competing firms or products in their total social context, it becomes obvious that to identify any one of these as the analogue of the organism rests upon a totally arbitrary act of selection, since what is a whole in relation to lower-order entities is itself a part in relation to higher-order entities. But if there is no social equivalent to 'organism', how can the concept of 'environment' survive either?

The point is that artefacts, firms, customs, institutions, etc., do not just compete in an environment—they *are* that environment, since they mutually affect one another and contribute to one

population, extended to the world of animals and plants, that suggested to Darwin the struggle for existence and the survival of the fittest as the source of evolution' (B. Russell 1946: 753).

[10] Some biologists may protest that comparative morphology has always been central to Darwinian theory, since it is integral to the proof of common descent. It is nevertheless undeniable that structural form is regarded as wholly subordinate in the evolutionary process to variation, adaptation, and selection.

another's existence. From one point of view the steam engine can be seen as a new type of organism competing with other types of organism such as the water-wheel or the horse-wheel. But it was also a means by which the society into which it was introduced—its 'environment'—was profoundly modified by it in its turn, since the steam engine not only revolutionized coal production, but for the first time allowed vehicles on land and sea to have a self-contained source of power, and also provided a convenient and cheap source of power for factory production that could be located anywhere, unlike the water-wheel. But the social effects of steam power can only be understood by a thorough analysis of the economic, social, and technological organization of the total society into which it was introduced. Natural selectionist attempts to explain social evolution merely ask 'Why did this change succeed?' and measure that success in terms of some relative frequency of the innovation, when what they should also ask is 'What were the effects of this change on the rest of the social system?' They do not ask this because as far as Darwinian theory is concerned it is an almost meaningless question, since the only effects of change (mutation) are on the relative frequency of genes or organisms.

The selectionists, in their structureless world of competing 'atoms', are indeed so obsessed with *competition* that they have entirely forgotten that the mutual interaction and *co-operation* of parts is an essential aspect of the generation of systems, as we saw in Section 4. So, too, a notable feature of invention is the way in which one aspect of technology is borrowed by another, or facilitates invention in another: thus clocks were a vital stimulus in the general application of gears in late medieval machinery; the suction pump and the cannon were important ingredients in the development of the steam engine, whose technology in turn greatly facilitated the development of the internal combustion engine. In none of these respects do inventions behave like mutations, and their significance is not so much that they give advantages to inventors or even investors—these advantages, even if present, are quickly lost—but in changing the total system. In addition, of course, there are many localized sources of change that have no resemblance to invention or mutation—the outcomes of battles, revolutions, political alliances, and so on. These are merely part of the continuing process of social life.

Indeed, we must repeat that merely because a particular

invention, such as the reciprocating steam engine, was quite rapidly replaced (either by the steam turbine or the internal combustion engine or electric motors) this does not establish any analogy with adaptive *failure* in the world of biological organisms. In systematic terms, the reciprocating steam engine helped to bring about the economic and technological conditions that made the engine itself obsolete within two centuries or so, and was therefore simply an accessory in a wider and more important process of development. By contrast, the swape (the counterpoised beam by which water is raised to irrigation ditches) has been in existence for thousands of years, but without the addition of steam power the counterpoised beam leads nowhere, whatever its longevity.

Societies, therefore, are systems of mutually interacting components, at different levels of organization, and of overlapping subsystems, and it is this set of interactions and mutual adjustments that is the basis of change and evolution.

(b) Altruism and selfishness[11]

In this subsection we shall examine in detail the consequences of trying to treat society as if it were nothing more than an aggregate of competing individuals.[12] This interpretation of society is an integral part of the 'inclusive fitness' theory, and we must first establish just what that involves.

(i) The concept of 'inclusive fitness'

This concept was introduced by W. D. Hamilton (1963; 1964*a, b*) in an attempt to account for the evolution by natural selection of 'altruistic' characteristics ' . . . where an animal behaves in such a way as to promote the advantages of other members of the species not its direct descendants at the expense of its own' (1963: 354). Standard examples are distastefulness in caterpillars, where in order to signal to a predator that a certain appearance is related to obnoxious taste, the carrier of the gene for distastefulness has first to be eaten; or alarm calls by birds which increase the risk to themselves from a predator by warning other birds of its presence. After reviewing some arguments against the theory of group selection he suggests (developing ideas of Fisher 1930 and Haldane 1955) that there is a way in which the theory of natural selection can be extended to the evolution of 'altruism':

[11] This subsection is an abbreviated version of Hallpike 1984*a*.
[12] The notable exponent of Darwinism, T. H. Huxley, long ago provided some telling arguments against such a view of society (Huxley 1894: 37–42).

As a simple but admittedly crude model we may imagine a pair of genes g and G such that G tends to cause some kind of altruistic behaviour while g is null. Despite the principle of 'survival of the fittest' the ultimate criterion which determines whether G will spread is not whether the behavior is to the benefit of the behaver but whether it is to the benefit of gene G; and this will be the case if the average net result of the behavior is to add to the gene-pool a handful of genes containing G in higher concentration than does the gene-pool itself. With altruism this will happen only if the affected individual is a relative of the altruist, therefore having an increased chance of carrying the gene, and if the advantage conferred is large enough compared to the personal disadvantage to offset the regression, or 'dilution', of the altruist's genotype in the relative in question. (Hamilton 1963: 354–5)

'Inclusive fitness' thus denotes not merely the 'fitness' or reproductive success of the individual organism, but of the particular genotype which that organism shares with his relatives, and the theory of inclusive fitness thus proposes the replacement of the *group* as the unit of selection by the individual or, more precisely, by genes shared by close relatives, and each organism is supposed to attempt to maximize the proportion of its own genes in the group of which it is a member. Individuals therefore follow strategies to increase their inclusive fitness, and have been selected *as if* they were doing a cost-benefit analysis before deciding on the approximate course of action in any given situation. To this end acts of assistance involving self-sacrifice will be of selective advantage only when they benefit a sufficient number of kin as opposed to non-kin, and the theory therefore indicates that the propensity for altruism and selfishness will be directly correlated with genetic relatedness.

The technical terms 'altruism' and 'selfishness' are thus basic to the theory, and it is important to see how they are defined:

An entity, such as a baboon, is said to be altruistic if it behaves in such a way as to increase another such entity's welfare at the expense of its own. Selfish behaviour has exactly the opposite effect. 'Welfare' is defined as 'chances of survival' [and, the implication must be, of reproduction], even if the effect on actual life and death prospects is so small as to *seem* negligible. One of the surprising consequences of the modern version of the Darwinian theory is that apparently trivial tiny influences on survival probability can have a major impact on evolution. This is because of the enormous time available[13] for such influences to make themselves felt. (Dawkins 1978: 4)

---

[13] Biologists are prone to rhapsodize about the immense amount of time available for evolution to occur. But immense by what standards? Five hundred million years

Sociobiologists such as Wilson, Dawkins, and Alexander have also maintained that it is possible to explain human as well as animal behaviour by this theory:

> . . . it resolved the ancient philosophical paradox whether humans are really selfish individualists or group altruists, and provided, I believe, the first simple, general theory of human nature with a high likelihood of widespread acceptance. (Alexander 1979. xii)

and,

> This general view of organic evolution I regard as firmly established; I do not expect any significant part of it to be retracted or altered in the future . . . the new view of natural selection provides a solid theoretical base from biology with which to pursue the questions of human sociality and the nature of culture. (Ibid., 65)

I shall argue, however, that when applied to human society the concepts of 'altruism', 'selfishness' (and related notions, such as 'investment') are logically confused, predictively empty, empirically false, and based on a comprehensive misunderstanding of the nature of social systems.

(*ii*) *Altruism, selfishness, and investment*

Hamilton's theory was developed to explain altruistic behaviour in species such as bees, ants, fish, rabbits, and birds where there is a close relationship between behaviour and genotype, a low level of intelligence and communicative ability by comparison with man, and, with the exception of the social insects, a low level of co-operative complexity. In such species, where individuals may not even have permanent social identities for purposes of recognition, and where it is not possible for individuals to inform others about which members of the group attempt to gain benefits without reciprocation, for example, so that each interaction can be treated

---

is certainly a very long time indeed for one man to write a novel, but it is almost infinitesimally brief for that same novel to be written by any kind of random process. Until one can calculate the probability of an event, therefore, claims about the amount of time available for it to occur are quite meaningless, yet biologists seem unable to provide any reliable quantification of the probabilities involved in organic evolution (see, e.g. Crick 1981: 87, and the discussions in Moorhead and Kaplan 1967). While evolution is the product of selection as well as variation, selection can only operate if variation can produce viable alternatives in the first place, which brings us back to the question of the probabilities involved.

in isolation from others, it may make sense for 'altruism' and 'selfishness' to be presented as quite distinct behavioural strategies, e.g.:

Blackheaded gulls nest in large colonies, the nests being only a few feet apart. When the chicks first hatch out they are small and defenceless and easy to swallow. It is quite common for a gull to wait until a neighbour's back is turned, perhaps while it is away fishing, and then pounce on one of its neighbour's chicks and swallow it whole. It thereby obtains a good nutritious meal, without having to go to the trouble of catching a fish, and without having to leave its own nest unprotected. (Dawkins 1978: 5)

Because such creatures cannot tell one another which member of the group has been making a meal of its neighbour's offspring (and may not even recognize one another individually), such strategies may pay off and it can be argued that, in a group of altruistic organisms, an individual with genes for selfishness would, through its descendants, spread those genes through the population at the expense of individuals with altruistic genes. But in the case of human society, where the members are a good deal more co-operative and intelligent than blackheaded gulls, they are aware that they live in a complex and interdependent form of association, so that if my neighbour needs help today I may need help tomorrow or next year, and they can also inform one another about which members of the group cheat. The more arduous the mode of life, or the more complex the problems to be solved, for example, the greater will be the benefits to *each individual* of mutual assistance, even if the people concerned do not necessarily realize this. So, if bodies are survival machines for genes, it is equally true that groups are survival machines for human bodies.

In this context, it makes very much less sense to present 'altruism' and 'selfishness' as though they were distinct strategies leading to quite different types of behaviour. No doubt, if one imagines certain isolated interactions, such as a man jumping into a river to save a drowning child or, on the contrary, a man who prefers to eat his sandwiches on the river bank and let the child drown, one can easily find illustrations of altruistic and selfish behaviour that are indeed very different. But the point is that in human society it is quite unrealistic to suppose that any individual could maximize his inclusive fitness as the sum of a series of isolated interactions of this kind. We therefore find that those individuals who follow elementary strategies of 'selfishness' and 'cheating', and persistently attempt to get without giving in social relations are not only rapidly detected but punished by sanctions ranging from contempt and low status to expulsion from the group or death. Correspondingly, rewards go not to the obvious spongers and cadgers and delinquents but to those who are perceived (rightly or wrongly) to contribute most to the welfare of the group. (I shall discuss exploitation in a moment.) Let me quote an instance from my own research in Papua New Guinea (Hallpike 1977*b*) to illustrate this.

The Tauade are pig-rearing shifting cultivators of the central mountains of Papua and, like many of the societies of this cultural area, have gradations of social status, with chiefs or 'Big Men' at the top, and 'Rubbish Men' at the bottom. The principal roles of the chiefs are the organization of feasts and dances, at which they make speeches on behalf of their group; the negotiation of peace between their group and others; and, to some extent, leadership in war. Their essential personal attributes are generosity, oratory, and political skills, and a willingness to accept compensation for wrongs rather than resort to violence at the slightest provocation. Typically, they maintain fairly stable polygynous unions of two or three wives. The rubbish-men, on the other hand, are the least effectual members of society: they are mean and avaricious, attempt to renege on their co-operative responsibilities such as contributing to feasts or making gifts on appropriate occasions, and are also said to be the worst thieves (theft being below the dignity of chiefs) and to be generally irresponsible. They are often unmarried, or have at most one wife. There is no doubt therefore that chiefs are reproductively more successful than the rubbish-men, and yet it is precisely the chiefs who are perceived to give the most to their groups.

But what sense does it make to say that the Tauade chiefs are *either* 'selfish' *or* 'altruistic' as these terms are defined in inclusive fitness theory? Their leadership requires more outlay of time and energy than is expended by the rubbish-men, but the benefits that accrue to them as a result are correspondingly greater, too. Sociologically speaking, we would say that the chiefs have greater effectiveness in social relations because they invest their social energies in a way that will reap the greater rewards, whereas the rubbish-men are socially ineffective because they think in terms of the immediate costs to themselves of socially useful actions rather than in terms of future rewards.

Thus in this society there are 'winners' and 'losers' in terms of social influence, but we gain no analytical advantage from trying to explain these differences as the outcome either of altruistic or selfish strategies, since as far as many instances of reciprocity are concerned, 'altruism' often turns out to be enlightened self-interest.[14] In other words, co-operation and competition in human society are not mutually antithetical modes of behaviour but are often mutually interdependent, so that in order to compete effectively one must be able to attract supporters and create networks of alliance and friendship, to which end assisting both kin and non-kin is often an intelligent strategy.

The essential vacuity of sociobiological theories of co-operation emerges even more clearly when we realize that Trivers (1971) advanced the argument that reciprocity even between non-relatives may also be of selective advantage (in order to account for reciprocal services between members of different species, such as cleaner fish and their hosts, where in the nature of things inclusive fitness cannot be involved). Trivers argues that 'reciprocal altruism' between non-kin can be selectively advantageous for the parties concerned, since each can expect to derive important benefits if the organism on which a benefit is conferred is prepared to reciprocate in kind when the original benefactor needs it in his turn. This will be especially true in the case of organisms such as man with a long life span, low dispersal rates, a high degree of mutual dependence and paternal care, the absence of rigid dominance, hierarchies, and the need for combat assistance. He concludes that it will not be necessary for the original beneficiary to reciprocate, and that systems of generalized reciprocity can develop in human society.

Trivers's theory of reciprocal altruism is certainly much closer to the facts of human co-operation than that of Hamilton. But the very reasonableness of the theory means, ironically, that the predictive value of inclusive fitness theory with regard to altruism and selfishness in human society is reduced to about zero. For we now have the predictions that in some circumstances people will give benefits to, or 'invest in', their kin, and that in others they will give benefits to non-kin. No doubt this is quite true, but it amounts to nothing more than the affirmation that *all* the various forms of human reciprocity are biologically possible, in so far as some

---

[14] I should like to make it clear that I do not believe that the social co-operation of human beings can be explained solely in terms of enlightened self-interest. The most elementary awareness of our fellow men tells us that sympathy and benevolence towards non-relatives, and love of our society, for example, are basic elements of human nature. But at this point I am simply concerned to show that, on their *own* assumptions (and not on mine), the arguments of the inclusive fitness theorists collapse when applied to the special conditions of human society.

argument of natural selection can, on the basis of these theories, always be constructed to 'explain' any act of reciprocity reported by social scientists.[15]

For humans, then, the surest method of ensuring social failure and, presumably, some corresponding decrease in inclusive fitness, is to follow simple strategies of 'selfishness' or 'cheating'. But human society provides at least two basic means by which some individuals can enrich themselves and their relatives at the expense of other members of the group. The successful person may gain control over some crucial resource such as land or cattle, or some crucial process, such as political leadership, and use this as a basis for exploitative relations with dependent individuals, who are induced to confer more benefits on the dominant individual than the costs to him of maintaining control over them. Or, the successful person may have some ability, such as specialized knowledge, that is valued by the rest of the group but is in short supply, and thereby extract more benefits from the rest of the group than the cost of supplying such services. In many cases, of course, there is no sharp distinction between these two basic ways of extracting payments from others, and politicians in particular (including Tauade chiefs) are fond of presenting relationships of the first kind as though they were of the second. But it is clear that social success as attained by these means will depend on a wide variety of specific abilities and personality traits, and is not some simple trait like 'altruism' or 'selfishness' that could conceivably be selected for, on a genetic basis.

We should now turn from the consideration of 'altruism' and

[15] The untestability of genetic theories of altruism would be even more complete if one were to follow Rushton *et al.* (1984), who suggest an alternative to the inclusive fitness theory: 'genetic similarity theory'. This postulates that individuals sharing similar characteristics, e.g. of physical appearance or personality, will be genetically disposed to behave altruistically to one another, even if they are *not* descended from a common ancestor. In real life, however, we have to take account of so many ways in which people can display similarities and differences—the whole gamut of physical variation, plus all the social variation of class, occupation, religion, ethnicity, etc. Resemblances in some characteristics will be counterbalanced by differences in others, and obviously certain characteristics such as race, class, and gender are likely to be more important than height (but what about a dwarf?), or degree of hairiness (but what about a woman with a moustache?). How are our genes supposed to perform the remarkably difficult task of calculating the extent to which another person does or does not resemble us? Is this a simple averaging procedure or are weightings involved, and so on? Once the actual implications of genetic similarity theory are followed through it becomes entirely unworkable because it demands extremely elaborate decision making procedures that would require something like a brain. The theory also assumes that co-operation in human society is based on friendship, which is a drastic over-simplification of the facts.

'selfishness' to the question of cost-benefit calculations in social relations: this is obviously an equally important aspect of inclusive fitness theory, since it is only in terms of the relations between costs and benefits that the question of why one individual should make a sacrifice to benefit another, perhaps unrelated, individual is raised at all.

Animals can only assist one another by doing something with their bodies, which inevitably involves energy expenditure and possibly danger as well, while the benefits of assistance are also restricted to physical welfare; therefore it is likely that there will be a reasonably close relation between costs and benefits. But while this limited basis for animal co-operation lends plausibility to the inclusive fitness theory at the level of birds, ants, and fish, it also severely reduces its relevance to human society, since one of the distinctive features of human society, besides its high level of co-operation and communication, is that it operates with all kinds of surpluses, a condition which potentially removes the necessity of any close relationship between the cost of bestowing a benefit and its value to the recipient. In human society there are many examples where large benefits, which clearly increase the reproductive chances of the beneficiary, are bestowed at little or no cost to the benefactor, e.g. the inheritance of property or an office from a deceased person, who can by definition no longer enjoy it himself, or the provision of surplus land to a person or group which needs it, of advice to the ignorant, of a job to a starving man, or of an honour conferred by a monarch or president. Thus, the resources from which the benefit is given (be they property, employment, knowledge, time or anything else) may not be needed, or be so abundant, or so easily renewable, that no sacrifice on the part of the benefactor is involved in their depletion, and hence no 'altruism' either. It is surely obvious that this asymmetry between the value of a benefit to a recipient and its cost to the benefactor, which we often find in human society, is made possible by surpluses of a kind for which there is no analogy in the animal kingdom.

Correspondingly, we also find that many benefits have no effect whatsoever on the welfare, or reproductive chances, of the recipients. This is partly because, as in the cases of many customary prestations, the value of the gift is primarily determined by its cultural significance rather than by any material importance. But it will also be recalled that Dawkins maintains that even effects on actual life and death prospects that *seem* so small as to be negligible may have cumulatively great effects on the selective process 'because of the enormous time available for such influences to make themselves felt', during which, it is presumed, even the slightest influences on survival probabilities have selective value. Dawkins seems to suppose that the relationship between benefits and chances of survival can be described by a continuous curve so that, for example, if doubling a man's salary increases his life chances by a certain amount, then giving him a rise of 1 per cent will also have some measurable effect on his life chances. Knowledge of the real world, however, tells us that the relationship is very often a discontinuous one, so that below a certain threshold benefits, such as giving someone a small piece of pork at a New Guinea pig feast, or inviting someone to tea in England, will have absolutely no effect on the survival of individuals and that therefore, however enormous the amount of time available, they can have no cumulative effect either. This will be especially true in societies where all adults have equal access to basic resources for survival and reproduction, and where reciprocity is governed by rules applying to all members of society. It follows that even when such benefits are bestowed they cannot be regarded as 'investment' in the way that the theory defines this. But to the extent that a good deal of reciprocity in human society is unrelated to the welfare of benefactors and beneficiaries, it is to that degree outside the predictive scope of the inclusive fitness theory.

The assumption that mutual assistance in human society must involve self-sacrifice is therefore a myth, once we consider a society as a long-term system of transactions. Human beings are sufficiently intelligent to recognize their mutual interdependence, and the organization of reciprocity is a response to this need that can be explained in terms of enlightened self-interest. Strategies of exploitation or the provision of valued services may be a means by which one individual extracts more benefits from another individual than it costs him to maintain the relationship with that individual, but to pursue such strategies requires a complex and variable set of personality traits so that they cannot be selected for genetically, especially since they will also be highly dependent on details of social organization.

Many benefits, moreover, do not even involve a sacrifice of welfare on the part of the donors, and may result in no measurable increase of the recipients' welfare either. In such a context, therefore, calculations of 'altruism' and 'selfishness' are meaningless as a basis for explaining co-operation and reciprocity, and there is consequently no reason for supposing that either of these behavioural strategies could have any distinctive genetic basis which could be subject to a process of selection. This being so, the distinction between kin and non-kin which is so crucial to the inclusive fitness theory does not have the significance attributed to it, as far as human society is concerned.

(c) *The mutual interdependence of competition and co-operation*
Because man's condition is essentially social, he is always dependent on one or more groups for physical and moral support: these groups may be the nuclear family, the clan, and the village or hamlet, at the more elementary level, and in more advanced societies may also include such groups as occupational guilds or unions, business firms, military units, and departments in large organizations. But prolonged and close association, whether based on blood ties, marriage, residence, or occupation, not only raises the level of solidarity and the intensity of affective relations in general, but also increases the possibility of conflict and the arousal of violent hostilities. Again, a perceived need for solidarity will render those who act in ways that are deviant or hostile to the interests of the group especially obnoxious to the other members.

Even the simplest band societies are themselves aggregations of nuclear families, and this subdivision or segmentation of societies into corporate groups becomes very much more pronounced as societies increase in size. Segmentation as the result of increased size or distance, or division of labour, thus operates on one hand to increase the solidarity of corporate groups but on the other hand, by this very process of nucleation or concentration of ties, it also tends to exacerbate the fragmentation and competitive potential of society. This complementary principle of fission and fusion, whereby groups may be allies in relation to other groups, but compete against each other at a more local level, was of course given its classical demonstration by Evans-Pritchard in his study of Nuer political organization (1940).

Traditional functional theory has assumed that because competition and conflict has the undoubted tendency to increase the internal solidarity of competing groups, it is therefore of functional value to society as a whole (e.g. Black-Michaud 1975). But as I have previously pointed out (Hallpike 1973), this type of argument relies on the arbitrary selection of one level of societal organization, e.g. the village or the clan, as normative and ignores the evident fact that, as among the Tauade or Konso or Yanomamo, villages and clans may not only fight one another regularly, but may also be related by various ties of marriage, exchange, and ritual in such a way that it is reasonable to describe them as being part of a larger society. The conclusion is therefore inescapable that societies have the inherent tendency to fission as well as to fusion, and that social co-operation leads by its very nature to competition, and vice versa. So, two business firms making one type of product such as beer clearly compete against one another at one level, but by that very fact have a vital interest in common as against those firms selling a different type of product, such as soft drinks. When we consider societies competing with other societies, or groups within a society competing with other groups we also find, as Walter Bagehot (1872: 51) expressed it, that the tamest are the strongest: those groups which can most effectively discipline their members are the best fitted for warfare, and for competition generally, as every general and trade union leader knows.

The interrelation of competition and co-operation emerges again when we consider that in many cases of competition, such as primitive warfare, or sport, while the opposing parties are in one sense enemies and are each trying to prove their superiority over the other, from another point of view they are united by their participation in the same activity. So, in primitive warfare, which is so often waged for the purpose of conferring glory and prestige on the male warriors, the combatants need each other since with no one to fight there would be no way for the men to display their military skill and courage. The same is obviously true of all forms of sport, and of economic, legal, and academic competiton as well.

Finally, we may note that competition, particularly within societies, has been an important factor in generating systems of law, decision-making procedures, and regulation in general. From all these points of view we reach essentially the same conclusion: that it is quite naive to elevate competition into the driving force of society, or to try to present it as operating independently from co-operation.

6. Adaptation in biological and social evolution

The idea of adaptation is not only basic to Darwinian evolution, but at first glance seems quite straightforward: some organisms are more efficient at survival than others and so leave more offspring than their less efficient competitors, thus perpetuating their more efficient characteristics through their descendants, and causing the less efficient characteristics of their competitors to die out. So Huxley writes that adaptation is all-pervading and of major importance: 'Adaptation cannot but be universal among organisms, and every organism cannot be other than a bundle of adaptations, more or less detailed and efficient, co-ordinated in greater or lesser degree' (Huxley 1974: 420). On closer examination, however, this apparent simplicity proves quite deceptive. So Lewontin says that 'There is virtually universal disagreement among students of evolution as to the meaning of adaptation' (Lewontin 1957: 395), and according to Simpson at the beginning of the chapter on adaptation in his book, 'the subject is so intricate that even here no more than a very general and summary statement can be attempted' (Simpson 1953: 160).[16] At the very beginning, let us be clear that for Darwinism the significance of adaptation cannot be understood unless the existence of rigorous competition between organisms is assumed.

(a) Competition under Malthusian conditions

As is well known, Darwin was greatly assisted in formulating his theory of natural selection by the insights of Malthus[17] on the inevitable population pressure of organisms on available food resources:

A struggle for existence inevitably follows from the high rate at which all beings tend to increase. Every being, which during its natural lifetime produces several eggs or seeds, must suffer destruction during some period of its life, and during some season or occasional year, otherwise, on the principle of geometrical increase, its number would quickly become so inordinately great that no country could support the product. Hence, as more individuals are produced than can possibly survive, there must in every case be a struggle for existence, either one individual with another of the same species, or with the individuals of distinct species, or with the physical conditions of life. It is the doctrine of Malthus applied with manifold force to the whole animal and vegetable kingdoms; for in this case

---

[16] I owe both these references to Harris 1960.
[17] See in particular Young 1969.

there can be no artificial increase of food, and no prudential restraint from marriage. (Darwin 1902:46-7)

The existence of rigorous competition is therefore an essential component of the Darwinian theory of natural selection: the less rigorous the competition, the less importance there is in improving the organic design:

Can it, then, be thought improbable, seeing that variations useful to man have undoubtedly occurred, that other variations useful in some way to each being in the great and complex battle of life, should occur in the course of many successive generations? If such do occur, can we doubt (remembering that many more individuals are born than can possibly survive) that individuals having any advantage, *however slight*, [*my emphasis*] over others, would have the best chance of surviving and of procreating their kind? On the other hand, we may feel sure that any variation in the least degree injurious would be rigidly destroyed. (Ibid., 58)

Some of those who apply Darwin's theory to social evolution tend to forget the vital importance of rigorous competition, and to suppose that 'efficiency' (however that be defined) will of its own nature inevitably tend to supplant 'inefficiency'. As Darwin said,

Nothing is easier than to admit in words the truth of the universal struggle for life, or more difficult—at least I have found it so—than constantly to bear this conclusion in mind. Yet unless it be thoroughly engrained in the mind, the whole economy of nature, with every fact on distribution, rarity, abundance, extinction, and variation, will be dimly seen or quite misunderstood. (Ibid., 46)

It is this assumption of rigorous competition (together with its consequences for reproductive success and failure) that gives adaptation its special significance in the Darwinian account of evolution. In a highly competitive situation, we can explain why variant form A has displaced variant form B by the superior adaptiveness of form A, and this superiority finds immediate expression in the relative reproductive success of A and B. It is only, therefore, on the assumption of high levels of competition that it becomes possible to claim that very minute adaptive advantages can be significant for reproductive success over long periods of time. In the absence of these conditions, therefore, the role of adaptation is at once reduced to the banal requirement that innovations must conform to natural laws and also have some degree of 'utility', whose definition in a social context must be extremely vague, e.g.

'desirable to at least some people', and 'not obviously self-defeating'. While adaptation in this weak sense will obviously be a general characteristic of social innovation, it is therefore nothing more than a limiting factor, and cannot aspire to the explanatory power which it assumes under the conditions that Darwin takes as the norm. Survival can therefore be evidence of *ineffectual competition* rather than of adaptive excellence.

Societies frequently have stable population levels and there may be an abundance of land, so there may be no necessity for any life or death struggle with their neighbours. We therefore find that although efficient warfare confers obvious competitive advantages on a society, there are or were large areas of the world where warfare was extremely inefficient, and waged not for land conquest or other political or economic gain, but for prestige and vengeance (see below, Chapter III, Section 1*d*). Such a state of affairs depends on the absence of any rigorous competition between groups, and the same is true of many cases of the inefficient use of the environment, which is possible, among other reasons, because all the societies in the area are equally inefficient. The ecological anthropologist Netting has argued that

No one but an arch determinist would claim that an environment demanded one and only one adaptation, but among the social and technological alternatives available, those that negatively affected the viability of the population adopting them would either be eliminated over time, or cause the extinction of that population. (Netting 1974*b*: 485)

But the conclusion does not follow. If 'negatively affect' means 'to make the group's survival impossible', then the proposition is tautologous; if it just means something like 'to create hardship', 'or to cause social friction', then no such result is predictable, because under conditions of weak or absent competition gross inefficiency can persist indefinitely.

We shall see that competition—between individuals, groups, and whole societies—tends to increase in rigour as societies become larger and more centralized, and internally specialized, and has reached an extremely high level with the emergence of societies such as our own. Military, political, economic, religious, and ideological competition between societies has, obviously, attained a hitherto unprecedented degree in the last few hundred years. It is precisely because competition is generally at a low level in primitive society that a rich profusion of social forms and beliefs which are (by our standards) of little or no practical necessity can flourish, and it is from these sources, pervaded with symbolic values, that some of mankind's most important institutions and ideas have grown. If primitive social life were in reality that rigorously demanding struggle in which only the fittest survived, many early institutions, practices, and beliefs would have remained stunted, or never have been introduced at all.

It is also worth emphasizing that adaptation is best at explaining how an existing population of organisms maintain their fitness in their specific environment. That is, it leads us to predict that any organic design will, over a sufficient number of generations, tend to become increasingly refined and efficient, up to a certain limit. But, unless the environment changes significantly, it is correspondingly difficult for the concept to explain the emergence of divergent forms:

The cultural ecologists of the 1950s and 1960s created a hypothetical (and often Panglossian) world of adapted cultural systems, in which it was becoming difficult to understand how change could ever occur. Cultural equilibrium- and system-models had become the main armaments of environmentalism, and they were leading the environmentalists into a dead end by doing such a fine job of explaining peoples' relationships with nature that change itself was becoming incomprehensible. (Rindos 1984: 17)

Similar reservations on the ability of the notion of adaptation to explain the emergence of novelty have been expressed by a leading biologist:

The conventional theory of evolution considers *adaptation* and *evolution* under the same terms of reference, both to be explained by random mutation, selective advantage, differential reproduction, etc. However, in my opinion, there is no scintilla of scientific proof that evolution in the sense of progression from less to more complicated organisms has anything to do with better adaptation, selective advantage or production of larger [numbers of] offspring. Adaptation is possible at any level of organization. An amoeba, a worm, an insect or non-placental mammal are as well adapted as placentals; if they were not they would have become extinct long ago. (von Bertalanffy 1969: 67)

(b) What is the level of adaptation?

If competition is fundamental to the notion of adaptation, we must also ask, competition between what? So biologists in recent years have debated whether selection operates at the level of the species, the individual, or the gene (see in particular the extensive literature cited in Hull 1981: 23–4; Boyd and Richerson 1982: 338; Rindos 1984:44–52). This problem is clearly not fatal for Darwinism, however. As Mary Williams has said,

> One level of selection may be more suitable than the other for studying a particular phenomenon, and the organism level may seem *primus inter pares* because we are more familiar with the phenomena for which it is most suitable, but *no* level of selection has absolute primacy over the others. (Williams 1973: 98)

But if the level of adaptation is a difficult problem for biologists, it is far more challenging for the social scientist. Every society comprises various institutions and subgroups which compete against each other, as do individuals, whereas the constituent organs and cells of an organism do not compete with one another. The student of society therefore faces the situation that what may be an adaptive strategy for one part of a society or for particular individuals may have adverse consequences for the rest of society: slave-owning is clearly adaptive for the masters, but less obviously so for the slaves; polygamy may be adaptive for men, but is it adaptive for women? And in what sense is it true that slave-owning and polygamy are adaptive for society as a whole?

In other words, competition and its attendant adaptations at one level may produce maladaptations at another, and even in biology it seems we cannot expect competition to produce adaptation as a matter of course. So Huxley quotes Haldane on the effects of competition between adults of the same species which

> renders the species as a whole less successful in coping with its environment. No doubt weaklings are weeded out, but so they would be in competition with the environment. And the special adaptations favoured by intra-specific competitions divert a certain amount of energy from other functions, just as armaments, subsidies and tariffs, the organs of international competition, absorb a proportion of the national wealth which many believe might be better employed. (Haldane 1932, cited in Huxley 1974: 484)

Huxley concludes:

> . . . we now realize that the results of selection are by no means necessarily 'good', from the point of view either of the species or of the progressive evolution of life. They may be neutral, they may be a dangerous balance of useful and harmful, or they may be definitely deleterious. (Ibid., 485)

We can generalize about social as well as biological adaptation in the following ways:

1. Because an institution exists, this does not mean that no other one would have been sufficient in its place,
2. Because an institution exists, it does not follow that it had to,
3. Because an institution exists, it does not mean that it is the best one possible,
4. Because an institution needs to exist, in order for a society to survive, it does not follow that it will actually appear. (Hallpike 1973: 169)[18]

7. Conclusions

It is obvious that the history and evolution of human society can be described as a process in which some types of thing become more frequent, while others become scarcer or vanish altogether. Biological evolution displays exactly the same characteristics, but this resemblance does not establish the relevance of Darwinian theory to social evolution, since all we are really elucidating are certain necessary aspects of change itself.

Societies are certainly not organisms, but still less can they be represented as populations of traits, social genes, or other notional entities, and the evident failure of the neo-Darwinian evolutionary model when applied to social systems basically derives from the impossibility of trying to explain the transformation of structured entities by a theory in which the concept of structure has no place. The structural properties of society in some ways resemble those of the organism, but while organisms are mortal, and can only perpetuate their design-type by reproduction, societies combine

---

[18] Eibl-Eibesfeldt (1979: 181–2) objects to these rather obvious propositions, contending that 'Points 1 and 3 say practically the same thing'. They do not. Point 1 refers to a situation in which there is *no* theoretically optimum solution to an adaptational problem, while point 3 refers to a situation in which the solution attained is *inferior* to the theoretically optimum. The distinction should be obvious. He also states that ' . . . points 2 and 4 have no heuristic value, since they are propositions that cannot be tested. Whether a structure that actually came into existence might also never have done so seems a question hardly worth quarrelling about, and whether an institution necessary for survival will really develop is not a question worth pondering' (ibid., 181–2). Point 2 asserts that not all institutions came into being because they were functionally necessary to a society (an example being the two-party system in British politics); while point 4 asserts that even if an institution is necessary to the survival or even well-being of a society, it will not automatically appear (an example would be disciplined leadership in an aboriginal society faced with attack by a colonial society). Both points are easily tested empirically, as these examples show.

reproduction and self-maintenance into the same process or, what amounts to the same thing, ontogeny and phylogeny are indistinguishable. There can thus be no basic particles of culture analogous to genes, and any attempt to discover such entities runs immediately into the insuperable problem of gigantic numbers. Co-operation and competition, so distinct in the organic realm, are closely combined in social systems at all levels of organization. In the same way, the distinction between organism and environment, which is fundamental to the Darwinian distinction between selection and variation, is largely meaningless in the context of social systems each of whose parts can affect all the others, and in which variation produced by the thought and behaviour of individuals is so greatly influenced by the society as a whole. It is therefore quite misleading to describe social innovation as random or blind in any sense comparable to genetic variation, and we must reject entirely the Darwinian exaggeration of selection at the expense of any interest in explaining the origins of innovation. We shall see, on the contrary, that an understanding of early forms and their potential transformations is crucial to any account of social evolution. Finally, while the concept of adaptation has a central place in Darwinian theory because of its links with reproductive success and the importance of a high level of competition, we shall see in the next chapter that these assumptions are highly questionable in the context of primitive society.

Most anthropologists have assumed that neo-Darwinism has answered the major questions of biological evolution, and that the only problem is applying it to the special properties of human society. The reader may by now have formed the impression that I am not entirely confident in the theoretical accomplishments of neo-Darwinism, and my doubts are shared by an increasing number of biologists, e.g. von Bertalanffy 1971, Webster and Goodwin 1982, Denton 1984, Ho and Saunders 1984. While it is logically possible, in view of the differences between organisms and societies, that Darwinism may still be the correct explanation of biological evolution, nevertheless, if the principles of random variation plus selection are so utterly incapable of explaining the development of fairly crude systems such as societies, how likely is it that they alone can explain the emergence of such amazingly ingenious and intricate systems as biological organisms? The emerging consensus among the biologists who reject neo-

Darwinism regards direction in evolution, the genesis of form, and the properties of structure as among the fundamental problems of evolutionary theory. In the words of Ho and Saunders, 'Our common goal is to explain evolution everywhere by necessity and mechanism with the least possible appeal to the contingent and teleological. Accidental variation and selective advantage—the foremost categories of explanation in neo-Darwinism—are thus relegated here to the last resort' (Ho and Saunders 1984; 5),

I do not, of course, maintain that the terms 'adaptation', 'variation', 'selection', 'competition', and 'survival', for example, cannot be used in discussing social evolution—they were after all originally borrowed from social discourse by biologists! But I have tried to show that they become radically distorted and, indeed, thoroughly misleading when they are brought back into social analysis from biology on the basis of Darwinian theory. It may be quite proper to describe a particular institution or custom as 'adaptive', or to refer to various aspects of social competition. Some ways of doing things are more viable than others, and in a process of social change some ideas, artefacts, etc., will become commoner than others. But to *explain* social evolution requires very much more than these processes, which are quite subordinate aspects of social systems.

III

The Survival of the Mediocre

1. The Survival of the Fittest

(a) Spencerian evolution

THE cultural selectionist theory of social evolution fails because it ignores the obvious structural properties of societies, but there is a more traditional theory, derived from Herbert Spencer, which fully recognizes these properties of social systems. Spencer was obsessed with those similarities between inorganic, biological, and social evolution which we noted at the beginning of the last chapter, and in the course of many volumes attempted to demonstrate that all these types of evolution conformed to certain universal principles of development in which a directional tendency was inherent, and not merely the result of selection:

From the remotest past which Science can fathom, up to the novelties of yesterday, that in which progress[1] essentially consists, is the transformation of the homogeneous into the heterogeneous. And now, must not this uniformity of procedure be a consequence of some fundamental necessity? May we not rationally seek for some all-pervading principle which determines this all-pervading process of things? Does not the universality of the *law* imply a universal *cause*? (Spencer 1891: I.35).

The universal law he proposed is that 'Every active force produces more than one change — every cause produces more than one effect' (ibid., 37). So it follows that

From the law that every active force produces more than one change, it is an inevitable corollary that during the past there has been an ever-growing complication of things. Throughout creation there must have gone on, and must still go on, a never-ceasing transformation of the homogeneous into the heterogeneous. (Ibid., 38)[2]

[1] Spencer is not using 'progress' here in a moral sense, but rather morphologically, as when biologists refer to 'higher' and 'lower' organisms.

[2] A later formulation of the Universal Law of Evolution incorporated the notion of development from rarefaction to condensation: 'Evolution is an integration of matter and concomitant dissipation of motion; during which the matter passes from an indefinite, incoherent homogeneity to a definite, coherent heterogeneity . . . ' (Spencer 1898: 396).

For Spencer, then, evolution is an inherently deterministic process, whereby certain 'higher' or more complex forms will inevitably evolve. On these assumptions about the nature of scientific laws, and the belief that the validity of a law is proportional to the number of its confirmations, he gathered voluminous evidence on the analogies between social evolution and the development of biological organisms both embryologically and at the level of phylogeny.[3] This obsession with bio-social analogy too often led him to treat the establishment of a resemblance as a scientific explanation, and some of the resemblances he detected are unconvincing, to say the least:

> If in an animal, any organ is worked so hard that the channels which bring blood cannot furnish enough for repair, the organ dwindles: atrophy is set up. And if in the body politic, some part has been stimulated into great productivity, and cannot get paid for all its produce, certain of its members become bankrupt, and it decreases in size. (Ibid., 290)

Despite this relentless and unfruitful pursuit of analogy, Spencer also gave considerable attention to the specific mechanisms by which evolution occurred, and in his view the struggle for survival was the basis of the whole process, both biologically and socially:

> As carried on throughout the animate world at large, the struggle for existence has been an indispensable means to evolution. Not simply do we see that in the competition among individuals of the same kind, survival of the fittest, has from the beginning furthered production of a higher type; but we see that to the unceasing warfare between species is mainly due both growth and organization. (Spencer 1893: II.240)

In the case of animals, the organs of perception and movement are improved by the competition between predators and prey, and these organic improvements have in turn led to superior types of nervous co-ordination, and so on.

> Similarly with social organisms. We must recognize the truth that struggles for existence between societies have been instrumental to their evolution. Neither the consolidation and re-consolidation of small groups into large ones; nor the organization of such compound and doubly compound groups; nor the concomitant developments of those aids to a higher life which civilization has brought; would have been possible without inter-tribal and inter-national conflicts. Social cooperation is initiated by joint

---

[3] It is frequently claimed, e.g. Toulmin (1981: 86) and D. T. Campbell (1965: 21–2), that Spencer's evolutionary model was based on embryological development alone, but this is incorrect.

defence and offence; and from the cooperation thus initiated, all kinds of cooperations have arisen. (Ibid., 241).

Thus the exigencies of primitive war select as leaders those men with the necessary qualities of courage and ability, and war leadership extends itself into civil leadership as well (ibid., 338). But all such leadership, being based on the personal qualities of an individual, is ephemeral, and can only become instituted on a permanent basis by being conjoined with the hereditary principle (ibid., 343). This hereditary authority is reinforced by beliefs in the special relation between the chiefs and ancestral spirits and deities (ibid. 348–9), and so on.

This is a perfectly sensible theory of the origin of political authority, even though in Chapter V we shall have occasion to modify it substantially, and throughout his writings one encounters many equally penetrating observations. So, for example, he pretty well anticipates Carneiro's very important concept of circumscription[4] as an essential element in the formation of the state:

Though, in regions where circumstances permit, the tribes descended from some original tribe migrate in all directions, and become far removed and quite separate; yet, where the territory presents barriers to distant migration, this does not happen: the small kindred communities are held in closer contact, and eventually become more or less united into a nation. (Spencer 1891: I.281–2)

He was also very conscious of the fundamental evolutionary significance of the increasing size of societies:

Mass is both a condition to, and a result of, organization. It is clear that heterogeneity of structure is made possible only by multiplicity of units. Division of labour cannot be carried far where there are but few to divide the labour among them. Complex co-operations, governmental and industrial, are impossible without a population large enough to supply many kinds and gradations of agents. And sundry developed forms of activity, both predatory and peaceful, are made practicable only by the power which large masses of men furnish. (1893: I.11)

For Spencer, then, societies are like organisms in all essential respects (1891: I.272–7), in which every part has some essential function in relation to the well-being of the whole, and whose evolution is a series of adaptive responses to the pressures of

---

[4] See below, Chapter V, Section 5a.

competition, the whole of this process exemplifying the famous
principle of the Survival of the Fittest.[5]

Spencer's theory resembles Darwin's in so far as both regarded
competition as the driving force of an evolutionary process leading
to optimal adaptive efficiency, and this has led to some confusion
among those anthropologists who have not realized that while
Spencer at once accepted Darwin's concept of natural selection into
his scheme of evolution, this was subordinate to the general
implications of his organic view of society which was essentially
un-Darwinian and, if anything, Lamarckian.[6] Random variation
has little or no place in Spencer's theory, and social adaptation and
advance is the direct response of a structured entity to its
environment.

But Spencer's approach to evolution therefore evades those
obstacles which are fatal to a neo-Darwinian cultural selectionism.
Recognition of the structural properties of society excuses us from
the futile search for the elementary particles of culture; competition
is stressed, but not to the virtual exclusion of co-operation, to which
Spencer ascribes equal importance; and whereas the selectionist
theory completely fails to grasp that innovations are not only
selected by the social environment, but are produced by that
environment and also change it, Spencer was well aware of this
essential interdependence between the components of social
systems.

Spencer's conception of society was shared by Durkheim,
Radcliffe-Brown, and the whole structural-functionalist school of
anthropology, although recognition of this theoretical debt has
been muted,[7] to say the least: Evans-Pritchard, for example, in *A
History of Anthropological Thought* (1981), makes only a few
allusions to the name of Spencer, and does not discuss his
significance. Spencerian evolution cannot therefore be treated as an
outmoded and eccentric deviation since, as Freeman implied in the
passage cited in Chapter I, it is a basic aspect of the whole
functionalist model.

The criticism of the Spencerian version[8] of evolution that will be

[5] As is well known, this phrase was invented by Spencer, not Darwin.

[6] For a discussion of some differences between Darwin's and Spencer's
evolutionary theories see D. Freeman 1974.

[7] As already noted, Radcliffe-Brown did acknowledge the value of Spencer's
evolutionary views, and more recently they have been vigorously defended by
Carneiro (1973), in particular.

[8] A number of modern sociologists, notably Parsons, Eisenstadt, and Smelser,

developed in this chapter is that while societies are certainly not mere populations of traits, as the selectionist would have it, they do not possess organismic properties to anything like the extent that Spencer believed, either: they may be structures, but they are very sloppy structures. The organismic conception of society faces three basic theoretical problems. The first is how to specify the functional requirements of any society in ways that are not empty and trivial; the second is to provide adequate criteria for identifying an adaptive or functional trait; and the third is to explain how groups of people can be expected regularly to produce institutions whose subtle

have attempted to apply functionalist theory to social evolution. Their work has been subjected to what is in many ways an excellent critique by Smith (1973), which is why I shall give little attention to it here, apart from a brief indication of my major criticisms.

One of the basic problems for functionalist theory, as we shall see, is the extreme difficulty of specifying any basic functional requirements for all societies that are not empty and trivial. So Parsons's list of 'pattern maintenance', 'integration', 'goal attainment', and 'adaptation', for example, seem little more than tautologous restatements of what the word 'society' means, and his theory of social evolution is essentially *descriptive* rather than explanatory. He claims, for example, that the basic process in social evolution is 'differentation', which involves every area of social organization and culture generally, not just the division of labour. Differentation, however, produces 'strain', and this in turn requires 'reintegration' by means of more generalized value systems and more specialized and flexible institutional forms to re-establish social equilibrium. As Smith rightly observes: 'So general and overarching are those conceptual processes that they can be discerned in every period and culture and trend, and yet leave us as ignorant as before as regards the why and how of the period, culture or trend. I am not here talking of small-scale changes, however potent or exciting for particular populations. It is the large-scale changes like the growth of urban life in river valleys, of centralized empires, of new world religions and ethics, or of new economic activities and groups like trade and merchants, which appear to be equally intractable material for a neo-evolutionary framework. A theory so general and abstracted from even these processes can only appear misleading and irrelevant' (Smith 1973: 45). Nor have I been able to find in the work of Parsons any explanation of how the individual members of a society are able unconsciously to develop, as a matter of course, those institutions which are functionally necessary. Again, Parsons justifies his theory by appealing to the authority ,of Darwin: 'Such basic concepts of organic evolution as variation, selection, adaptation, differentiation, and integration are our concern—appropriately adjusted to social and cultural subject matter' (Parsons 1977: 48), but he makes no attempt to examine the implications of Darwinian theory and to incorporate it into his account of social evolution in an informed way. A further source of weakness in these functionalist theories of evolution is that they have clearly been formulated on the basis of Western industrial society, which is taken as the norm by which all evolutionary development is to be assessed (see Smith 1973: 35-7). Yet it must surely be obvious that any theory of social evolution should begin with those societies that for the greater part of human history have actually been typical—primitive societies. It is precisely here that functionalist accounts of social evolution are weakest: Parsons's discussion of primitive society, for example, in Chapter I of *The Evolution of Societies* is enormously over-simplified and displays very little anthropological knowledge.

adaptive and functional properties they will normally have no means of understanding or of producing voluntarily. We shall first examine the problems of functionalism, but by way of clarification it is important at this point to say something about the two concepts of adaptation and function.

In principle one may define a functional custom as one which helps to maintain the efficiency of some system of relationships within a society, and an adaptive institution as one which contributes to the survival of the society in its natural and human environment, especially through the survival of its individual members, and responds to changes in that environment. But in practice the distinction is often hard to maintain, since efficient social systems would also, by that very fact, seem likely to be better adapted than inefficient ones. (To complicate matters further, a functional institution can also be described as one that is well adapted to other institutions in the society). Merton defines 'functions' as: '. . . those observed consequences which make for the adaptation or adjustment of a given system: and dysfunctions, those observed consequences which lessen the adaptation or adjustment of the system . . .' (Merton 1967: 105). The two concepts largely overlap, therefore, and present a number of essentially similar theoretical problems, but they are not identical. So, the concept of adaptation is related particularly to the whole issue of technological determinism and the extent to which social institutions are dependent on the ecology and associated modes of production. The concept of function raises separate problems about the nature of social systems, and whether or not they are holistic entities that have needs or necessary conditions of existence, to which specific institutions make an essential contribution.

(b) *The functionalist illusion*

Durkheim and Radcliffe-Brown wrote persistently of the 'normality' or 'health' and the 'pathology' of social systems, which have needs or ends, or 'necessary conditions of existence' (Radcliffe-Brown 1952: 178). This theory encounters three basic difficulties: (1) how are these systems' needs or 'necessary conditions of existence' to be identified?; (2) what specific need does each institution fulfil? and (3) by what process could individuals, unbeknown to themselves, be expected as a matter of course to develop institutions that meet these needs?

In an attempt to answer the first question, Aberle *et al.* (1950) proposed four basic states under any of which a society would no longer exist:

(*a*) biological extinction or dispersal of the members
(*b*) apathy of the members
(*c*) war of all against all
(*d*) the absorption of the society into another society.

In relation to these basic limiting conditions they then proposed the following functional prerequisites;

(1) provision for adequate relationship to the environment, and for sexual recruitment
(2) role differentiation and role assignment (the allocation of certain essential tasks)
(3) communication
(4) shared cognitive orientations
(5) a shared, articulated set of goals
(6) normative regulation of means
(7) the regulation of affective expression
(8) socialization
(9) the effective control of disruptive forms of behaviour.

That is, if all these 'needs' are not satisfied, one or more of states (*a*) – (*d*) will occur. But as Cancian observes, 'The needs are so broad that almost any social process can be as contributing to at least one of them' (Cancian 1968: 34), and, 'Since almost all societies survive, barring sudden catastrophes, it is impossible to test a statement of the form "X is necessary for survival" if X is universal' (ibid.,35).

The same criticism can be made, even more forcefully, of the vacuous concept of 'social solidarity' which was basic to Radcliffe-Brown's variety of functionalism. As numerous critics have pointed out, there are no means of establishing any objective tests of this concept: item (9) on Aberle's list, 'the effective control of disruptive forms of behaviour' is very weak precisely because, like 'solidarity', what is actually disruptive will depend to a considerable extent on culturally relative norms of disruptiveness.

Any functionalist explanation that is intended to be a real explanation and not just a recapitulation of the facts must not only establish a precise need, but also demonstrate that a particular institution exists because it satisfies this need in an appropriate and effective way. Is it possible to improve on the precision of the list of needs of Aberle *et al.*? One might suggest that any enduring society is likely to encounter problems in the following areas of its organization:

(1) leadership and social co-ordination
(2) the division of labour by gender and age
(3) rules for the allocation and control of scarce resources and property
(4) reciprocity and co-operation
(5) dispute settlement
(6) the regulation of relations with the supernatural
(7) relations with other communities, including recruitment.

The basic forms of relationship in primitive society are derived from descent, relative age, gender, and residence, but these are so general in nature that no specific functional connections can usually be established between them and the general needs or problems faced by a society. So, for example, a segmentary lineage system or an age-grading system may, simultaneously, satisfy all the items (1)–(7) in my list.

Cancian's objection that no precise connection can be established between general needs and specific institutions therefore retains its force, not only because of the generality of the needs in question but because of the multi-functional nature of descent, relative age, gender, and residence. The concept of function only makes sense when we can ask 'What is this institution for?' as the physiologist can ask, 'What is this organ for?' Once we have established this, we are then in the position to ask how a particular aspect of the institution helps it to attain its goal. But the broader the goal, the less valuable is the notion of function, and when we come to society as a whole, its goals, in any meaningful sense of that word, are so broad as to make the use of the concept of function entirely pointless.

The problem of functionalism can be approached from another direction. This is the problem to which I have already alluded: assuming that an institution is functional, and that this function is not of some limited and obvious kind, then by what possible process could a mass of individuals, all unaware, have developed it? It is highly significant that no functional theorist has ever been able to provide any explanation of this singular and striking phenomenon, other than one based on natural selection, or on the assumption that whatever is adaptive will, somehow, appear.

Sztompka's *System and Function* (1974) is one of the most

thorough and sympathetic treatments of functionalism in recent years, and he gives close attention to this central problem. One possible explanatory mechanism is the 'rational' hypothesis that all members of a society 'have a full and adequate knowledge of the social goals (global preferred states of the system or social requirements), as well as of the best means to achieve them, and they take this knowledge into account as the basic motivation behind their own actions' (ibid., 147). This hypothesis merely assumes what it sets out to prove, namely, that people actually realize what is objectively functional for their society and try to accomplish this. Sztompka largely concedes the point, and his reference to limited cases of 'rational social planning based on the scientific diagnosis of the relevant situation' does nothing to restore plausibility to the hypothesis. We observed in Chapter I that the notion of social evolution as guided by conscious purpose is fundamentally untenable.

An alternative is what he calls the normative hypothesis, ' . . . the integration of individual and social goals is brought about by the full internalization by the members of a society of that society's norms and values, and the consequent motivational importance of internalized norms and values in guiding individual actions' (ibid., 148). But, as he very pertinently remarks, even if we know how social norms and values are transferred into individual rules and purposes, 'we are still left with the crucial problem of why these norms and values themselves are fitted to the preferred states of the system or to its functional requirements' (ibid., 149).

Next, he considers the 'structural' hypothesis that the link between the functional requirements of a society and individual goals is 'the result of the direct influence of existing structural arrangements on the motivation of the individual acting within the framework of these arrangements' (ibid., 150). But, as Sztompka says, this approach suffers from the same defect as the normative hypothesis in so far as it gives no explanation of why this structure rather than that had become dominant in the first place.

What, then, is Sztompka's solution? He concedes that there has simply not been enough time in human history for the probabilistic assumptions of random mutation to be applicable; that competition between societies only rarely leads to the elimination of societies; and that in reality there is a good deal of functional inefficiency in societies. Instead, he believes that

a *generalized notion of evolution* [i.e. one not restricted to the specific properties of biological evolution] parallel to the generalized notion of systems, could probably suggest the mechanism we are seeking. Although the task remains to be performed, its eventual completion seems to promise the solution of the teleological dilemma in functionalist thinking. (Ibid., 146).

This, rather obviously, is no solution at all, and our second line of enquiry thus leads us to the same conclusion as the first: that **functionalism is a myth, and that where functions exist they are, unless of recognizable value to the people themselves, either of** accidental origin, or else an illusion in the mind of the anthropologist. To illustrate this we may briefly consider two typical functionalist explanations of particular institutions. Gluckman, for example, advanced the theory that civil wars in the Zulu and Swazi states actually tended to strengthen rather than to weaken tribal unity, since the kingship itself was the prize for the competing factions who, rather than abolishing the monarchy, or fleeing from its rule, wished to maintain it for themselves:

At this stage of political development, where an integrating economic framework was lacking in the kingdom, civil wars did not break the national unity, but preserved that unit as a system. I am tempted to go further and suggest that a periodic civil war was *necessary* to preserve that national unity: sections fought for the kingship, and not for independence from it. (Gluckman 1954: 78).

Quite apart from the problem of why and how leaders of factions should have behaved in a way that, unknown to themselves, was necessary for the solidarity of their society, the actual analysis seems factually incorrect:

The evidence, even for Zulu and Swazi, does not support Gluckman's main thesis. It is true that, both here and among other Bantu, rebels or conspirators usually aim at usurping the chieftainship, and not at breaking away to found tribes of their own. But, as shown by our examples, the outcome of their attempts almost always was the flight or secession of one section, and there are even instances of men who seceded without making a bid for the chieftainship. Indeed, of the eight tribes whose histories were summarized in the preceding section, five broke up into two or more separate tribes each (Xhosa, Tawana, Pedi, Letswalo, Venda), and the three others (Zulu, Swazi, Kgatla) were all permanently deserted by groups whose descendants now belong to other tribes. This can hardly be regarded as valid ground for maintaining that civil war 'strengthened' tribal unity, let alone was 'necessary' for its preservation. (Schapera 1956: 175–6)

We may conclude with an example from Papua New Guinea. Dr Margaret McArthur has described (McArthur n.d.) how the

Kunimaipa have a taboo against eating one's own pigs, and a breach of this taboo is supposed to lead to various forms of sickness. Pig feasts, at which large quantities of pork are given to members of neighbouring groups as well as one's own, are basic institutions of Kunimaipa life, and these occasions are organized by leaders who must be able to establish peaceful relations with neighbouring groups in order to allow guests to travel in safety. Gluckman concludes:

. . . we start here with what seems . . . to be a rather silly, indeed childish, superstition, and we end with a widespread system of international trade which contributes to an international peace in which the leaders of each group have the greatest interest, in order that they may be able to maintain their own positions among a very irascible and quarrelsome set of people. (Gluckman 1967: 62)

The taboo on eating one's own pork and that of close relatives does not in fact have the consequences which Gluckman supposes. In the first place, it would be quite possible for groups of relatives within each community to exchange pork, without this leading to any system of reciprocity between different groups. Secondly, far from being peaceful affairs, Kunimaipa pig feasts, like those of the other language-groups in the Goilala Sub-District, are essentially competitive and are part of the general system of agonistic relations and inter-group hostility that is normal in New Guinea. In particular, they are typically the occasion of widespread adultery, and violence and killings associated with this; and the pig herds increase to such a size before the feasts that they cause much damage to gardens, and many quarrels between neighbours.

Moreover, even if Gluckman's interpretation of the consequences of the taboo on eating pork were correct, we are still faced with a daunting task of explanation. Are the Kunimaipa supposed to have a subconscious intuition of the sociological consequences of their taboo? This scarcely seems likely: even Gluckman says

. . . I cannot help puzzling about how a custom of this sort, with all its widespread effects, originated. We may never know the answer: yet increasing research on primates and archaeological evidence seems to suggest human society evolved not from a situation in which one family group established relations with other independent family groups, but more probably among a troop or company of manlike beings, who slowly established rules which compelled sharing. (Ibid., 63)

This, of course, even if true, tells us nothing about how the taboo on eating one's own pork originated among the Kunimaipa.

One suspects in fact that the symbolic association between the exchange of food and the exchange of women (found in many areas of New Guinea and elsewhere) provides a more immediate clue to the origin of this taboo than is to be found in speculation about early hominids. So Mead records the following set of associations among the Arapesh:

> Other people's mothers
> Other people's sisters
> Other people's pigs
> Other people's yams which they have piled up
> You may eat,
> Your own mother
> Your own sister
> Your own pigs
> Your own yams which you have piled up
> You may not eat.

(Mead 1940: 352, cited in Hage and Harary 1983: 159)

There is, however, one feature of society that is universal, has some beneficial consequences, and is not intended by the people as a whole. The social characteristic I have in mind is that of 'cross-cutting ties', a concept particularly associated with the work of Gluckman. The essence of the idea is that people who are enemies in terms of one set of relations are constrained by other social ties:

> . . . men quarrel in terms of certain of their customary allegiances, but are restrained from violence through other conflicting allegiances which are also enjoined on them by custom. The result is that conflicts in one set of relationships, over a wider range of society or through a longer period of time, lead to the re-establishment of social cohesion. (Gluckman 1963: 2)

As an example of such a process he quotes Colson's study of the Tonga of Northern Rhodesia (now Zambia). In this case a man of clan A kills a man of clan B. The two clans break off relations, and apparently in days before colonial rule the men of B residing in A's territory would flee home, and vice versa. Women of clan A married to men of clan B are threatened and insulted by other men of that clan, which upsets their husbands and is an additional factor disposing clan B to accept the compensation offered through the good offices of the affines of both clans, so that peace is restored.

Up to a point, as Gluckman says, the principle of cross-cutting ties is indeed a very general and important aspect of all social life, so general and so important, in fact, that one is led to ask if it is not simply a necessary aspect of society as such. For if a society were composed of a number of groups which existed in complete isolation from one another, in what sense would they constitute a single society at all? Given that the very nature of 'society' involves the existence of relationships between the members of different groups, it also follows that some of these relations will be positive, and others negative: as we noted in Chapter II, co-operation and competition are inextricably linked in all human interaction.

The fact that cross-cutting ties *must* exist in all societies means therefore that we can never appeal to them for an explanation of any specific institutional form. For example, in Chapter IV we shall examine some aspects of Konso society, the organization of whose towns is marked by the dispersal of lineages throughout the various wards of each town. But it is vacuous to claim that this feature of Konso society can be explained by the functional value of cross-cutting ties, since the people themselves can give a much more precise explanation. 'We do this', they say, 'because we do not like to be dependent on our kinsmen, and because our neighbours and friends are in some ways just as important as relatives.' Here, the form and extent of cross-cutting ties between ward and lineage members can be explained by specific features of Konso values and social organization, making any appeal to the functional necessity of cross-cutting ties quite superfluous.

There is, moreover, no guarantee at all that the mere proliferation of cross-cutting ties will in and of itself lead to social harmony. As I have previously pointed out at length (Hallpike 1973, 1977*b*, and see also Warner 1937: 127–9; Ferguson 1984: 16–17), where the groups so linked have no internal cohesion or effective leadership, and where the ethic of vengeance is important, the very proliferation of such linkages may actually be the basis for an extension of violence. It can thus be shown that the case of cross-cutting ties is not an exception to the generalization that societies are not systems that miraculously maintain themselves in some optimum state of internal harmony unbeknown to their members. When we examine such claims, they either prove to be analytic statements about the very meaning of the word 'society', or accidental, or illusion on the part of the ethnographer.

(c) Adaptationism

When we call something 'adaptive' we imply that it 'conforms to requirements', especially those of natural laws, and that it is perceived as useful or desirable by those who introduce or retain it. In these two basic senses culture is certainly adaptive, but this elementary truism will be challenged by no one. The question is, first, whether it is the adaptive advantages of an institution that explain its survival and spread to different societies, and secondly, if so, how people can regularly produce such institutions whose adaptive and functional value they do not understand. This is an essential point. For if organisms could consciously change their own design in the pursuit of optimal adaptive strategies, the whole Darwinian hypothesis would be superfluous and, in the same way, if societies were governed by conscious purpose we should not need a theory of social evolution either. There is no problem in explaining why people trade, build houses, or control vehicles by traffic-lights. But when we are trying to explain institutions whose adaptive advantages are not so obviously attributable to purpose, the Spencerian concept of evolution becomes in one respect indistinguishable from the Darwinian, since both, ultimately, are concerned with consequences, with survival in a state of rigorous competition. Whether we are Darwinians or Spencerians, therefore, we would expect to find that those forms which are most widespread, and have the greatest capacity to survive are those which, in a competitive milieu, have shown themselves to be the best adapted.

Durkheim expresses an idea that has become part of the common stock of anthropological thought:

It would be incomprehensible if the most widespread forms of organization would not at the same time be, *at least in their aggregate*, the most advantageous. How could they have maintained themselves under so great a variety of circumstances if they had not enabled the individual better to resist the elements of destruction? On the other hand, the reason for the rarity of the other characteristics is evidently that the average organism possessing them has greater difficulty in surviving. The greater frequency of the former is, thus, a proof of their superiority. (Durkheim 1964*b*: 58)

In view of the frequent inability of individuals to explain their customs and institutions, many theorists have therefore supposed that societies must be treated as natural, adaptive systems comparable to organisms, each of whose parts has some function in relation to the necessary conditions of existence of the society and its members. So while many anthropologists would reject the application of Darwinian principles to society, their implicit assumptions are nevertheless saturated with ideas of adaptation to the environment, produced by some sort of selective process whereby inefficient or maladaptive institutions are weeded out. These assumptions have seemed especially justified in the case of primitive society, whose remarkable elaborations of systems of marriage and kinship, age, reciprocity, and symbolism appear to resist practical, utilitarian explanation. In such cases there is an almost irresistible temptation to search for that hidden level of adaptive significance beneath superficial appearances:

The more we study the culture of people both 'savage' and 'civilised', the more it becomes apparent that no social institution comes into being and continues to flourish unless it has a definite function to fulfil in the culture of which it forms a part. (Wedgwood 1930: 6)

According to Malinowski:

The functional view of culture insists therefore upon the principle that in every type of civilization, every custom, material object, idea and belief fulfils some vital function, has some task to accomplish, represents an indispensable part within a working whole. (Malinowski 1926: 133)

Kluckhohn expresses the same idea when he says:

no cultural forms survive unless they constitute responses which are adjustive or adaptive, in some sense, for the members of the society, or for the society considered as a perduring unit. (Kluckhohn 1967: 79)

The following passage by a leading authority on kinship is replete with the kinds of adaptationist reasoning we are discussing:

The study of kinship is the study of what man *does* with these basic facts of life — mating, gestation, parenthood, socialization, siblingship, etc. Part of his enormous success in the evolutionary struggle lies in his ability to manipulate these relationships to advantage. And this is important. He does not simply play games with them for sheer intellectual excitement. That is sport reserved for anthropologists, and perhaps some Australian Aborigines. He utilizes them in order to survive, and beyond survival, to prosper. At some level he is bound by circumstances to adopt one mode of adaptation rather than another; but he is free to vary this within limits and to his advantage. I am not implying that he does this as a result of conscious choice, indeed this can rarely be the case, but that natural selection can, as it were, take advantage of his powers of choice and intelligence to make him exploit possibilities to their fullest range, and probe modes of adaptation and advance that are unknown and unknowable even to the most intelligent of his primate cousins. No Australian Aborigine sat down and worked out a blueprint for the complicated systems of kinship and marriage for which he is justly famous; but his ability to conceptualize and classify was as much a factor in this successful development as the claws of the tiger or the neck of the giraffe were in the survival and success of these species. (Fox 1967: 30–1)

In a similar vein, the adaptive value of warfare in New Guinea is alleged to be in rectifying man – resource imbalances (Vayda 1971); ritual cycles among the Maring maintain the correct size of pig herds (Rappaport 1968), large scale human sacrifice among the Aztecs was really to provide high quality protein from cannibalism (Harris 1979: 334–40); the combination of matrilocal residence and patrilineal descent reduces the risk of feuding (Murphy 1957; see also Otterbein (1968), who supplies strong evidence that this proposition is factually correct). Matrilateral cross-cousin marriage provides more effective social cohesion than patrilateral cross-cousin marriage and is therefore much commoner (Lévi-Strauss 1969: 445–6). The cow is sacred in India because of its manure and its value as a draught animal (Harris 1978: 141–2). The segmentary lineage has been selected for in tribes that are involved in predatory expansion against their neighbours (Sahlins 1961). Divination by hunters in North America is actually a randomizing technique which allows them to find more game than they would by conscious judgement (Moore 1957), and so on.

All these alleged cases of adaptive institutions assume that a material or functional benefit must be the real explanation for the existence of the institution, and that the explanations given by the people themselves are irrelevant, if not actually false and deluded. For Durkheim, indeed a scientific account of society and its evolution depended on the elimination of all explanation based on the purposes or needs of individuals, in favour of purely causal explanation:

. . . the fact that we allow a place for human needs in sociological explanations does not mean that we even partially revert to teleology. These needs can influence social evolution only on condition that they themselves, and the changes they undergo, can be explained solely by causes that are deterministic and not at all purposive. (Durkheim 1964b: 93)

The biologist can at least produce a plausible explanation for the adaptive features of organisms: they result from natural selection operating on the accumulation of random mutations in millions of individuals over thousands of generations. But we saw in the previous chapter that this solution is not available to the student of social evolution, because the number of possible trait combinations is far too large, the number of societies far too small, and the time span of social evolution far too limited, for any model based on random mutation of single traits plus selection to have a chance of working.

It is essential to realize that no anthropologist has been able to give any other explanation of how, unbeknown to themselves, groups of people should have been able to develop these wonderful adaptive systems, whose subtle adjustments to the demands of the environment are only detectable to twentieth-century science. Instead of a genuine Darwinian explanation, what we are in fact typically given is a low-grade organicist theory in which it is assumed that adaptive traits will automatically emerge by some compulsion from the environment or from the social system itself. Nor is any attention given to the extent of competition between societies or types of adaptation, or to the penalties of failure and to how, exactly, maladaptive institutions will be weeded out. Again, it is simply assumed that they will disappear. According to Rappaport, for example, 'Human adaptation resides ultimately in wholes through the mobilization of which the ambitions of separate men may be subordinated to common interest while at the same time the operation of society may be reviewed and tempered by the psychic and physical needs of the humans who compose it' (Rappaport 1978: 101). But how does this process occur?

To talk in general terms about the adaptiveness of institutions is easy enough, but let us remind ourselves of what was established in the previous chapter about the essential requirements for using the notion of adaptation in a truly explanatory way. First, it is essential to be able to specify in precise terms the trait whose presence and survival one wishes to explain, and to specify with equal precision the adaptive value which this trait confers, and on whom. What is adaptive for one level or type of group (the family or the individual) may be maladaptive at higher levels, or vice versa. Second, we must be able to show that it is the *adaptive* aspects of the trait that explain its survival, and this in turn is most effectively demonstrated by showing that there is a high level of competition and that success or failure in adaptation will have a significant effect on societal or individual survival. Third, an adaptive argument must always be based on existing circumstances, not on possible future circumstances: arguments of the second type are completely unfalsifiable, since one can *always* say, 'Even if this characteristic of society is, at the moment, adaptively neutral, or even rather maladaptive, it might be adaptive if appropriate conditions arose in future.' Selection can only operate on the basis of actual conditions and on what is actually present in relation to them. Fourthly, let us remember that the great strength of the Darwinian theory is that it can claim to provide a means by which elaborate and efficient systems can develop without conscious purpose.

Darwinism is a logically coherent and empirically testable theory, and no adaptationist argument can claim to be a genuine explanation of a social feature unless it can give a convincing account of how it could have originated. By this I do not mean some precise historical reconstruction of each institution, for which the necessary information may often be inadequate or non-existent, but a general theory which can at least explain in principle why we should expect adaptive institutions to be the rule rather than the exception, and which is sufficiently precise to be related to specific institutions, in the same way that the natural selection theory is used to explain specific organic traits in terms of their adaptive value. Without such a theory, the sociological use of adaptationist argument becomes the empty assertion that whatever is, is necessary, and is also vulnerable to the objection that any apparent case of adaptation is merely fortuitous.

Anthropologists seem oblivious to these problems, however, and use the concept of adaptation as a kind of 'Open, Sesame!' to explain every puzzling institution. Misled by the apparent simplicity and obviousness of the idea, they ignore all the requirements for its valid use, and their so-called 'explanations' degenerate into the unfalsifiable belief that survival is itself the proof of adaptive value. If further confirmation of this belief is required, a search is made for *any* beneficial consequence of a practice or institution, which is then asserted to explain it.[9] They do not seem to notice that the central problem remains unsolved: just how are societies regularly able to produce the right adaptive responses without any conscious

---

[9] The philosopher of science, R. Harré, provides a good illustration of this enterprise: after observing that 'A cursory glance at the relation between social practice and local social requirements suggests that even the most pessimistic commentator must be impressed by the rather high degree to which practices are adapted to needs', he gives as an example 'The expressive practices of football hooligans [which] are very nicely adapted to resolving and remedying the humiliations they perceive themselves to have received in the world of work and school' (Harré 1981: 163–4)

understanding of these problems on the part of their members? So, according to Marvin Harris,

Countless studies of extant sociocultural systems and bio-organisms have been made to discover the functional status of sociocultural and biomorphic structures. In both realms the results of these studies indicate that bio-organisms and sociocultural systems are largely if not exclusively composed of positive-functioned, that is, useful traits. (Harris 1960: 60–1)

As far as human society is concerned, this must be one of the least substantiated claims in the history of anthropology. No doubt, if by 'useless traits' one means those that are dangerous, painful, and disgusting, or obviously self-defeating or suicidal, then indeed such traits must be few and far between. But if Harris's claim had more force than this, why has the ingenuity of countless anthropologists been so taxed over the years to explain the *usefulness*, in any objective sense, of such institutions as Australian 4- and 8-section systems, prescriptive alliance, *gada* systems among East Cushitic societies, human sacrifice, the intricacies of the Indian caste system, and the exposure of corpses and the prevalence of warfare in New Guinea? It is precisely because primitive and traditional societies are littered with such cases of institutions that serve no apparent practical purposes—however valuable or practical they may seem to the indigenous people themselves—that anthropologists such as Harris have been driven to ignore the native explanations and invent their own, based on the belief that all mankind has the primary aims of security, greater reproductive efficiency, and optimum energy yields. So I remarked that:

'function' has frequently the covert significance of 'What a twentieth-century materialist rationalist intellectual from Europe or America thinks is a sensible allocation of labour and resources'. When such a person encounters primitive societies, he is baffled by their indifference to *his* criteria of what is sensible, and therefore casts about for some hidden reason which will be the *real* explanation for their behaviour. (Hallpike 1973: 459)

Biologists, like anthropologists, have also indulged in facile, *post hoc* rationalizations that treat any kind of 'good' result from a trait as a sufficient and obvious explanation for its existence. As G. C. Williams has said:

A frequent practice is to recognize adaptation in any recognizable benefit arising from the activities of an organism. I believe that this is an insufficient basis for postulating adaptation and that it has led to some serious errors. A benefit can be the result of chance instead of design. The decision as to the purpose of a mechanism must be based on an examination of the machinery and an argument as to the appropriateness of the means to the end. It cannot be based on value judgments of actual or probable consequences.[10] (Williams 1966: 12)

Williams therefore emphasizes the necessity for biologists to specify a precise function for each trait or organ whose adaptive significance they are trying to explain: vision for the eye, dispersal and reproduction for the apple, hearing for the lateral line in fishes, and so on. Social functions, however, are much harder to specify than biological functions. No doubt, in modern society especially, there are institutions whose basic functions are fairly clear—local government in the Western democracies, for example—and we know that in the last hundred years or so there has been a great deal of experiment in an effort to produce more efficient forms; but even here the question of cultural values has to be considered, not just cost-effectiveness. When we come to primitive societies, which are ascriptively rather than functionally differentiated, (see below Chapter III, Section 3) the problem of establishing the precise function of a given institution becomes very difficult indeed, because each institution may have multiple functions and, conversely, there need be no relation between one type of function and one type of institution. Explanations based on superior adaptiveness must therefore depend on the precision with which the function or goal of the alleged adaptation can be defined: the vaguer the function, the weaker the explanation.

In the last chapter we also established that genuinely adaptationist solutions derive their force from the existence of a high level of competition, and it is to the level of competition in primitive society that we must now direct our attention, since if the condition of a high level of competition is not met, the whole adaptationist enterprise becomes drastically weakened.

---

[10] According to another leading biologist: 'I call that approach to evolutionary studies which assumes without further proof that all aspects of the morphology, physiology and behaviour of organisms are adaptive optimal solutions to problems *the adaptationist program*. It is not a contingent theory of evolution or hypothesis to be tested since adaptation and optimality are *a priori* assumptions. Rather, it is a program of explanation and exemplification in which the purpose of the investigator is to show *how* organisms solve problems optimally, not to test *if* they do.' (Lewontin 1979: 6)

(d) The level of competition in primitive society

As Darwin emphasized, we cannot understand the full significance of adaptation unless we also realize the importance of competition since, clearly, the lower the level of competition, the less important does adaptation become. For Spencer, too, competition was the *sine qua non* of social evolution.

The level of competition can be understood in a number of different ways. First, it will depend on the number of variant forms that are available at any one time and place, and secondly on the importance that attaches to choosing the right variant. If there is only one possible way of doing something, no matter how important that something may be, clearly no competition between ways of doing things exists, and if there are many ways of doing something but all are equally viable, then also the level of competition will be low or absent. In industrial society, for example, there are many different ways of organizing sales or production, and choosing the right variants will make the difference between the success and failure of a business. Thirdly, there may be competition between groups of people as well as between ways of doing things, and here we would assess the level of competition in terms of the penalties paid by those who lose.

If we consider the question of variant forms, it is clear that in many small-scale primitive societies the level of variation is very much lower than in large complex states. In New Guinea, for example, we find remarkable similarities of social organization and cultural values from one end of this enormous island to the other, and a similar tendency to homogeneity can be found in many other areas of the world. Secondly, as we shall establish in detail in the next chapter, there is ample evidence that a wide variety of institutional forms are equally viable in more or less any primitive environment. To this extent, then, we must conclude that as far as variant forms are concerned, there is a low level of competition in primitive society.

Turning to actual physical competition between groups, the level of this is most appropriately assessed by the nature of primitive warfare. In the words of Carneiro, 'Cultural selection, which operates even on traits of little or no adaptive value, acts with special intensity on traits directly concerned with survival. And since there is generally no greater challenge to a society's existence than war, it is here that we find selection operating most rigorously.'

(Carneiro 1970: xii). While some anthropologists (e.g. Divale and Harris 1976; Carneiro 1970; Otterbein 1970) suppose that primitive societies are typically in highly competitive relations with their neighbours, this belief is not supported by the evidence. No doubt, there are many instances of population movements that are associated with warfare (e.g. the Kukukuku (Hallpike 1978); Ok (Morren 1984); Jivaro (Ross 1984)), but in order to be of evolutionary significance competition must involve significant gains and losses of a permanent nature. It is well established, however, that in many areas of the world warfare among acephalous societies does not typically lead even to land conquest, let alone the extermination or conquest of whole societies, nor to any significant military innovations (like those which gave such dramatic success to the Zulu, for example).[11]

It is quite clear that in general primitive societies are not sufficiently well organized, either politically or militarily, to destroy or subjugate their neighbours, especially since their neighbours are likely to be similar in social organization. This kind of competitive success as a rule is only obtained by societies with considerable political centralization and military discipline, and is by no means typical of primitive society generally. Otterbein's table shows this clearly (see Table 1).

Turney-High's classic survey of primitive warfare (1971) has shown that the primitive is essentially a warrior rather than a soldier, that is, an armed civilian, not under proper military discipline, who fights basically as an individual, pursuing his own aims or those of his kin. Turney-High regards the following criteria as indicating whether or not a society has reached the 'military horizon', that is, is capable of using military force as an instrument of political aims:

1. Tactical operations
2. A definite system of command and control, with a hierarchy of command, discipline, and planning
3. The ability to conduct campaigns, as opposed to mere raiding
4. This in turn requires the organization of adequate supply
5. Warfare must be motivated by clear aims of the subjugation of the enemy.

---

[11] Andreski (1968: 7–19) maintains that there is a univeral state of competition in all societies for wealth, power, and prestige.

Table 1

Political System	Reasons for Warfare		
	Defence (including revenge), plunder, or prestige	Political control	
Centralized	7	9	16
Uncentralized	30	0	30
	37	9	46

$\chi^2 = 20.98$ $p = <.001$

Source: summarized from Otterbein 1970: 69, Table 14.

With regard to tactical operations, Turney-High singles out a number of typical deficiencies in primitive warfare:

(*a*) Lack of co-operation: the formation often fails to fight as a unit, and there is a tendency to individual heroism and self-reliance.

(*b*) Lack of troop specialization: 'Lack of specialization is just as much a mark of primitivity as is lack of specialized tools in the material culture of peace, or lack of division of labour in social and economic life' (ibid., 53).

(*c*) Lack of concentration of force at the critical point:

Violation of concentration at the critical point is so prevalent in primitive war as to be one of its features. The warrior, in contrast with the soldier, almost always yields to the temptation to accomplish useless little victories, the slaughter of one man or the crushing of one small party. This fritters away the force's strength so that more often than not no real advantage is acquired by the victor nor permanent injury done to the defeated. (Ibid., 53)

(*d*) Lack of exploitation of victory: in true warfare,

The mere defeat of the opposing force is not the sole aim of the attacker. He is not like the boxer who is content to win a technical decision 'on points', but seeks to administer a knock-out. The purpose of war is to impose our will upon the enemy, and this must be accomplished by completely breaking down his resistance by capturing or destroying his armed forces. Accordingly, the attacker, having driven the enemy from his position, must *exploit his success* by inflicting all possible damage upon his defeated opponent. Local successes are promptly followed by utilizing the supports and reserves to press the defeated enemy. (Ibid., 103, citing *Tactics and Techniques of Cavalry*, 6th ed., 1935, p. 6)

Because in many cases the aim of subjugation is lacking, and warfare is often pursued for the sake of prestige, 'The end of the enemy would have meant the end of manhood society, the *raison d'être* for the male population' (ibid., 104).

Thus primitive war can display the following characteristics of correct tactical operations:

1. Aggression: the intent to close with the enemy
2. Sometimes, correct formations
3. Use of terrain
4. Surprise
5. Simplicity of plan.

It is weak, however, in other aspects of tactics, almost necessarily, given the frequent lack of specialization, discipline, co-operation, and planning, tactics usually only found in societies with professional armies, e.g.:

6. Troop specialization
7. Co-operation between tactical units
8. Concentration of force at the critical point
9. Mass and the economy of force—using the right number of men to accomplish the mission in hand
10. The exploitation of victory.

With regard to the next item on the 'military horizon', the need for discipline and command structures, the uncentralized nature of the warrior society, dominated by the search for glory, goes together with indiscipline, the lack of clear command structure or professionalism, and the voluntary nature of participation in military exploits. Thus the Assiniboin Indians

. . . never fully accomplished their missions, and the chief cause of failure was insubordination. No man could make plans, carry them out, or actually lead. The nominal Assiniboin head chief was only leader of his own band, which contained many men who considered themselves his equals. Everyone's advice was asked and nobody's taken. A party might look fair on setting forth, but soon old personal grudges cropped up and the party was disrupted by disputes. In the end, a large percentage of the army drifted home in detached parties. (Ibid., 61–2)

Self-selection for the leadership and the voluntary recruitment of those who wished to join war parties is evidently a very inefficient means of selecting a body of troops. (Not all primitive societies however, conducted war in this way: thus the Jivaro, an acephalous society of South America, were able to decide collectively to go to war, to make up a party, and elect a real leader who could give orders and be obeyed. He alone made plans and decided the disposition of forces, and the young warriors pledged themselves to obey him without question.)

But in addition to having an effective leader and a committed body of soldiers, it is necessary to have a hierarchy of command:

. . . in working out the combat functions of even so small a unit [as the modern platoon or squad], good team work often requires that the men working at some distance from the squad leader shall be supervised by someone. In large commands the subordinate commander is even more indispensable. No human can direct more than just so many other men; no master mind can care for all details of supervision. A hierarchy of junior commanders is essential. So likewise is some type of staff to care for details. (Ibid., 75)

Primitive war typically has weak development and articulation of command functions, such that hierarchies, chains, and specialization of command are usually poorly developed.

The organization of supply, that is, the movement from place to place of essential material, especially food, is a crucial aspect of true war, and the absence of a proper supply function is a very clear mark of primitive war. While sporadic raiding can be maintained indefinitely across borders between groups living on their own land, prolonged campaigning involving the pursuit of an enemy across hostile or unknown territory requires a level of supply normally not attained by primitive society. Hence such wars ordinarily come to no real end, and the status quo is not fundamentally changed. Supply and the prosecution of campaigns are only necessary when the aim is the political subjugation of the enemy, but this is quite untypical of primitive society.

(e) Primitive warfare as an adaptive trait

The evidence concerning primitive warfare not only provides strong support for the view that effective competition at this level of social organization is weakly developed, but can also be used to test the theory that the frequency and survival of traits is directly related to their adaptive advantage. No one, of course, would maintain that people will not fight over land or anything else which is valued and in short supply, but a real test for the adaptationist position is frequent warfare in the *absence* of competition over scarce resources. Just such a case is provided by New Guinea, an area with low population densities, but high levels of warfare and conflict generally.

A number of ecological anthropologists, such as A. P. Vayda and R. A. Rappaport, have attempted to argue that despite appearances, warfare may indeed be an adaptive device that prevents pressure on land resources.[12] The society Vayda studied are the Marings of the Madang and Western Highlands Provinces, but as he himself admits, 'The fact is, however, that when we were doing our field work in the 1960s we could find no clear evidence of such population pressure anywhere in the Maring region except in the Kauwatyi and Kundagai territory, where there were tracts of permanent grassland and degraded secondary forest' (Vayda 1971: 20). Nor do we find that there was any significant relationship between aggression and land shortage, according to Vayda himself:

Some of the smallest Simbai Valley clan populations, living at the edge of a vast expanse of unoccupied forest extending eastwards along the Bismarck Range, fought as often as did some of the large clan cluster populations of the Central Maring area, where there are not only higher population densities, but also such other indications of greater pressure on resources as shorter fallow periods for garden plots . . . (Ibid., 6)

When people were actually driven out of their territory, the casualties do not seem to have been very heavy:

When some 300 Tyenda were routed following the Kauwatyi's surprise raid, 14 Tyenda men, 6 women and 3 children were killed. The 600 Manamban lost only 8 men and 3 women in the course of being routed by the combined forces of the Kauwatyi and Tukumenga (although there had been 20 other Manamban deaths at the fight ground previously). If these figures indicate the heaviest mortality suffered in Maring wars, it may be questioned whether routs in general were effective in decisively altering the capacity of groups to defend and use land. (Ibid., 13)

Nor does routing usually appear to have deprived the losers of their land more than temporarily:

I have accounts of 21 routs. In seven of these the groups did not even leave their own territory and took refuge in portions of it at some distance from the borderlands where the enemies had engaged them. Among the 14 other cases the members of some routed groups fled across the Bismarck Range or

---

[12] This, of course, is directly traceable to Malthus. See e.g. Davie 1929: 11.

the major rivers, but there were others when they remained closer and, indeed, sometimes continued to maintain a claim to their territory by going to it for food. (Ibid., 13)

In 13 of these 14 cases, the defeated groups returned to their territory. The only group which failed to do so was the now extinct Worau, 'that had been living on the south side of the Jimi River, where it had been attacked by an alliance of the Mindyi and Kumom clans' (ibid., 11). When some groups returned to their territory after being attacked, they re-established their prosperity, made appropriate sacrifices to the ancestor spirits, and replanted the boundary stakes to signify that they would not relinquish any land. Not all groups did this, and by not replanting the stakes would leave some territory vacant to be annexed. It is significant, however, that Vayda adds, 'Informants stated this as a possibility but were unable to cite any recent examples' (ibid., 17).

Vayda summarizes the facts of land redistribution as follows:

The fact remains that most groups in recent decades have held on to their own lands after warfare. (Ibid., 19)

It also seems that the majority of fights, of varying degrees of severity, led to peace without any territorial conquest at all. (Ibid., 19–20)

In fact, it was not merely the majority of routs that were not followed by land conquest: no rout except one had this result. In the face of all this evidence, presented by Vayda himself, that the level of Maring warfare and its causes had no ascertainable relation to land shortage and population redistribution, he still maintains the utility of an ecological explanation:

In other words, even if territorial conquests had only been an infrequent rather than a regular aftermath of Maring warfare for a considerable time, the warfare remained the kind that could, through an already institutionalized systemic process, lead again to the adjustment of man/ resource ratios whenever demographic and ecological conditions changed sufficiently to make it appropriate for this to happen. (Ibid., 22–3)

And he appends the note, 'when, if ever, such conditions obtained throughout the Maring area is problematic'. The 'already institutionalized systemic process' is illustrated in Figure 1.

This looks very impressive, but on closer inspection we can see that this 'institutionalized systemic process' represents nothing more

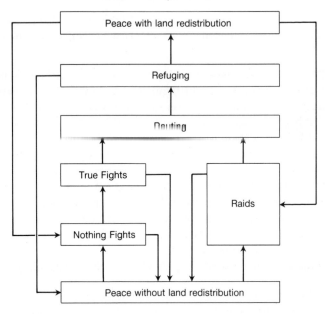

Figure 1. Phases of the process of war and peace among the Marings
Source: Vayda 1971: 19.

elaborate than the possibility that a group may, if sufficiently determined and strong, chase another group off its land permanently, instead of allowing them to return as is usually the case. Even if this were as efficient and complex an adaptive mechanism as Vayda claims, he gives no thought to explaining its development, or showing how, despite being manifestly inoperative throughout living memory, it has been retained in the 'cultural repertoire'. He simply assumes that, being adaptive, it must have been evolved and maintained in existence. It is also quite fallacious to explain an existing institution on the basis of its hypothetical value in the future.[13]

[13] Some of these points were initially made in my paper 'Functionalist interpretations of primitive warfare' (1973). The only noteworthy attempt at a rebuttal was by Professor Netting (1974), and see my reply to this (Hallpike 1974*a*). Vayda merely responded 'In a future book on war, peace, and the structure of adaptive response processes, I shall be correcting some of Hallpike's many misinterpretations' (Vayda 1974: 141). When this book was eventually published (Vayda 1976), the only reference to my criticisms was in a footnote (p. 107, n. 2), 'Some critics of my New Guinea case study have misconstrued my objectives in so far as they have assumed that the study was part of a programme designed to show the

Sillitoe has made a general survey of New Guinea societies and compared population density with the frequency with which land is the object of conquest in war, and he concludes that

although some groups occasionally fight wars to gain land, this in fact is a rare occurrence. This is not surprising, because few groups have approached, let alone exceeded, the carrying capacity of the land they occupy. The data throw considerable doubt on attempts to explain war in New Guinea by ecological factors alone. (Sillitoe 1977)

As Ember (1982) and Ferguson (1984: 30) have pointed out, however, there is a strong correlation between population density and the frequency with which victorious groups take over the land of those whom they defeat. So, if we arrange Sillitoe's data into societies with low (<20 p.s.m.), moderate (20–100 p.s.m.), and high (100+ p.s.m.) population densities (Sillitoe 1977: 73, Table 2), and into four categories of land conquest (1, never; 2, rarely; 3, sometimes; and 4, normally (ibid., 73 Table 3)), we find the correlation shown in Table 2 of $p = < .001$

This is a very strong correlation but, of course, it only establishes an association between population density and the consequences of victory, and leaves unexplained the high levels of warfare that also occur all over New Guinea in areas of low population density as

pre-eminence or universality of certain environmental causes of warfare.' The critics he referred to were myself, and Dr K-F Koch, whose *War and Peace in Jalémo* (1974) had concluded independently from my 1973 paper that ecological explanations were quite inadequate to account for Jalémo warfare. Our criticisms of the Maring case study were that it did not even explain the *Maring* data, let alone the data for the rest of New Guinea, or farther afield. In 1977 I published my account of Tauade warfare, and showed in detail, as Koch had done for the Jalémo, that warfare among the Tauade could not be explained by ecological factors. Neither at the time of field work, nor in the traditional society, was there any evidence of man/resource imbalances, and warfare was shown to be a product of social organization and a particular value and belief system. In some ways warfare was facilitated by the particular environment and technology of the Tauade, but was certainly not produced by these factors. Vayda, in his review of the book (1979), adduced no fresh arguments in defence of his position (which I had further criticized in Hallpike 1977*a*, and which Sillitoe (1977) had subjected to a major and unfavourable survey). Vayda simply denied my arguments, which he described as 'arbitrary', and even questioned my data on the lack of population pressure on available land. Vayda and McCay (1978) attempted to reply to various criticisms of ecological explanations, but they did not address themselves in any effective way to the objections raised by myself and others. Their article is interesting, however, in conceding that warfare may be related to the motives of individuals. On this, see also Peoples 1982. For further analyses of ecological explanations of primitive warfare see King 1976 and Lizot 1977. A recent volume of essays defending the ecological theory of warfare (Ferguson 1984) fails to rebut the basic objections of its critics (see Hallpike 1985*b*).

The Survival of the Mediocre

Table 2.

	Population density			
Warfare Categories	Low	Moderate	High	N
1	**5**	1	0	6
2	1	10	6	17
3	0	0	2	2
4	0	0	1	1
	6	11	9	26

$\chi^2 = 21.38$ df = 6 $p = <.001$[14]
The cell in bold type contributes 9.49 to the total χ^2 value.

well. The obvious interpretation is that warfare occurs throughout this area for reasons unrelated to scarcity of resources (Koch 1974, Hallpike 1977), but that where people are also short of land this will be a simple reason for using their customary pattern of warfare to secure more.

Materialist explanations of primitive warfare are also prone to a false antithesis between cultural factors (warfare for prestige and revenge) and material factors (warfare for scarce resources). On this basis it is then assumed that if warfare confers any material benefits on the victors, therefore it must really have been waged for material reasons. The fallacy here is quite obvious, since there is no reason why plunder and land conquest and even extermination should not *also* satisfy the desire for revenge or glory. And even where material gains are made, the costs in death and injury may be irrationally high. In our own society, for that matter, whose economic activities are alleged to be based on utilitarian motives, wealthy men continue to pile up fortunes long past the point when they can derive any material benefit from doing so, while criminals steal and murder for gains they might have achieved more efficiently by legitimate means. Material profit is therefore an unreliable indicator of material motive.

If adaptationist arguments are unconvincing explanations of primitive warfare in situations where resources are abundant, are they necessarily more successful in showing that warfare is adaptive where resources are scarce?

Another ecological theorist of warfare, Netting, is at least willing to concede that 'Warfare in technologically primitive societies has long been enigmatic because it does not do what it is popularly

[14] This value of p corresponds with that obtained by Ember (1982: 646) from different calculations.

supposed to do. In many cases, primitive warfare results neither in large-scale killing nor in the conquest of enemy territory and appropriation of resources' (Netting 1973: 164). In typical adaptationist fashion he assumes that 'A general explanatory model must at least begin with such biological observations as "the function of much conflict appears to be the control of food and reproduction through the control of territory and the maintenance of well organized dominance hierarchies that serve to reduce the amount of fighting in a group" (Nader 1968: 326)' (ibid. 164).

Accepting Vayda's model of warfare as a response to social tensions produced by population pressure on resources, he is naturally much exercised to explain cases of warfare which, despite apparent pressure on resources, do not lead to population redistribution by land conquest, as among the Kofyar of Northern Nigeria.

The Kofyar practise the intensive cultivation of millet and other crops on terraced and manured fields, being also 'favoured by local conditions of rainfall, dependable water, good soils, and a terrain that discouraged invasion' (Netting 1973: 166), so it is not surprising that population density should be high-290 p.s.m. in 1952. Apparently it was about double this earlier in the century, and while at the time of fieldwork the Kofyar showed no obvious signs of malnutrition, they do seem to have suffered food shortages in earlier years when densities were higher.

Netting obtained accounts of warfare between the villages, which have always been stable and coherent units, with effective mediation and sanctions against internal violence. His data show that while formalized battles took place, the line of warriors never engaged in hand to hand fighting, although ambushes occurred with greater likelihood of loss of life, and one party of warriors was sometimes successful in raiding and looting an opposing village. But in 37 hostile encounters of all types there were apparently only 56 deaths (1.5 per encounter) and these were equally divided between the combatants (ibid, 171). (See also Netting 1974*a*.)

Even more important was the fact that none of the adversaries gained any territory by occupying farmlands or house sites. The rewards of plundering another village were not high. One Bong man whose homestead was burned told of losing three goats, some chickens, all his hoes, and five bundles of *acha* (*Digitaria exilis*). Such a loss was significant but not irreplaceable, and the victim suffered no major hardships. Many looters came away empty-handed. War did not alter village boundaries nor did it materially benefit more than a few individuals. (Ibid., 172)

Despite the rather unpromising support which his data give to an ecological theory of warfare as a means of adjusting man/resource ratios among these people, Netting, like Vayda in the case of the Marings, is not discouraged. Following Wynne-Edwards (1962) he maintains that if there is population pressure on the environment warfare can function as a homeostatic device to restore equilibrium to the system. In order for this to happen two processes must occur: one is the transmission of information on the imbalance of the system, while the other restores the balance of the system when necessary. Netting concedes that no rectification of imbalance actually occurred, but maintains that Kofyar warfare nevertheless performed the other function of a homeostatic system by acting as a means of transmitting information of resource imbalance:

Kofyar warfare in all its varieties appears to have been an expressive, rather than an instrumentally effective institution. Fighting acted to transmit information to the participants concerning the relation of their population to their resources. It signalled disequilibrium, but did not directly rectify it. (Ibid., 172)

Since they were well aware of the shortage of food from their daily experience (e.g. ' . . . stories of an earlier period mention seasonal hunger, begging, and children crying for food', as well as frequent theft (ibid., 167)) the Kofyar must have been remarkably obtuse if they needed to make war on one another in order to communicate these self-evident truths, especially since they also took no notice of this 'information' they were allegedly giving themselves. Indeed, not only did Kofyar warfare fail to rectify the population pressure on resources, it actually made it very much worse, since this mode of warfare was essentially concerned with boundary maintenance, which entailed the loss of areas of bush land between the competing villages so that in consequence it could no longer be used for agriculture:

The ambushes that menaced travellers and farmers in outlying fields served to further contract and solidify the effective boundaries of individual settlements. War thus induced increasing nucleation and the creation of new massive borders in the shape of no-man's lands between rival alliances . . . (Ibid., 173)

It appears that as the boundary-defining activity of warfare increased in frequency and severity, *both* sides lost access to important resources. (Ibid., 173)

Rather than reducing competition, warfare seems to have caused a quantum jump in the pressure of population on a shrinking available environment. (Ibid., 173-4)

Warfare did, ultimately, reduce Kofyar overpopulation but only through the indirect route of disease. The abandonment of large areas to bush and subsequent tree cover allowed the tsetse-fly to flourish in increasing numbers, and with them sleeping sickness became much more prevalent, while cerebro-spinal meningitis, always endemic in the area, seems to have increased through overcrowding. There is also some evidence that men delayed marriage until after 30 in order to prove themselves first as warriors, and that this may have had the effect of restricting the birth rate. It is no doubt true that populations limit themselves by increasing their liability to disease but this would have occurred anyway in the Kofyar case without recourse to warfare, simply as the result of malnutrition and associated illnesses.

In so far as the raiding activities that are typical of primitive warfare often involve the destruction of dwellings, animals, crops, trees, and other food reserves, we can assume that on balance its ecological effects will certainly be harmful, but not so harmful as to extinguish the groups which practise it.

(f) The survival of the mediocre

Why, then, is primitive warfare so common if it is not adaptive? The answer is clearly that there are a number of very widespread factors that lead to it: the aggressive propensities of young males, lack of effective social control in acephalous societies, mutual suspicions between different groups, revenge, the self-maintaining properties of social systems, problems in developing mediatory institutions, religious associations between success in warfare and vitality in general, and so on. Warfare of the primitive type continues to exist indefinitely because of these factors, until the development of the state or colonial conquest replaces these forms of warfare by those of 'true' warfare, in Turney-High's terms. We have here an excellent example of the principle that the mere survival of a social feature may have nothing to do with adaptive advantage, but instead be a case of the survival of the mediocre, one of the fundamental principles of social evolution.

(*i*) *Some cases of early technology*

A good example of the persistence of an unimpressive design is the Oldowan hand axe, the oldest of which so far discovered is dated to about 2,600,000 years before the present. It consists of a water-worn pebble about the size of a fist, from one end of which a few chips were knocked off to produce a rough edge that could be used for hacking, mashing, scraping, grubbing for roots, and breaking bones to extract the marrow. This tool remained in use for at least two million years until the development of the Acheulian hand axe, made of flint, which gave a sharper edge.

To argue that the Oldowan hand axe persisted for so long because it was marvellously adapted is clearly absurd: as a piece of technology it was crude in the extreme, and very far from the most efficient use that could have been made of stone even at that time, as subsequent developments in the later Palaeolithic and the Neolithic showed quite clearly. It persisted because it was perceived to have *some* use, because no one could think of how to improve the design, and because no alternative and superior version was available from some other culture. If, however, only tools of a Neolithic level of efficiency could work at all, clearly no human technology would ever have got started.

The principle of the survival of the mediocre is even better demonstrated by the history of horse-harness, since this example comes from a much later period of history, when technology was incomparably more advanced. The harnessing of horses to pull wheeled vehicles was first invented in early Mesopotamia, and was of the 'throat-and-girth' type. This, in the words of Joseph Needham,

consists of a girth surrounding the belly and the posterior part of the costal region, at the top of which the point of traction is located. Presumably in order to prevent the girth being carried backwards, the ancients combined it with a throat strap, sometimes narrow, more often broad, which crossed the withers diagonally and surrounded the throat of the animal, thus compressing the sterno-cephalicus muscle and the trachea beneath it. The inevitable result was to suffocate the horse as soon as it attempted to put forth a full tractive effort, accompanied by the lowering and advancing of the head. (Needham 1965:304–5)

The modern type of harness, whose early form was developed in China during the Ch'in dynasty or previously in the Warring States period, is based on a padded collar which 'bears directly upon the sternum and the muscles which cover it, thus linking the line of traction intimately with the skeletal system and freeing fully the respiratory channel. The animal is now able to exert its maximum tractive force' (ibid., 305). The difference in efficiency between these two types of harness is dramatic. The French cavalry officer Lefebvre des Noëttes carried out practical tests, and found that two horses harnessed in the throat-and-girth manner could produce a tractive effort of only half a ton whereas a single horse with collar harness could easily draw one and a half tons, a sixfold increase in power (ibid., 312). As Needham says,

The really astonishing thing about the throat-and-girth harness is the immense spread which it had both in space and time. We find it first in the oldest Chaldean representations from the beginning of the −3rd millennium onwards, in Sumeria and Assyria (−1400 to −800). It was in sole use in Egypt from at least −1500, where it is shown on all paintings and carvings of chariots and horses, and it was likewise universal in Minoan and Greek times. Innumerable examples occur in Roman representations of all periods, and the empire of the throat-and-girth system also covered Etruscan, Persian and early Byzantine vehicles without exception. Western Europe knew nothing else until about +600, nor did Islam. Moreover, the south of Asia was almost entirely in reliance upon this inefficient harness, for it is seen in most of the pictures of carts which we have from ancient and medieval India, Java, Burma, Siam and other parts of that area. Central Asia, too, has it, e.g. at Baamiyaan. One of its last appearances occurs on a bas-relief of the +14th century at Florence in Italy, where it may be a conscious archaism. (Ibid, 307–8)

This capacity of the mediocre to survive was obviously due, in the first place, to the fact that it *seemed* to work: if horses with throat-and-girth harness had not been able to take a step, or had dropped dead from strangulation, even the most slow-witted teamster would have realized that something was amiss. Since it seemed to work, therefore, there was no pressing incentive to improve it, and no competing alternative was available. But if the users of horses had had to invent the collar harness at a single stroke, they would probably never have succeeded, and therefore the fact that a very inefficient form of harness did work, after a fashion, was the essential basis of subsequent evolution.

It is of course quite true that even though the Oldowan hand axe and the throat-and-girth harness are not optimally adaptive, they are relatively more adaptive than grubbing for roots with one's bare hands or not being able to use draught animals at all. But no one would deny that people can devise moderately satisfactory solutions to perceived problems. The essential point is that early and mediocre solutions can survive indefinitely in situations of low competition, and that there is no evident pressure[15] to produce optimal solutions. Examples of such phenomena abound, e.g.:

One might perhaps think of the most ancient form of the granary as a simple stack on the ground. Although this is a very inefficient form of storage (the dangers of losses to birds, rats and other vermin are obvious), it is extremely undemanding to make, and this charm has ensured its long survival. Markham, deploring its use in +17th century England, exhorted his readers at least to raise the stack on a platform out of the reach of rats, and to turn the ears of the corn inwards so that they would suffer less damage from wind and rain. (F. Bray 1984: 403–4)

The adaptationist might object that this type of granary at least optimizes convenience, just as, I suppose, lying in bed all day can be said to optimize comfort, but at this point the notions of adaptation and efficiency have entirely parted company. All we can say is that people do things because they find them desirable in *some* way, but this is very far from a genuine adaptationist argument.

(ii) The adaptive value of divination

One of the oldest and commonest practices is divination, which is also one of the most puzzling for the adaptationist, who has to explain why an obviously misguided practice should have such capacity for survival. Moore (1957) proposes that in some cases divination may actually have positive effects, even though these are not understood by the people concerned. His argument is based on the use of scapulimancy by the Montagnais-Naskapi of the

---

[15] Even when there is, 'necessity' is a very poor mother of invention. A further example of this is provided by the history of road making. It seems that until McAdam in the early nineteenth century, European road builders from the time of the Romans had been dominated by the image of earth as soft and weak and of stone as strong and hard, and had therefore failed to realize that it is actually the subsoil that bears the whole weight of the traffic. The function of the stone surface is not, therefore, to provide strength, but a waterproof covering for the subsoil. Unless the subsoil is kept dry by a waterproof covering and proper drainage, any stone surface will either break up, or, as in the case of Roman roads using mortar, require an enormous expenditure. McAdam's analysis of the fundamentals of road making (1821) shows how long it can take for people to grasp fairly elementary principles, and the history of European road making is an excellent example of the interminable survival of the very mediocre indeed.

Labrador Peninsula, as described by Speck (1935), for locating game. The shoulder blade of the type of animal to be hunted is held over hot coals and oriented in relation to the local terrain, and the pattern of cracks and spots produced by the heat is believed to give precise information on the direction and location of the game which the hunter has previously dreamed about. As Moore says, the pattern of cracks and spots is not under the control of the diviner, and is therefore an effective randomizing procedure that is quite independent of where the hunters expect to find game:

Without the intervention of this impersonal mechanism it seems reasonable to suppose that the outcome of past hunts would play a more important role in determining present strategy; it seems likely their selections of hunting routes would be patterned in a way related to recent successes and failures. If it may be assumed that there is some interplay between the animals they seek and the hunts they undertake, such that the hunted and the hunters act and react to the other's actions and potential actions, then there may be a marked advantage in avoiding a fixed pattern in hunting. Unwitting regularities in behaviour provide a basis for anticipatory responses. For instance, animals that are 'overhunted' are likely to become sensitized to human beings and hence quick to take evasive action. (Moore 1957: 71)

If he is correct in assuming that the use of this randomizing procedure may lead to more hunting success (and he concedes that there is insufficient evidence to show this), his explanation raises the further problem of how the people themselves could have discovered a technique whose theoretical principles are quite unknown to them and would probably be repugnant if they were explained. And even if Moore's theory of possible benefits from divination is valid here, there is no reason to believe that it can account for the enormous variety of divination elsewhere. Yet Moore proposes that his analysis of this case 'is potentially relevant to all situations in which human beings base their decisions on the outcome of chance mechanisms', although he can provide no evidence for this assertion, or even any way of testing it. His only explanation of how this general principle of randomizing techniques might have been discovered is: 'it is possible that through a long process of creative trial and error some societies have arrived at some approximate solutions for recurring problems' (ibid., 73).

But if the people do not understand the true principles involved, how are they to know that they *have* arrived at an appropriate solution? By the success of the results? But these are, on Moore's

own admission, difficult to detect. By the disappearance of those
societies that do not practise divination? Surely a drastic penalty for
such an omission, especially since there are many instances of
societies surviving perfectly well without it. It seems, therefore, that
the attempt to explain the origin and survival of divination on the
basis of trial and error, and selection by adaptive consequences, is
distinctly unpromising.

There is in fact a much simpler explanation for the widespread
occurrence of divination. In the first place, people naturally seek
guidance and reassurance in difficult situations: one method is to
allow a variety of non-human agencies to communicate with human
beings, and for this to occur these supposed agencies must therefore
be free to communicate without interference by conscious human
manipulation. Secondly, people consult oracles to discover which of
a number of quite sensible acts they should perform—oracles
cannot therefore tell them to do bizarre or downright foolish things
like trying to hunt without weapons, for example. In the ordinary
course of events, therefore, there is no reason to suppose that the
advice of oracles will be any worse than ordinary human advice and
sometimes, if Moore's hunting hypothesis is valid, it may even be
better. Divination will not therefore conflict with the facts of life in
any obviously maladaptive way.[16] So Evans-Pritchard says of his
own experience of using oracles among the Azande: 'I always kept a
supply of [oracle] poison for the use of my household and
neighbours and we regulated our affairs in accordance with the
oracles' decisions. I may remark that I found this as satisfactory a
way of running my home and affairs as any other I know of'
(Evans-Pritchard 1937: 270).

I believe this to be a typical case of evolution. A practice is
instituted for limited and quite comprehensible reasons. It *seems* to
work, although it is not really very successful for the most part, but
it is not noticeably harmful either, and so can survive indefinitely. It
also has two structural properties that later prove to be highly
significant: a randomizing procedure, and rigorous rules for the
manipulation of objects in a game-like manner. Such rules for the
manipulation of objects lead to various games of chance and skill—

---

[16] On the virtual impossibility of providing any empirical refutation of oracles and
magic to those who believe in them, see Evans-Pritchard 1937, and a brief survey in
Hallpike 1979: 466–74.

dice, cards, and chess, for example.[17] These in turn are ideal situations for the discovery of the laws of probability when mathematical techniques have sufficiently advanced.[18] By ignoring adaptation, and explaining the origins of divination in terms of certain simple motives and definitions of reality, and its survival in terms of the inability of people to detect the fallacies underlying the practice and its harmless consequences, we are able to reach a far more satisfactory understanding of the problem than if we assume that a practice can only survive if it has a superior adaptive value unknown to its believers.

We have also supplied a structural answer to the question 'How did people discover randomizing techniques?' that is far more specific than vague notions of 'creative trial and error'. This is that 'randomness', in practical terms, only means 'uninfluenced by human guidance'. The believer in oracles reduces human influence to the minimum so that the influence of whatever is behind the oracle may be at a maximum, but from our point of view this is exactly the same as randomization. This is a simple gateway to randomizing techniques, and to those other consequences already mentioned, that is easily discovered by primitive man, though he does not realize what he has found (as I have shown in my analysis of primitive notions of probability, Hallpike 1979: 451–66). Again and again we shall see that the history of innovations is an exploration of the structural properties of natural and cultural phenomena, and that there are in many cases what may be called easy routes by which structures may be developed and which, later, will also provide easy routes for human understanding (as with games of chance and the discovery of the laws of probability).

(iii) Conclusions

Let us now return to Durkheim's proposition that 'It would be incomprehensible if the most widespread forms of organization[19] would not at the same time be, at least in their aggregate, the most advantageous'. Far from being incomprehensible, it is easy to see that there are a number of sources from which widespread social traits will emerge, which can survive indefinitely, and which may

---

[17] See, for example, Joseph Needham's discussion of this subject in the section 'The magnet, divination, and chess' (Needham 1962: 314–34).
[18] See Hacking 1975, Chapters 6 and 7.
[19] In which he included crime (Durkheim 1964b: 70).

still confer no significant adaptive advantage. The first and most obvious is the nature of human beings themselves. Magic, for example, is more or less universal, and of enormous antiquity, and the explanation for this derives from the general disposition of all human minds to make those mental associations on which magic is based. We may also cite dualistic opposition, especially of left and right, the ubiquity of black, white, and red as the primary symbolic colours, and the equally universal symbolic forms of reversal and inversion. There is no evidence that any of these forms exist as collective representations because they are of adaptive advantage. The second source of widespread traits is the nature of social organization itself. So, for example, there are only four possible types of descent (patrilineal, matrilineal, double, and cognatic), and three types of marriage (polygyny, polyandry, and monogamy). Obviously, the fewer the possible forms, the more widespread they must be. Thirdly and very importantly, a number of different factors or situations may all produce similar consequences (equifinality). An obvious example is primitive warfare, as we have already noted. Of course, in a trivial sense all these institutions are adaptive in so far as they must conform to reality and also be seen as useful or desirable in some way or other by real people, but these are necessary conditions for just about anything that occurs at all in society.   .

While in the conventional Darwinian acceptation of things capacity to survive is evidence of superior adaptive efficiency, this in fact relies on the special assumptions of a high level of competition and the co-presence of variant forms. Such conditions are often lacking in the circumstances of primitive society, where first and inefficient attempts can survive indefinitely because they satisfy some desire (which may not be of objective practical value, e.g. magic), and because the people concerned are unaware of how the invention or institution might be improved. This lack of awareness will also be compounded by cultural isolation and consequent ignorance of other and possibly better ways of doing things. Primitive warfare and magic are, from a practical point of view, a waste of time. But they lay the foundations of important evolutionary developments and they can only do this because of the capacity of the mediocre to survive.

So, if one's military aim is merely to raid one's neighbours rather than to conquer them, and they, too, have similarly restricted ambitions, then a number of such societies can survive together in the same area, and maintain this level of inefficiency more or less indefinitely. Or, again, kingship of a mainly ritual nature does not require the organizational efficiency of a centralized bureaucratic state. But both primitive warfare and divine kingship lay the foundations for the evolution of more potent institutions.

The concept of the survival of the mediocre raises the question of why the mediocre should appear in the first place. It must be obvious that the first forms of anything will be those that are the easiest to produce: granted the basic similarity of the human mind throughout the world, we can therefore expect that *ease of production* in the circumstances of primitive life will often be the best explanation for the generality of any particular cultural trait, and what is easy to produce at a first attempt is typically inefficient.

So, for example, if we consider the origins of writing, we find that wherever it emerges as an independent invention it *always* begins with the graphic representation of concrete objects, and it does this because this is very easy for all normal human beings. The next step is to use written signs to express speech sounds, and Gelb (1963: 66–7) suggests that the particular problem this was initially designed to solve is the expression of proper names which may have no phonetic resemblance to the name of any concrete objects.[20] The syllabary is the next stage in the evolution of writing, and last of all is the alphabet. There was undoubtedly a highly contingent element in the emergence of every independent writing system, with regard to exactly when, where, why, how, and by whom, but the process of development is from the easy to the difficult.

The development of number shows a similar progression. The earliest and most widespread form of counting is tallying—the successive enumeration of objects to assess their total. This is commonly performed by the use of small objects, by making marks, and by use of the fingers. The next stage is the development of verbal terms to express this operation, and in consequence ordinal terms can then be distinguished from cardinal terms and odd from even numbers. The understanding of addition always precedes that of the other mathematical operations, and when numbers acquire written form we always find that the earliest forms are tallying marks, as in Roman numerals, letters, or characters and that the concept of place as an expression of numerical value is a much later

---

[20] A similar suggestion was made by Spencer (1898: 349).

development. In exactly the same way, we shall see, the evolution of the state shows a progressive development from certain common early forms of institution by a succession of structural transformations, each of which depends on the properties of earlier forms.

It is clearly false to suppose that all early writing was in the form of pictures of objects because this was more adaptive than other forms; this was the *only* form it could have taken, just as tallying is the only possible early form of arithmetic. From this point of view, trying to explain the universal features of the early forms of anything in terms of their adaptive advantage must be mistaken. Indeed, all that we can conclude is that an innovation should not be seriously maladaptive if it is to survive. These considerations bring us to the problem with which this chapter began, which is how groups of people manage to construct highly functional and adaptive institutions, unbeknown to themselves.

The simple answer is that in the case of primitive social organization it is extremely difficult to be maladaptive, because almost everything will work, with small groups and subsistence technologies under conditions of limited expectations and absence of effective competition. Rather than being a universal feature of all societies, then, functional and adaptive efficiency is actually an emergent property of society, and I shall suggest later that it is related in general to significant increases in the size, centralization, and specialization of society, and in particular to the emergence of the state, when for the first time the whole of society is subordinated to a clear and distinct set of goals—the maintenance of the authority and power of the monarch. Our conclusions on the survival of the mediocre apply also to human cognitive representations of nature and society, which we may now consider in detail.

2. Thought and adaptation

Human society differs essentially from associations among animals by its dependence on shared cognitive representations of reality, involving a common body of categories, rules, and values. This at once creates a profound difference between organic and social evolution in terms of adaptation to reality:

Social science has to do with human beings in their self-created universe of culture. The cultural universe is essentially a symbolic universe. Animals are surrounded by a *physical* universe with which they have to cope: physical environment, prey to catch, predators to avoid, and so forth. Man, in contrast, is surrounded by a universe of *symbols*. Starting from language which is the prerequisite of culture, to symbolic relationships with his fellows, social status, laws, science, art, morals, religion and innumerable other things, human behaviour, except for the basic aspects of the biological needs of hunger and sex, is governed by symbolic entities. (von Bertalanffy 1971: 208)

(a) Ideology and illusion

Thought, especially in the form of religion and ideology in general, is often represented as too impotent and too mistaken to have any decisive influence on society. Radcliffe-Brown, for example, considered the suggestion 'as absurd as to hold a quadratic equation capable of committing a murder' (Radcliffe-Brown 1948: 30), and in similar vein Harris depicts thought as overwhelmed by material reality:

To take a familiar example: during the late 1960s many young people believed that industrial capitalism could be destroyed by a 'cultural revolution'. New modes of singing, praying, dressing, and thinking were introduced in the name of a 'counter culture'. These innovations predictably had absolutely no effect upon the structure and infrastructure of US capitalism, and even their survival and propagation within the superstructure now seems doubtful except insofar as they enhance the profitability of corporations that sell records and clothes. (Harris 1980: 72)

In this scheme of things, what we may call the world view of each society is determined by the basic requirements of physical survival and the need for orderly social relations, and these adaptive and functional needs are met primarily at the level of action. So Mary Douglas writes that 'It is misleading to think of ideas such as destiny, witchcraft, *mana*, magic as part of philosophies, or as systematically thought out at all' (Douglas 1966: 89). She goes on to argue that these beliefs are the result of solving the urgent practical problems of everyday life: 'These questions are not phrased primarily to satisfy man's curiosity about the seasons and the rest of the natural environment. They are phrased to satisfy a dominant social concern, the problem of how to organize together in society. They can only be answered, it is true, in terms of man's place in nature. But the metaphysic is a by-product, as it were, of the urgent practical concern' (ibid., 90–1).

The requirements of biological and technological adaptation, and of social function, thus provide the basic needs of a society, and these needs exert themselves below the level of conscious thought, through actions and sentiments (e.g. Radcliffe-Brown 1952: 155). Thought is thus reduced to a sort of froth on the surface of society, at best giving some indication of the deeper currents of causality but often being nothing more than gibberish and self-deception that disguise underlying realities. So Durkheim said in a famous passage,

. . . it is an essential postulate of sociology that a human institution cannot rest upon an error and a lie, [otherwise][21] it could not exist. If it were not founded in the nature of things, it would have encountered in the facts a resistance over which it could never have triumphed. So when we commence the study of primitive religions, it is with the assurance that they hold to reality and express it . . . When only the letter of the formulae is considered, these religious beliefs and practices undoubtedly seem disconcerting at times, and one is tempted to attribute to them some sort of a deep-rooted error. But one must know how to go underneath the symbol to the reality which it represents and which gives it its meaning. The most barbarous and the most fantastic rites and the strangest myths translate some human need, some aspect of life, either individual or social. The reasons with which the faithful justify them may be, and generally are, erroneous; but the true reasons do not cease to exist, and it is the duty of science to discover them. (Durkheim 1947: 14–15)

For Durkheim, of course, supernatural beings were nothing more than projections of society, and the very categories of space, time, causality and classification were derived from social groupings. For Marx 'The religious world is but the reflex of the real world' (*Capital* 1967: I. 79). According to Fortes (1959: 66) 'The Tallensi have an ancestor cult . . . because their social structure demands it', just as for Leach the various spirits of Kachin religious ideology 'are nothing more than ways of describing the formal relationships that exist between real persons and real groups in ordinary human Kachin society' (Leach 1964: 182).

And even if a people's world-view does conform overtly to what the anthropologist regards as their objective needs and situation, this can be explained on general adaptive principles:

According to the tenets of Darwinian evolutionism, upon which modern thinking of biological and cultural evolutionism is based, the selection of

[21] The translation reads 'without which' for *sans quoi*, which makes nonsense of the passage.

morphological and behavioural traits is by virtue of the adaptive advantage that they confer to the species in question. Following from this principle we would assume that the development within the genus *Homo* of the capacity for seeing reality in markedly different ways enhanced survival by allowing local groups to develop world views appropriate to their particular habitats. (Kearney 1984: 110)

But the proposition that ideas about the nature of things, whether natural, social, or supernatural, cannot affect behaviour and social institutions is manifestly absurd. While equations cannot commit murder, the ability to solve them has enormously enhanced man's control of his environment, and while American capitalism was fortunately immune to the delusions of the 'counter culture', the whole of American society has been profoundly affected by the political ideas of those who drew up the American Constitution. Similarly, if people believe that their own well-being and that of their crops and herds depends on the performance of certain rituals, and that only certain persons are qualified to perform these rituals, this definition of reality must have powerful consequences for their society and its development. We shall see that religion is almost universally a vital source of political authority, but this has always been repugnant to the rationalist tradition, which has found it easier to believe that the sacred functions of kings were cynical impostures to gain the more abject submission of their people, or that they evolved in order to increase social solidarity. As Hocart has said,

Ritual is not in good odour with our intellectuals. It is associated in their minds with a clerical movement for which most of them nurse an antipathy. They are therefore unwilling to believe that institutions which they approve of, and which seem to them so eminently practical and sensible as modern administration, should have developed out of the hokus-pokus which they deem ritual to be. In their eyes only economic interests can create anything as solid as the state. (Hocart 1970: 35)

In the 1950s preparations began for the building of a new cathedral at Coventry, to stand beside the ruins of the old cathedral destroyed by German bombs.[22] Coventry's City Council had from the very beginning opposed the building of a new cathedral. They had even sent a Council deputation to London to see the Minister of Works, in an attempt to have the Cathedral's building licence revoked, arguing that the enormous number of bricks required

[22] This account is quoted from an article on Coventry by Alan Maitland in *This England*, 13.4 (1980), 50.

would be better used in old people's homes, hospitals, and schools. The councillors insisted on priority for new law courts and a police station, and asked for a building licence for new swimming baths rather than one for a cathedral which, they argued, was unnecessary. The Minister told the Lord Mayor that, after considering the deputation's arguments he intended issuing a building licence nevertheless, and in a covering letter explained why:

The Cathedral is not a building which concerns Coventry and Coventry alone. The echo of the bombs which destroyed your city was heard around the world. We cannot tell how many people are waiting in this country and abroad for this church to rise and prove that English traditions live again after the blitz. The threat of far worse destruction is with us today, demoralising and corrupting our thoughts. We have never had a greater need for acts of Faith.

When one claims that this or that institution in primitive society—kingship, warfare and head-hunting, age-grading systems, athletic contests, feasts, and so on—is to be explained by religious purposes, one may be misinterpreted as claiming that primitive man is like those in favour of a new Coventry Cathedral: primarily interested in acts of Faith, symbolic gestures, and other affirmations of unworldly and 'impractical' values, and only secondarily or not at all in down-to-earth, utilitarian conveniences like swimming baths, hospitals, schools, and police stations. In reality, of course, our conception of religion as other-worldly and impractical is a fantastic anachronism in the context of just about all pre-industrial societies. In discussing the public works, such as irrigation canals, which are ascribed to the kings of Egypt and Ceylon, Hocart makes the crucial observation:

It would be an error to put such works in a category by themselves as 'utilitarian' in opposition to 'religious' works such as temples. Temples are just as utilitarian as dams and canals, since they are necessary to prosperity; dams and canals are as ritual as temples, since they are part of the same social system of seeking welfare. If *we* call reservoirs 'utilitarian' it is because *we* believe in their efficacy: *we* do not call temples so because *we* do not believe in their efficacy for crops. What *we* think has nothing to do with the matter, but only what the people we are studying think . . . (Hocart 1970: 217)

Granting, then, as we must, that people's representations of the world will fundamentally affect their behaviour, the problem is to decide how far reality can, as it were, force itself on human understanding through some process of adaptation, by which error will be corrected by a crucial confrontation with the facts, and which will induce representations to reflect in some way the basic necessities and imperatives of life. As the following two sections will show, this adaptationist approach to thought is inadequate.

In the first place, we can only interact with our environment as we understand it, not as it 'really' is. The environment does not interpret itself, and it is quite possible for mistaken or inadequate ideas, by seeming to work, to survive indefinitely. As Febvre said, 'What finally matters is the idea adopted by the people—the political group—with regard to their geographical position, of its characteristics and advantages or inconveniences, though this idea may be quite wrong or have no basis in reality' (Febvre 1925: 225). Quite apart from mistaken ideas, social institutions, especially before the emergence of the state, can be organized on very different principles, *all* of which are viable, and the result is that it is extremely difficult for a society's world-view, by which it interprets both nature and its own institutions, to come into those conclusive confrontations with the facts envisaged by Durkheim. But, as I have repeatedly emphasized when discussing social institutions, what is false or inefficient or simply unprovable may nevertheless have great developmental potential, and this is not only true of that aspect of social life and thought we term 'religion', but also of the whole range of human imagination with which our ancestors laid, unknowingly, the foundation of vast developments.

(b) Adaptive aspects of thought

There is no doubt that thought is the primary means by which human beings adapt to their environment, but the belief that there is a world of facts 'out there' which is simply reflected by individual perception and intelligence is by now a thoroughly discredited epistemology. The almost infinite volume of stimuli require some filtering process if they are to be manageable at all, and each type of organism will focus on those kinds of stimuli which are most appropriate to it. Whether one considers the physiology of perception, cognitive psychology, linguistics, or the theory of art one finds that, more or less independently, these various branches of knowledge have come to the same conclusion: that, far from being a blank slate, man can only make sense out of the vast multitude of stimuli by actively and selectively concentrating on a narrow range of these stimuli that yield the maximum of relevant information, and largely ignoring the rest.

At the most elementary level of visual perception, for example, we cannot make sense of what we see until we grasp that the world is composed mainly of solid, non-deformable objects of which only one can occupy a given place at any one time. In order to gain as much information about these objects as possible, our brains concentrate on those areas of an image where light intensities vary most abruptly because these are apt to reveal surface boundaries. Separating figure from ground requires, among other things, object recognition, and this in turn involves the ability to recognize the same object from a number of different vantage points. This requires the detection of such readily identifiable geometric features of the overall shape as 'generalized cones' (see Marr 1981, Stent 1981). So Gombrich, the theorist and historian of art, says:

An image in this biological sense is not an imitation of an object's external form but an imitation of certain privileged or relevant aspects . . . The artist who goes out to represent the visible world is not simply faced with a neutral medley of forms he seeks to 'imitate'. Ours is a structured universe whose main lines of force are still bent and fashioned by our biological and psychological needs, however much they may be overlaid by cultural influences. We know that there are certain privileged motifs in our world to which we respond almost too easily. The human face[23] may be outstanding among them. (Gombrich 1963: 5–6)

In rather similar vein Rosch 1977 showed that much classification of natural phenomena in ordinary life does not rest on a 'digital' enumeration of discrete properties as the basis of ascribing a thing to a certain class but rather upon an analogue procedure in which things are assimilated to a prototypical image of the ideal thing—be it bird, colour, facial expression, or whatever. These ideas are supported by the work of Berlin and associates on folk classification. They find that the genus is the basic classificatory concept in folk taxonomy, rather than such general terms as 'plant' or 'animal' (which may not even be named), or terms at highly

---

[23] 'In the normal individual the ability to identify people by their faces is itself quite remarkable. At a glance one can name a person from facial features alone, even though the features may change substantially over the years or may be presented in a highly distorted form, as in a caricature' (Geschwind 1979: 189). According to Geschwind this ability is located in a specific area of the brain, lesions of which produce the condition known as 'prosopagnosia', inability to recognize faces.

particular species or subspecies levels. Examples would be 'oak', rather than 'tree' or 'post oak', 'quail' rather than 'bird' or 'blue quail' and so on. They conclude that 'generic taxa are the basic building blocks of all folk taxonomies. They represent the most commonly referred to groupings of organisms in the natural environment, are the most salient psychologically and are likely to be among the first taxa learned by the child . . .' (Berlin, Breedlove, and Raven 1973: 216; and see Berlin 1974: 262).

The same organization of experience in selective, purposive and coherent ways is also to be found at more general levels of culture. The psychologist Osgood and his associates have shown that there seem to be three basic dimensions in terms of which we assess the social and natural world, those of Evaluation, Potency, and Activity. Typical concepts of the Evaluation dimension are 'good/bad', 'helpful/unhelpful', 'sweet/sour'; of the Potency dimension 'big/ little', 'strong/weak', 'deep/shallow'; and of the Activity dimension 'fast/slow', 'noisy/quiet', 'sharp/dull'. As Osgood says, these basic dimensions are cross-cultural universals because, like the geometry of solids, prototypes, and genera, they are fruitful and economical ways of organizing relevant experience:

> What is important to us now, as it was back in the age of Neanderthal man, about the sign of a thing is, first, does it refer to something *good* for me or *bad* for me (is it an antelope or a saber-toothed tiger)? Second, does it refer to something which is *strong* or *weak* with respect to me (is it a bad saber-toothed tiger or a bad mosquito)? And third, does it refer to something that is *active* or *passive* with respect to me (is it a bad, strong saber-toothed tiger or a bad, strong pool of quicksand which I can simply walk around)? Survival, then and now, depends upon the answers. (Osgood, May, and Miron 1975: 395)

(And while Evaluation, Potency, and Activity are the main dimensions of semantic space, there are numerous others of general cultural importance, such as social/non-social, predictable/ unpredictable, superficial/deep, and so on.)

The human mind therefore grasps reality by a highly selective and structured attention to certain restricted features of it, an attention which is essentially active rather than a mere passive reception of sensations. This same activity and selectivity is also evident in our cognitive as well as our purely perceptual understanding of the world. Piaget and other developmental psychologists have shown us that cognition is not purely imitation, but

... an active and selective process, dominated by a constant interaction between accommodation and assimilation, a process in which the child's physical manipulation of objects plays a fundamental part in his gradual co-ordination of his sensory impressions and constructions of reality. Such a theory of cognitive development is radically opposed to empiricist theories which regard learning as the bit-by-bit accumulation of data, such that the child's thought is simply a crude copy of external reality and adult models which slowly adds details to achieve a more refined fit, because it is a theory that stresses the internal organization of knowledge as an essential foundation of stability and growth. (Hallpike 1979: 7)

Cognition develops on the basis of actions and their co-ordination, through imagery and concrete symbols, and through the mastery of conventional sign systems of which language is by far the most important, and cognition, like perception, obviously has the 'goal' of adapting the organism to its environment. In one respect it must enable people to solve urgent problems of existence: 'Is that a real bear or only a shadow?': 'Is this plant poisonous?'; 'If we soak it in water for a day will it be safe to eat?' and so on. We may call this 'convergent' thinking because it attempts to reach a single correct answer to a problem. So, for example in the standard Piagetian test for conservation of quantity, if liquid is poured from a short fat vessel into a tall thin one, the correct answer to the question 'Is there the same amount of liquid in the second glass as in the first?' is 'Yes'. There are innumerable such problems of daily life, and as I showed in my exposition of Piaget's work in *The Foundations of Primitive Thought* (1979), the human mind has gradually come to a more correct understanding of such basic features of the world as space, time, causality, probability, number, measurement, and so on.

I also showed that, as in all other aspects of culture generally, early and inefficient forms have enormous potential for survival because of the undemanding nature of the social, technological, and natural environment of primitive society. So, to take one example, probabilistic reasoning is a very late cognitive development, and without it all sorts of false inferences will be made, but members of primitive societies and early states can nevertheless survive quite well without this kind of understanding.

(c) Divergent thinking and adaptation

There is another aspect of the human mind which has so far scarcely been mentioned, and that is its capacity for metaphorical or symbolic association. This emerges as soon as the child is capable of image-based thinking (at the beginning of the pre-operatory stage of Piaget's scheme of development), and is clearly basic to all thought and culture:

The possibility of metaphor springs from the infinite elasticity of the human mind: it testifies to its capacity to perceive and assimilate new experiences as modifications of earlier ones, of finding equivalences in the most disparate phenomena, and of substituting one for another. Without this constant process of substitution neither language nor art, nor indeed civilized life would be possible. Psychoanalysis has made us familiar with the wide range of substitutions which enables man to find gratification in goals far removed from his original biological needs . . . The term 'transference', used by psychoanalysts to describe this process happens to mean exactly the same as the Greek word '*metapherein*' . . . (Gombrich 1963: 14)

Symbolism and metaphor in general accommodate to the natural properties and associations of objects, but also assimilate these properties and associations into cultural systems of meaning in a selective and coherent way. Thus, since most animals are much hairier than human beings, some cultures may use these differences to express the distinction between the realms of culture and nature, as in myths which describe the first men as very hairy, and also as ignorant of fire and the rules of correct behaviour to their kin. But in other societies (or in the same society, in different contexts), the symbolic opposition between 'hairy' and 'hairless' may not be related to the nature/culture distinction at all, but to the categories of youth and age; in this case 'hairy' will symbolize the health and vitality of young people, whereas 'hairless' will signify the baldness and infirmity of old age. Again, we may find that cutting the hair is symbolically appropriate to many rites of passage, and that shaven hair signifies the assumption of a new status.

Symbolic and metaphorical association therefore impose order on the world, (see for example Lloyd 1966 for the importance of this type of thought in the development of Greek philosophy) but the structures and properties derive from the mind. All ideologies and collective representations therefore accommodate to experience, but because they are based on the symbolic and metaphorical processes we are considering, they also assimilate that experience to the purely cognitive structures of those who create them. This involves not only the distortion of reality, but also the capacity to transcend its limitations; this is true of all levels of thought, including modern science:

Time after time, people have been able to construct remarkable theories on the basis of very little evidence, often rejecting much of the available evidence on obscure scientific intuitive grounds as they sought to construct theories that are deep and intelligible. Furthermore, although the creation of new theory is an achievement of the gifted few, it has been possible through most of the history of science for others, less talented, to comprehend and appreciate what has been accomplished. The theories that have been constructed, regarded as intelligible, and generally accepted as science has progressed have been vastly underdetermined by evidence. Intellectual structures of vast scope have been developed on the basis of limited and (until fairly recently) fairly degenerate evidence. (Chomsky 1980: 250)

For example: 'Led by their mystical view that the sphere is the perfect figure, just as 10 is the perfect number, the Pythagoreans introduced the conception that the earth and the heavenly bodies are spheres. This important advance is among the many in the history of science in which the formation of general ideas on theoretical grounds has preceded and not followed practical observation' (Singer 1943: 21).

In this type of thinking there is often no single right answer as in convergent thinking, because its strength lies in the generation of novel and fertile associations of ideas, and for this reason it is often referred to as divergent thinking:

Most of the aptitude factors identifiable as belonging in the category of creativity are classifiable in a group of divergent-thinking abilities. These abilities, by contrast to convergent-thinking abilities, emphasize searching activities with freedom to go in different directions, if not a necessity to do so in order to achieve an excellent performance. Convergent-thinking abilities proceed toward one right answer, or one that is more or less clearly demanded by the given information. (Guilford 1970: 186)

Again and again in the conclusions of psychologists who study creativity, we find a small number of related factors: fluent and divergent associations of words and ideas; unusual responses;

tolerance of ambiguity; the ability to toy with elements and concepts; category width and the capacity to 'take the world in large lumps'; and risk-taking in thought (e.g. Rogers 1970).

Huizinga long ago noted the essential resemblance between play and ritual, in so far as both constitute formal activities that take place outside the constraints of immediate material interests, and create a different world in a time and space of their own, according to their own rules:

More striking even than the limitation as to time is the limitation as to space. All play moves and has its being within a play-ground marked off beforehand either materially or ideally, deliberately or as a matter of course. Just as there is no formal difference between play and ritual, so the 'consecrated spot' cannot be formally distinguished from the play-ground. The arena, the card-table, the magic circle, the temple, the stage, the screen, the tennis court, the court of justice, etc., are all in form and function play-grounds, i.e. forbidden spots, isolated, hedged round, hallowed, within which special rules obtain. All are temporary worlds within the ordinary world, dedicated to the performance of an act apart.

Inside the play-ground an absolute and peculiar order reigns. Here we come across another, very positive feature of play: it creates order, is order. Into an imperfect world and into the confusion of life it brings a temporary, a limited perfection. Play demands order absolute and supreme. The least deviation from it 'spoils and game', robs it of its character and makes it worthless. The profound affinity between play and order is perhaps the reason why play . . . seems to lie to such an extent in the field of aesthetics. (Huizinga 1955: 10)

The play-ritual complex is not only a structure governed by rules, but also has the potential of creating a different reality. At the level of the child who is playing at being something else,

The child is *making an image* of something different, something more beautiful, or more sublime, or more dangerous than what he usually *is*. One is a Prince, or one is Daddy or a wicked witch or a tiger. The child is quite literally 'beside himself' with delight, transported beyond himself to such an extent that he almost believes he actually is such and such a thing, without, however, wholly losing consciousness of 'ordinary reality' . . .

The sacred performance [however] is more than an actualization in appearance only, a sham reality; it is also more than a symbolical actualization—it is a mystical one. In it, something invisible and inactual takes beautiful, actual, holy form. The participants in the rite are convinced that the action actualizes and effects a definite beatification, brings about an order of things higher than that in which they customarily live. (Ibid., 13–14)

Not surprisingly, therefore, religion and ritual, magic and divination have been the source of many aspects of science, the pictorial arts, sculpture, drama, and sport,[24] and have generally provided mankind with larger purposes than those of immediate day-to-day survival.

It is a great mistake, then, to regard this type of thinking as merely an escape from the constraints of reality into undisciplined fantasy, since its primary object is to impose order. Myth, symbolism, and the arts can therefore express important truths, both about society and the physical world. There are certain features of nature and society of which all cultures seem to be aware, to a greater or lesser degree, and certain beliefs about the nature of the world and man which seem more or less universal: the assumption that social organization is closely associated with the natural world, so that ritual, in particular, can be effective in changing the world; the belief in powerful invisible beings who control aspects of nature and society, and in magic, witchcraft, and divination. Many societies also have some idea of fate or destiny, which is commonly linked to the intentions of supernatural beings. We also find that a number of basic categories and their opposites are integral aspects of the world views of most societies: the distinction, in some form or another, between nature and culture, or the wild and the tame; between sacred and secular authority, and between purity and impurity; notions of harmony and conflict in both society and nature; the problems of the origin of man and of one's own society, and especially the belief that the legitimation of the social order is provided by an account of how it originated; the nature of social inequality and its justification; and other very general categories of existence such as good and evil, active and passive, flux and stability, and so on.

In one sense, all these categories accommodate to real aspects of nature and society—they are certainly not pure fantasy, elaborated out of touch with reality; but this does not mean that they are testable hypotheses that can be refuted by evidence. On the contrary, these categories order and select the evidence itself, and are thus beyond the kind of refutation to which factual propositions are liable. Not only are these world views essentially classificatory rather than predictive, empirical models, but they employ modes of thought that are refractory to empirical testing—symbolic and

[24] Most ball games, for example, have a religious origin: see Simri n.d.

metaphorical association, and qualitative rather than quantitative thinking.

We have established, then, that it is only possible to understand the world by reconstructing our representations of it in selective and coherent ways, and therefore by utilizing such conceptual relations as logical implication, metaphorical association, and various types of symbolic relations, all of which are the properties of *thought*, and not of reality itself. The environment does not interpret itself, nor does it tell people when they have only half or quarter solved a problem.

It is therefore quite possible for men to develop representations of reality which are false, or at best unprovable, yet which are perfectly viable as the basis of social institutions and a wide range of behavioural patterns over an indefinitely long period of time. The belief that society is closely associated with the working of nature and that there are powerful invisible beings who control both would be obvious examples, as would belief in ancestral spirits, witchcraft, and divination. The standard Durkheimian response would be, as we have seen, that although such beliefs may be false they survive because they satisfy certain needs or provide certain essential functions such as social solidarity or confidence in the future. But such alleged functions are far too vague to explain the existence of any specific beliefs and, moreover, a psychological or social need cannot by itself explain the origin of ideas that are claimed to satisfy those needs:

. . . if magic, myth, ritual, 'animism', psychomorphic causality, and so on are the spontaneous products of the human mind when it exists in a certain environment, then the whole question of the fundamental social value of religion and magic proposed by Durkheim is raised in quite new terms. For it can now be maintained that while religion and its attendant rituals, with magic and sorcery, may have the *effect* of cementing social bonds, this so called 'function' will be a mere spin-off from a more basic propensity of the human mind to think in religious and magical terms when in a certain milieu. (Hallpike 1979: 64)

Because, in short, the world is a very baffling place, we may expect that human understanding of it will initially be inadequate because it will be based on more elementary thought processes than those which become available as culture advances. Yet, these more elementary representations will *seem* perfectly adequate to those concerned. Indeed, all systems of thought, including scientific theories, have by reason of their dependence on selectivity and imagery a built-in bias against some area of experience. Primitive thought is less systematic and explicit than the thought of societies such as our own, and therefore in such societies it is very much harder to bring it to any crucial confrontation with the facts, so that it can be shown to be inconsistent or inadequate. But science itself is based on conceptual structures that may be highly resistant to refutation by experience, as Fleck[25] very rightly says:

Once a structurally complete and closed system of opinion consisting of many details and relations has been formed, it offers enduring resistance to anything that contradicts it . . .

In the history of scientific knowledge, no formal relation of logic exists between conceptions and evidence. Evidence conforms to conceptions just as often as conceptions conform to evidence. After all, conceptions are not logical systems, no matter how much they aspire to that status. They are stylized units which either develop or atrophy just as they are or merge with their proofs into others. Analogously to social structures, every age has its own dominant conceptions as well as remnants of past ones and rudiments of those of the future. It is one of the most important tasks in comparative epistemology to find out how conceptions and hazy ideas pass from one thought style to another, how they emerge as spontaneously generated pre-ideas, and how they are preserved as enduring, rigid structures owing to a kind of harmony of illusions. It is only by such a comparative investigation of the relevant interrelations that we can begin to understand our own era. (Fleck 1979: 27–8)

(d) Conclusions

We may therefore sum up the significance of thought for social evolution in the following way:

1. For man, above all other organisms, thought defines the nature of·reality. We have seen, of course, that thought is a means by which we discover certain truths about the world which are necessary for our survival, but beyond this elementary level the basic properties of thought which allow us to make these discoveries—selectivity, logical implication, metaphorical and symbolic association and classification, and the internal structuring of world views—are also the basis for representations that cannot be said to accommodate to reality precisely because of the

---

[25] Fleck's ideas in many ways anticipate those of T. S. Kuhn (1970).

predominance of their assimilative aspect.

2. So the fact that men inhabit a world whose very nature depends on their definition of it raises a crucial issue of adaptation: What is a problem, and what is a fact? Obviously, if there were no objective, stable world of things 'out there', it would be pointless to debate the extent to which people did or did not accommodate to it, but the point is that people can only accommodate to their environment as they understand it. Cognitive representations may not, therefore, be correct, and yet they may be quite convincing to those who hold them, and may be able to persist for an indefinite period of time without correction.

3. Proto-ideas have great generality, and thus easily comprehend both social and natural phenomena. Just as early social institutions have within them the germs of extremely important developments that can remain dormant, so too we can find many instances of proto-ideas that have similar developmental possibilities. The ideas of elements, magical causes of disease, the notion of the cosmos as an organic, harmonious unity, the idea of law as binding both nature and man alike, etc., are all capable of great development and contain the embryonic form of powerful insights. We find here the enormous significance of the vague, over-generalized, and the plastic, which is the essential foundation of later development. It follows, then, that it is senseless to expect these early ideas to be closely adapted to their environment.

4. Religious ideas in particular have been of the greatest significance because they have prompted man to all kinds of exploration of his world, and to all kinds of endeavours that he would never have undertaken if he had from the beginning operated on the basis of what we would consider his immediate material advantage.

5. We have seen that it is a cardinal error to impose our distinction between the 'religious' and the 'practical' on pre-industrial man since it is both anachronistic and ethnocentric. Primitive man is just as 'practical' as we are: the difference lies in his view of the world, and hence his notion of how to *be* practical.

6. Thought is also fundamental to evolution because societies are systems of ideas as well as systems of action. Any association of people interacting on a permanent basis will generate a body of accepted rules, categories, and values, some in the form of an explicit ideology, and others below the level of conscious

articulation that will be detectable only to the more reflective members of the society, if at all. While a number of basic themes recur in the world views of many societies, each society will develop and elaborate on some themes at the expense of others. In this way certain core principles develop, which exercise great influence over the evolutionary development of each society. This is the subject of Chapter VI.

3. From ascriptive to functional organization

Without at this point becoming involved in the difficult question of stages of evolution, we may usefully distinguish between societies whose organization is predominantly ascriptive, and those whose organization is predominantly functional. (This distinction is, of course, intended as one between ideal types, and does not imply that the transition from one type to the other will be sharp or discontinuous.)

Linton (1936: 115–28) distinguished between 'ascribed' and 'achieved' status in the following terms:

Ascribed statuses are those which are assigned to individuals without reference to their innate differences or abilities. They can be predicted and trained for from the moment of birth. The *achieved* statuses are, as a minimum, those requiring special qualities, although they are not limited to these. They are not assigned to individuals from birth but are left open to be filled through competition and individual effort. (Ibid., 115)

Ascribed status therefore derives primarily from attributes of birth, that is, membership of particular descent groups, or a particular group of ancestors and relatives; secondly, from gender; while relative age, and the seniority dependent on it, is the third major basis of ascription since growing older, like being born to specific parents, is an inescapable reality that has nothing to do with individual abilities or effort. But while, as Linton says, 'The bulk of the ascribed statuses in all social systems are parcelled out to individuals on the basis of sex, age, and family relationships' (ibid., 126), it is quite possible to extend the principle of ascription more widely: '. . . there are many societies in which purely social factors are also used as a basis of ascription. There seems to be a general tendency for societies to divide their component individuals into a series of groups or categories and to ascribe to such categories differing degrees of social importance' (ibid., 126).

Ritual status is a notable example of this. In primitive societies especially we find that all sorts of groups and categories based on birth, age, or gender also have ascribed to them a wide variety of ritual statuses and symbolic attributes that may have little or no relation to the actual capacities or abilities of these groups and categories. It is therefore quite possible for occupations and statuses which are actually achieved to have, notwithstanding, a number of attributes which are ascriptive. By this I mean attributes which are not functionally necessary for the satisfactory performance of the occupation or role, but which are felt to be inherently or necessarily associated with it.

The forms of social organization of an ascriptive type are extremely flexible, and are well suited for organizing a wide variety of social activities and functions in general. For this reason we usually find that while certain roles may have ritual status, in this type of society it is very difficult to find any institutions that are distinctively religious, political, legal, economic, or military. Rather, these are often only aspects of a single institutional form so that, for example, a kinship structure or an age-grouping organization may have a variety of political, economic, legal, religious, and military functions.

These basic social formations readily give rise to certain common structural forms: segmentary articulation; dualistic opposition; symmetries and asymmetries of relations, especially of reciprocity; cycles; alternations; and what one may call 'total structures', such as moieties, or the tripartite functions of Indo-European society, where a fixed number of subunits is considered necessary for the proper functioning of the whole. The essential simplicity of these structural forms allows systems of great elaboration to be constructed on the basis of a few elementary principles: Australian 4- and 8- section systems, East Cushitic *gada* systems, Micronesian systems of 'money', and so on. But we shall see in the case of the *gada* systems that these institutions, despite their elaboration, are not functionally necessary to the societies in which they exist.

This propensity to elaboration is an extremely significant aspect of primitive society in particular. As Linton says:

There is always a point beyond which further elaboration of behavior does not yield returns in increased efficiency which are commensurate with the labor involved. However, existing cultures show that such limits bear little relation to culture growth. All societies have elaborated their responses to certain situations to a point beyond that of maximum relative utility. Even in the case of tools and utensils, where the disadvantages of such a course would seem most obvious, we have plenty of examples of quite unnecessary expenditures of labor and materials. Hundreds of tribes ground and polished their stone axes completely, although such instruments cut no better than those ground only at the bit and are actually more difficult to haft. The Imerina of Madagascar make their spade-handles of fine cabinet woods, palisandre, spotted ebony, and the like. Such handles are neither more nor less efficient in use than those of ordinary wood, and trees from which they are made do not grow in the tribe's territory. A good spade-handle will cost a laborer in the rice fields a week's wages and its purchase will entail short rations for several weeks . . .

Similar tendencies toward unnecessary elaboration can be observed in all other phases of culture. Some societies have developed an extreme elaboration and formalization of the rules governing the behaviour of their members toward each other. Such elaborations contribute somewhat to the ease of social intercourse, but they impose a real burden upon the individual both in the labor of learning them and in the constant attention and frequent thwarting of personal inclinations which they call for. Even if they make for greater ease of existence within the society, they do not seem to give the society as a whole any noticeable advantage over other societies in which the regulations are less elaborate and formal.

In the field of religion this tendency toward needless elaboration is even more marked. The variety of religious beliefs and practices is almost infinite, yet the system developed by each society appears to meet all its members' needs. Some groups have developed elaborate creeds and philosophies, while others have barely attempted to rationalize the rites which they perform, yet the satisfaction to the worshipper seems to be the same in both cases . . . This tendency toward unnecessary and in some cases even injurious elaboration of culture is one of the most significant phenomena of human life. It proves that the development of culture has become an end in itself. Man may be a rational being, but he is certainly not a utilitarian one. (Linton 1936: 87–90)

A good example of such elaboration is provided by the form of 'money' on Rossel Island in the Pacific. There are two categories of this money: *ndap*, consisting of individual pieces of *Spondylus* shell, and *nko*, each consisting of ten shell discs, probably from the giant clam. *Ndap* money is of higher value than *nko*, and they are respectively regarded as men's and women's money. *Ndap* has 22 grades (of which the 13 highest grades have individual names, reckoned by shape and colour), and *nko* has 16 grades. The value of each grade of each category is determined by custom, rather than by supply and demand:

> There are special uses for each denomination and they are not freely interchangeable. It is not possible, for instance, to use in payment several pieces of lower denomination instead of a higher unit, or several *nko* moneys instead of a *ndap* money. Tradition has fixed the amount and the denomination of the units which are payable on every ceremonial occasion. Such ceremonial occasions are connected with marriage or various kinds of festivities such as the slaughter of a pig, or the eating up of a man sentenced to the cooking pot for some minor offence. (Einzig 1966: 63)

> The parities between the various values of *ndap* follow a very peculiar system. The higher values are not simple multiples of the lower values, but represent a lower value plus the equivalent of the accumulated interest on the lower value for a certain period. Thus, if somebody borrows number 4 for a brief period, he has to repay a number 5. If the loan is for a longer period, he has to repay a number 6, or an even higher number, according to the length of the period. There is, however, no arithmetical proportion between the length of the period and the interest due for the loan. This system operates for all units up to number 17; numbers 18–22 follow different rules. Debtors borrowing units up to number 17 need not even repay a higher unit than number 17. Anyone borrowing a higher unit has to repay the same unit, and interest is paid in the form of a smaller unit. Number 18 is regarded as sacred and can only be passed from one holder to another in a crouching position. Numbers 19–22 are considered even more sacred. (Ibid., 62)

A common attempt to rebut the idea of social evolution relies on the remarkable elaboration of such institutions in primitive society. So, it is pointed out, modern Western society has an extremely simple kinship system (the terminology usually being 'Eskimo' in type); in our society there is also nothing like the formal age-grouping systems of East Africa, nor do our rituals for the most part compare in richness of symbolic detail with those of many primitive societies.

Those who rely on such facts to claim that primitive societies are just as complex as our own but in different ways fail to notice that such institutions are basically ascriptive in nature, rather than functional, like the state, professional armies, or business corporations. The view that I shall advance in this book is that in small-scale societies, with only a few thousand members at most, and with rudimentary subsistence economies, a very wide range of institutional arrangements will *all* work perfectly well, because the demands on functional and adaptive efficiency are very low. What we find is that a limited number of institutions, based on such ascriptive principles as kinship and affinity, gender, age, and ritual status perform all those 'functions' which, in more complex societies are differentiated. At this level of organization it is therefore quite possible to organize, for example, money on Rossel Island by ritual and symbolic principles without impairing such funcuonal cfficicncy as is necessary, but which would be impossible for a society of much larger scale with a market economy. It is also possible to use a few simple principles, such as symmetrical and asymmetrical oppositions, or alternation based on gender and generation, to produce very elaborate institutions of little or no functional importance.

Functional efficiency of organization only becomes of major significance with political centralization and the emergence of the state, bureaucracy, professional military organization, large-scale trade and public works, and a high level of division of labour. It is therefore societies with these features that I categorize as 'functionally differentiated'. Once it becomes necessary to maintain a central government, to allocate official tasks, to prevent rebellion, to raise and distribute the necessary revenues, to organize truly effective military forces, to organize large-scale public works such as irrigation, and so on, we are in a very different world from that of the society based on ascriptive institutions.

It is therefore perfectly sensible to ask 'What was the function of military tenure in Norman England?' or 'What is the function of a bank in a monetary economy?', but meaningless to ask 'What is the function of Australian 8-section systems?' or of East Cushitic generation-grading systems. Anthropologists who have spent so much time trying to give functional or adaptive explanations for this type of institution have therefore been the victims of an illusion: that because societies like ours have many institutions that are genuinely functional, therefore this same degree of 'functionality' occurs in all societies, and that if we were sufficiently ingenious we should be able to detect it in primitive societies too.

The consequence of the development from ascriptive to functional organization is the dissolution of the elementary ascriptive categories of the earlier stages, particularly those based on descent and age, so thoroughly imbued with ritual and symbolic values and concepts, and the growth of purposive institutions for specific ends; pragmatic substitutability, the growth of rational calculation, and the assessment of institutions in terms of efficiency and power. But it is essential to note that the transition from ascriptive to functional institutions does not mean that all the early types of institution simply disappear. What in fact often happens is that their significance becomes transformed—the sacred king into the political ruler; religious ritual into drama and sport; alchemy into chemistry; and so on.

The true significance of the ascriptive stage is that it allows the development of a wide variety of social and cultural forms at the ritual and symbolic level into genuinely functional institutions when the size of the society increases, and differentiated political, economic, military, and legal institutions appear. Only when societies become differentiated in this way can we talk of the 'goals' of specific institutions, and only when one can specify goals can one effectively use the concept of function at all. The demands of bureaucratic, military, and economic efficiency require the increasingly precise specification of goals, and the freedom to allocate tasks on the basis of individual capacity in order to meet those goals.

It is precisely because these pressures are low in primitive society that a wide variety of rather inefficient institutions can survive quite easily. Primitive warfare, ritual authority, symbolic exchange, divination, and magic, for example, are in many respects inefficient or based on false premises, but they are the foundation of more efficient forms. In other words, it is at the primitive, ascriptive level of development, where adaptive and functional requirements are low, that man is free to produce social structures that are not dictated by minute adaptive requirements, but which are capable of transmutation into genuinely functional and adaptive institutions when the circumstances are appropriate. It is the very fact that humans in primitive society are not confined to a limited response to the here-and-now, but are free to create institutions and belief systems pregnant with developmental possibilities, that has allowed social evolution to occur at all.

But this is not to say that societies in which true functional organization has developed will necessarily operate their institutions efficiently. The course of history since the emergence of centralized states has been the record of ceaseless attempts to master the arts of government and of political economy, in which incompetence and folly are more obvious than wisdom and clear thinking. In many ways the evolution of society has been in the direction of instability, recurring rebellion, and periodic collapse: so China during the epoch of the Warring States, medieval Europe, and the Germany of the Thirty Years' War were far less orderly than the majority of primitive societies. Not only do large centralized states generate unprecedented difficulties of government for their rulers, they also give them unprecedented power, and the abuse of this power and attempts to restrain it have also been enduring themes of civilization.

Again, it must be emphasized that many ascriptive features survive quite easily in more functionally organized societies. The distinction between sacred and secular authority can be found in modern industrial society, although not as clearly as among the Galla, the Konso, and the early Indo-Europeans. Another distinction, between brain-work (especially where it involves the activities of government) and manual labour, appears in almost every society that can support a class that does not make an immediate contribution to the economy. Generally, we find that mental work is regarded as superior to manual work, and that the scholar, priest, and administrator are treated as on a higher plane entirely than the peasant. Under the Chinese Empire, for example, the classes of society were ranked in order of merit as officials, farmers, artisans, and merchants. Fighting, too, is usually regarded as superior to tilling the soil, and competes for social supremacy with mental work in many societies. Nor does the development of the modern state necessitate the pursuit of utilitarian goals alone. Indeed, the desire for glory, power, and prestige, often in the form of useless wealth objects and other symbols of success, is as powerful in our own type of society as it is in primitive society:

The orthodox economists, as well as Marx, who in this respect agreed with them, were mistaken in supposing that economic self-interest could be taken as the fundamental motive in the social sciences. The desire for commodities, when separated from power and glory, is finite, and can be fully satisfied by a moderate competence. The really expensive desires are not dictated by a love of material comfort. Such commodities as a legislature rendered subservient by corruption, or a private picture gallery of Old Masters selected by experts, are sought for the sake of power or glory, not as affording comfortable places in which to sit. When a moderate degree of comfort is assured, both individuals and communities will pursue power rather than wealth: they may seek wealth as a means to power, or they may forgo an increase of wealth in order to secure an increase of power, but in the former case as in the latter their fundamental motive is not economic. (B. Russell 1960: 9)

Political theories and ideology, which are so conspicuous in modern society, have also led to a type of confusion and irrationality for which there is no parallel in primitive society.

IV

Environmental Determinism and Social Variability

1. Adaptationism as environmental determinism

WE have yet to consider the possibility that the environment might exercise so compelling an influence on man that his adaptations have been more or less forced on him by its demands. In such a case, his behaviour and social institutions would simply be effects of certain material causes, requiring only the most elementary calculations of immediate benefits. Obvious examples would be the transhumance of pastoralists such as the Nuer, or infanticide to prevent overpopulation where food resources are limited. Adaptationist arguments that minimize the degree of human choice do not, of course, then have the problem of explaining how people can unconsciously make the *right* choices. Again, arguments for the primacy of selection over orthogenesis in social evolution would be greatly strengthened if it could be shown that each type of environment and its associated technology inevitably produces a distinct type of society.

In the previous chapter I maintained that because of the small scale and rudimentary technologies of primitive society, a wide range of institutions will all work perfectly well. This, of course, is quite contrary to adaptationist theories and, indeed, the power of the environment to require specific adaptive responses is often seen as maximal in the case of primitive societies, because their rudimentary technologies place them almost entirely at the mercy of nature. As a recent book expresses it:

. . . the less sophisticated a people's technology which mediates between their physical environment and their social and cultural forms, the greater determining power the former has over the latter. Here, where class relationships are absent, the more purely material aspects of historical materialism exert the most force in shaping world view and culture in general. (Kearney 1984: 6[1])

[1] One critic has described this type of assumption as ' . . . the rather Victorian notion of primitive people fighting off imminent starvation and struggling continuously for survival in an environment they could not control' (Rindos 1984: 18). See also Sahlins 1974: 2–3.

A classical statement of the cultural materialist position is this:

. . . hunting, herding, gathering, fishing, farming, mining, manufacturing, and transportation will influence, each in its own way, and in proportion to its magnitude, the form and content of a social system . . . A hunting people will have one type of social organization as a consequence of this kind of activity, i.e. the use of certain technological implements; an agricultural, pastoral, or industrial people will have another cast to its social system. (Leslie White 1959: 20–1)

One way of testing the validity of this theory that is commonly used is, in fact, quite ineffectual. This is to consider a single society and demonstrate that its organization is consistent in various ways with the mode of subsistence. All that such case studies can establish, however, is that in the societies concerned the people can in practice organize themselves to perform such subsistence activities as they actually perform! But what else would one expect to find? Necessary subsistence tasks that were left undone because the people could not organize themselves to carry them out? In which case, obviously, the people would all be dead, or the tasks would not really be necessary at all. Or, might one expect to find people organized into groups for performing subsistence tasks that were never accomplished? Markets where nothing is sold, or fishermen who never use their nets, perhaps? Single case analyses of this type, especially those which are also confined to a single point in time, are evidently pointless because they tell us nothing of the alternative types of social organization that would be *equally* capable of peforming the necessary subsistence tasks, and they also take it for granted that no alternative modes of subsistence are possible either.

2. The cross-cultural evidence

In order to discover if it is really true that the mode of subsistence is associated with markedly different types of social organization we must obviously proceed by comparing a number of societies, first holding the mode of subsistence constant and varying the societies and, conversely, considering some closely related societies that differ markedly in their mode of subsistence. In this section, therefore, we shall consider the main types of subsistence— gathering, hunting, fishing, pastoralism, shifting agriculture, intensive agriculture, and irrigation agriculture—and see what aspects of social organization can be predicted on this basis.

Despite the generally acknowledged difficulties attending cross-cultural surveys, it is obvious that, in principle, the hypothesis proposed by White is quite easily testable and that without attempting to test it we can say little or nothing of general significance about the ways in which adaptation to the physical environment requires specific types of social organization.

One major problem in cross-cultural research for many years was to obtain a representative sample of societies so that on the one hand distortions produced by diffusion of common origin ('Galton's Problem') are minimized, but that, on the other hand, all the regions of the world are proportionally represented. Despite my earlier criticisms of cross-cultural research (Hallpike 1971, and references to other critics of cross-cultural research cited there), I would agree that Murdock and White (1969) have produced a world-wide sample of 186 societies that is much superior to previous samples, and which can provide the basis for the comparison of economies and social organization that we are attempting here.

Another major problem in this type of research has been the reliability with which the different variables are coded. Some variables, however, such as mode of descent, settlement pattern, and type of economy inherently produce less disagreement among coders than others, and it is only variables of this type that have been used here. I have also excluded, as a matter of course, those variables which the coders consider in any way ambiguous or unreliable.

The Murdock–White sample has been coded for type of subsistence economy (Murdock and Morrow 1970), which together with the coding of the *Ethnographic Atlas* enables us to group the societies of the sample into the following categories: Gathering, 10; Hunting, 15; Fishing, 13; Pastoralism, 16; Shifting Agriculture, 25; Intensive Agriculture, 19; and Irrigation Agriculture, 15: that is 113 societies in all, not 186, since societies with mixed economies were omitted for obvious reasons. Societies were chosen for each economic category because they were coded as 'D' by Murdock and Morrow (1970), signifying that a particular mode of subsistence 'contributed more to the local food supply than all other techniques combined'. But only 3 societies in the Gatherer category were coded as 'D', and 7 in the Hunter category, so in order to increase the size of these categories in the sample I also included societies coded as 'I', in which a particular mode of subsistence 'contributes more to the local food supply than any other mode of subsistence but less than half of the total food consumed'. The sample of Agricultural societies was composed of those coded as 'D' for agriculture, and this sample was then further distinguished into the three categories of Shifting, Intensive, and Irrigation agriculture on the basis of the coding in Column 28 of the *Ethnographic Atlas* (Murdock 1967). The category 'Horticulture' in Column 28 of the *Atlas* was omitted because of its ambiguous status ('semi-intensive agriculture'), and because there were few societies in the category, all but one in the Pacific.

Once the Murdock–White sample has been arranged on the basis of economy, it is evident that a regional bias reappears so that, for example, North America is over-represented in the Fishing category, and Africa in the category of Shifting Agriculture, but this is an unavoidable consequence of the fact that economies vary on a regional basis (see Barry 1968, Table 2). It would, of course, be most advantageous statistically if the size of the total sample could be increased, but to be statistically important this increase would have to be by a factor of at least 10, and this would only reintroduce that problem of diffusion and common origins which has been avoided as far as possible by the Murdock–White sample, and would also require us to draw upon many inadequately described societies.

Murdock and Wilson (1972) have coded the sample for type of settlement and community organization, and their study forms the basis of the cross-cultural survey to be conducted here, although I have also used the *Ethnographic Atlas* for two variables, 'Slavery', and 'Segregation of Adolescent Boys'. Unless otherwise indicated, all symbols and their definitions are direct quotations from Murdock and Wilson 1972. (The cross-cultural study of types of political organization by Tuden and Marshall (1972) unfortunately contained too many cases of societies either lacking the relevant institutions, or else the data upon them, to be statistically useful for my purposes.)

It must be emphasized that the variables which I have selected are by no means the only ones which could be tested cross-culturally in relation to type of economy. But those discussed here are of a basic and elementary nature and it therefore seems most unlikely that they would not reflect any important influences from the economy, where such influences existed.

The predictive value of the various economies falls into three categories. In Category A, the correlation between rows (representing economies) and columns (representing social traits) is extremely strong and quite uncontestable (p = <.0001) although in the one borderline case a few cells exert a disproportionate influence on the χ^2 value. In Category B (p = .01–.04), the correlation between rows and columns has some significance but we generally find that this is derived from only a few cells in each table. In Category C (p = .13–.94), there is no evidence from these data of any relationship between the rows and columns of the tables. In the following tables Gathering = G, Hunting = H, Fishing = F, Pastoralism = P, Shifting agriculture = A(1), Intensive agriculture = A(2), and Irrigation agriculture = A(3).

Category A

1. *Permanence of settlement*

As one might expect, type of subsistence is an extremely reliable predictor of the degree of permanence of settlement:

B   Migratory or nomadic bands, occupying temporary camps for brief periods successively throughout the year.

S   Semi-nomadic communities, occupying temporary camps for much of the year but aggregated in a fixed settlement at some season or seasons, e.g. recurrently occupied winter quarters.

R   Rotating settlements, i.e., two or more permanent or semi-permanent settlements occupied successively at different seasons.

T   Semi-sedentary settlements, occupied throughout the year by at least a nucleus of the community's population, but from which a substantial proportion of the population departs seasonally to occupy shifting camps, e.g. on extended hunting or fishing trips or during pastoral transhumance.

I   Impermanent settlements, occupied throughout the year but periodically moved for ecological reasons or because of untoward events like an epidemic or the death of a headman.

P   Permanent settlements, occupied throughout the year and for long or indefinite periods. P is used instead of I in default of specific evidence of impermanence.

Table 3. Settlement type

Subsistence type	B	S	T	I+P	Total
G	6	3	1	0	10
H	8	5	1	0	14
F	2	4	3	3	12
P	10	3	1	1	15
A(1)	0	0	0	25	25
A(2)	0	0	1	18	19
A(3)	0	1	0	13	14
Total	26	16	7	60	109

$\chi^2 = 92.4$ df $= 18$ $p = <.0001$
I and P were conflated because of evident ambiguities in the coding.

We should note, however, that within each subsistence category some variation occurs, as here in Fishing, and that this tendency will increase dramatically when we examine most of the other variables. We shall also discover that for most variables there is a marked tendency for one or two forms of organizations to be overwhelmingly preferred in all types of subsistence.

2. Population density

It has long been recognized that population density is also very closely related to mode of subsistence, e.g. Murdock and Wilson 1972: 276 (Table 4). This correlation is strikingly confirmed in Table 4.

A Less than one person per five square miles.
B From one person per square mile to one per five square miles.
C From 1.1 to 5 persons per square mile.
D From 5.1 to 25 persons per square mile.
E From 26 to 100 persons per square mile.
F From 101 to 500 persons per square mile.
G Over 500 persons per square mile.

3. Community size

The population size of the focal or typical community is ranked by a numerical symbol in one of the following categories:
1 Fewer than 50 persons.
2 From 50 to 99 persons.

Table 4. Population density

Subsistence type	A + B + C	D + E	F + G	Total
G	10	0	0	10
H	15	0	0	15
F	9	2	1	12
P	13	3	0	16
A(1)	3	16	6	25
A(2)	3	10	6	19
A(3)	4	2	9	15
Total	57	33	22	112

$$\chi^2 = 77.91 \quad df = 12 \quad p = <.0001$$

3 From 100 to 199 persons.
4 From 200 to 399 persons.
5 From 400 to 999 persons.
6 From 1,000 to 4,999 persons.
7 From 5,000 to 49,000 persons.
8 50,000 persons or more.

Table 5. Community size

Subsistence type	1+2	3+4	5+6	N
G	6	4	0	10
H	8	6	1	15
F	8	4	1	13
P	9	4	3	16
A(1)	5	12	6	23
A(2)	2	5	12	19
A(3)	0	7	6	13
Total	38	42	29	109

$$\chi^2 = 38.97 \quad df = 12 \, p = .0001$$
Categories 7 and 8 were omitted because there were only 3 cases.

Community size is also very closely related to economy, at the $p = .0001$ level, but there is considerable variability within each subsistence category as far as pastoralists and all agriculturalists are concerned. We shall see in the next chapter that community size is also closely related to complexity of social organization in general.

4. *Household form*

A capital letter indicates the prevailing form of household relative to its family composition and component dwelling units.

L Longhouses or other large communal dwellings, the entire community residing in one or a very few such structures, each occupied by a social group larger than an extended family.

A Apartment houses or other multi-family dwellings (exclusive of long-houses) whose residents do not constitute a familial group.

H Family homesteads, in which a single family, whatever its composition, occupies a single residential structure in a cluster of structures which may also include important outbuildings (e.g. granaries or stables) and/or separate quarters for dependants (e.g. slaves, servants, or unmarried youths).

F Family dwellings, in which each family, whatever its composition, occupies a single residential structure without important outbuildings.

C Multi-dwelling households, in which a larger familial unit occupies a compound or cluster of residential structures, and each dwelling houses a component nuclear or polygamous family.

I Multi-dwelling households, in which a larger familial unit occupies a compound or cluster of residential structures, and each dwelling is occupied by an individual married man or woman rather than by married pairs.

J Multi-dwelling households, in which a large familial unit occupies a compound or cluster of residential structures, and each dwelling is occupied by a married woman with her children, the husband residing with his wives in rotation.

M Mother-child households, in which each married woman with her young children occupies a separate dwelling, the husband residing elsewhere, e.g. in a men's house.

The overall statistical significance here is very high indeed, but this is an excellent example of the danger of attaching undue importance to purely statistical significance, since in reality only 3 cells, those printed in bold type, are together responsible for nearly half of the total χ^2 value of 58.19, and without these cells the table as a whole has no significance at all. We also note that variable F, 'family

Table 6. Household form

Subsistence type	H	F	C	I	J	Total
G	0	6	3	0	0	9
H	0	13	1	0	0	14
F	3	8	1	0	0	12
P	1	6	5	0	4	16
A(1)	5	8	0	7	2	22
A(2)	6	7	2	3	1	19
A(3)	2	9	4	0	0	15
Total	17	57	16	10	7	107

$\chi^2 = 58.19$ df = 24 $p = .0001$
Variables L, A, and M were omitted because they had only 4 cases between them.

dwellings, in which each family, whatever its composition, occupies a single residential structure without important outbuildings' accounts for more societies than all the other variables combined. These are typical features of the data: so, as already mentioned, we generally find that one or two organizational forms are preferred in all types of subsistence and that while in some cases there are important relations between particular economies and particular features of organization, this level or correlation is confined to very few cells in the tables.

None of these results will come as any surprise to the anthropologically informed reader, of course, but it is rather more surprising that these are the only variables out of the 14 tested here that are very strongly and consistently related to modes of subsistence in terms of statistical significance, and even the Household Form variable is, as we have seen, a largely spurious association, since it is so heavily influenced by only three cells.

When I say that no other factors of social organization are nearly as closely associated with subsistence as these, it will at once be objected that such phenomena as literate bureaucracies, empires, and industrialism are only associated with agriculture. This, of course, is quite true, and no one would suggest that hunting and gathering, or fishing, could form the basis of a military empire, but for the time being I am concerned with those features of society which, like modes of descent, polygyny, or succession to local political office, are not the distinctive or exclusive features of centralized states. Just why it is that centralized states can only arise on the basis of certain forms of subsistence (but will by no means *necessarily* do so), will be discussed in the next chapter.

Category B

5. *Descent*

A capital letter indicates the prevailing rule of descent.

M The principal consanguineal kin groups are based on matrilineal descent, e.g. matrilineages.

P The principal consanguineal kin groups are based on patrilineal descent, e.g. patrilineages.

D Double descent prevails, both matrilineal and patrilineal descent groups being present.

A The principal consanguineal kin groups are based on ambilineal descent, e.g. ramages.

B Descent is bilateral, i.e. ancestor-oriented descent groups are absent, and kinsmen are aggregated only by consanguineal and/or affinal ties between individuals, as in personal kindreds or kiths.

Table 7. Mode of descent I

Subsistence type	M	P	D	B	Total
G	0	2	0	8	10
H	1	1	1	12	15
F	3	3	0	6	12
P	2	11	1	2	16
A(1)	3	12	3	6	24
A(2)	1	14	0	4	19
A(3)	1	6	0	8	15
Total	11	49	5	46	111

$\chi^2 = 40.62$ df = 18 $p = .002$
Variable A omitted because there were only 2 cases.

It is clear that patrilineal and bilateral (cognatic) descent are overwhelmingly the most popular choices of descent system in all types of society, the only significant relations between a particular economy and descent system being the heavy preponderance of bilateral descent among hunters and gatherers, and the relative importance of patrilineal descent among pastoralists.[2] Even so, the

[2] It should be noted, however, that according to Murdock (1949) and Schneider and Gough (1961) matrilineal descent and matrilocality are associated with economies in which women make a predominant contribution, e.g. horticulture, and which lack the plough and large domesticated animals.

Environmental Determinism

Table 8. Mode of descent II

Subsistence type	M	P	D	B	Total
F	3	3	0	6	12
P	2	11	1	2	16
A(1)	3	12	3	6	24
A(2)	1	14	0	4	19
A(3)	1	6	0	8	15
Total	10	46	4	26	86

$\chi^2 = 19.39$ $df = 12$ $p = .08$

5 cells in bold type are responsible for nearly half of the χ^2 value. Interestingly, if we omit the hunters and gatherers and recalculate the data, significance disappears entirely, and $p = .08$.

6. *Compactness of settlement*
A capital letter indicates the degree to which the focal or typical community is a dispersed or concentrated settlement.

C   Compact settlements, e.g. nucleated villages or concentrated camps, whether of circular, linear, or amorphous shape.

D   Dispersed settlements, e.g. neighbourhoods of isolated family homesteads, bands whose members live in dispersed family camps, or villages with dwellings strung out at appreciable intervals along a highway, shore, or river bank.

H   Settlements composed of spatially separated subsettlements, e.g. sedentary hamlets or clusters containing two or three families of nomadic groups.

P   Partially dispersed settlements, e.g. a central village or town core with satellite hamlets or family homesteads.

Surprisingly, correlation between this variable and mode of subsistence is not very strong, at $p = .01$, and one third of the χ^2 total is provided by only 3 cells. As can be seen from the table, variable C is the commonest type of settlement in all forms of economy, except intensive agriculture.

7. *Community Leadership*
A capital letter indicates the form and complexity of political organization within the focal or typical community.

Table 9. Settlement pattern

Subsistence type	C	D	H	P	Total
G	5	3	2	0	10
H	11	4	0	0	15
F	8	5	0	0	13
P	9	4	3	0	16
A(1)	11	4	5	5	25
A(2)	4	7	2	6	19
A(3)	12	1	1	1	15
Total	60	28	13	12	113

$\chi^2 = 34.83$ df $= 18$ $p = .01$

O   The focal or typical community lacks centralized leadership, political authority being dispersed among its component households or other segments, which remain essentially autonomous.

X   The focal or typical community lacks centralized leadership, but such leadership exists at a higher level of political integration.

H   The community has a single leader or headman but lacks other political offices other than, at most, an informal council of elders.

D   The community had dual or plural headmen with distinct but co-ordinate authority but lacks a complex system of subordinate political statuses.

F   The community has a single leader or headman with one or more functional assistants and/or a formal council or assembly, but lacks an elaborate or hierarchical political organization.

E   The community has a single leader or headman plus an elaborate or hierarchical system of subordinate political statuses.

C   The community lacks a single political head but is governed collectively by a committee, a council, an age-grade organization, or the like.

U   The political organization of the local community is too complex to be appropriately coded under any of the foregoing symbols, as when religious functionaries play important political roles.

Table 10. Type of leadership

Subsistence type	O	H	D	F	C	Total
G	2	5	1	2	0	10
H	2	8	0	4	1	15
F	1	6	0	3	1	11
P	1	0	0	3	3	15
A(1)	2	3	1	**16**	1	23
A(2)	1	4	1	6	4	16
A(3)	1	**0**	2	9	0	12
Total	10	34	5	43	10	102

$\chi^2 = 40.72$ df = 24 $p = .018$

Variables X and E were omitted because of too few cases (3 each); U only had 5, and is also uninformative.

The correlation here for the whole table is a little lower than variable 6, and we find the typical feature of a few cells being responsible for about half the χ^2 value. It is also clear that variables H and F are the commonest in all modes of subsistence.

8. *Slavery* (This coding is derived from Murdock 1967 as defined for Column 71, p.166)
The forms and prevalence of slave status, treated quite independently of both class and caste status, are indicated by the following symbols:
    H   Hereditary slavery present and of at least modest social significance.
    I   Incipient or non-hereditary slavery, i.e. where slave status is temporary and not transmitted to the children of slaves.
    O   Absence or near absence of slavery.
    S   Slavery reported but not identified as hereditary or non-hereditary.
The 4 cells in bold type contribute more than half of the χ^2 value. Here again, without the hunter-gatherers, Table 11 would have much less significance.

9. *Community integration*
A capital letter indicates the predominant factor or factors contributing to the solidarity of the focal or typical community.

Table 11. *Type of slavery*

Subsistence type	H	I	O	Total
G	0	0	10	10
H	1	3	10	14
F	4	2	5	11
P	6	2	5	13
A(1)	11	5	5	21
A(2)	4	5	10	19
A(3)	4	1	7	12
Total	30	18	52	100

$\chi^2 = 23.76$ df = 12 $p = .02$

Variable S was omitted because there were only 4 cases, and because of ambiguous classification.

O The focal or typical community is notably lacking in social integration, at least as compared with its constituent local segments or with some large political unit of which it forms a part.

I The focal or typical community is distinguished from other neighbouring communities by a sense of common identity, e.g. a common dialect or subculture.

K The focal or typical community is integrated by kin ties, whether these are consanguineal or affinal.

S The focal or typical community is integrated primarily by common social or economic status, e.g. membership in a social class or participation in a common economic activity.

P The focal or typical community is integrated primarily (not incidentally) by common political ties, e.g. through allegiance to a particular chief or by interdependence through patron–client relationships.

R The focal or typical community is integrated primarily by a common cult or religious affiliation or by a civil-religious system of offices, the religious element in either case transcending in importance all other types of local bond.

C The focal or typical community is primarily integrated, not by common kinship, social status, worship, or political allegiance, but by the choice, fact, or accident of common residence.

Table 12. Basis of community integration

Subsistence type	I	K	P	R	C	Total
G	1	4	0	0	5	10
H	1	5	2	3	4	15
I'	?	6	2	1	2	13
P	0	13	0	0	1	14
A(1)	2	14	2	4	3	25
A(2)	2	6	2	1	4	15
A(3)	3	1	1	5	3	13
Total	11	49	9	14	22	105

$$\chi^2 = 37.43 \quad df = 24 \quad p = .04$$

Here, $p = .04$, and four cells are responsible for over half the χ^2 value. As we already know, residential ties are proportionally of greater importance among hunters and gatherers than other types of economy, except advanced agriculturalists, and ties of kinship are proportionally more significant in pastoral societies than in any others. Kinship and residence are the two most significant bases of community integration in all societies, except irrigation agriculturalists.

Category C

10. *Marital residence*
A capital letter indicates the prevailing practice of residence after marriage.

A   Avunculocal residence, i.e. with or near the maternal uncle or other male matrilineal kinsmen of the husband, including cases where men preferentially and typically marry a MoBrDa and reside matrilocally.

B   Ambilocal residence, i.e. optionally with or near the parents of either the husband or wife depending upon personal choice or circumstances, where neither alternative exceeds the other in actual frequency by a ratio greater than two to one.

M   Matrilocal or uxorilocal residence, i.e. with or near the female matrilineal kinsmen of the wife.

N   Neolocal residence, i.e. where spouses establish a common

household at a location not determined by the kin ties of
either.
P   Patrilocal or virilocal residence, i.e. with or near the male
patrilineal kinsmen of the husband.

Table 13. Type of residence

Subsistence type	B	M	P	Total
G	3	3	4	10
H	2	3	7	12
F	1	2	7	10
P	0	1	14	15
A(1)	1	5	18	24
A(2)	0	1	15	16
A(3)	1	3	10	14
Total	8	18	75	101

$\chi^2 = 17.52$ df = 12 $p = .13$
Variable A had only 4 cases and was therefore omitted, as was N, with 7.

This result has no significance.

11. *Segregation of adolescent boys* (This coding is derived from
Murdock 1967 as defined for Column 38, p.161)
Several degrees and modes of segregating boys at or approaching
puberty are indicated by the following symbols.
A   Absence of segregation, adolescent boys residing and
sleeping in the same dwelling as their mothers and sisters.
P   Partial segregation, adolescent boys residing and eating with
their natal families but sleeping apart from them, e.g. in a
special hut or in a cattle shed.
R   Complete segregation, in which adolescent boys go to live as
individuals with relatives outside the nuclear family, e.g.
with grandparents or with a maternal or paternal uncle.
S   Complete segregation, in which adolescent boys go to live as
individuals with non-relatives, e.g. as retainers to a chief
or as apprentices to specialists
T   Complete segregation, in which boys reside with a group of
their own peers, e.g. in bachelor dormitories, military
regiments, or age-villages.

Table 14. Segregation types

Subsistence type	A	P	R	S	T	Total
G	5	1	0	2	1	9
H	9	1	0	0	0	10
F	7	0	2	0	0	9
P	8	2	0	0	2	12
A(1)	13	4	2	1	1	21
A(2)	9	3	0	0	3	15
A(3)	14	0	0	1	0	15
Total	65	11	4	4	7	91

Conflating P+R+S+T gives us a $\chi^2=8.53$, df=6, p=.2, a result with no significance.

12. Intercommunity marriage

A capital letter indicates the extent to which the community as a whole forms an endogamous or exogamous unit.

A The focal or typical community is agamous, marriages both within and outside the community being permitted and roughly equal in frequency, i.e. with frequencies of between 40 and 60 per cent.

B The focal or typical community is agamous, but endogamous unions are in fact appreciably more common than intercommunity marriages, i.e. with a frequency of between 61 and 89 per cent.

C The focal or typical community is agamous, but exogamous unions are in fact appreciably more common than marriages within the community, i.e. with a frequency of between 61 and 89 per cent.

N Local endogamy is strictly enjoined or strongly preferred, marriages with members of other communities being rare or exceptional.

X Local exogamy is strictly enjoined or strongly preferred, marriages with a member of the same community (at least with the exception of levirate and sororate unions) being rare or exceptional.

Table 15. *Type of marriage*

Subsistence type	A	B	C	N	X	Total
G	4	1	4	0	1	10
H	5	5	0	1	4	15
F	6	1	4	0	2	13
P	4	1	5	1	5	16
A(1)	6	6	5	0	6	23
A(2)	3	5	4	3	4	19
A(3)	2	5	4	2	2	15
Total	30	24	26	7	24	111

$$\chi^2 = 25.15 \quad df = 24 \quad p = .4$$

This result has no significance.

13. *Local political succession*

A capital letter indicates the mode of succession to political leadership within the focal or typical community.

O   There is no community headman or council.

A   Succession to the office of headman, if such or an approximate equivalent exists, is through appointment (not merely acquiescence) by some higher political authority.

S   Succession is based primarily upon seniority or age, as under gerontocracy.

D   Succession is based on divination, dreams, or the like.

I   Succession is not appointive or hereditary but is achieved primarily by informal consensus or the recognition of leadership qualities on the basis of the acquisition of personal influence, wealth, or prestige.

R   Succession is not appointive or hereditary but is achieved through some formal electoral process, e.g. selection by a council or body of electors.

P   Succession tends to be hereditary, by a son or other patrilineal kinsman of the predecessor.

M   Succession tends to be hereditary, by a sister's son or other matrilineal kinsman of the predecessor.

L　Succession tends to be hereditary, but passes not to a particular category of kinsman but to a member of a ruling lineage or other privileged group selected for his personal qualifications by some electoral or appointive procedure.

Table 16. Type of succession I

Subsistence type	O	A	S	D	I	R	P	M	L	Total
G	2	1	1	0	4	0	1	1	0	10
H	2	0	0	0	7	0	6	0	0	15
F	1	0	2	0	5	0	2	3	0	13
P	2	0	2	0	0	2	7	1	1	15
A(1)	2	1	1	0	5	3	8	2	2	24
A(2)	3	3	1	0	1	6	4	0	1	19
A(3)	1	1	0	0	3	5	4	1	0	15
Total	13	6	7	0	25	16	32	8	4	111

Omitting A, D, and L because of low numbers of cases, and conflating the rather similar categories of I + R, and P + M, we have the results shown in Table 17.

Table 17. Type of succession II

Subsistence type	O	S	I+R	P+M	Total
G	2	1	4	2	9
H	2	0	7	6	15
F	1	2	5	5	13
P	2	2	2	8	14
A(1)	2	1	8	10	21
A(2)	3	1	7	4	15
A(3)	1	0	8	5	14
Total	13	7	41	40	101

$$\chi^2 = 13.34 \quad df = 18 \quad p = .77$$

This result has no significance.

14. *Forms of family*

A capital letter indicates the social composition of the predominant form of the family, regardless of its residential distribution.

E The predominant form of family organization is a large extended family, i.e. one normally embracing the families of procreation of at least two siblings or cousins in each of two adjacent generations.

F The predominant form of family organization is a small extended family, i.e. one normally embracing only one family of procreation in the senior generation but at least two in the next generation. Such families usually dissolve on the death of the head.

S The predominant form of family organization is a 'stem family', i.e. a minimal extended family consisting of only two related families of procreation (disregarding polygamous unions) of adjacent generations. But see 'Q' below.

M The predominant form of family organization is an independent monogamous family, polygyny being forbidden or disapproved.

N The predominant form of family organization is an independent nuclear family, polygyny being permitted but having an incidence of less than 20 per cent.

P The predominant form of family organization is an independent polygynous family, the incidence of polygyny being 20 per cent or higher. In cases of doubt about incidence, N rather than P is indicated.

Q The predominant form of family organization is an independent polyandrous family or a stem family with polyandry.

Table 18 shows no significant relation between these variables and type of economy.

We are now in the position to supply a reasonably well informed reply to the hypothesis proposed by Leslie White and others. Hunters and gatherers are certainly different in many respects from the other societies, but apart from this the claim that each mode of subsistence entails or determines some distinctive form of social organization is a gross exaggeration. What one finds instead is that economy is a very strong predictor of population density, permanence of settlement, and community size, but that beyond

Environmental Determinism

Table 18. Forms of family

Subsistence	E	F	S	M	N+P	Total
G	0	4	1	0	5	10
H	3	5	0	1	6	15
F	4	3	1	0	5	13
P	1	5	1	1	7	15
A(1)	5	8	3	1	8	25
A(2)	4	4	3	1	7	19
A(3)	1	6	3	0	5	15
Total	18	35	12	4	43	112

$\chi^2 = 14.23$ df $= 24$ $p = .94$

Variable Q was omitted because there was only one case, and N and P were conflated because of uncertainties in the coding. This result has no significance.

these variables the predictive value of economy becomes very irregular with regard to household form, slavery, compactness of settlement, community integration, (besides the importance of kinship for pastoralists), and community leadership. It has no relation at all to form of family, marital residence, descent (excluding hunters and gatherers), intercommunity marriage, local political succession, and segregation of adolescent boys.

It also appears that there are certain forms of social organization that are extremely common, irrespective of economy: the small extended family, and the polygynous family, patrilineal and cognatic descent, compact settlements, elective or hereditary succession to office, community leadership by a single headman with or without a formal council as well, and patrilocal residence, to mention some of the most important.

The obvious conclusion is that these types of social organization are satisfactory in a very wide range of social circumstances, or, to put the matter another way, if one has a simple subsistence economy, with only a few hundred people to organize, the same few principles of residence, descent, marriage, leadership, etc., will work in almost all of them. Numerous other alternatives, however, are often possible as well, and for the most part have little or no relation to specific types of subsistence. Those anthropologists, then, who expect to be able to prove that in *this* particular environment, with *that* technology, only a specific type of social organization will work, are simply deceiving themselves. No such precise correlation exists because the ascriptive principles on which primitive societies are organized—descent, age, gender, ritual status, residence, etc.—are extremely flexible and adaptable to a very wide range of circumstances.

At this point, however, the materialist might object that the major economic categories used in the cross-cultural survey are so general that they do not allow the subtler influences of the environment on social institutions to be detected. Let us therefore meet this objection, such as it is, by a detailed examination of a small number of societies. In the next section we shall consider the arguments and evidence produced by a cultural materialist that the pastoral economies of the ancient Indo-Europeans and the East African Dinka, Nuer, and Masai cause essentially the same types of society and religion.

3. Two types of pastoral society

My second method of assessing the relationship of environment to society involves holding the type of economy constant and varying the societies.[3] Just such an approach has been adopted by Lincoln in his *Priests, Warriors, and Cattle* (1981), in which he compares two societies of cattle pastoralists: the Indo-Iranians and East Africans, or, more specifically, the Dinka, Nuer, and Masai. (Since these East African societies are an arbitrary selection from a large number of pastoralists in the area I shall henceforth refer to them as the DNM.) Basing his analysis on the ideas of Hultkrantz (1966, 1974) in particular, and what seems to be a generally Marxist view of society, he attempts to show that in the organization of society and religion there is an extensive similarity in essential features between the two cultures, and that this is causally determined by their common reliance on cattle as the principal form of livelihood:

In religious matters the resemblances were overwhelming. Both groups had pantheons that focused on celestial sovereigns; both practised animal sacrifice as the chief ritual act; both had well established priesthoods; both had groups of martial spirits that were related to the warrior bands; both had myths telling of the creation of cattle; and both had myths of the first cattle raid.

The resemblances were not limited to matters of religion, however. Social organization was also very similar. A priestly class was well established in each case and stood at the head of the social hierarchy. Warriors were also exalted above the general lot and composed a separate social class. Some

---

[3] For a similar treatment of three Eskimo societies see Damas 1969.

subgroups were ruled by a king, while in others the leadership was more diffuse. For both East Africans and Indo-Iranians, social organization tended to be on a small scale, and the most important unit of organization was the herding party. This is in keeping with the facts that the two cultures are essentially pastoral and the base of their economies is the possession of cattle. (Ibid., 3)

We shall shortly examine the more detailed parallels which Lincoln claims to establish between the two cultures, but at this point it is worth introducing the specifically ecological factors which he believes responsible for this 'overwhelming resemblance':

. . . it is necessary to recognize the truly generative role of ecology with regard to culture and religion. It is not enough simply to state that culture is based in ecology. One must go further and put it more strongly: the given features of ecology serve to mold or shape culture, which in turn serves to mold or shape religion . . .

Given the practice of cattle keeping as a starting point, two features seem to follow almost automatically, namely cattle raiding and cattle sacrifice. The first is born of the natural desire to increase one's own stock of the most prized and valuable commodity. The second is born of the equally natural desire[4] to share one's goods with whatever deities there may be out of gratitude, desire for blessings, desire to feed and maintain the deities, or other such motives.

The existence of these two separate modes of action, both of which have cattle as their focus, leads eventually to the development of specialists who make it their business to perform either raiding or sacrifice as well as possible. These are the warriors and the priests, who develop subtleties of practice within their respective areas of concern and pass their knowledge on to the generations that follow. As the two groups refine their specialties to an ever greater degree, they become more separated from one another and tend to harden into classes.

Devoted to different activities, each class tends to develop different modes of valued conduct. The warrior cultivates strength, bravery, loyalty to comrades, and so forth; the priest cultivates his ties to the sacred and his knowledge of correct ritual procedure. Ultimately two completely different *Weltanschauungen* evolve. (Ibid., 173–4)

Having established the general outline of Lincoln's theory, we may now examine some of the more detailed resemblances which he claims to exist. In the case of both societies we are told that cattle are the essential element in a ritual cycle, as Figure 2 shows.

[4] While it is undeniable that ideas of sacrifice to deities are extremely common, in what sense can belief in such deities be described as 'natural'? Lincoln does not attempt to answer this question. But if belief in deities is not natural, how can the idea of sacrifice to them be natural either?

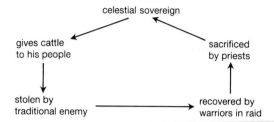

Figure 2. The East African cattle cycle
Source: Lincoln 1981: 35.

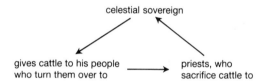

Figure 3. The East African priestly cycle
Source: Lincoln 1981: 37.

Here, sacrifice is regarded as an exchange in which gifts of cattle are given to the celestial sovereign and return gifts are received from him. Priests view this exchange as the paramount religious act, absolutely crucial for the well-being of the community and indispensable for the maintenance of continued prosperity. The myth of the first sacrifice governs the practice of all sacrificial offerings, and this practice emphasizes the proximity of the priest to the celestial sovereign, who bestows all cattle. (Ibid., 37)

Just as we can separate out a priestly cycle from the larger cattle cycle, so it is also possible to isolate a 'warrior cycle'. In large measure, priests are irrelevant to the lower half of Figure [2]. The central event here is the cattle raid, whereby cattle originally lost are recovered. Even the celestial sovereign seems somehow foreign to this part of the cycle, and insofar as divine support for the warriors' endeavors is present, it seems to come from deities specific to warriors, such as the Nuer Spirits of the Air, rather than from on high. Thus, the workings of a separate warrior cycle can be outlined (Figure [4]), and it will be noted that the warrior cycle has no point of contact with the priestly cycle, save that both share a concern for the welfare of the tribe and that obtaining cattle is understood as the means of preserving the tribe's welfare in both cases.

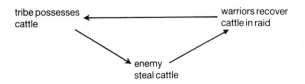

Figure 4. The East African warrior cycle
Source: Lincoln 1981: 38.

It is also necessary to note that the religious forms observed by the warrior are different from those of the priests. We have already seen how the chief ritual concern of the warriors is the increase of their own strength for battle by means of charms, potions, magical acts, and the eating of meat. It seems that they also have a theology somewhat different from that of the priests. (Ibid., 38)

By this he means that to the priests the celestial sovereign is the most important deity, whereas the warriors are more closely attached to the Spirits of the Air, which inhabit a realm intermediate between sky and earth, and which may possess a prophet who will lead the warriors on a raid.

Lincoln claims that a similar religious organization based on cattle existed among the Indo-Iranians, as shown in Figure 5. (The 'real' cycle differs only in the actions of the warrior class, who, instead of handing over the cattle to the priestly class, sometimes steal and eat them.)

Lincoln provides a more detailed list of alleged correspondences between the 'East African' and Indo-Iranian cattle cycles on pp. 171–2, some of which will be discussed presently. For the time being, however, I am simply concerned to establish those general resemblances between the two cultures that Lincoln claims to have discovered.

It is at once obvious that Lincoln's account of the two cultures is highly selective. The researches of Dumézil, for example, have shown that Indo-Iranian, and Indo-European society as a whole, was divided not into a two, but a three 'class' or 'function' pattern: priests, warriors, and food-producers. Lincoln, however, tries to dismiss the reality of the third function altogether, in an obvious

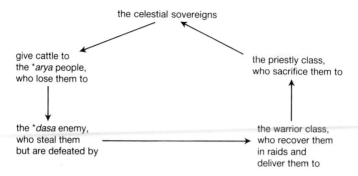

Figure 5. The (ideal) Indo-Iranian cattle cycle
Source: Lincoln 1981: 160.

attempt to produce a greater appearance of similarity between the Indo-Iranian and the DNM:

> Certainly Dumézil is right in making this division, but there are problems with regard to his 'third function' that bother me. The category is terribly general, and I am inclined to see it as something of a catch-all, including everyone in society who was not a priest or a warrior. Thus I do not see it as a 'function' in the same sense that members of the first two groups were identifiable by a specialized vocation, and I would simply call it the 'third class' or better, 'the commoners'. (Ibid., 51 n. 6)

We shall consider the evidence against this view in detail later (Chapter VI); suffice it to say here that Lincoln's interpretation of the third function is quite unsound: the members of the third class were, economically, the food producers (farmers and herdsmen) and, politically, the freemen—very different from mere peasants.

It is also clear that Indo-Iranian society was distinctly more specialized than DNM society. The Indo-Iranian priests were evidently the hereditary guardians of an elaborate corpus of oral mythology and ritual texts which required long years of apprenticeship, and were handed down in each priestly family, but this is very different from the knowledge required of Masai and Dinka priests. In these societies the tribal mythologies are common property, as is the knowledge of ritual procedure, and Lincoln's attempt to portray these priests as the possessors of an esoteric and complex body of knowledge is therefore quite contrary to the facts.

In the same way, it seems that in Indo-Iranian society there was a clear distinction between the priestly families and those of the professional warriors, presumably the sons of families wealthy in herds and perhaps slaves, who could thus be relieved from the duties of herding to specialize in military activities. In DNM society, however, while some men are richer in cattle than others, we cannot talk of any kind of 'class' of priests or of warriors such as seem to have existed among the Indo-Iranians. This is for two reasons. First, as a general principle, when we find that particular clans are termed 'priests' and others 'warriors', this does not mean, in an African context, that members of each clan may only perform one kind of social function. Thus, while only the *beny* (spearmaster) alone of the Dinka *provide* the Master of the Fishing Spear (priest), this does not mean that all the (male) members of such clans have priestly status, and do not fight. Secondly, as we shall consider in more detail shortly, warrior status throughout East Africa generally is much more a matter of age than clan, just as ritual status is closely associated with elderhood.

Nor do we find among the Nuer and Masai that sacrifice, which Lincoln regards as uniquely associated with priestly status, is in reality the exclusive prerogative of priests. In the case of the Nuer, as Lincoln concedes, ' . . . the Nuer are fiercely egalitarian and such "priests" as they have are considered no better than any other man. They do not hold any special prerogatives, do not even preside at sacrifice, and the functions they do retain are as much juridical as religious' (ibid., 48). The Masai do, indeed, have one clan, the Engidong (Fosbrooke 1948: 14), from which the *laibon* (priest) of each tribal section is chosen. While this official had a ritual responsibility for blessing the warriors before a raid, and was rewarded with a share of the booty, there is no suggestion that only he, or any of the lesser ritual experts, had any exclusive right to sacrifice. In particular, the sacrifices associated with the age system seem to have been performed by the elders (Bernardi 1954: 274, 277). Nor is there any evidence that the members of the Engidong clan as a whole had any priestly status, and this also applies to the members of those Dinka clans who provide the Master of the Fishing Spear.

It is also worth noting that the descent group organization of the Nuer and Dinka differ significantly from one another (see Lienhardt 1958: 130–1), and that both differ even more from the Masai in this respect: 'Masai society is divided into two moieties *en daloshi*, pl. *in daloishin*, which seem to provide a basis for clan organization. Every Masai is found in one or the other of the two moieties.

These are named after cattle, one: *orok kiteng*—the black cattle, the other: *oodo mongi*—the red bulls' (Bernardi 1954: 266). Fosbrooke also adds that the *orok kiteng* (*laiser, l'oorokiteng*) are regarded as the right hand of the tribe, and the *oodo mongi* (*molelian, l'oodomongi*) as the left hand (Fosbrooke 1948: 41), and we also find a similar left/right opposition in the age-grade system (ibid., 24 ff.) Nothing comparable exists either in Dinka or Nuer clan and age organization.

Nor does the Dinka evidence support Lincoln's claim that 'the priests remain a class apart from the warriors and exalted above them' (Lincoln, p. 41), or that the Dinka themselves perceive the relationship as one between superiors and inferiors (ibid., 46–8). According to Lienhardt the relationship is seen as ideally comparable to that between mother's brother and sister's son:

In Dinka thought, if such dual leadership, either of the tribe or the subtribe, is to be harmoniously maintained, the master of the fishing spear and the war-leader should be maternal kin, and in any subtribe or tribe, those descent groups which traditionally have provided the master of the fishing spear and the war-leader should have a classificatory kin-relationship through a woman . . . Such kinship through a woman is thought to be in some respects closer than agnatic relationship, and kin of these categories are ideally supposed to live together in amity, showing each other a courtesy and even affection more markedly than agnatic kin. The maternal uncle— who often brings up his sister's eldest child in his own home—is the peacemaker between his own children and those of his sisters, and is the pivot of relationships between members of his own and other exclusive agnatic groups living in the community. The sister's son is similarly the peacemaker between the children of the different wives of his maternal uncle, since he stands in the same relationship to all of them. (Lienhardt 1958: 119)

Lincoln's account of the DNM also drastically underestimates the importance of the age-grading system in their social organization. The age system is of least importance among the Nuer, but is clearly of great importance in Dinka society where the installation of new age-sets is under the control of the Masters of the Fishing Spear. For the Masai, however, the age-set system is the basis of their society:

The importance of the age grade system to the Masai social organization cannot be over-estimated. It regulates a man's conduct in relation to his fellow men; it is the basis of such political organization as the tribe possesses; together with clan and kinship it regulates a man's sexual life;

organized religion, certain economic activities, and above all military organization are dependent on the age grade system for their existence. (Fosbrooke 1948: 25)

In relation to Lincoln's theory it is of particular importance to note that advanced age is seen as conferring ritual status, in opposition to the relation between youth and warlike activities (Bernardi 1954: 312). This sacred/secular opposition of age and youth is a basic theme in East African societies generally, whether pastoral or agricultural, which must be set against any priestly/warrior specialization on a descent group basis, but it is a theme which Lincoln entirely ignores.

With regard to formal age organization we find, then, a very marked gradation in importance and formal structuring from the Nuer through the Dinka to the Masai (which is hardly consistent with the ecological hypothesis), so that among the Masai it is the basic principle of the whole social order. There is, however, no trace of such an institution among the Indo-Iranians. Lincoln argues that 'The insistence of such texts as RV 5.59.6, 5.60.5 on the fact that the Maruts[5] are all the same age would point to age-set organization' (Lincoln, p. 125 n. 94). (The Maruts, Avestan Fravasis, 'were martial figures located in the atmospheric region beneath the heavens and were associated with storm phenomena in some ways' (ibid., 96).) But this is extraordinarily slender evidence on which to base the deduction that Indo-Iranian society as a whole was therefore based on a system of age grades, and we must also remember that in Nilotic and Nilo-Hamitic society *elderhood* is the essential complement of warriorhood, with important political and religious functions. Lincoln provides no evidence whatsoever that Indo-Iranian society was or could have been organized on the basis of rule by elders.

If there is no evidence of age-grade organization in Indo-Iranian society, the Nuer, Dinka, and Masai have no trace of another institution that distinguished Indo-European society as a whole— the assembly. This institution (which is discussed in detail below, Chapter VI, Section 3*h*) was both secular and religious in nature. It was the setting for debates and word duels, for law suits and the punishment of criminals, and it was the occasion at which prominent men gave audience, and when the free men attended with arms to approve or reject the policies of their leaders. Nothing

[5] Warrior spirits led by the god Indra.

resembling this can be found at all in the societies studied by Lincoln, although a reasonable parallel seems to have existed among at least some of the Galla, e.g. Legesse 1973: 93–8, Knutsson 1967: 172.

It appears, then, that in social organization the Indo-Iranians and the Dinka, Nuer, and Masai were markedly different, and that the similarities involve nothing more than a differentiation between warriors and priests, a similarity which is not, of course, confined to pastoral societies at all. Even here, as we have seen, it radically distorts the evidence to represent the priest/warrior distinction as based on class, or as involving some kind of struggle for supremacy, as Lincoln does at various points throughout his book.

In religious beliefs, too, those 'overwhelming similarities' which Lincoln perceives are quite illusory. To begin with, both Evans-Pritchard and Lienhardt make it very clear that the Nuer and the Dinka conceive their Supreme Being to be one: 'Whether they are speaking about events which happened *ne walka*, in the beginning or long ago, or today, God, creative Spirit [*kwoth*] is the final Nuer explanation of everything' (Evans-Pritchard 1956: 6). Similarly, says Lienhardt, 'All Dinka assert that Divinity is one, *nhialic ee tok*' (Lienhardt 1961: 56). But it can, admittedly, also be said that the Nuer and Dinka perceive Spirit or Divinity as having more specific manifestations or 'refractions':

nhialic is also a comprehensive term for a number of conceptions which differ considerably from each other. Powers, of which the most important religiously are those I have called free-divinities and clan-divinities, are distinct from each other, though of most of them the Dinka may say simply *ee nhialic*, 'it is Divinity'. This unity and multiplicity of Divinity causes no difficulty in the context of Dinka language and life . . . (Lienhardt 1961: 56)

Evans-Pritchard describes how the spirits of the air are related to God in a similar way:

. . . the spirits of the air are, nevertheless, being Spirit, also God. They are many but also one. God is manifested in, and in a sense is, each of them. I received the impression that in sacrificing or in singing hymns to an air-spirit Nuer do not think that they are communicating with the spirit and not with God. They are, if I have understood the matter correctly, addressing God in a particular spiritual figure or manifestation. They speak to God directly or they speak to God in, for example, the figure of *deng*, whichever mode is most appropriate in the circumstances. They do not see a contradiction here, and there is no reason why they should see one. God is not a particular air-spirit but the spirit is a figure of God . . . The spirits are not each other but they are all God in different figures. Consequently, if one asks a Nuer whether a sacrifice is to God or to a spirit of the air the question makes no sense to him. Nuer pass without difficulty or hesitation from a more general and comprehensive way of conceiving of God or Spirit to a more particular and limited way of conceiving of God or Spirit and back again. (Evans-Pritchard 1956:51–2)

Lincoln, however, will have none of this:

Such an argument . . . cannot be accepted. In order to see monotheism, one is forced to deny the reality of other deities. Clearly they are not the equals of the celestial sovereign, and it would appear that they are not completely independent of him. But they are real, none the less, and they cannot be ignored or argued away. (Lincoln 1981: 18)

Even the brief quotations which I have given from Evans-Pritchard and Lienhardt show clearly that they do not claim the various spirits or powers can be ignored or treated as non-existent, or that the people regard them as unreal. The ethnographers are trying, with a wealth of detail and subtle analysis, to explain the difficult idea of the one and the many in the conception of the divine; the whole point of *Nuer Religion* and *Divinity and Experience* is that the kind of simplistic dichotomy between monotheism and polytheism assumed by Lincoln is quite inadequate to the facts, and radically distorts the theology of the Nuer and the Dinka.

The distinction between monotheism and polytheism is certainly not clear-cut, but there seems no doubt that Indo-Iranian religion attributed very much more independence to its deities than the Nuer and Dinka do to the various divinities and spirits of their religion, and it is this very obvious and inescapable Indo-Iranian polytheism, of course, which has impelled Lincoln to deny the evidently greater degree of monotheism among the Nuer and Dinka. Indeed, on the Indo-Iranian pantheon by comparison with the DNM he says:

There [amongst the DNM] one god dominated the pantheon in a relatively uncomplicated state of affairs. Among the Indo-Iranians, however, numerous different deities may be discerned: an otiose sky god (*Dyaus); a large group of associated deities (the forerunners of the Adityas and the Amesa Spentas), headed by two major figures: a legal sovereign (*Mitra) and a magical sovereign (*Varuna); and finally, a separate demiurge (*Twarstar). (Lincoln 1981: 60)

He claims that despite these obvious and important differences, nevertheless 'much can be seen that closely resembles the characteristics of Ngai, Kwoth, or Nhialic: all reside in the heavens, play a role in the creation, and rule over the world, dispensing favors and punishments to man' (ibid., 60). At this point, however, we have entirely lost touch with the theory that ecology determines the main forms of religious belief, since these characteristics of the DNM idea of God can be found in the beliefs of societies all over the world quite independently of any kind of ecology.

A further major difference between the religious systems of the Indo-Iranians and the DNM emerges later, when he concedes:

Among these differences perhaps the most noteworthy is the appearance of a single warrior god, a towering figure whose importance at times rivals that of the celestial sovereigns. In East Africa . . . there exists a vague group of lesser deities, such as the Nuer Spirits of the Air, who are concerned with raiding and other warrior matters. Among the Indo-Iranians a similar group existed . . . who were martial figures located in the atmospheric region beneath the heavens and were associated with storm phenomena in some ways. Also, the personification of the storm wind, *Vayu . . . often cuts a martial figure. But transcending these in importance is the one deity who must be considered the warrior par excellence among the pantheon of the Indo-Iranians, the god *Indra . . . (Ibid., 96)

Not only does Indra have no counterpart among the DNM, but even the claim that the DNM warriors have their own deities, 'such as the Nuer Spirits of the Air' is actually false (with the exception of the Nuer). Lienhardt's account of the Dinka makes no reference to any free or clan divinities which are in any way peculiarly associated with warriors, nor do we find such beings in Masai belief either. Lincoln has therefore taken a solitary and exceptional belief (that of the Nuer Spirits of the Air and their relation to warfare) and claimed that it is common to the Dinka and Masai as well, in order to give more substance to his theory.

Again, Indra is closely associated with intoxication and the furor of the warriors entering battle:

. . . the strength of *Indra is not inherent; he is not mighty by nature, nor does he possess great physical power at all times. Rather, he enters into a state of furor just as human warriors do . . . becoming invincible only at those times when he is in such a state of frenzy. He is, furthermore, ultimately dependent on men for his strength, and it is the purpose of their cultic activity to bring him to this state of increased power. Thus they offer

him songs and libations of the intoxicating *sauma . . . both of which have
the effect of invigorating and fortifying him. (Ibid., 99)

The furor of the warrior in battle is a well-attested feature of
many Indo-European societies, and was induced by drunkenness
obtained from alcohol. What parallels to this do we find among the
DNM? Lincoln refers to vigorous songs and dances, and to a report
that the Masai drink a decoction of certain tree barks in fat and
water (ibid., 30), and to the practice of eating large quantities of
meat to build up their strength. Fosbrooke, however, specifically
notes that 'Another duty, or rather, restriction placed on the moran
[warriors] was abstinence from tobacco and beer' (Fosbrooke
1948: 31). Evans-Pritchard (1940: 127–8) gives a fairly detailed
description of the conduct of cattle raids against the Dinka, but does
not mention any 'frenzy' on the part of the warriors, nor does
Lienhardt in his publications on the Dinka. We may conclude that
here, too, a very distinctive feature of Indo-Iranian religion and
society is almost completely absent from DNM society, despite the
availability of alcoholic beverages to the Masai, Nuer, and Dinka.

Finally, we must ask if Lincoln is correct in his theory of the
religious significance of cattle among the DNM. He says:

> The cattle procured by the warriors become, at least in one sense, part of a
> 'national herd' belonging to the entire tribe. And it is in this sense that they
> are offered up to the celestial sovereign in sacrifice, returning the gift that he
> bestowed on his tribe and creating a bond of reciprocity whereby he will
> again give more cattle. Such sacrifices are offered, not by the warriors who
> have procured the cattle for the tribe, but by priests or other ritual
> specialists who are particularly close to the celestial sovereign and
> particularly interested in cattle. (Lincoln 1981: 34)

We may first observe that Lincoln is wrong to treat the herd as, in
native eyes, being seen as ideally replenished and maintained by the
activities of the *warriors*, since in reality the herd of a social group is
conceptualized as being descended from its ancestors in the same
manner as its human owners. So Evans-Pritchard says,

> Nuer conceive of the ancestor of a clan, and likewise the ancestors of its
> component lineages, as having possessed a herd, the descendants of which
> have had, and continue to have, though distributed among different
> families, a constant relationship with the descendants of their original
> owners and are still thought of as one herd. This ancestral herd is a fiction,
> for the cattle are being constantly dispersed and replaced by others at
> marriages, but conceptually it is an enduring collectivity. There is ideally a

constant attachment, the clan and its herd forming a joint community down the generations, so much so that a common, perhaps the commonest, explanation of a division in the clan is the fighting of bulls of the ancestors of the divided parts. (Evans-Pritchard 1956: 258)

It is also clear that Nuer, Dinka, and Masai warriors spend a great deal of time raiding cattle from one another rather than from foreigners.

Secondly, sacrifice is for a wide variety of purposes: for fertility and for health, for the expiation of sins, to avert calamity, and so on, and while all these peoples naturally wish their herds to be maintained by divine protection, it quite misrepresents the significance of sacrifice to depict it as *primarily* intended to acquire more cattle. Finally, as we have seen, sacrifice is not the exclusive responsibility of a priestly class among the Nuer or the Masai.

At this point it is necessary to remind ourselves that Lincoln has been discussing a small sample of East African pastoralists (which he persists in calling 'East African'). In the next section we shall give detailed attention to the Borana Galla, who are exclusive cattle pastoralists but whose religious and social organization differ markedly from Lincoln's model. Indeed, another Nilo-Hamitic society of pastoralists, the Karimojong, from the same area as the Masai, have a religious and social organization that is very different from Lincoln's model as well.

While 'It is through the medium of cattle, their greatest value, that Karimojong seek contact with their deity (*Akuj*), who is regarded as the source of all values' (Dyson-Hudson 1966: 94), sacrifice is not the prerogative of any priestly class, since no such class or role exists at all in Karimojong society. Instead, ritual authority as well as political leadership is exercised by the elders:

Although credited with wisdom in worldly matters, their most important characteristic in Karimojong eyes is an ability to intercede with the deity for assistance. Their principal obligation is to turn this ability to the advantage of society through periodic public performance of ritual, designed to control the environment for the benefit of the political community as a whole or for any recognized segment of it gathered together. (Ibid., 212)

It also seems clear that Karimojong religion is even more unambiguously monotheistic than that of the Nuer and Dinka:

Akuj is the non-personalized deity of the Karimojong, occupying the regions of the above, manifested in sun, moon, stars, and the sky itself, and utilizing on occasion 'spirits' (wind, lightning) as the active agents of its purpose. Deity is the creator of all things, and in its gift lie equally prosperity and disaster according to the material conditions it causes to transpire in the world. Though manifest in nature, the deity thus controls it, and may alter natural conditions at will: in the Karimojong phrase 'God is great'. (Ibid., 212)

One's general impression of Lincoln's theory is that it relies on a highly selective use of evidence from a small and arbitrary list of East African societies. To be sure, both the Indo Iranians and the East African societies recognize a distinction between sacred and secular authority, but this is an idea that can be found all over the world and has nothing whatever to do with pastoralism as such. Both peoples believe in the existence of certain deities, and sacrifice cattle to them—as do many agricultural societies as well. And both peoples engage in stock raiding, from foreigners and from one another, for which purpose they naturally desire supernatural protection. Beyond this, as we have seen, the resemblances which Lincoln claims to have discovered are illusions produced by the desire to fit the facts into a preconceived model.

These two cases show that even cattle pastoralism can support very different social and religious systems, and we must also remember that there are numerous types of pastoralism (see, for example, the taxonomy developed by Goldschmidt 1979: 17–18). This is not to say, however, that pastoralism has no social consequences by comparison with agriculture. I would agree with Baxter, for example, that sedentarism tends to narrow the range of social relationships, whereas pure pastoralism, in particular, 'appears to build up sets of social relationships which, within the tribal economy, are territorially and socially widespread and which are utilized as sources of help and as protection against the vagaries of fortune' (Baxter 1975: 224). This tendency probably applies to patterns of marriage as well: 'pastoral marriage links tend to be spread far, those of partial agriculturalists to be less spread, and those of sedentarists to be near' (ibid., 217 n.). Baxter also suggests that 'inequalities of wealth are likely to be greater among sedentary than pastoral peoples, even when overall wealth is lower than it is among pastoralists' (ibid., 218). This, too, may be correct but requires extensive cross-cultural investigation. But while one does not wish to deny that pastoralism may have such effects on social organization,[6] they are likely to be rather vague: so Baxter himself

[6] Baxter proposes that egalitarian values and manners are the product of the relations between people and their herds: 'A herding unit which has a herd or flock

agrees that 'it appears doubtful that dependence on stock is, in itself, a criterion which can be used to distinguish a sociological type' (ibid., 206). Goldschmidt, however, claims that within the general pastoralist category, the herding of large animals in arid lands produces a distinctive type of social organization, value system, and world-view (Goldschmidt 1979: 19, Fig. 1). Examples of such traits are alleged to be segmentary patrilineages, age-sets, bride price, military skills (especially for young men), self-determination and independence, high concern with status, initiation with bodily mutilation, divination, a view of the world as hostile, and lack of interest in witchcraft. These characteristics seem in fact to have been derived from his field-work among the Sebei of East Africa, not from any extensive (and essential) cross-cultural comparison which would have shown him that these traits are also to be found among other societies with quite different economies.

Even within the small area of East Africa that we have been considering we found that Nuer and Dinka societies have close similarities to one another because they have common origins, and that both are very different from the social organization of the Masai which, like the Karimojong, is based on an age rather than a kinship structure. Nuer and Dinka society, however, are very different again from that of their immediate neighbours, the pastoralist Murle, whose social organization is based on four drum chieftainships (B. A. Lewis 1972). If we had time, we might also consider the social organization of Bantu pastoralists, such as the Ila-Tonga of Zambia who have matriliny and dual descent. Rather than ecology, it seems that historical relationship (often indicated by membership of a common language family) is a more reliable predictor of social organization and religion. So the Nuer and Dinka are members of the Nilotic language group, unlike the Masai and Karimojong, who are linguistically Nilo-Hamitic, and the Murle, who are members of the Isolated Didinga-Murle language group (Tucker and Bryan 1956: 87–91). As we shall see, it is often possible to predict more about a society if we know its language

too numerous for it to manage must seek extra labour or pass some of its stock to be tended by others who have less. These facts ensure a comparative equality of stock units from the points of view of tendance and consumption of the food they produce. This, I suggest, is the source of the famed egalitarianism in manners and in lifestyle of the East African pastoralists' (ibid., 217). This seems to me an implausibly limited origin for so broad a cultural characteristic. The Konso, for example (see below, Section 4a), are as democratic and egalitarian as any East African pastoralists, but have had intensive agriculture for many centuries.

group than if we know its environment. This is not because there is some Whorfian connection between a society's language and its culture, but simply because linguistic affiliation is often good evidence that the societies in question share a common origin. (As this book goes to press, I find that Jorgensen (1980: 98) has written in almost identical terms about the Indians of the west coast of North America.) I shall demonstrate this in the next section by an ςxamination of three societies in Ethiopia which speak East Cushitic languages but which have very different modes of subsistence, and it will become clear that they nevertheless share a common culture whose expression is largely unaffected by the ecological differences. Our study of East Cushitic societies will also complement the results established so far, because in this case it is the economies rather than the social organization that will provide the major variation.

4. East Cushitic societies and ecologies

The final test which I shall apply to the theory of environmental determinism involves holding the social organization constant and varying the type of ecology. Ethiopia is a country of great ecological and cultural diversity and the society which I studied there, the Konso, is one of a number which speak East Cushitic languages. The societies in this language group have a number of distinctive features of organization and general culture, one of which, the *gada* or generation-grading system, is actually unique to them.[7] On the basis of a comparison between three Galla groups—the Ambo, Meca, and Borana—and the Konso, Dassanetch, and Iraqw (of Tanzania), Lewis detects the following fundamental principles of social organization:

(a)   They all maintain an interest in descent and genealogy—but relegate it to a minor role, at best, for group and joint action.

(b)   They all operate with a sense of neighbourliness, community, and local contiguity for everyday affairs—and for political affairs as well.

[7] According to Stewart 'The view that [*gada* systems] are found only among speakers of East Cushitic languages (Haberland 1963: 169) needs to be modified, since it is doubtful whether Dassanetch is Cushitic, and the status of Konso is unclear (Tucker and Bryan 1956: 56; Tucker 1967: 660, 678)' (Stewart 1977: 17). The status of Konso had already been made quite clear (Hallpike 1972: 3), where I state the Konso and Borana Galla languages share 46% of cognates, almost the same as Bender's more authoritative figure of 44%. According to Bender, the linguistic status of Dassanetch is also East Cushitic (Bender 1971: 174).

(c) Movement from community to community is easy, and families (sons and brothers) readily split up and move to different communities. Within the community, co-operation is enjoined upon people, regardless of descent background, merely because they are neighbours.

(d) Free choice of associates and associations is also basic. Sometimes this means changing locale, sometimes it means joining voluntary associations such as the *iddir*, and sometimes it means changing alliances. But in each case there is considerable freedom of choice.

(e) Most of the peoples we have dealt with have, or had, formal assemblies of the elder males of communities and districts, often featuring formal and elected positions of leadership.

(f) With the partial exception of the Boran *k'allu* none of these groups recruits its leaders on the basis of descent group membership or inheritance; all depend for their leadership upon the self-selection of men of achievement, men of wealth, diviners, or men of responsibility and a civic sense who stand out in councils. (H. S. Lewis 1974: 154–5)

Fortunately for the purposes of testing our hypothesis their economies are very diverse, and we can thus establish with some precision the extent to which the characteristic features of East Cushitic society do or do not vary in some manner which is clearly determined by their ecology. (There will also, of course, be some variation that has no discernible relation to the ecology at all.) I propose to examine three societies: the Konso, who are terrace and manure agriculturalists, growing sorghum and maize on the lower slopes and wheat and barley on higher ground, with limited numbers of cattle, sheep, and goats; the Sidamo, who are dependent on the *ensete* plant which has entirely different agricultural requirements from the cereals of the Konso, and who also have large herds of cattle as well as sheep and goats, so producing what amounts to a dual economy; and the Borana Galla, who are exclusive cattle pastoralists, but who also have sheep, goats, and horses. The Konso and Borana are members of the Lowland Group of East Cushitic languages, while the Sidamo belong to the Highland Group, and are related to one another linguistically by the percentages of cognates shown in Figure 6.

(a) The Konso

The Konso, numbering 55,000–60,000, are the immediate neighbours of the Borana, and live about a hundred miles to the south-west of the Sidamo. While, as we shall see, their culture is thoroughly typical of the Eastern Cushites, it is important to note

Fiɡuɾe 6
Suuɾce. Deⁿder 1971: 171, 175.

that, despite the close relation between the two languages, the Konso are not simply Borana who have taken up agriculture:

. . . we should beware of thinking in terms of a basic Konso stock which split off from a proto-Galla people, wandered around in southern Ethiopia, and finally came to rest in Konso. Konso family traditions show that the present Konso population is derived from all the surrounding areas. Moreover, the Konso are markedly shorter and more negroid than the Borana. They are clearly an amalgam, both physically and culturally, in which other stocks than Galla are represented. (Hallpike 1972: 4)

One source of this amalgam is the Werizoid language speakers (Gauwada and Tsamai in particular), who, although members of the Lowland East Cushitic Language Group, seem to have no pastoral tradition. (On the relation between Konsoid and Werizoid languages, see Black 1973).

The Konso Highlands are a small range of mountains running roughly east-west in a bend of the Rift Valley, and are bounded by the Sagan River to the east and south. The area traditionally inhabited by the Konso is about 200 square miles, and the population density therefore about 250 p.s.m. In the parts traditionally cultivated there is an altitudinal range from about 5,000 to 6,000 feet, and a dry montane climate. Since their conquest by the Amhara in 1897 they have begun cultivating the lowland area of the north, which has considerably increased their food supply. The main crops, in the lower and hotter areas, are millet (sorghum) and maize, and on the higher ground wheat and barley. Cotton and coffee are important cash crops. (See Hallpike 1970a for a detailed description of Konso agriculture.) Rainfall in this area is about 26 inches per annum, but much of this comes in the form of thunderstorms, and in half the year very little rain falls. The terrain is extremely mountainous and stony, and the soil is preserved by the construction of stone terraces. These follow the contours of the hillsides and their principal function is of course to prevent the violent rainstorms from washing away the fertilized soil and crops. Pressure of population on available land is heavy and no fallowing occurs. Consequently the fields require large quantities of manure, which is supplied by the herds of cattle, sheep, and goats, and also by dried human faeces. Grazing land is scarce, and the stock are kept in stalls in their owners' homesteads, only being taken out to graze along walled paths which keep them off the fields. No use of the plough is possible in most of this area, and all cultivation is by hoe and digging stick. Some *ensete* is grown on the higher and wetter land, but although it is apparently indigenous to the area the Konso do not esteem it highly, and it is a very minor crop. Cattle, on the other hand, are not only essential for agriculture but of great religious importance.

The Konso are most unusual in this part of Africa for living in walled towns, averaging about 1,500 in population (Hallpike 1970*b*, 1972). The largest town, Degato, has a population of around 3,000 (more at an earlier date), and its walls are a mile in circumference (see Hallpike 1972: 27–39, 60–86). These towns are certainly ancient features of Konso society, and in some cases at least have been produced by the consolidation of previously separate settlements. Each town is divided into two sections, and there is a rule that a man born into one section can never live in the other. Each section is further divided into wards which are each governed by an elected council of elders, as are the towns themselves. As we shall discuss in more detail later, ward membership is not based on kinship and each ward contains members of many different lineages. Each married man has his own homestead, which is a fenced compound containing sleeping huts, kitchen, granaries, and stalls for the stock. Narrow paths make their way through the towns between blocks of such compounds.

The ward is responsible, first and foremost, for burying its dead, a task from which kin are specifically disqualified. Ward members also have mutual obligations of hospitality and assistance, and individuals are completely free to reside in any ward they please within their own section.

Descent among the Konso is based on nine named exogamous patrilineal clans which are dispersed among all the towns. These clans now have no corporate existence in the form of leaders' or elders' councils such as we shall find among the Sidamo, and it is only at the lineage level that Konso descent groups become corporate. While every lineage belongs to one of the nine clans, it does not do so according to any segmentary scheme, and neither clans nor lineages have apical ancestors, nor are genealogies kept beyond about the fourth ascending generation, though senior lines in a lineage may remember direct ancestors for up to about eight generations. There is however considerable evidence that the Konso descent system was at one time of a segmentary type resembling that of the Sidamo and Borana.

1. In the Garati region there are still named sacred places where the clans are supposed to meet if there has been serious quarrelling between their members, and eight of the nine clans meet in pairs at four locations (Hallpike 1972: 88, Table 2). Elsewhere I was told that there should be no intermarriage between some of the clans (ibid., 89), and there is a tripartite religious grouping of the clans that conforms to these exogamic relationships and the associations at the sacred places.

2. There are major differences in the size of the clans (ibid., 88, Table 20). These show that the largest clans are those of the greatest ritual importance. On these indications, the original segmentary organization of the clans may have been as shown in Figure 7.

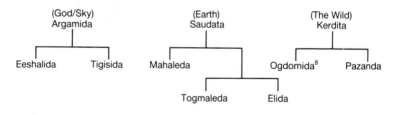

Figure 7

3. There are well over a dozen priests who are entitled to wear the silver bracelet (as do the regional priests Bamalle, Kalla, and Gufa) instead of the five iron bracelets of the ordinary lineage head. These 'intermediate' priestly families are of great eminence, and their status becomes much more intelligible if interpreted as a relic of a now forgotten segmentary system, in which these families

---

[8] Although the Konso conventionally refer to the nine clans, in one region there is a tenth clan, Ogdomida.

would have been the heads of major segments. Within each town, moreover, there are also some lineage heads of great ritual and social importance, and others who are quite obscure.

4. In one region, Garati, it is said that the line of eldest sons of junior wives of a lineage head can, over several generations, become the heads of new lineages, though this was not apparently a recognized custom in the other two regions.

5. The erosion of the corporate solidarity of the clans and the whole segmentary system may well have been brought about by the growth in importance of the towns, which would have intensified the basic East Cushitic tendency for kin to disperse. Thus I was told that 'our ancestors liked to move about to make themselves big' and for the man who wished to found a new lineage it would have been distinctly advantageous to move from his natal town, where his influence would have been overshadowed by the head of the senior lineage, to a new place of residence in which there would have been no lineal superior. I have a small amount of data that give tentative support to this possibility. For example, the Kalla line of regional priests is supposed to have been the origin of the lineages shown in Figure 8, whose towns of residence are shown in brackets.

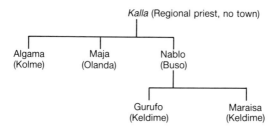

Figure 8

While this evidence is not conclusive, it does strongly suggest that the Konso originally had a segmentary descent system basically similar to that of the Borana and the Sidamo.

Each lineage has as its ritual leader a priest, *poĝalla*, and it is knowledge of one's relationship to the *pôgalla*, not any precise genealogical reckoning, that maintains the unity of the lineage. The *poĝalla* sacrifices on behalf of his lineage each year to bring them and their stock life, health, fertility, and prosperity. He also mediates in disputes between lineage members, and acts as spokesman for members of his lineage when they are involved in legal disputes with those of other lineages. While land and stock may only be inherited patrilineally, the lineage itself does not own any property. All land, stock, houses, and other real property are owned by individuals who can dispose of them as they please. Only if a man dies without heirs will his closest relatives within the lineage inherit; normally, however, property is divided among a man's sons, the eldest receiving a double share of land and his father's principal homestead, since he is expected to set up house with his father after marriage. The remaining sons live scattered through the town of their birth, or may even move to a friendly town nearby.

The Konso are extremely emphatic that they dislike living near the other members of their lineage; while the lineage may pay the fines of its members when they are punished by the town, and rich members of the lineage may assist poor members who are short of food, it is clear that the Konso resent the kind of dependency on the lineage that these and other benefits involve. Women are regarded as marginal to the basic institutions of town, lineage, and *gada* system. Marriage only concerns the immediate relatives of bride and groom: in Garati region it is said that no bridewealth is paid, and in Takadi region that only small presents are exchanged. Bridewealth, and compensation for murder, which are both forbidden, are compared to selling a person—an idea that is most abhorrent to the Konso.

Just as wards are made up of people from different lineages, another type of organization, the working party (Hallpike 1972: 78–80), is composed of men (and in some cases women) who come from different wards and lineages, despite the fact that every ward and lineage has sufficient members to form a working party. These working parties (the large comprising about 30, and the smaller about 10 members) are named and persist for an indefinite period. Members pay an annual fee which goes to the purchase of a bullock for a feast and sacrifice for the benefit of the members, and on such an occasion each working party will perform its own dance in one of the public places. Each has an elected leader, who negotiates for work on its behalf, and this consists of labour in the fields of those who have too much land to cultivate themselves, and other jobs such as housebuilding and threshing grain. Rich men as well as poor are members of working parties, and they are in no way a 'class' phenomenon but rather a kind of social club. Work on community tasks, however, such as repair of town walls, paths, dams, and cattle pools is the responsibility of the warrior grade under the authority of the ward or town council.

The towns are therefore the centres of daily life, and the highest level of organization at which there is effective dispute settlement and mediation and the punishment of criminals. (Towns also form alliances, but permanent groups of this type only comprise two or three members; see Hallpike 1970*b*.)

Beyond the towns are what we may call 'regions': three named areas, each under the ritual leadership of a particular priestly family (Hallpike 1972: 180–221), who live in large, ancient homesteads in the fields. Around the homestead is a sacred lawn of grass, and close by is a sacred wood. The priest of each region is responsible for supervising the *gada* system of his region. The main difference between *gada* systems and the normal type of age-set system is that in the *gada* system one's initiation into the system does not depend on one's chronological age, but upon where in the system one's father is at one's birth. (Stewart 1977: 87 describes this as 'paternal linking'.) I shall give a brief description of the system as it works in the Garati region as an illustration. The diagram (Figure 9) shows a series of grades, with Ukuda at the top, and Farida at the bottom.

Farida is essentially the grade of childhood; Hrela are the warriors, who may also marry; they comprise the police force of the town, acting on the elders' authority. Kada is the first of the elders' grades, and their functions involve political and judicial decision making, and the ritual offices of blessing Hrela and the land. Orshada are simply more senior elders, and Gurula is the grade in which men retire from active life, though they retain the capacity to bless. (The two grades of Gulula and Ukuda are in practice unfilled, because they are relics of an earlier system based on a nine-year cycle: see Hallpike 1972: 205–6.)

Recruitment into this system is governed by the following rules:

Everyone, as soon as he is born, is placed in a grade whose rank is solely dependent on the grade of his father. Secondly, the interval between the father and all his sons is always two grades and nothing else. Thirdly, no one may marry before he reaches Hrela grade. Fourthly, every eighteen years there is a great festival called Kadabaha. At this time everyone in Garati moves up one grade, simultaneously. No movement between grades can take place at any other time. (Hallpike 1972: 181)

The peculiar consequence of such a system is that a man is always in the same grade as the rest of his brothers, irrespective of the

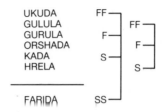

Figure 9. The Garati *gada* system

actual age differences between them, and it is also by the same rule possible for a man whose father is in Gurula, for example, to be born into Kada. For various technical reasons this seldom happens (Hallpike 1972: 183–4; Stewart 1977: 85–7), and the rule forbidding marriage before Hrela also prevents men being born so far outside the system that they are of mature age before they may even enter Farida. Nevertheless, there will obviously be greater difficulty in maintaining a correlation between the average age of each grade and the social age norm for that grade, than there will be in normal age-set systems. In an earlier form of the Garati system, moreover, entry into the system depended on whether the father was an eldest son or a younger son, and on the birth order of the son himself, which I have termed 'sibling seniority grading', and Stewart names 'birth order paternal linking' (Stewart 1977: 106).

Despite the extremely elaborate nature of the Konso *gada* system (of which I have only given the most abbreviated description here) it has very little importance in the practical regulation of social life, other than preventing the marriage of men until they reach Hrela grade. While the ceremonies of promotion occur under the supervision of the regional priest, the *gada* grades have no elected officials or councils of any kind, and it is also quite unrelated to the system of clans and lineages. Even at the level of town organization, ward and town councillors are elected on the basis of actual age and ability, not primarily on the basis of grade membership (Hallpike 1972: 67–71). In these repects the Konso *gada* system differs markedly from that of the Borana and Sidamo, in both of whose societies the grades are corporate groups with elected officials; in Borana society the *gada* system is closely associated with the moieties of Gona and Sabbo, and in Sidamo society it is closely integrated with the clan system. This isolation of the Konso *gada* system seems to have been produced by the growth of the towns, which have become the centre of all political and judicial decisions. In the same way, as already mentioned, the dominant influence of the towns seems also to have eroded the corporate nature of the clans. But despite what *we* would consider the practical irrelevance of the *gada* system, the Konso regard it as supremely important, and it remains as vital a part of their society as the age systems of other East African societies, including pastoralists. They were extremely interested in discussing it, and when asked why they had it, replied 'To make the crops grow'. By this they meant that it is the basis of social harmony, which in turn is necessary to obtain the blessings of rain and fertility. It must also be observed that, because of the principle of paternal linking, *gada* systems are inherently more difficult to operate than ordinary age-grouping systems, which do not require marriage restrictions, and in which age is easily correlated with grade membership.

The regional priest, therefore, has no political authority based on the *gada* system enabling him to prevent violence between the towns, and in fact warfare was a common occurrence before the Amhara conquest. But he could call upon the services of prominent priests in different towns to act as peacemakers when towns were about to fight. They were supposed to run between the lines of warriors and cast down their sacred staves as a means of enforcing peace. In addition, each religion has a pair of sacred drums which are also symbols of moral and religious authority, appealed to as a means of restoring peace. These drums are blessed by the regional priest and circulate among the most notable priests of each town in the region. The homestead of the regional priest, like that of every *poĝalla*, is a sanctuary, and no priest may use weapons or have any association with death.

Central to this appeal for peace is the concept of the sky God, Waĝa, who is the god of morality and rain. It is believed that Waĝa is particularly concerned that men shall live at peace, and that he withholds rain from towns which are guilty of too much quarrelling. Originally he is said to have lived close to earth, and to have made himself known to individual men, but a woman angered him and he went far away. For this reason, it is said by some that women are excluded from all religious ceremonies, but in fact they are more accurately described as excluded from ceremonies for the warrior grade. The craftsmen—smiths, weavers, potters, and tanners—are also excluded from religious ceremonies (see Hallpike 1968), and form a despised group whose status is hereditary.

Konso religion, like that of the Borana and Sidamo, is therefore essentially monotheistic, but like many other peoples the Konso also believe in spirits. The traditional name for these is *oritta*, and they are generally regarded as malevolent. But there is no place for individual prayer to God in Konso religion, and it seems possible that requests for help in sickness and other troubles of a personal nature were made to such spirits. Certainly today essentially the same cult of spirit possession by *iyanna* spirits as described by Hamer and Hamer (1966) for the Sidamo exists among the Konso and the Borana (see Hallpike 1972: 315–21).

Finally we may note the importance of certain basic Konso values: these are, first, a great emphasis on toughness and courage in warfare and hunting. In traditional times the penis of a dead man was cut off and worn on the killer's wrist, and the men's clubhouses are still adorned with clay pots of a phallic nature; 'stones of manhood', pillars made of basalt, were erected in public places to commemorate victories in battle over hostile towns, and a man who kills a lion or leopard is allowed to hold a triumph ceremony, in which he parades through the town ringing a bell, being kissed by the women who call him 'our bull'. Secondly, wealth is greatly admired, and a rich man may commission a series of statues to commemorate himself after death. These will show the hero, flanked by several wives (only rich men can afford more than one wife), several emasculated victims, a leopard to show his prowess in hunting, and a row of stones to commemorate the fields which he bought during his lifetime. Only a rich man, too, would be able to afford such statues.

But on the other hand the Konso also have a high regard for peace, *nagida*, which is sanctioned by their religious beliefs, and genuinely strive to prevent quarrels growing beyond control, and they have a strong fear of unbridled emotion.

A second aspect of their idea of *nagida* is the emphasis they place on discussion, *dehamda*. Differences of opinion should be settled by discussion, not violence, though they recognize that if one person is really intransigent, force may be the only solution . . . It is in discussion that *dugada* manifests itself. *Dugada*, truth, in a rough translation, is a very important quality among the Konso. It has the connotation of honesty, and impartiality, and absence of self-seeking. They know that most of the time men fall below this standard and ironically refer to the grave as the *porra dugada*, the 'road of truth', because only the dead tell no lies. (Hallpike 1972: 133)

(b) The Borana

The Borana are notable as a pastoral people inhabiting the hot, dry lowlands of northern Kenya and southern Ethiopia who traditionally had no reliance on any form of agriculture and who 'live entirely off milk, blood and meat provided by their herds of cattle, camels, sheep and goats' (Baxter n.d.: 52).[9] They trade skins, meat, and stock to obtain cloth, tea, sugar, tax money, and other necessities and luxuries that they cannot supply themselves (ibid., 52). According to Haberland (1963: 4–7), the Borana, like the other Galla peoples, were not originally pure pastoralists at all, but highland dwellers with a mixed economy. He presents convincing arguments that the archaic agricultural system was a barley monoculture without manure, using the hoe rather than the plough, and that the domestic animals were cattle and sheep. The continued religious reverence of the Borana for barley, which they cannot grow; the adjustment of their calendar to the rainy season of the highlands, despite the fact that the seasons of the lowlands are quite different; and the religious importance of the centre post of the house, even though the lowland shelters of the Borana are too simple to require such a feature, are further evidence of their highland origin. Among many Ethiopian peoples (as we shall see in the case of the Sidamo), cattle are herded in the lowlands by the young men, while the rest of the society lives in the highlands and is primarily dependent on agriculture. In some cases it is known for this economic difference to lead to a permanent split in the society concerned, and Haberland suggests that some time before the beginning of the sixteenth century population pressure forced the Galla to divide into a number of different tribes, and that in this process the Borana became a purely pastoral society.

Settlements are unstable, seasonal agglomerations of families, numbering from 2 to 20 homesteads, with an average of 7. Each homestead comprises a man, his wife, and their children (Baxter

[9] Dr Baxter informs me that in recent years the Borana have suffered much economic hardship, and that few can now survive by pastoralism alone. The description of the Borana in this section should therefore be taken to refer to their traditional society and not necessarily to present conditions.

n.d.: 50). Kinsmen in a camp tend to be siblings, or parents and children (especially eldest sons), or affinal chains of siblings, e.g. △ ○=△ ○=△ ○ (Legesse 1973: 34–5). There are, however, many unrelated persons in a settlement, and it should be stressed that genealogical ties *per se* are not the basis of residence, and that friendship networks and age-set loyalties are of equal or greater importance (ibid., 36). In particular, younger sons do not usually herd their portion of the family stock together, but in widely dispersed locations (ibid., 35). 'Boran divide their herds and flocks into five units: milch cows, dry cows, milch camels, dry camels, and the flock of sheep and goats. Each are normally herded in different places. Ideally a brother should reside with each unit of the family herd, but obviously in practice other kin, affines or stock associates must frequently substitute for non-existent siblings' (Baxter 1975: 216 n.). As Dahl (1979: 271) also observes, there are sound ecological reasons for the dispersal of family herds, but there are clearly other ways in which this can be done besides the dispersal of brothers. Each settlement or village has a 'Father' who is the senior elder present. 'He is usually someone respected, rich in stock and generous, who can afford to sacrifice coffee beans every day and to tide over the others with milk and meat in hard times' (Baxter n.d.: 51). According to Legesse (p. 36), the Borana in Ethiopia arrange their huts so that the most senior man's homestead is on the extreme left of the semicircle (looking outward).

Wells are essential for the Borana, both in Ethiopia and Kenya. According to Baxter, those in Kenya may be up to 17 men deep, while more open wells may be 3 men deep (Baxter n.d.: 40–1), and it seems that in Ethiopia the wells are not only deeper (up to 30 men?), but are capable of yielding a more permanent and copious supply of water. So Legesse states (p. 42) that an important corporate activity of clans and lineages is the digging and maintenance of wells and other sources of water such as dams. Again, it seems that in Ethiopia it is possible to maintain larger numbers of people in the vicinity of the wells than in Kenya. But Legesse also notes:

. . . The strange attraction of Borana to the well complexes is difficult to explain. Borana could, presumably, live by the rivers where the pastures are plentiful and the supply of water practically unlimited . . . It appears that the wells have become the centre of social activity and are an emotionally charged focus of Borana society. (Legesse 1973: 43)

Dr Baxter, however, informs me that rivers are avoided because of tsetse-fly, and according to Dahl (1979: 269) the Borana consider the quality of well-water to be superior to that from the rivers.

Borana society is divided into two patrilineal exogamous moieties, Sabbo and Gona. The members of these, and of their component clans, are dispersed throughout Borana country, but members of both moieties must be present at all deliberations (Legesse 1973: 39–40). At the head of each moiety is a religious leader, the Kallu, of whom more will be said presently. Gona is divided into two sub-moieties, and Sabbo into three (although Dr Baxter informs me that these are essentially two). These sub-moieties are further subdivided into clans, sub-clans, and lineages. Kin groups perform some ceremonies associated with birth and marriage, but the most important ceremonies are performed by the *gada* classes.

Baxter states (p. 102) that 'Clansmen should render each other every sort of assistance, contribution to fines, hospitality, help in herding, gifts in misfortune and distributions from fortune's bounty', but in practice, it seems, 'It is to those people he addresses as *milo* [close clansmen] that a Borana turns when he needs assistance, and it is them that Borana mean when they say that clansmen love and assist each other' (ibid., 104).

It should also be noted that in a society of such pronounced individual mobility between residence groups, the moiety and clan system is constantly used by the Borana as a means of identifying other Borana who are strangers to them, and of providing a set of conventional relations between the Borana and the Sakuye and Warta tribes who live among them.

While there is no inheritance of land, or even of grazing rights, cattle are inherited patrilineally. The eldest son, *angafa*, is his father's heir, and according to Legesse redistributes the herd at his inheritance to his younger brothers as he sees fit. (See also Dahl 1979: 275–7 for further details.) Since cattle are essential as bridewealth he thereby controls the marriages of his younger brothers, and this is apparently a major cause of friction between brothers, and an important factor in their dispersal (Legesse 1973: 25). Baxter, however, conveys a somewhat different impression, since he says that this abuse of authority by eldest brothers is 'rigidly checked', and that

for day to day usage, the herd may be considered as administered jointly by the group of male siblings. When the joint herd is large enough to maintain separate homesteads, unless they are particularly fond of each other, brothers usually live in different villages. The different sorts of stock of such a group of brothers, and the brothers themselves, may be scattered all over Borana country (Baxter n.d.: 50).

Baxter also suggests that in course of time the beasts which are being looked after by one agnate for another gradually become detached from their original owner and are inherited by the warden's heirs (Baxter 1966: 126–7). This may counteract the influence of primogeniture and prevent the development of an aristocracy of wealth

The eldest son, as heir, is the only son who conventionally remains with his parents after he has married (Legesse 1973: 32), just as among the Konso. Although bridewealth is an essential basis for marriage, it should be noted that the necessary transactions only concern the immediate agnates of the groom—his father, brothers, and father's brothers while the mother's brother exerts considerable moral influence. By African standards the amount of bridewealth is small: only one cow to the bride's mother, and a cow and two bulls to the father (ibid., 32). The polygyny rate does not seem high: the census taken by Legesse shows only 20 men with 2 wives of 298 married men, or 6.7 per cent, perhaps a slightly lower percentage than for the Konso.

Women are seen as occupying a marginal social status, 'Borana conceptualize the family as a group of males surrounded by a "border" of alien and alienable females through whom they are linked with other families and descent groups' (ibid., 24). Women are associated with domestic life (only married women build huts, which are very simple structures with no heavy timbers), and their roles are seen as 'indoors', in opposition to male roles which are 'outdoors' (ibid., 20). Baxter notes, however, that 'Borana women tend to marry at a distance, they have considerable social respect, and are secure from divorce' (Baxter 1975: 217 n), whereas Konso women marry close at hand, and are not secure from divorce. While the Konso regard women as occupying a marginal social status (as do the Borana according to Legesse), I should say that the status of women among the Konso is fairly high, especially in the case of older women.

The age system, like that of the Konso, is of the *gada* type. The system is a sequence of ten grades, *luba*, each of eight years' duration, so arranged that boys in the first grade are the sons of men in the sixth grade; those in the second grade are the sons of the men in the seventh grade, and so on (a five grade interval, therefore, between fathers and sons, or 40 years). There is an eleventh grade, *gadamoji*, whose members assume ritual responsibilities of purity and special sanctity: they are supposed never to carry a spear, use harsh words, beget a son, or commit adultery (Baxter n.d.: 279). For reasons too complex to discuss here (see Legesse 1973; Hallpike 1976*a*; Stewart 1977), the relation between the nominal status of the grades and the actual ages of the average members has become disturbed, so that men are presently being born about five grades too high in the system. As a result, a series of true age-sets, *harriya*, has long existed to organize the young men, in particular for military purposes. It therefore seems that membership of a *luba* involves little corporate solidarity, but that among members of the *harriya* there is a very strong and genuine feeling of solidarity. According to Baxter, age-mates should always assist each other in every way in their power, and an age-mate may take personal property belonging to another (except stock) without danger of litigation (Baxter n.d.: 420). Age-mates conventionally use obscene language to one another in a joking way, which is normally forbidden to adults; they hunt together, assist one another in watering stock, attend dances together, and a married man should offer his wife to an age-mate on the first night that he stays with him (ibid., 421).

We are now in the position to examine Borana political institutions, and it must first be emphasized that there is no centralized authority which can impose its decisions on the people:

The 'Peace of Boran' is not merely a passive absence of strife, but an active principle of co-operation and commonalty. This is most obvious in the fact that this warrior people, with a name but no settled habitation, dispersed very thinly over a country that extends for nearly four hundred miles from North to South, throughout recognize and obey a common law though there is no centralized political or judicial authority which can impose direct sanctions to enforce that law. (Ibid., 13)

In particular, the Peace of Boran dictates that there should be no violence, and that disputes must be taken to the appropriate judicial authorities; Baxter (1966: 117) records that violence between Borana is almost unknown, even in times of severe hardship. In this respect the Borana differ markedly from the Nuer, for example. Peace, *nagaia*, is clearly a basic Borana value and essentially similar to the Konso *nagida* in both its social and religious significance.

The ritual head of each moiety, as we have seen, is the Kallu, who inherits his office by primogeniture on the male line. Each Kallu has his own large village, close to plentiful supplies of water and grazing ('it always rains well wherever the Kallu sleeps'), although these villages may be moved to new sites when all the firewood within carrying distance has been cut down. In the Kallu's village reside various legal and calendrical experts, diviners, representatives of clans with special ritual responsibilities, servants, and herdsmen to tend the large numbers of cattle given to the Kallu, from which he makes gifts especially to Boran who have lost their herds (Baxter n.d.: 189–90). The Kallu's approval, with that of the council of his lineage, is necessary in the election of all principal heads of the Borana political system. Each *gada* class recruits 6 senior gada councillors, three of these councillors from each moiety' (Legesse 1973: 48).

But the Kallu have no power to give any executive orders, though they may apparently veto proposed raids if they hear of them, and even send messengers after the raiding parties to forbid them to continue. Indeed, there is clear opposition between the Kallu and warfare: no Kallu may go to war, and the Kallu and his sacred emblems provide sanctuary, so that no one touching them may be harmed. In all these respects they resemble the regional priests of the Konso.

Theoretically, the Kallu is the final court of legal appeal, but in practice it seems unlikely that he is ever required to act as such. For practical purposes judicial functions are performed by the officials of Gada grade (the grade which holds political authority for eight years). The senior official is the Abba Gada, or Abba Boku, whose office is primarily ritual, but he is assisted by numerous other elected officials, and there are also specific war leaders. These officials also travel throughout Borana country during their term of office (ibid., 85), and there are elders at the local level to hear disputes.

It is also of particular interest that the Borana have the idea of an assembly of the whole nation, the *Gumi* Gayo, or 'assembly at the well of Gayo'.

Gumi Gayo is by far the most inclusive event in Borana political life. They think of it as the assembly with the highest degree of political authority. To impress this idea upon strangers Borana say, 'What the *gumi* decides cannot be reversed by any other [lower] assembly'. It is interesting to learn that this body, which holds the ultimate authority, is neither the gada assembly nor the Kallu councils. It is, rather, the assembled representatives of the entire society in conjunction with *any* individual who has the initiative to come to the ceremonial grounds. In their idiom it is *gumi* (the multitude) which sits in judgement. In theory any individual has a right to attend, to take full part in the deliberations, and to bring any matter to the attention of the *gumi*. (Ibid., 93)

Borana beliefs in God (Waq) and spirits appear to be essentially the same as those of the Konso, and we find a similar emphasis on the values of peace, bravery, and wealth throughout their culture.

(c) *The Sidamo*

The Sidamo are located between Lakes Abaya (Margherita) and Awasa, roughly a hundred miles north of the Konso, and numbering approximately 600,000 (Hamer 1976b: 327). Although they are members of Bender's (1971) Highland East Cushitic Language Group (hence the much lower percentage of cognates), there has clearly been significant cultural contact (as late as the sixteenth century) with the Borana (Hamer 1970: 50), and they are still neighbours with the Guji and Arussi Galla.

Population density was estimated by Smeds as about 385 p.s.m. in eastern Sidamo (Smeds 1955: 34). Their economy is notable for its dependence on the *ensete* plant (*Ensete edule*), though they also grew maize, and coffee as a cash crop, and also for the marked divergence of ecology between lowland and highland regions. But despite the great differences between their economy and those of the Borana and the Konso, we shall see that the basic features of East Cushitic society are plainly visible in Sidamo institutions.

'The ensete, being a *hapaxapanth* (i.e. a plant which perishes entirely after the fruitescence) and living in a highland climate, needs 3 to 6 years to build up a store of carbohydrates in the leaf sheaths, necessary for the following florification and fructification' (Smeds 1955: 16).

When ready for cutting, the pulp is scraped from the leaf sheaths and pseudostem and placed in pits lined with leaves to ferment for two to three months, when the resulting flour is ready to be baked or made into porridge (ibid., 23–4).

The plant is propagated by shoots from the stem of the six-year-old plant, which are removed from the seed beds to plantations where they are planted very close together (ibid., 20). Large quantities of manure are required to maintain soil fertility, and for this large numbers of cattle are kept:

Of the village area mapped in the neighbourhood of Arbigona . . . only 16.4% was cultivated area, 6.0% bamboo groves and hayfields, and 77.6% pastures. But, this large pasture area is not enough for the grazing of the animals of the farmers, a large part of the herds being now and then, especially during the dry season, sent up to Garamba [a high, wet area of mountain pasture].

The manure is not collected from the pasture, but from the houses, where the animals are kept during the night in separate partitions, the dung being collected in baskets and carried out to dungheaps inside the plantations, or more often in the fenced yard. (Ibid., 20)

The cultivation process only requires the soil to be turned over with digging sticks before the rainy season, and then periodic weeding. 'The only assistance necessary to support the members of the nuclear household is that provided by three or four male agnates in the spring digging, and a reciprocal exchange of labor among village women at the time of harvest' (Hamer 1967*a*: 76).

Quite apart from their significance as providers of manure, cattle are valued as wealth, and men desire stock as well as land. Cattle are not only sent up to the high Garamba plateau, but are also kept on a long-term basis in the lowlands. If, however, a man is to have a large herd of cattle he must strengthen and maintain his kinship ties with people in the lowlands. The Sidamo thus have what amounts to two economies:

So different are the middle and high altitudes from the lowlands that they attract people with different value interests. Those who live permanently in the lowlands are willing to put up with the heat and malaria for the sake of a continuous diet of milk and butter in contrast to persons who prefer the ensete and vegetable diet of the cool, damp, and relatively healthy highlands. When a man is young the practice is to spend much of the rainy season with his herds in the lowlands, returning to the plateau to harvest his coffee and prepare the land for planting. As his sons mature the seasonal care of the stock in the lowlands is delegated to them. Practically all highland dwellers have some agnatic or affinal kinsmen who live permanently in the lowlands and may be entrusted with the herd during the absence of the owner or his sons. These people return periodically to the highlands to participate in various rituals and to have their sons initiated into the generational class [*gada*] system. It is the generational class system which provides support for the political bonds between the two ecological zones by linking diverse descent groups through the process of generational complementarity. (Hamer 1970: 55)[10]

The Sidamo live in villages (*kaca*) averaging about 25 households, each comprising a man, his wife, and unmarried

[10] This is an excellent example of the multiple uses to which such institutions as *gada* systems can be put.

children. The huts of the households are 'scattered across the hills and interconnected by a number of winding footpaths. Villages are grouped around plateaux which along with forest land are treated as common property for the purposes of grazing and the gathering of firewood' (Hamer 1970: 52). About 50–60 per cent of male household heads in each village are of the same lineage (of about three generations in depth), but each village has, as these figures indicate, a very substantial number of 'strangers' who are, however, treated as members of the clan on whose land they have settled (except for marriage purposes) (Hamer 1967a: 76). The reason for this high percentage of strangers is that 'The pursuit of wealth leads men to seek to expand their initial patrimony of land and cattle by obtaining gardens and pasture in clan areas other than their own' (Hamer 1970: 55). This may be the immediate justification, but the Sidamo clearly conform to general East Cushitic norms in this basic aspect of social organization.

Large scale labour for housebuilding, clearing paths, damming streams or cleaning ponds for the water supply to the villages is provided by the working party, *olauw* (a term which also means 'district') (Hamer 1970: 63). An *olauw* comprises the young male population, in the age class of initiates (not the elders), and is drawn from a number of contiguous villages, and so may number some hundreds of individuals. It is therefore divided into groups of forty to fifty men called *cinanca*, each under a foreman. Traditionally, these were the only work groups larger than the extended family (Hamer 1967a: 77; 1970: 54).

The village is thus the basic political unit, where decisions over the allocation of unused land and the settling of disputes between members are the responsibility of the assembly of adult males (*songo*) who are members of the Elder (*cimessa*) grade (Hamer 1970: 54), but higher levels of authority are at the *olauw*, sub-clan, and clan. We must therefore consider the organization of the clan, and how it is related to the age-system.

The Sidamo are organized into a number of segmentary patrilineal clans governed largely by elders whose position is supported by a generational class system . . . In the past, segmentation occurred as a result of population increase and subsequent scarcity of land for grazing and cultivation. A group of agnates would move into vacant territory and in time develop into a new sub-clan. There is no term for lineage, but it is important for a man to be able to trace his descent to the founder of a given sub-clan, *bosello*, as well as to be able to claim descent from a common clan (*gurri*) ancestor for purposes of prescribed marriage exogamy and land rights. Thus these descent groupings constitute the basis of territorial divisions with sub-clans being further divided into district, *olauw*, and village, *kaca*, units. At the head of each clan and sub-clan is a chief, *Morte*, whose role is largely ritual, though he does have the authority to mediate disputes between individuals and descent groups. Nevertheless, government at all four levels is by an assembly of elders known as the *songo*, with the individual having the right of appeal to the clan assembly of elders in matters of law and custom.

The one exception to this overall Sidamo structure is the Aleta cluster of thirteen clans located in the center of Sidamo territory. To protect themselves from hostile action by the clans to the north as well as against the Gugi in the south and the Jamjam to the east, these people have in the last 150 years established a tribal *Morte* and *songo*. Instead of clan generational classes, the Aleta peoples have simply projected this system to the more inclusive tribal level, without changing the decision-making status of the elders. (Hamer 1967*a*: 74–5)

But since clan membership *effectively* depends upon residence, and authority within each clan is based on generational status as determined by the *gada* system, Sidamo social organization essentially conforms to the East Cushitic model.

Each clan has a ritual leader, the Woma:

So important are the attributes of this gerontocracy in maintaining peace and harmony that they have been personified in the position of *Woma*, the ideal *cimessa* [elder]. In fact, informants with historical knowledge were unanimous in their opinion that the *Woma* position existed before the *Lua* or the *Gadane* and *Morte* roles had been established. A *Woma* is more than a competent mediator or ritual functionary such as a *Gadane* or *Morte*, for he combines in addition to their abilities the wisdom associated with very old age. Though there is variation from one clan to another in the selection and functions of these dignitaries certain general principles apply to all, such as the requirement that candidates must have survived two cycles of the *Lua*, and while they need not come from the senior sub-clan or, in the case of the Aleta, from the oldest clan in the tribe, they must be selected by members of that descent group. A *Woma* must always be available for consultation, so that the elders from the countryside may meet daily at his homestead to enjoy the satisfaction of associating with such a prestigious person as well as to form a perpetual *songo* for resolving disputes. (Hamer 1970: 67)

There are evidently close resemblances here to the Borana Kallu and to the Konso regional priests. The Woma of the Holo and Garbico clans is described as

exempted from physical labour and representatives from all the Holo and

Garbico lineages pay homage by bringing him bulls and honey . . . . Perhaps, however, the most symbolic privilege of the postition is the deference etiquette which requires that no one, regardless of age or rank, may pass in front of a Woma . . . On the other hand there are restrictions that a Woma may only have one wife, must not travel far from his home, must invariably display dignity of deportment, and should always be available to negotiate disputes. (Hamer 1967*b*: 332)

The Sidamo clan system is therefore more closely tied to the *gada* system than is that of the Borana, but we must remember that the clan is in practice a residential group, almost half of whose numbers are not real members of the clan.

Let us now examine how the *gada* system of the Aleta works. There are three basic grades: Pre-initiates, Initiates or warriors, and Elders (*cimessa*), and five generation classes or sets: Fullassa, Hirbora, Morgissa, Darara, and Wawassa. The basic rule is that all sons join the class four below that of their father, and promotion occurs every 7 years, but there is no class in which marriage is forbidden, and so over-aging can and does occur (Hamer 1970: 57). It is interesting to note that the circumcision[11] of elders, which is also a feature of the Borana system (Legesse 1973: 128) and was once also of the Konso (Hallpike 1972: 193, Stewart 1977: 83), is also present in the Sidamo system, despite the absence of a ban on marriage below a certain generation set. This suggests that the circumcision of elders is primarily symbolic of an opposition between sacred status and sexual activity, and was only secondarily intended as a device to prevent over-aging.

Though Hamer is describing the Aleta system, this seems essentially the same as that described for the Garbico by Stanley and Karsten (1968), although the Garbico do have a means of dealing with over-aging not apparently used by the Aleta (see Stanley and Karsten 1968: 95, 97; Stewart 1977: 107).

Each *Lua* has its leader and assistant leader (*Gadane* and Jet-lawa), who are appointed shortly before their *Lua* is initiated into the warrior grade. The selection is under the control of the elders, although the exact procedure is not clear in Hamer's account. According to Stanley and Karsten (p. 96), the *Lua* of the initiates'

---

[11] The circumcision operation among the Sidamo must apparently be carried out by a non-Sidamo (Hamer 1970: 64). I record the same requirement for the Garati Konso (Hallpike 1972: 193), and for the Takadi Konso, except that in this case the operator is a craftsman (ibid., 199).

fathers appoints a selection committee from their sons' *Lua* charged with finding the most appropriate man to fill the office of Gadane.

Once chosen the *Gadane* and his assistants are recognized as permanent leaders of the new *Lua*. The class leader having been formally designated must perform three major roles: that of officiant at ritual sacrifice for members of the *Lua*; as peacemaker in the settlement of disputes; and as organizer of the initiation rituals. Though he is the official head of his *Lua* and in the opinion of some informants commands more loyalty than men feel for their descent groups, he is in no way a military leader. His role as a man of peace is such that when the men of his class raid cattle from other tribes he goes part of the way and blesses their work, but never participates in the ensuing combat. (Hamer 1970: 60)

The *Gadane* thus seems very similar to the Abba Boku of the Borana. The *Gadane* and *Jet-lawa* may also function as peacemakers for the Sidamo: 'This is so much a part of their role that they must become living symbols of harmony by avoiding acrimonious debate with others and any participation in the military activity so highly esteemed by men' (ibid., 60). Hamer also notes that the *Gadane* can only sacrifice if he is an elder, because the slaughter of cattle is the exclusive prerogative of elders (ibid., 60 n.1), and until he becomes an elder he can only call the *Lua* together for the sacrifice.

The Sidamo believe in a sky God, Magano, who was originally much closer to Man than he is today:

It seems, however, that he became angry with mankind and returned to the sky, where he influences the course of events only in a distant and most indirect fashion. This sky god, Magano, is seen as a punishing deity who seems in the main to be concerned with the giving and taking of life. (Hamer and Hamer 1966: 393)

Hamer does not say, however, if he is particularly associated with rain. The Sidamo also believe in spirits, *shatana*, which were sent by Magano, 'The *shatana* are thought to have an influence on such important aspects of everyday life as childbirth, health, and the reproduction of cattle' (ibid., 393). Spirit possession of a kind very similar to that which I have described for the Konso also occurs among the Sidamo.

The influence of the dead is also of great importance:

This deference [to elders] continues after death, for when a man dreams of his dead father it is invariably of a demand by the latter to be honoured with the offering of a bull, ram, or honey. Dreaming is considered one of the most important channels of communication with the supernatural world and to fail to honour the request of a dead father is to risk an untimely death.

(Hamer 1967b: 327–8)[12]

Women and craftsmen (potters, tanners, smiths, and one other unnamed occupation) are certainly excluded from full participation in one very important ritual, the 'feeding of Abo', the craftsmen on the grounds of their impurity (and the alleged greed for meat by the tanners) (Hamer 1967b: 334), but the reason for the exclusion of the women is not given.

In their values, Sidamo clearly conform to the dominant pattern of East Cushitic society: 'the ultimate aim in any Sidamo dispute is the restoration of good will and harmony within the community' (Hamer 1970: 54). All the information on the function of the elders as a class, the *Gadane* of the various *Lua*, and the clan heads, such as the Woma, testify to the importance which the Sidamo attach to peace and social harmony. Again, wealth and bravery are highly esteemed:

There is much in Sidamo folktales, mythology, and in the data provided by contemporary elders to indicate that a high valuation of wealth and a concern about exchange practices are of considerable historic depth. In traditional tales men of wealth are always treated with deference, for this attribute is not only important in itself, but is usually associated with bravery and outstanding oratorical ability. (Hamer 1967a: 80–1)

The importance attached to bravery is confirmed by the cattle raiding duties of the newly initiated *Lua*, who were supposed to undertake 'numerous cattle raids in which they might demonstrate skill in taking large numbers of cattle under dangerous conditions' (Hamer 1970: 62). Indeed, for a man to make a daring raid on someone's pen and remove all the animals conferred even more prestige than killing an Arussi, Guji, or Jam-Jam.

(d) Conclusions

Our survey of these three peoples provides ample support for Lewis's description of the basic principles of East Cushitic society. The subordination of descent to the ties of residence and neighbourhood is not as marked among the Sidamo as it is among

12 Of the Konso I said, '[Ghosts] are thought still to be in contact with their surviving relatives and descendants, returning in dreams either to the lineage priests or their immediate surviving relatives. When a man or woman dies, he or she will return a short time after death, in a dream, to demand the sacrifice of a bull, which will be carried out' (Hallpike 1972: 161).

the Borana and the Konso, but it is quite clearly a very important aspect of Sidamo society. Also, there is some variation in the degree to which the *gada* system is related to the descent system: strongly among the Sidamo, weakly among the Borana (only at the moiety level), and not at all in the case of the Konso. The solidarity of the descent group in Sidamo society seems related to its role in land acquisition: 'In the past, segmentation occurred as a result of population increase and subsequent search for land for grazing and cultivation. A group of agnates would move into vacant territory and in time develop into a new sub-clan' (Hamer 1967*a*: 74). Among the Borana, however, this basis of descent group solidarity is lacking, even though the wells provide a focus for clan and lineage co-operation, while the Konso have been settled on their present land for very much longer than the Sidamo, so that there has been no vacant land to allow expansion and segmentation. The Konso towns, too, have had an important effect on the clan and *gada* system, both of which have had their corporate solidarity almost completely eroded by these large and stable residential groups. (It should be noted, however, that ecologically speaking there is no reason why the Sidamo, too, should not live in towns of equal or greater size than those of the Konso.)

But while the economies and settlement patterns of these three peoples vary enormously, it is quite clear that they have had remarkably little effect on the general principles of East Cushitic society, and we have therefore confirmed that economy is a weak predictor of social organization and culture when we consider a few societies in detail, just as it is at the more general level of the cross-cultural survey in Section 2 of this chapter. Freedom of association and the relative subordination of kinship, voluntary associations, the political and ritual importance of elderhood, the circumcision of elders, the emphasis on generational seniority, the status of the eldest son, the *gada* system, elected officials, Kallu-type priestly mediators, the emphasis on peace, wealth, and bravery, the generally 'democratic' ethos, and ideas of God and the spirits, for example, are quite capable of finding expression in *any* of the simple economies that we have considered. In this connection the reader will find it highly instructive to compare the Sidamo with the Semitic-speaking Gurage (Shack 1966), who are also intensive cultivators of *ensete*: the two societies differ greatly in social organization, values and religion, despite the fact that their ancestors were Sidamo who were conquered by Semitic speakers. It should also be added that of course I am not claiming that the particular *elements* of East Cushitic societies are unique to them (with the exception of the *gada* system). My purpose here has simply been to demonstrate that a distinctive combination of social characteristics may be largely unaffected by type of economy and environment.

The materialist belief that the environment simply causes social adaptation is therefore quite unfounded. Where the technology is simple, there are many different ways of accommodating to the environment, and when societies are small in scale, a wide variety of institutions will all be adequate, because the same institution may serve many different purposes.

V

The Direction of Evolution

1. Introduction

AT this point in the book the reader may protest, 'But surely, if your objections to adaptationism are sound, they also destroy any possibility of explaining those *directional* features of evolution which you emphasized at the beginning of the book? If "anything goes", why should the state, for example, have developed on numerous unrelated occasions?' To answer this objection we must go back to some conclusions established in Chapter II.

The direction of any evolutionary process can, in principle, have only two kinds of origin: in the internal properties of the organism or society, or in external, environmental factors. The selectionist model denies that the direction of evolution could be the result of the internal properties of the organism (orthogenesis), because it assumes that variation is blind; any apparent direction is therefore the result of selection pressures alone. This model may be valid for the particular conditions of biological evolution in which there is typically a clear distinction between organism and environment. In such a case organic variation is not a direct response to environmental conditions; the environment is not itself changed by new variations in the organism; and the appearance of one variant form will not affect the probabilities of other variant forms.

We have seen, however, that this model does not apply to social systems and their evolution, because here there is no clear distinction between the 'organism' and the 'environment'. One of the distinctive characteristics of social systems, therefore, is that *variation itself changes selection pressures*, in such a way that the probability of certain new types of variation ceases to be random or blind and becomes highly directional.

In social systems, moreover, adaptation is far weaker as a selective agency than it is in biological evolution. We observed when discussing the survival of the mediocre in Chapter III that the survival and spread of social traits may have little or no relation to any adaptive advantage: an institution may be widespread because it expresses some basic disposition of human nature, or because there may be only a very limited number of organizational possibilities, or because it is simply easy to produce. So, for example, warfare is universal in primitive society not because it is adaptive, but because there are many different factors producing it.

The selectionist model also has a strong tendency to operate on the basis of single traits, whose adaptive advantages are then compared with those of variant forms. But we observed in Chapter IV that all important social institutions (including artefacts and types of economy) have *many* properties: agriculture, for example, not only permits a larger population per unit area than any other type of economy, but also sedentarism, expansion of settlement size, more elaborate systems of exchange and prestation, the payment of tribute and taxes, and the support of specialists who do not produce food, and it also changes the nature of property relations between people and land. But the more numerous an institution's properties, the more various may be the reasons for its adoption and the more likely it will therefore be to occur. While Cohen (1977) suggests that population pressure was responsible for the shift to agriculture, it is clearly possible that agriculture was adopted for other reasons than this: for example, cultivation of crops facilitates residence in larger and more permanent settlements than would otherwise be possible, and this may be desirable for a variety of reasons (see Maybury-Lewis (1967) on the reasons for Akwe-Shavante villages, for example). Also, the growing of crops permits large-scale systems of exchange, such as those found throughout the Pacific and New Guinea and this, too, is a possible reason for the shift to agriculture in some areas. As Bray concludes, 'It is unlikely . . . that the same combination of factors operated in every case, and most archaeologists today would agree that there can be no universally valid model for the adoption of agriculture' (Bray 1984: 34).

If we take the case of urban settlements, it is also clear that these may occur for an equally wide variety of reasons: for defence or trade, or as centres of religious worship or of government, and so on. Patrilineal descent groups, for example, have also been produced by many different factors, and the same is true of warfare, the state, and all the other institutions of major importance. A condition in which many different starting points may lead to a similar conclusion is known as 'equifinality', and is a very important factor in giving direction to social evolution.

In addition, since institutions only exist in association with other institutions, their *combination* must also lead to important new developments; the technological case we considered was the Chinese invention of gunpowder and cannon, which was the outcome of a variety of unusual Chinese institutions and cultural traditions. In this chapter our example will be the rise of the state, which we shall see is the result of a combination of fairly common institutions in a mutually reinforcing way.

This combinatorial approach to innovation, based on the multiple properties of institutions, is then quite different from that of the selectionists. The selectionist model tends to think of innovation very much in terms of a variation in an existing form (whether that form be an artefact, idea, or institution), and of the selective advantage of one variant form by comparison with another. While there are plenty of examples of such types of innovation—an easy and a difficult spelling of a word, different types of paintbrush, and so on—social innovation cannot be restricted to this type of variation alone, which is essentially atomistic and takes no account of the relations between institutions, by which they facilitate and inhibit one another.

It is also important to note that because institutions have multiple properties, some of these may remain latent[1] and unsuspected by

---

[1] It might be argued that my emphasis on the importance of multiple properties of institutions, many of which can remain latent, is nothing more than Merton's concept of 'latent function'. This is not so. Merton (1957) agrees that not everything in a society must be functional for the society as a whole, and emphasizes the need to be aware of functional alternatives, but his celebrated distinction between 'manifest' and 'latent' functions does nothing to overcome the basic defects of the theory, nor is his notion of latent function the same as the latent properties of institutions. '*Manifest functions* are those objective consequences contributing to the adjustment or adaptation of the system which are intended and recognized by the participants in the system; *latent* functions, correlatively being those which are neither intended nor recognized' (ibid., 51). Manifest functions are thus (1) purposeful, and (2) adaptive, while latent functions are (1) non-purposeful, but (2) nevertheless adaptive. But how are we to define adaptive or functional? Merton admits, 'Embedded in every functional analysis is some conception, tacit or expressed, of the functional requirements of the system under observation . . . this remains one of the cloudiest and empirically most debatable issues in functional theory. As utilized by sociologists, the concept of functional requirement tends to be tautologous or *ex post facto* . . . ' (ibid., 52). But if we have no means of establishing the functional requirements of a society, the distinction between manifest and latent *functions* is at once reduced to the banal distinction between intended and unintended *consequences*. And since he has already conceded that not everything in a society need function for the good of society as a whole, and that some aspects of a society may even be dysfunctional, we cannot even be sure that these consequences, whether intentional or unintentional, will actually be adaptive. (See also Rex

the people concerned. An example is the hierarchical structure of various types of institutions, such as those of kinship, residence, age-grouping, mediation, and warfare. All hierarchies have certain structural properties that allow the relations between large numbers of persons to be co-ordinated, because they drastically reduce the number of interactions in a network that are necessary to disseminate information. (These properties will be discussed in detail below, in Section 4.) While it is unlikely that the people involved will have any conscious understanding of these properties, they nevertheless continue to exist in latent form, and will assume great importance under appropriate conditions; and they are important factors in allowing states to co-ordinate very large numbers of people.

These basic differences between biological and social evolution in the nature of variation and selection mean that while orthogenesis must be excluded from a Darwinian account of biological evolution, it is easy to see how it can be normal in social evolution, without lapsing into teleology, vitalism, or mysticism of any kind.

If we examine any particular institution, therefore, expecially in primitive societies, we may find that it is of little or no adaptive advantage. It survives because it is perceived as 'desirable' in some way, and because there are no effective competitors, but its evolutionary significance may lie in its latent developmental *potential*, rather than in its actual utility at a particular point in time.

We are now approaching an understanding of how social evolution can be directional, yet not be the result of conscious purpose or of selection. Because certain institutions, such as agriculture, large dense settlements, patrilineal descent groups, and privileged access to the supernatural, have multiple properties, there is a high probability that they will occur frequently; secondly, some of these properties will be of high developmental potential, but this potential may only be realized under certain conditions; and thirdly, it is possible for a combination of institutions to bring about the conditions under which this potential is realized.

It is, I suggest, in the multiple properties of institutions (used here in the widest sense to include ideas and inventions) and in their combination that we find the true solution to the problem of blind variation: the blindness does not consist in random trial and error at 1961: 73–4.) It is quite possible however to discern structural *properties* of institutions that are latent, as well as those that are manifest, without involving ourselves in the conundrums of functionalism.

all, since institutions may be originated for some clear purpose and be regarded as quite satisfactory by those concerned, but consists rather in the latent and unrecognized properties of those institutions and in their potential for being *combined* in unsuspected ways with other institutions. One example of such a process, the Chinese development of gunpowder, was discussed in detail, and the state is another excellent example of these principles of social evolution at work, and is of particular importance since it is one of those 'watersheds' of social change noted at the beginning of this book, which has occurred at many different times and places, and is of very great developmental potential.

In the case of the state, for example, relations of authority are latent in a number of very elementary and widespread institutions and forms of organization, all of which may be mutually reinforcing. For example:

1. The allocation of tasks by gender. In all known societies women's work is primarily concerned with domestic tasks and child-rearing. This division of labour has the additional property of placing women at a political disadvantage in relation to men, who are freer to meet together to co-ordinate plans and to spend long periods in each other's company away from home.

2. The structure of descent groups. Where the principles of unilineal descent groups and primogeniture exist, the potential of senior and junior lines within the descent group is created. It seems that there is a more or less universal tendency to ascribe greater prestige, and often considerable authority, to the representative of the senior line of a descent group.

3. Religious authority. In most societies, it is believed that some types of person in particular are best qualified to obtain supernatural benefits for the rest of the group, or the whole society. Seniority of descent and elderhood are the most typical bases of religious authority.

4. Mediation. Religious status can provide authority and some kind of sanctions for a mediator in the absence of secular powers of coercion.

5. Relative age. In some societies, differences of age are in-stitutionalized into actual group hierarchies. Political decision making and religious functions are typically ascribed to elders, and military functions to the younger men. This type of institution is well suited to the development of elective office.

6. Spokesmanship. There is a strong tendency for all groups to favour representation by their most effective champion.

7. War leadership. In all forms of warfare, some men achieve leadership over others. Successful warfare is often regarded as conferring religious as well as practical benefits such as plunder.

8. Managerial functions. In many societies there are complex systems of exchange over which, as in warfare, some men succeed in acquiring control.

9. Redistribution. In many societies, lineage heads or religious functionaries are rewarded by some kind of tribute from their dependants in reciprocation for the benefits which they are believed to confer. Tribute of this kind may then be redistributed differentially, to relieve hardship or reward services.

It is clear that all these institutional features (seniority of descent and or relative age, religious office, spokesmanship, war leadership, mediation, managerial functions, and redistribution) will mutually reinforce one another, especially where unilineal descent groups and religious authority are well developed. The result is what we may call 'institutional pathways' all converging on a single point—the emergence of centralized political authority, with a monopoly of armed force, that will usually be legitimated on the basis of descent and religion, and perform all the other useful functions of redistribution, mediation, spokesmanship, war leadership, and so on.

But, it must be emphasized, this is not a functional explanation of the origin of the state. No appeal whatever is made to any alleged systemic needs of society as a whole, or to arguments that this process is governed by some super-organic controlling principles. Nor, of course, is it claimed that these institutions exist *in order that* subsequent evolution may occur. The argument is based solely on the observable properties of certain widespread institutions, and on the equally observable fact that these properties are mutually compatible and reinforcing.

The reader may reply that, at the least, these institutions are of adaptive value, and that the increase of centralized authority, too, can be explained in terms of its superior adaptive advantages. It certainly seems clear that the formation of the state must be explained in terms of the perceived benefits conferred by earlier forms of authority, since effective means of coercion and exploitation are weak at this point in social evolution. Thus the various institutions I have described are certainly perceived as useful by real people, although as we have seen, there is no point in employing the concept of adaptation to 'explain' this obvious truth. It must also be emphasized, however, that the 'utility' of these institutions has a considerable subjective element. Thus, the warfare may be pointless, the religious beliefs mistaken, the elaborate systems of exchange wasteful of energy, and the lineal descent groups in no way essential for the functioning of society. The fact that institutions are perceived as useful by individual people is therefore a necessary but not sufficient condition of the directional properties of evolution; this can only be explained by the properties of the institutions themselves.

It will also be remarked that I have given a highly abstract analysis of these institutions. In any real society, however, they will exist in the most complicated relationship with one another which the members of the society will not be able fully to understand, even though they will be able to say how they think *particular* institutions are beneficial. Still less, therefore, will they be able to grasp the process, which may extend over many generations, by which their society is evolving from, say, the level of 'tribal' organization (to use Service's classification) to that of the state. Goldman's (1970) analysis of the evolution of Polynesian society, for example, elucidates an enormously complex process that cannot possibly have been understood by the actual participants. In order to explain such a process, therefore, one must resort to the structural properties of each society's institutions and their developmental potential: to be sure, the perception by individual people of the benefits, imagined or otherwise, of their institutions and practices will be an integral part of this evolutionary process, but we gain no analytical advantage by bringing in the notion of adaptation to explain the process as a whole.

The inherent weakness of an adaptationist explanation of state development may be clarified by the reflection that the state has not in fact been the culmination of the history of most societies. This is not because tribes or chiefdoms are more adaptive for these societies, but because of certain structural properties of political authority that act to limit its growth.[2] One is the fact that it is very

[2] I am not of course suggesting that structural features of political authority alone are sufficient to explain the absence of the state. The society may not have an economy that can support the necessary population, it may lack certain essential institutions, the condition of circumscription may be absent (below, in Section 5*a*) and so on.

difficult to extend political authority beyond the boundaries of the community in which it originates—hence the importance of warfare in the establishment of the state. Another is that, while unilineal descent groups are the commonest basis of political authority, the very principles of descent and inheritance may provide legitimation for other rebellious claimants to that authority. A third is that before rulers can acquire a monopoly of force it is extremely easy for subordinate authorities to establish their autonomy, a process which tends to be self-maintaining. It seems to me that to invoke the concept of adaptation to 'explain' both the emergence of the state, and the fact that in most cases it does not emerge, is to propose a theory that is inherently unfalsifiable and hence fundamentally unscientific.

In this chapter we shall therefore be concerned primarily with the emergence of the state, as a central problem in the direction of social evolution, but the development of the state is also closely related to those other aspects of social evolution that were emphasized at the beginning of the book. In the first place, it is directly linked to major increases in societal size; secondly, it involves a radical transformation of society in which many of the ascriptive principles typical of primitive society are gradually submerged by those of a truly functional nature: for the first time the whole of society becomes subordinated to a few simple goals, chiefly the desire of rulers to perpetuate their control over their subjects. Thirdly, this process can also be described as one that involves the increasing simplification and rationalization of social life, and a progressive tendency for modes of government to become increasingly similar: early states have more in common than do chiefdoms or tribes, and industrial states resemble one another more than do early states. Finally, on the basis of these conclusions, we shall be in the position to assess the contribution of modes of production to this evolutionary process.

The analysis of the process of state formation can be greatly clarified if we begin with a concrete example taken from another of those East Cushitic societies which were introduced in Chapter IV. The purpose of this example is to show how some ascriptive institutions typical of primitive society become transformed into truly functional institutions, but the reader should note that in some respects the case of Jimma represents an unusual course of state formation.

2. The emergence of an East Cushitic State

One of the clearest examples of the transition from ascriptive to functional organization is provided by the emergence of the Galla kingdom of Jimma in Ethiopia at the beginning of the nineteenth century. (The following account is taken from H. S. Lewis's excellent book *A Galla Monarchy* (1965).)

The Galla who eventually formed this particular kingdom (one of a number of Eastern Galla monarchies) seem to have shared all those social institutions and values which we have already encountered in our previous examination of East Cushitic society. So, descent groups were not localized, and controlled no property as corporate groups: 'The nuclear or joint family is free to move and settle in communities with members of other descent groups. The local community tends to be a hillside or district with dispersed homesteads rather than a nucleated village, and the people living in the area interact regularly as neighbours' (ibid., 27).

Leadership was not based on descent, but on ability and character, and in formal terms derived from the *gada* system. As among the Borana, sets passed through five grades, each of eight years' duration, in which the distinction between elders and warriors was fundamental (ibid., 27). Again like the Borana, each set elected a few of its number to act as officials: the *abba boku* was 'chairman' and principal mediator; the *abba dula* or *moti* was war leader; *abba sa'a*, perhaps 'chief of public finances'; the *irresa*, some kind of ritual functionary or priest, and *dori* and *raba*, 'assessors' or 'judges' (ibid., 28). 'The *abba boku* ('father of the sceptre') or *hayu* chaired assembly meetings [council meetings, rather than meetings of the whole set] and was the chief speaker and representative of the group. He might also be called upon to tour his territory as an arbitrator' (ibid., 27). But the actual authority of the *abba boku* was very limited, and was essentially confined to a mediatory role at meetings of the *gada* councils, when disputes were settled, and he could not even enforce payment of compensation (ibid., 28).

It seems, however, that another elected official, the *abba dula* or *moti*, the war leader, had very much more substantial secular authority:

Soleillet says that in time of war 'the able-bodied, the warriors, gather together; they elect the *abba dula* . . . , a sort of dictator, who will command the country while hostilities last' . . .

War leadership was the major source of power in Galla society, and this had consequences for the whole social structure. Wherever we find chieftainship or kingship among the Galla, the name of the leader is invariably *abba dula* or *moti*. Furthermore, Massaja, who lived among the Meca for many years, describes an extremely revealing occurrence in Lagamura. In a war between Lagamura and Celia (two Galla groups) a raid was led by three *abba dula*, each with his own following. Celia suffered a complete defeat and its people fled. Normally when the spoils of war were distributed land was returned to the old owners, in return for compensation. In this case, however, the people did not come back for a while, so the three *abba dula* decided to divide the land among themselves. When the original owners returned to the land they found that they were now tenants and subjects of the three chiefs. Some of the war leaders' own followers resettled on these newly conquered lands. The Lagamara chief with the largest following was declared the first *abba dula* of Celia. (Ibid., 29–30)

Similar developments are noted by other contemporary European sources. The great importance of warfare as the source of land in these historical circumstances thus clearly allowed certain hierarchical elements of Galla culture to overwhelm the essentially egalitarian nature of the *gada* system. In this system, as Lewis sums it up:

In most Galla areas for which we have information—Harar, Shoa, Wellega and elsewhere—we find this ideal pattern, which might be called 'republican'. Political membership and leadership was based largely on common residence and on achievement ('universalistic criteria'); officers were elected; they served strictly limited terms and could not succeed themselves; and they held functionally specific positions with closely defined tasks. There was also an insistence on thrashing out problems in open council meetings. (Ibid., 29)

But other aspects of the culture permitted a different line of development in the circumstances of land conquest:

In spite of the Galla ideals of rotation of offices and authority, there is definite evidence that Galla political life had other facets not encompassed by the *gada* system. Galla culture produced important men of wealth and power, many of whom could be independent of the *gada* system. These men arose primarily through success in warfare and through control over trade. (Ibid., 29)

We noted in the previous chapter that respect for wealth and bravery is a highly developed aspect of the East Cushitic value system, together with economic individualism in general, and among the Western Galla, too, land '. . . could be bought and sold freely. In return for animals, cash, slaves, or any other medium of exchange, anyone, even a stranger, might buy land' (ibid., 30).

Warfare and trade, in conditions of freely alienable land, thus allowed the rise of powerful landed families, who could operate on their own behalf largely independently of the *gada* system. The absence of corporate kin groups also allowed great mobility:

> It is clear that landless people, artisans, immigrants, conquered peoples, and relatives settled on the lands of *abba lafa* [landowners] and increased their wealth and importance. The more a man increased his landholdings, the more tenants and followers he attracted.
>
> Massaja also shows us this kind of development in recounting the rise to power (in the 1850s) of Gama-Moras, who became king of the Gudru. Gama-Moras, a man whose wealth was derived from trade, drew to himself not only kin and tenants, but a small army of riflemen as well. Indeed, Salviac also tells us that 'the landlords raise from among their clients little troops of volunteers to join the forces of the tribe or to march, under private command, to the defense of the estate and of wronged friends'. (Ibid., 31)

For a time *gada* authority and that of the war leaders who had become landowners coexisted, but in the end monarchical rule triumphed in numerous areas, and the *gada* system was finally eclipsed. We shall see, however, that the kingship which emerged was also characteristic of East Cushitic society, in that, having its origins in war (and trade, to a lesser extent), it was entirely secular in nature, with none of the sacred attributes so prominent in the neighbouring West Cushitic monarchies of Kafa, Hadya, and Janjero.[3]

The Kingdom of Jimma finally emerged by the processes already described from the amalgamation of perhaps nine original groups of which one, the Diggo, ultimately became supreme by military conquest of the others in 1830 under Abba Jifar I. At its largest extent (1875), the kingdom covered about 5,000 square miles. An estimate of its population in 1861 was 150,000, and in 1936 300,000 (ibid., 48). It is interesting to note that while the original and conquered inhabitants of what became Jimma territory were probably Kafa, ' . . . there are, in Jimma, no major group

---

[3] It seems likely that Jimma and a number of other Galla states developed in this area because further expansion was prevented by the powerful monarchies of Shoa and the West Cushitic states. A similar process of circumscription occurred in the case of the Zulu because of the lack of vacant land for expansion, and is also reported by Carneiro (1970*b*) for the Inca. Lewis plausibly argues that the mere diffusion of the idea of kingship from these West Cushitic and Shoan states was not enough for the development of the Jimma monarchy, especially since Jimma kingship was significantly different from these.

distinctions on the basis of ethnic origin. This seems to be generally true in all Galla areas, and may be one aspect of the 'universalistic' nature of Galla society and culture' (ibid., 38).

Very early in Abba Jifar's reign he became a Muslim and an energetic proselytizer for his new faith: this development may well have been related to that lack of any sacred basis for monarchy in traditional Galla culture which we have previously noted. 'Islam was probably useful to the early kings, allowing them to break more fully with the traditions of the past and from the rituals and associations of the *gada* system' (ibid., 131). By changing the ground rules of sacred and secular authority, the new king could remove his principal disadvantage under the *gada* system in which he was wholly secular, and at least become Defender of the Islamic faith under the new system. By 1882 most of the people had been converted to Islam (ibid., 42).

An orderly succession to the throne in the male line became established, and although Abba Jifar II recognized the suzerainty of the Ethiopian Emperor Menelink II in 1882, he managed to retain internal control over his kingdom until his death in 1932; hence the existence of living informants who could still remember how royal administration had worked by the time of Professor Lewis's fieldwork (1958–60).

When we examine the institutions of the state of Jimma it is at once obvious that they were 'functional' in a precise and meaningful sense: they were all 'for' something, and that something was the maintenance of political power by the king. It can be said that central authority everywhere is confronted by certain problems to which there are various possible solutions, some more efficient than others. These centre on how the king is to be chosen, how his subordinates are to be chosen, how they are to be paid or otherwise rewarded and maintained, and in general how the state is to be protected from rebellion and anarchy.

The recruitment of officials from descent groups with the traditional right to hold certain posts has always proved inefficient—the system is inflexible and limits the availability of the most able men. The granting of land as a means of payment for official service has also led to problems in many cases since, particularly in conditions of poor communications, there is a marked tendency for such feudal officials to make themselves into hereditary rulers of their own fiefs, and whenever possible to throw off any allegiance to the monarch. Solutions to this problem include the dispersal of fiefs, the requirement that fief holders come regularly to court or provide hostages to the king, or the constant movement of the king through his domain. Better still is the payment of such officials from taxation raised by other officials, and frequent postings from place to place. The separation of fiscal, administrative, and military functions is also a valuable technique in preventing the problem of the overmighty subject.

In terms of these functional criteria, we shall see that the administration of Jimma, at least by the time of Abba Jifar II, had become highly efficient. Many aspects of this efficiency, however, derive from the distinctive features of the earlier society, whose developmental potential became manifest under new conditions:

1. The king was not the theoretical owner of all Jimma land, but simply the largest landowner of the *abba lafa* class. While he owned all barren and unclaimed lands, and could allocate these at will to followers and officials, grants of land were not the basis of any system of fiefs given to royal officials and their descendants: 'Because the Galla have a pattern of individual land ownership which allows for the accumulation of estates by an *abba lafa*, it was easily conceivable to them that the king was simply the greatest *abba lafa* in the land' (ibid., 75).

2. 'The king was not politically bound to the members of his own family and descent group' (ibid., 76). Here again, the relative unimportance of kinship in Galla society meant that the king was not obliged to give special privileges or consideration to any relatives merely because they were relatives. Brothers were usually given provinces to rule, but disloyalty meant exile to another kingdom, and in general the king was free to use, or not to use, the services of his relatives at his own discretion:

The appointment of relatives of the king to high office was by no means automatic. Sons and brothers of the king could be by-passed, exiled, or removed from office. For example, Abba Jifar took away provinces from one of his sons and one of his grandsons when they were found to be guilty of corruption deemed excessive by Jimma standards. Brothers and sons of the kings were likely to be appointed as provincial governors, rather than as ministers. (Ibid., 81)

Nor did any clans have hereditary rights to specific offices.

3. All appointments to ministerial office were entirely in the hands of the king, and none was, in principle at least, hereditary:

The governing of Jimma Abba Jifar was accomplished through appointed officials—not through hereditary chiefs or representatives of tribal or descent groups. Below the king were hundreds of officials in a great many categories: governors, market judges, border guards, tax collectors, couriers, military officers, overseers of artisan labour, jailers, palace officials, and many others . . . The king held all rights to appoint, transfer, promote and demote officials, and he could devise new positions or mark off new districts. (Ibid., 80–1)

Officials were mainly recruited from the members of the king's family, from wealthy landowners who would not therefore need to extort money from the peasants, and from those who had no family influence at all: slaves of the necessary ability and foreign mercenaries. In this category might also be included the affinal relatives of the king who were often used in government since, as outsiders, they were dependent on him alone:

Immigrant Muslim merchants, or their descendants, were often given important positions, especially those relating to trade or to Islam and its practice. The *k'adis* were often of immigrant origin, as were the men who held the post of *nagadras* (chief of trade and markets). (The *nagadras* was generally also made a governor of a province.)

Abba Jifar made great use of slaves. In addition to the many official functions they performed in the palace, slaves served as jailers, stewards of the king's lands, market judges, and provincial governors . . .

Some men caught the eye of the king through valor in war; others, especially slaves and traders, won recognition because of their loyalty, special skills, or usefulness. Many regional governors, however, gained their positions through their wealth and their ability to get close to the king. In order to compete with other wealthy men, the *soresa* [men of wealth and importance] of the kingdom would bring the king presents and try to spend time at court. (Ibid., 85–6)

4. A clear distinction was drawn between government remuneration and private wealth, and the one form of remuneration that was not allowed was that obtained by direct taxation of the people. (Lewis does say, however, that for high officials, especially governors, 'there were opportunities to take bribes, get some free labor, and collect occasional fees or tribute' (ibid., 87).)

Government officers in Jimma were rewarded in a number of ways depending upon their origins, needs, and functions. Palace officials were supported directly from the king's storehouses and table. Foreign mercenaries, the chiefs of the tollgates, and perhaps some other officials, were paid salaries . . .

Ideally, the king did not give regular payment to wealthy men who served him. In the minds of the people of Jimma, the governors and highest ministers were men of wealth who served for honor, power, and the chance of advancement, and to whom the king gave presents and land only 'from love'. The land which governors and officials owned was not government land, even if granted by the king, but private, inheritable property . . . When the king wished to appoint a poor man or a slave to a high post outside of the palace he would give that man a grant of private land, and thus create a new notable. By creating and using notables the king made an essential separation between private and governmental resources A man's private land allowed him the wealth and leisure to carry out his functions as a state official. (Ibid., 86–7)

5. The king's council, comprising the *abba gurmu* ('assistant' or prime minister), the *abba dula*, war minister, and a few confidants, aided the king by carrying the burden of a great deal of administrative work, but was advisory only, and had no right to control or supervise the king.

6. There were a large number of provinces—sixty, in fact. These were arbitrary divisions made by the king which did not correspond with any older *senyi* (descent group) areas, or with the estates of nobles. Being so many it was therefore difficult to co-ordinate rebellion, and being relatively small, any rebellion would have been localized. 'Governors were not representatives of the people who lived in their provinces They did not necessarily have their homes and lands in their districts, although they might. They were appointees of the king, and served where the king wanted them to' (ibid., 89).

7. Governors were responsible for organizing corvée labour for work on the king's lands, and on the good roads which were a notable feature of the kingdom (ibid., 92). But they had no control over military units or over taxation, although they had to assist in these matters; military and fiscal administration were the responsibility of other officials:

The kings of Jimma insisted upon the separation of their administrators from armed forces and from tax revenues. By maintaining a central standing army, by going directly to the lowest freeman for recruitment in case of all-out war, the king circumvented the military potentialities of his landowning subjects and his regional governors. Similarly, the king insisted upon collecting taxes through his own specific officers, rather than permitting provincial administrators to collect them themselves or to levy additional major taxes for their own support. Furthermore, by forbidding governors either to pursue bands of outlaws or to take the life of any of their subjects, the king increased the governors' dependence upon him, and correspondingly decreased the subjects' dependence on their governors. (Ibid., 117)

8. As well as receiving tax revenue (which supported the standing army of mercenaries), the administration, and the rewards to faithful followers, the king also controlled trade. 'The kings were the patrons and overseers of the craft specialists, the foreign traders, and the markets' (ibid., 94). All markets were under the jurisdiction of royal officials, and all foreign merchants required the king's permission to trade. Each class of artisans—smiths, potters, and weavers—was, through its appointed chief, directly subordinate to the king, and the chief's duty was to ensure that each craftsman contributed either his time or his products to the king (ibid., 97).

9. A census was taken for tax purposes each year, and records kept by means of knotted cords.

10. The king maintained a standing army of 1,500 mercenaries from other areas, plus two groups of 400 men each, serving for one week in rotation. One group was recruited locally, the other from the provinces. In peacetime these two groups had various non-military functions, such as tax collecting, acting as royal messengers, and general corvée work, while the mercenaries were permanently stationed at the royal palace as guards, unless in pursuit of bandits. They also acted as executioners and as a general police force.

11. Large defensive works, especially deep ditches and elaborate gates, were maintained on the borders of the kingdom by corvée labour, the border itself being an unpopulated no-man's land:

> In order to defend the border of the kingdom, Abba Jifar and his predecessors awarded land to men who would serve as border guards. Trusted and resourceful warriors were given positions as governors of the provinces along the boundaries, and the soldiers under their command were rewarded with grants of land from the king. These frontier troops, called *k'oyye*, were to fight off surprise attacks and to spread the alarm through the kingdom. Along these borders were *gono* drums which were beaten to relay the warning to the palace and to neighbouring regions. (Each drum had someone assigned to man it.) (Ibid., 108)

Lewis also notes, significantly, that

> Of course, the frontier defense functioned to keep people in as well as out. Soleillet describes leaving Jimma at the K'ank'ati *kela* (gate) as follows:

'The guards arrived and after having taken the names of the people who wanted to leave they made us jump over the first enclosure. A second line of defense is formed by three rows of spiny stakes in the middle of which is built a guardhouse; we came, finally, to a gate and a ditch which we passed over on a drawbridge.' (Ibid., 108–9)

12. There was a hierarchy of courts, at the apex of which was the king, and only he was legally able to order capital punishment. The lowest level was that of the elders of the community, above which was the district court and the provincial court. There were also religious judges (*k'adi*) and market courts. Capital punishment was rare, and in cases of homicide the family of the victim was usually persuaded to accept compensation. Enslavement and confiscation of property were, however, common punishments.

The *gada* system was incompatible with the monarchical system in the following respects:

Even before the foundation of the kingdom its political functions had been weakened by the growth of strong leaders but that so few traces survived to the 1960s indicates that the element of *gada* were under attack from several directions.

Gada had at least three important functions: (1) it was the basis for an assembly for arbitration, a tribunal; (2) it was the basis for recruitment of leaders and the appointment of political tasks; (3) it provided a system of age status, of ritual, and of life-crisis rites. It was evidently a long time before *gada* was totally replaced as an assembly of elders, since such meetings continued throughout the nineteenth century, although with restricted jurisdiction and disassociated from the rest of the *gada* system. Those who attended were elders representing families and kingroups rather than all the members of a particular age grade and set, and the system of cutomary law they represented was decreasing in influence due to the development of both Islamic and executive legal systems. The other political connotations of *gada*, and its leadership patterns, were more directly attacked by the powerful organization of the monarchy with its monopoly of force and its economic power. Landlords, war leaders, kings, governors, and market administrators all undercut these aspects of *gada*.[4]

The other blow to the *gada* system was the adoption of Islam, which meant not only a new god and new spirits but also new festivals, new religious practices, and a new system of rites of passage. Circumcision now had to be done early in life rather than after the fourth grade, as it had been in *gada*. Cattle could no longer be speared for ritual purposes (which had been basic

---

[4] It is interesting to note, however, that the pilgrimage to the Abba Muda, the sacred leader of the Galla people, was still continuing from Jimma as late as 1928 (Huntingford 1969: 85).

to *gada* ceremonies) but had to have their throats cut and the proper Muslim prayers said. Islam, as the faith of the king and the great men of the kingdom, had high prestige and it soon spread to the whole population. With this replacement of its several functions through new institutions, it is understandable that *gada* has not survived. (Ibid., 130–1)

The rise of the Jimma kingdom is a classic example of the working of those evolutionary principles described in this book. A typical East Cushitic society, with distinctive attitudes[5] to kinship, seniority, peace, individual land tenure, the distinction between sacred and secular authority, and individual achievement, is placed in a situation in which true warfare for conquest, as opposed to raiding, develops (as it could not, for example, among the Konso). The specific features of the *gada* system and attitudes to individual achievement allow a type of war leadership to arise, based on a position of authority within the *gada* system, which eventually consolidates itself on a permanent basis of monarchy. The earlier society was therefore 'pre-adapted' in a variety of ways to produce the state when the appropriate circumstances arose, not least in the various elective offices of a highly specific nature that were part of the *gada* system.

We thus find certain universal features of social evolution—the importance of warfare and trade, and the necessity for a basis of authority, in this case the *abba dula*—around which monarchy can develop. The centralized political organization is also marked by far higher division of labour, especially in government, greater individualism and substitutability of personnel, and by much greater functional efficiency in general. The whole process was very rapid—two or three generations at most—and involved a simultaneous change in a wide variety of variables.

An existing structure thus accommodated itself to certain features in its environment, but assimilated them to its own distinctive structural features, and advanced to a new evolutionary level in the process. Certain basic features of East Cushitic society were able to survive unchanged, while others, in particular the *gada* system, were dissolved.

[5] But it must also be emphasized that the relative unimportance of kinship and the radical distinction between sacred and secular authority, which are important features of East Cushitic society, normally work *against* the emergence of the state, which, as we shall see, typically depends on strong corporate descent groups and the ability of those endowed with sacred authority to assume responsibility of a political nature, including the conduct of warfare.

3. The roots of authority

(a) Benefits and dependency

As Service (1975: xii–xiii, 71–2) has emphasized, one of the central problems of social evolution is to explain how an initial condition of equality develops into unequal ranking in terms of status, and ultimately of social class, and, in particular, how informal leadership of the kind typical of band societies develops into formal political office. For it is not pseudo-historical speculation to claim that since in hunter-gatherer societies leaders can influence other men only by example, based on respect for their age and experience (and in some cases their genealogical status), and since all societies were once based on hunting and gathering, therefore the first condition of man was that of equality. Nor could the development of political authority have been based on coercion: one man cannot dominate his fellows by mere violence, since they can either hit him back or run away and live elsewhere. R. Cohen (1978) rightly supports Service (1975) against Fried (1967) in maintaining that it is *not* the case

. . . that early states originate from the efforts of powerful groups in society using coercive force, or its threat, to protect their proprietary and unequal rights over resources. Once it comes into existence, as an evolved form of socio-political organization, the early state is clearly stratified, and a ruling class does, ubiquitously, have unequal access to coercive power and wealth. It would seem, therefore, that Marxist theory describes the results rather than the causes of state formation. (Cohen 1978: 51; and see also Claessen and Skalnik 1978c: 646)[6]

The origin of political authority must therefore be explained not by coercion but in terms of its perceived advantages for the ordinary person, and by the properties of certain institutions. The propensity to obey authority is not only the product of institutional forms, but

[6] It has also been maintained that the early state was the product of class stratification based on military rather than economic inequality. According to Oppenheimer, 'The State may be defined as an organization of *one class* dominating over the other classes. Such a class organization can come about in one way only, namely, through conquest and the subjugation of ethnic groups by the dominating group. This can be demonstrated with almost mathematical certainty' (Oppenheimer 1923: iv). Oppenheimer supposed that the first states were produced by the armed force of pastoralists, who employed slaves captured in war as herdsmen, and later subjugated agricultural societies. (In the New World, without pastoralism, hunters are supposed to have subjugated agriculturalists.) It is worth noting that the ethnographic data which Oppenheimer used to support his theory were of remarkably low quality, and quite unacceptable from a scholarly point of view even at the time he was writing.

motivated by dependency, of which the basic types would seem to be the following:

1. With the domestication of crops and animals, and the consequent increase in size and permanence of population noted in Chapter IV, descent groups can assume major importance in the control of these resources, and of the land which supports them. The individual thus receives essential support from his descent group, and this in turn will mean that the development of authority within the descent group must have great potential significance for the individual members.

2. It appears to be a more or less universally accepted principle that not all persons are considered equally qualified to obtain supernatural benefits on behalf of the group or the society as a whole. To this extent, the many will regard themselves as inherently dependent on the few for such benefits.

3. In all societies disputes are inevitable. While it is in no way inevitable that mediation and dispute settlement are bound to develop as a response, it is clear that where these do exist those who exercise mediatory functions are (*a*) necessarily in a minority, and (*b*) are perceived to confer a benefit on those who need them.

4. Almost all societies engage in warfare, and some men are more adept in planning and leading war parties than others. Here again, a minority is legitimately perceived as conferring benefits on the majority by leading them to victory.

5. For reasons that will be discussed shortly, tribute is frequently paid to heads of descent groups, ritual authorities, and other such persons, who are typically under an obligation to redistribute their wealth. This may take the form of a type of social insurance whereby the misfortune of some can be relieved.

6. Many societies have important ceremonial occasions which benefit from co-ordination by a leader: I am thinking in particular of New Guinea, where Big Men play an essential role as organizers of feasts and large-scale exchanges of pork.

7. Almost all groups, or whole societies, will have matters of importance to negotiate with other groups or societies, and the man who acts as spokesman will be perceived as conferring an important benefit on the rest of the group.

8. Especially where individuals are displaced from their natal groups and have to migrate elsewhere, it will be to their advantage if they can place themselves as clients under the protection of a person of influence in their host group who can defend them, and it will also

be to their patron's advantage to be able to recruit strangers as his dependants.

While, therefore, ethnographic literature is full of examples of the difficulties of leaders in being obeyed, it is clear that there are also many occasions of dependency which tend to make authority more acceptable (see, for example, Southall 1956). It will be noted that our discussion of dependency is entirely at the level of the conscious, short-range motivation of individuals, and makes no appeal to any adaptationist or functionalist presuppositions. We also recall here our discussion of the significance of the individual as the efficient cause of structural elaborations, from Chapter I.

Motivation is one thing, however, and the properties of institutions are another. We shall now examine certain structural properties of ascriptive institutions which, despite their very elementary nature, are fundamental to evolution.

(b) Lineality and seniority of birth

Lineality, usually patrilineality, is an extremely common mode of reckoning descent.[7] While cognatic descent groups can control resources if they have a common residence (e.g. in Polynesia, see Goldman 1970), a lineal basis of reckoning descent is particularly appropriate for this, while the division of society on the basis of descent also makes ritual and political specialization of function much easier as well. While we now have no means of knowing how or why lineal descent actually arose, it seems likely that many factors contributed—residence, the co-operation between men, the control of property, theories of biological inheritance, religious beliefs about ancestors, and so on. Just as there have been many roads to statehood, no doubt there were also many to unilineal descent. This is not enough by itself, however, to form a basis for authority. The principle of birth order (which is independent of lineality, and can be found in cognatic societies) provides such a basis, and the belief that the eldest child, especially the eldest son, has a unique status is extremely common. Again, there are doubtless many factors both social and psychological that are responsible for this, e.g. the first-born child changes the status of a man and woman into that of parents, it typically receives more

---

[7] Radcliffe-Brown (e.g. 1952: 48) and his followers have regarded unilineal descent groups as a virtual necessity for social solidarity. Needless to say, this is quite unfounded, and they are absent or weakly developed in many perfectly viable societies.

attention than subsequent children, and is in a position to dominate its junior siblings from early childhood onwards. Whatever the reasons for this institution, it certainly did not appear because it was for the good of society; but in combination with lineality it produces the possibility of senior and junior lines within the descent group and on this basis has provided an extremely common source of authority. The senior line, which is that descended through eldest sons from the founder of the group, often exercises authority over the descent group as a whole. This seems invariably to be at least of a ritual nature, whether or not there is a cult of ancestor worship, and often includes mediation in the disputes of members, and acting as their spokesman or representative. In some cases the descent group head may have considerable authority over the lives of his dependants.

Over successive generations lines of descent necessarily acquire greater genealogical distance from one another. This frequently leads to segmentary structuring of the descent group, so that it acquires an internal hierarchy. In some cases, this may be the basis of fission, whereby the leaders of sub-groups establish their autonomy from the original descent group, but in other cases the segmentary extension of descent group membership, aided by legal fiction, allows quite large populations to represent themselves as all descended from some mythical ancestor, so that the whole society may be based on the model of a segmentary descent group (or a small number of these).

Tribute is often given to the head of the descent group by its members in recognition of the religious and social services which he performs for them, and in this way, and because of his control of the assets of the group in some cases, the basis of a system of redistribution is laid.

At any one time, the members of a descent group are necessarily related to one another according to their generational seniority, as distinct from their relative seniority by birth, and generational seniority necessarily involves seniority in terms of age. Some societies may therefore exercise the option of conducting descent group affairs by the generation of elders. Royal succession in the Shang dynasty of China, for example, seems to have been on the basis of generational rather than lineal seniority within the royal clan (see below, Chapter VI, Section 2a).

The actual working out of these structural principles in real societies is, of course, much more variable and flexible than may be implied by the highly abstract account which has been given here. In the Konso lineage, for example, the ritual and moral authority of the *poĝalla* is simply inherited through eldest sons, and among the Bantu and Hottentots of southern Africa the kinship system 'stresses the importance of seniority in terms of descent, and the hereditary head of every group has recognized authority over all its other members. It is upon this basic pattern that the system of centralized government has been developed' (Schapera 1956: 123). But where the descent group is very large the succession to authority may be qualified by other criteria, such as age and ability. So Fortes describes the basis of authority in the lineage of the Tale of West Africa:

> Every lineage is subject to the authority of its senior male member (*kpeem*). In a lineage of narrow span, i.e. with common ancestry four or less generations back, he is the most senior by generation; in lineages of wider span, age is the criterion, since generation seniority is no longer determinable. Throughout the social structure seniority confers authority.
>
> The authority wielded by a lineage *kpeem* varies with its span. In the lineage round which a joint family is built up, the head has complete moral and ritual authority; he has the right to dispose of his dependants' labour, property, and persons, and he can use force or ritual measures to assert his authority. In a lineage of greater span, the head has only moral and ritual authority over his co-members other than his own dependants. The greater the lineage span, the older is the *kpeem*, the more prestige, respect, and honour attaches to his status, though it confers purely moral and ritual authority. (Fortes 1940: 251–2)

In Polynesia the principle of seniority by descent certainly provides the essential structural principle:

> Polynesian social structures are literally built upon the principle of seniority. Kin groups are traditionally organized around the relative seniority of descent lines. At the most elementary level of organization, the household, a distinction is drawn between the status and authority of senior and junior members. (Goldman 1970: 15)

But while *mana* is primarily obtained through descent it can also be achieved, especially by success in war or craftsmanship, and the concept of descent is broader than seniority alone: 'Polynesia takes account of primogeniture, of senior descent lines, of sex line, of genealogical depth, and, in the overall, of genealogical distinction (that is, the history of the line). Each individual criterion of genealogical distinction establishes sharp divisions, but the combination of these four factors reopens ambiguity' (ibid., 9).

Despite these qualifications, however, it is clear that the principles of lineality and birth order are among the most important foundations of political authority from which the state develops. The basic importance of descent for chiefly authority is attested by ethnography from all over the world (e.g. Mair 1962; Schapera 1956; Fortes and Evans-Pritchard 1940; Goldman 1970, etc.), and clearly persisted into early states. In confirmation of this Claessen found from a survey of twenty-one early[8] states that in every case, except two for which no data were available, plus the exceptions of Jimma and Ankole, the sovereign's status was justified by his genealogy (Claessen 1978: 558), and 'In eighteen cases it was found that the heads of at least a number of clans (or lineages, or comparable groups) were classified with the aristocracy. In most cases these clan dignitaries were connected to the ruler's family by matrimonial ties, or even descended from junior branches of these' (ibid., 568). Jimma was the only exception, and for two cases data were insufficient.

(c) Age

While members of all descent groups are necessarily stratified on the basis of generational level, and hence of age, formal systems of age-grouping are relatively uncommon but, where they exist, possess a number of important structural properties.

The age principle is, as such, quite independent of descent and of residence, and in fact it seems that age-grouping systems always incorporate members of different descent groups and would, of course, be virtually redundant if they did not. As Eisenstadt (1956) has emphasized, systems of age-grouping are thus 'universalistic' in character, in so far as descent is irrelevant to membership, and they are also inherently egalitarian. For these reasons they are well suited to the development of achieved, elected office.

Formal systems of age-grouping (including *gada* systems) permit a clear differentiation between a number of social functions: the political and the military, the judicial and the executive, and the sacred and the secular, so that in each case the political, the judicial, and the sacred are associated with the elders, while the military, the executive, and the secular are associated with the younger men.

Formal age-grouping systems are much less common than lineal descent groups, but they have certain properties that may facilitate the development of centralized government. As noted, they cut

[8] 'Early' is used here in a typological, not a chronological sense.

across descent-group membership and help prevent the fragmentation of society along lines of kinship. Where some degree of political authority already exists, this property of age-grouping may therefore reinforce that authority. Such systems also lend themselves to the development of elective office in ways that were well illustrated in the rise of the state of Jimma. The category of elderhood, which is given corporate existence by age-grouping systems, is inherently opposed, in the functions of blessing and mediation, to the brute force of the warriors, who are subordinated to the wisdom and religious authority of their seniors. This distinction between authority and force is an essential political principle on which all early states rely, and which is well taught by age-grouping systems.

Writing of the Bantu chiefdoms of southern Africa, Schapera says:

The trend towards centralization is reinforced by other factors, notably the widespread grouping of the people into age-sets whose creation is regulated by the chief. The initiation ceremonies undergone simultaneously by the members of each set, their organization into a single named body always headed by a member of the royal family, the mutual obligations imposed upon them and distinguishing their age-mates from all other adults, and the many activities that they are called upon to carry out collectively, give them a strong feeling of solidarity cutting across parochial attachments to kin or local group. The age organization serves therefore as an effective means of binding people together, and except for the chieftainship and the hierarchy of regional authorities it is perhaps the most conspicuous factor in the promotion of tribal unity. (Schapera 1956: 123)

(d) Religious authority

Members of all pre-industrial societies perceive themselves as dependent on supernatural forces in their quest for health, fertility, and prosperity— for life, in fact—and we have already noted the universal belief that not all persons are equally qualified to perform religious acts on behalf of the group or for society as a whole.

1. Religious capacities are very widely believed to be inherited, and there is a common belief that eldest sons inherit more of these capacities than their junior siblings.

2. It also seems to be a very generally accepted principle that religious capacity is more closely associated with older persons than with younger ones.

3. When an ancestor cult exists, it seems that the representative of the senior line normally has special or even unique religious access to the ancestors.

4. The inheritable nature of religious capacities means that whole descent groups may have special religious status, in the sense that they are all priests, or are the group from whom alone priests must be selected. In these respects religious functions fit very well with the basic features of descent and age systems.

5. Religion is also well suited to be the basis of secular authority because it is possible for people in societies with very low levels of political co-ordination to have clear ideas of a total moral and religious order that transcends the little communities of daily life. This sacred order may be in the keeping of supernatural beings who punish wrongdoers and reward the good, and these beings can be approached by men through ritual. Where crime is also sin that threatens the whole community, a powerful sanction for the enforcement of law is placed in the hands of priests, elders, and mediators.

6. Sacred office, because of the benefits which it is believed to confer, and because it may be seen as the basis of a wider moral and religious community, can easily transcend the limitations of local groups based on residence and descent, and become the focus of a much wider loyalty, e.g. the Kallu of the Galla peoples. Among the Bantu, the chief acts as priest for the tribe as a whole. 'This he does not so much *ex officio* as because he personally is the senior living descendant of the tribal gods, and therefore the proper person to intercede with them' (Schapera 1956: 125).

Because of these benefits, religious leaders often receive tribute, which they can redistribute to those in need. They also, in their capacity of representing the whole society as spokesmen in relation to the gods, easily acquire subordinate officials to whom religious, economic, and judicial functions can be delegated, and are also often closely associated with victory in war so that one of their chief functions is to ensure success in battle by their blessings and sacrifice. As Hocart said,

In this quest of life all the actors do not play the same part; they must, in virtue of the very structure of ritual, have different roles assigned to them. There is a president, for instance, there is a master of ceremonies, and others we shall learn to know. This ritual organization is vastly older than government, for it exists where there is no government and where none is needed. When however society increases so much in complexity that a coordinating agency, a kind of nervous system, is required, that ritual organization will gradually take over this task. (Hocart 1970: 34–5)

There is a clear continuity in this religious component of political authority from the chiefdom to the state: 'In most, if not all, ethnographically known chiefdoms or ranked societies, the leaders play a central role in the religious system and exercise some form of control over religion or supernatural symbols (e.g. Service 1971: 162; Fried 1967: 137; Sahlins 1958, 1968; Mair 1962)' (Haas 1982: 180). And religious authority is a more or less essential basis for its legitimacy and acceptance by the people at the level of state organization (cf. R. Cohen 1978: 62–3; Claessen and Skalnik 1978c: 646). In his study of twenty-one early states, Claessen found that eighteen rulers had sacred status, in two cases the data were inconclusive, and in only one, Jimma, was the king clearly regarded as lacking any sacred status. In fourteen cases the ruler acted as spokesman for his people in relation to the supernatural, in six cases data were inconclusive and only in the case of Jimma did the ruler have no such role although he was 'defender of the faith'. In every case except three, on which no data were available, the ruler had ritual duties, and in five cases was the high priest as well (Claessen 1978: 555–9).

Though leaders in many societies can combine sacred and secular authority, there seems no doubt that many societies also perceive these functions as somewhat incompatible. In particular, we often find, as Needham (1980: 63–105) has discussed in detail, that the sacred is associated with physical weakness—with elders, for example, with women, with the left hand, with abstention from warfare, and even with outcast groups (e.g. the Fuga craftsmen of the Gurage, Shack 1966). Where a clear division between the sacred and the secular exists before the emergence of the state, it may therefore be difficult for the holder of a sacred office to assume political authority involving the use of force as well.

(e) Military organization

1. In the nature of things, warriors tend to be recruited from the younger members of society (except for a few experienced leaders) and, of course, from men and not women. Military activities will therefore be closely correlated with age organization (whether or not this is formalized into an age-grouping system).

2. Even when warfare is not employed for conquest, it often possesses religious significance, being regarded as a life-giving practice conferring wealth, abundance, and vitality on the victorious group.

3. There is frequently a ritual complementarity between the warriors and those, such as the elders or priests, who bless them and ensure their success by ritual means. Or, where hereditary chiefs exist, they will often be expected to preside over the military activities of their subordinates as part of their religious duties, even if they do not personally lead their warriors in battle.

4. Above the simplest level of small-scale raiding, warfare is an activity which obviously benefits from planning, co-ordination, and leadership, and some men are outstanding in this respect. Hierarchical organization and effective discipline, where they can be achieved, produce even more effective military organization.

5. Successful warfare may yield plunder (including land), and this may give important redistributive powers to war leaders.

Mere violence, however, cannot lead to permanent institutions of political authority, and to my knowledge there is no instance of military activity *by itself* ever having led to the emergence of even chiefly authority. While men may give temporary allegiance to someone who can lead them on successful raids, this is not a sufficient basis for political authority since it is dependent solely on the ephemeral personal qualities of the leader. It seems clear from the ethnographic evidence that war leadership within the political community will only lead to the strengthening of social control and of centralized authority, in particular, if there already exist some institutions which can act as a nucleus of permanent authority. The prime examples of such institutions are, of course, descent groups, age-groups, and the religious offices associated with them. According to Schapera, 'chieftainship seems to have been a traditional feature among all our peoples, whether or not they expanded by subjugating other groups. The main effect of conquest usually was to enhance the chief's power, not to create it . . . (Schapera 1956: 134). Fried's conclusions on the relation between the emergence of the state and warfare generally coincide with those of Schapera (1956) and Service (1975). In particular, he holds that 'Warfare serves to institutionalize rank differences only when these are already manifest, or at least implicit, in the society in question' (Fried 1961: 134); and 'There is no evidence that warfare makes chieftains of individuals of exclusively military renown; instead, warfare brings new kin-units to the fore and may establish the legitimate and pre-existing head of such a kin-group as the new chief or paramount chief' (ibid., 144).[9]

But once some basis of political authority is established, it seems quite clear that while 'State formation is *not* caused by war [it] is greatly *promoted* by war, or by the threat of war and by social stress . . . ' (Claessen and Skalnik 1978b: 626). Warfare is certainly the basic means by which the political authority of one group can be extended to other groups which have no other reason for accepting it. So while chiefly authority seems to rest primarily on genealogical and religious foundations, the emergence of the state itself seems highly dependent on political conquest. Claessen's survey of twenty-one early states shows clearly that the sovereign has a very close association with warfare. In eighteen cases he was supreme commander (three cases of insufficient data), and in ten he personally participated in combat (Claessen 1978: 563).

Having shown how a variety of common institutions have the latent property, especially in combination, of leading to centralized authority we may now examine the way in which these institutions have another latent property, that of co-ordinating large numbers of people.

[9] Otterbein (1970: 27) argues, following Spencer, that subordination tends to arise first in warfare, and then to become gradually transferred to the political realm. In Table 2 (ibid., 24) from a survey of 36 societies we have:

Political system	Degree of military subordination	
	High	Low
Centralized	2	13
Uncentralized	7	14

From these data he argues that if the opposite theory were correct, and political centralization arose before military subordination, the distribution of societies in Table 2 would show lack of military subordination in politically uncentralized societies. But this assumes that either military subordination or political centralization must come before the other. There is in fact no reason to assume any such thing, and these data are equally compatible with the theory that military subordination may develop independently of political organization, but that without some basis of political authority, e.g. in genealogy or religion, military subordination will not be able to produce this. And, as Cohen says, 'Subordination exists across many facets of uncentralized social and political life—in hunting, religious ceremonies, family life, *rites de passage*, and so on. Why must we attribute increased subordination in government to only one institution at the pre-state level and test only for that feature while disregarding the others?' (R. Cohen 1978: 46).

4. Societal size

My aim here is to show, first, that the various types of institution considered in the previous section have certain structural properties that greatly facilitate the co-ordination of large social networks and, secondly, that these large networks have distinct properties of their own. We observed in Chapter I that the ability to co-ordinate increasing numbers of people is one of the outstanding features of more advanced forms of social organization. It is also clear that the higher the population density in an area, the easier it will be to develop communities of large size. Do these facts therefore justify the conclusion that increases in population density cause the state to appear? It is well established (e.g. Claessen 1978: 544–5) that by far the commonest economic basis for the state is agriculture; we noted in Chapter IV that there is a very strong association ($p = < .0001$) between mode of subsistence and population density such that the highest population density is produced by agriculture, and that there is also a very strong correlation between mode of subsistence and community size ($p = .0001$). On the other hand, the state has only developed in a minority of societies, yet the majority of societies are agricultural. It is therefore likely that there are many societies with sufficient population density but which have nevertheless not developed the state.

We know that this is indeed the case: for example, the Chimbu of Highland New Guinea have densities in the range of 350–450 p.s.m. (Brown 1978: 102), but their social organization is not appreciably more elaborate than in areas with only a small fraction of this density; or again, the Ifugao of Luzon island in the Philippines have comparable population densities, but also a very simple type of social organization. The Konso have approximately 250 p.s.m., and Netting reports *c.* 500–600 p.s.m. for the Kofyar (above, Chapter III Section 1*e*). On the other hand it is well known that in other areas with population densities below 1 p.s.m. quite elaborate social institutions may develop e.g. the Borana Galla, some Australian Aboriginal societies (Berndt and Berndt 1964), and the Gê-speaking peoples of Brazil (Maybury-Lewis 1967, 1979). High density of population may therefore simply produce a large number of small, uncentralized, autonomous communities instead of a single centralized state or chiefdom. Conversely, Claessen's survey of twenty-one early states showed that nine were of high density and ten of low density (Claessen 1978: 538). Indeed, Fortes and Evans-Pritchard long ago pointed out on the basis of modern censuses that the population density of some African states is actually *lower* than that of some stateless societies (Fortes and Evans-Pritchard 1940: 7–8). This was disputed by Stevenson (1968) and Harris (1969: 537–8), but Goody (1977) has shown conclusively that this can in fact be the case (Goody 1977: 540, Table 1). While for various historical reasons these inverted ratios are likely to have occurred after the emergence of the state in these areas, we can still draw the broad conclusion that population density is merely an index of the abundance of a vital raw material—people—and has by itself no power to determine how that raw material will be used.

On the fundamental issue of societal size let us then be clear that we are discussing the size of communities, of *integrated networks* of people, and not merely gross population totals within a specific area. The relation between *social* size and types of organization has long been recognized, by Plato and Aristotle in their speculations on the ideal size of polities, and in more recent times by sociologists such as Spencer, who observed that 'as population augments, divisions and sub-divisions become more numerous and more decided' (Spencer 1893: I. 437–8).[10] On the assumption, then, that we are discussing the sizes of different communities of differing levels of organization, it is well established that community size is closely related to organizational complexity (e.g. Forge 1972).

So Carneiro, using a sample of forty-six single-community societies, showed that there was a close correlation between population size and the number (205) of organizational features present in the society. Some of these traits are: craft specialization, service specialization, sumptuary laws, slavery, towns, cities, formal political leadership, advisory councils, state treasury, state ministries, judicial process, code of laws, hierarchy of priests, temples, census taken, and military conscription (Carneiro 1967: 235 n. 2). The results are summarized in Figure 10.

From a sample of twenty-four societies randomly selected from Murdock's World Ethnographic Sample (1957) of 560

---

[10] Simmel (1902) was one of the first sociologists to make a specific study of the effects of size on social organization, but his analysis, although interesting, is rather vague and unsystematic, and while Michels (1915) formulated his 'iron law of oligarchy' with the question of size in mind his study, too, is inconclusive on the actual effects of size on organization. For further references see Terrien and Mills 1955: 11.

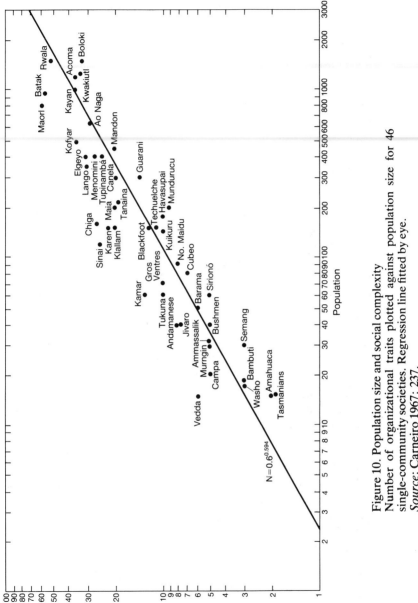

Figure 10. Population size and social complexity
Number of organizational traits plotted against population size for 46 single-community societies. Regression line fitted by eye.
Source: Carneiro 1967: 237.

Table 19. Relationship between upper limit of community size and differentiation of political authority

Rank Order of Societies	Community Size	Political Authority
Kaska	1	6
Caribou Eskimo	2	2.5
Kutubu	3	10
Xam	5	2.5
Naron	5	6
Mataco	5	6
Tiwi	9.5	2.5
Ojibwa	9.5	10
Bacairi	9.5	10
Acholi	9.5	17
Guahibo	12.5	2.5
Timucua	12.5	15
Ontong Java	13	15
Chamorro	15	10
Lango	15	10
Samoa	15	18.5
Cuna	17	21
Omaha	19	20
Teton	19	13
Didinga	19	18.5
Huron	21	15
Tswana	22.5	22
Ashanti	22.5	12
Thai	24	24

Source: Ember 1963: 239[11]

contemporary and historical societies, Ember found a clear relationship (see Table 19) between community size and the

[11] These conclusions on the relation between size and organization are supported by studies of a wide variety of organizations in modern industrial society, especially with regard to the criteria of Complexity and Formalization. By 'complexity' is meant (*a*) the number of levels of the hierarchy (vertical); (*b*) the numbers of divisions or departments (horizontal); and (*c*) the number of job titles (division of labour). By 'formalization' is meant (*a*) the number of rules and regulations; (*b*) the existence of punishments or sanctions for deviation. Hall, Haas, and Johnson (1967) found significant relations between size of organization and complexity and formalization in a study of 75 widely different organizations. See also Strauss *et al.* 1974: 109–13 for a useful survey of research on the relation between the size and structure of organizations.

differentiation of political authority, ' . . . as measured in terms of the number of different types of political officials (full or part time, with formally or informally delegated authority) who participate in the initiation of government activities on all levels of political integration in the society' (Ember 1963: 232–3). In order to gain more complete understanding of the structural transformation involved here, it is necessary to examine the mathematical, or graphical[12] properties of social networks, some of which are very remarkable. The first steps in this direction were taken by Graicunas in 1933 (Graicunas 1937); an expert in organizational management, his basic concern was the optimum number of subordinates for an executive, and he produced a number of formulae to express the exponential increase in relationships resulting from each extra individual in the group. His work was extended to family groups by Bossard (1945), and generalized by Kephart (1950).

In any social network there are three basic types of interaction: I, individual–individual; II, individual–group; III, group–group. Because increasing size of population is commonly thought of in simple arithmetic terms (a population of a thousand is only ten times greater than one of a hundred, for example), the truly astonishing exponential increases in the number of relationships that are generated by very modest arithmetic increases in group size are commonly overlooked, despite the profound significance which this has for social organization.

Let us begin with the potential relations (PRs) of type I in any network of n members. Assuming that relationships are symmetrical—that if A interacts with B, B interacts with A—the number of PRs is given by the formula $1/2(n^2 - n)$ (Graicunas 1937: 186; Kephart 1950: 545), as shown in Table 20. In the case of type II relations, the formula for all individual–subgroup relations is given by the formula $n(2^n - n - 1)/2$ (Kephart 1950: 547), as shown in Table 21. It will be observed that the number of type II relations rises much more rapidly than type I relations. One of the most important formulae is that for the sum of type I + II + III relations, as follows: $1/2(3^n - 2^{n+1} + 1)$ (Kephart 1950: 548), as shown in Table 22.

---

[12] In pure mathematics, graph theory is concerned with the properties of points joined by lines. See in particular Hage and Harary 1983.

Table 20

n	PRs
2	1
3	3
4	6
5	10
6	15
7	21
10	45
20	190
30	435
50	1225

Table 21

n	PRs
2	1
3	6
4	22
5	65
6	171
7	420
10	5,065
20	10,485,550
30	16,106,127,000
50	281,474,980,000,000,000

Table 22

n	PRs
2	1
3	6
4	25
5	90
6	301
7	966
10	28,501
20	1,742,343,625
30	1,029,444,900,000,000
50	358,948,990,000,000,000,000,000

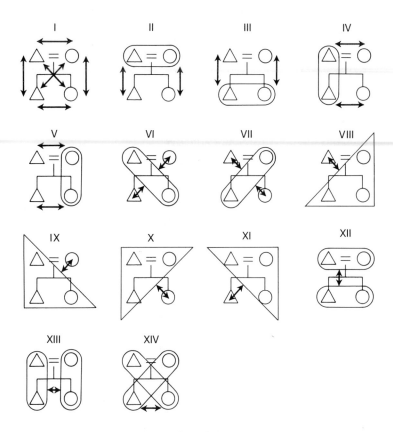

Figure 11

So, taking an imaginary family of father, mother, son, and daughter, 25 PRs are generated in the case of a sum of types I + II + III relations, as illustrated in Figure 11.

It is obvious that various means must be found to reduce drastically these gigantic numbers of PRs and, to begin with, it is fairly clear that actual relations (ARs) will be constrained by such basic factors as age and gender. Thus, in our imaginary family of Fig. 11 the PRs [M + F] <——> [S + D], or [F + S] <——> [M + D] will very often be realized in day-to-day relations, but such combinations as [S] <——> [M + F + D], or [M] <——>[F + S + D] are much less likely to have any permanent significance. But these constraints do not take us very far, and we must now examine a number of structural properties of institutions which have the effect of drastically reducing the PR:AR ratio. The first of these is the *specialization* of relations.

Let us begin by referring to our imaginary family in Fig. 11. In this case the relationships are of the following types:

1. Affinity (Parent–Parent)
2. Descent (Parent–Child)
3. Consanguinity (Sibling Sibling)
4. Genealogical distance (all 'first-order' relatives)
5. Generational level (Parent–Child).

If these types of relationship are explicitly differentiated from one another, it is then possible for specialized forms of each to be elaborated. For instance, there are 6 possible forms of relation 2 (Descent), as shown in Table 23.

Table 23. (m = male; f = female)

1.	m–>m (patrilineal)
2.	f–>f (matrilineal)
3.	(m–>m) $^+$ (f–>f) (bilineal, combination of (1) and (2))
4.	(m–>f) $^+$ (f–>m) (alternating)
5.	(m–>m)//(f–>f) (parallel, disjunction of (1) and (2))
6.	m/f–>m/f (cognatic)

Types 4 and 5 are not in fact socially feasible options as the basis of descent *groups*, though they can be the basis of inheritance of property and other rights on an individual basis.
Source: Needham 1974: 47

Once relations of descent, for example, have been isolated from others it then becomes possible to allocate different rights and statuses according to a number of principles of descent simultaneously. So Needham observes that in Penan society of Borneo the descent name is transmitted by mode 1, marital residence by mode 2, inheritance of movable property by mode 5, and group membership by mode 6 (ibid., 47). And once particular types of relationship have been isolated, or 'abstracted', it is also possible to elaborate upon them. So lineal descent can be made the basis of clearly bounded groups that can then engage in further social relations such as the exchange of women in very elaborate ways (e.g. systems of prescriptive alliance).

These principles of order, which depend on the specialization of different categories of relationship, allow people to co-ordinate the relations between hundreds of persons without difficulty, despite the gigantic numbers of PRs that are involved. By distinguishing different categories of kin it allows rules of behaviour and priorities of values to be established, and all this is accomplished by a process of *simplification* whereby the complicated relationships of kinship, for example, are disentangled from one another and each given specialized treatment. In other words, lineality has the structural property of allowing the coordination of large numbers of individuals, particularly when lineal descent groups are internally organized on hierarchical principles.

The construction of *hierarchies* provides a further very powerful means of reducing the PR : AR ratio. Residential groupings and subgroupings, such as those of Konso towns, councils of elders or royal courts, all bureaucratic and military hierarchies, the 'spokesman' function, the sending of delegates or representatives to decision-making bodies, markets, and the division of labour generally all have the property of allowing the co-ordination of social networks of very large scale because they employ the hierarchical principle. So too does military conquest when the vanquished communities are allowed to retain their organization and to communicate with the central government by intermediaries.

The graphical properties of hierarchy are therefore of fundamental importance in understanding how societies have been able to co-ordinate increasingly large numbers of people, and we must now examine these properties in more detail. Let us suppose there is a group of n members, and that it is necessary for an item of information to be communicated to them all. If there is no established sequence of individuals for this purpose, then the total number of interactions that must occur to ensure complete communication will be $1/2(n^2 - n)$, and many redundant interactions will take place, since some people will be giving the information to those who already know it. Thus, in a group of 8 members, for example, there will be 28 interactions. This number of interactions can be drastically reduced by two simple devices: if one member has the job of telling all the other members of his group; or, if there is a fixed sequence or chain of members along which the information is always passed, again, from one initiating member. These types of network organization reduce the required number of interactions to $n - 1$, e.g. in our group of 8 members to 7 interactions, as shown in Figure 12.

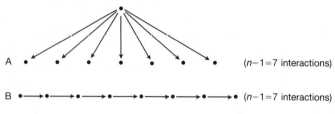

Figure 12

In case A one man has a great deal of work to do: he must remember to tell all the 7 members of his group, and he will take 7 times longer to do this than if he had to tell only one man. In case B, the work-load on each individual is minimal, but there is no improvement in the time factor, which remains the same. But now let us arrange the group of 8 in a hierarchy, as shown in Figure 13.

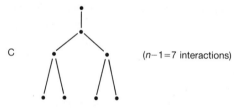

Figure 13

The number of interactions remains the same, but the work-load has been cut to 2 members each (1 in the case of the leader), and because there is now a number of parallel chains the time factor has also been reduced drastically. We may conclude, therefore, that fixed communication sequences greatly reduce the number of interactions necessary for ensuring the transmission of information, and that hierarchical networks, in turn, greatly reduce both work-load and transmission times. They also have the property of facilitating specialization of function.

It is very important to remember, however, that the graphic properties of institutions we are considering may well be largely unsuspected by the people concerned or regarded as trivial. We noted, for example, that there are a number of reasons for the widespread occurrence of patrilineal descent and primogeniture, which will be sufficient to explain them without reference to the graphic properties of hierarchies. But by producing hierarchies, fixed sequences, and specialized relations people are, unknown to themselves, laying the organizational foundations by which very large numbers of individuals can be co-ordinated when other factors permit societal size to increase. Nor do the co-ordinating properties of hierarchies, fixed sequences, and specialized relations exist because they are functionally necessary for society, or because they are of adaptive advantage. They are simply the structural properties of a wide range of institutions.

Organizational networks of types A and B also occur frequently throughout society: A, for example, appears in another form as the 'spokesman' function.

Thus, let us suppose that we have two groups of 50 members each, and that these two groups wish to negotiate some matter with one another. If all the members of the two groups (total 100) were to talk to every other member, total PRs would be $1/2(n^2 - n) = 4950$, whereas if each group were represented by a spokesman to whom each member of the group gave his opinion, PRs for each group would be $(n - 1) = 49$, total PRs = 98, + 1 for the meeting of the two spokesmen, = 99, as opposed to 4950, a reduction by a factor of 50. (Where group size increases, the factor of reduction becomes progressively greater.) But the members of these groups need not understand this, and their desire for a spokesman may well be motivated by the simple wish to have their group led by its most effective champion.

Hierarchies can also be considered as networks of sub-groups, and the general importance of sub-groups, or sub-assemblies of parts generally, in the generation of complex structures needs to be emphasized here. H. A. Simon illustrates the fundamental importance of this principle by a parable of two watchmakers, Hora and Tempus. The watches they made all consisted of about 1000 parts, but while Tempus had so designed his watch that if he had one partly assembled and had to put it down, it immediately fell to pieces and had to be rebuilt again from scratch, Hora's were designed using the principle of sub-assemblies. Each sub-assembly contained ten elements, and 'ten of these sub-assemblies, again, could be put together into a larger sub-assembly, and a system of ten of the latter assemblies constituted the whole watch' (Simon 1965: 65–6). Simon proves that Tempus will complete an assembly only 44 times per million attempts, while Hora will complete 9 out of 10. While in one sense the actual mathematics of this example are arbitrary, the general principle is of the greatest importance in social evolution, since, especially where larger societies are concerned, growth is usually by the absorption of entire communities, whether by peaceful amalgamation or by conquest: 'As they grow more populous, multi-community societies appear to elaborate their social structure more slowly than single-community societies. The reason for this seems to be that societies grow larger primarily by aggregation, that is, by incorporating into themselves smaller, previously independent societies' (Carneiro 1967: 238).

There are two other ways of reducing the PR : AR ratio that we have not considered. One is the restriction in the type of relation: by this I have in mind commercial relations in our type of society, where forming a relationship does not commit one to any relationships with any of the relatives or friends of the other party; the scope of the relationship itself is likely to be very narrow, and potentially limited in time.

Secondly, one finds in all societies that PRs are drastically reduced by localization of range; hence ARs may be far less than the total membership of the network itself. Or, relationships may be sequentially activated, one group of people at one time, and a different group at another.

It should also be noted that not all relationships are of equal significance in the working of a network. Thus, in a typical primitive society, relations between adult males will be of prime importance, between adult females of secondary importance, and relations between children of very little importance. Thus in calculating the size of a network one can often divide the total population by a factor of five or so.

So far, we have been examining various ways in which the structural properties of institutions have the effect of reducing the number of interactions necessary for social co-ordination. We may now consider certain properties of group size that affect the structure of large societies. Even in hierarchical systems, of course, absolute numbers at each point in the hierarchy may grow beyond the point of effective co-ordination. When members of groups have to interact with *all* the other individuals of the group, the number of PRs rapidly exceeds the limits of co-ordination. Caplow suggests that in groups where *all members interact with one another individually*, 'Primary Groups', the limit is about 20 (Caplow 1957: 487), and points out that

> Most of the organized groups in any society are found within the limits of the *small group*.[13] These include practically all households, play groups, cliques, gangs, councils, and conspiracies. Also included are the basic units of larger economic, military, and political organizations: work crews, infantry platoons, and precinct committees. (Ibid., 487)

In the case of Medium groups (50–1000) the distinctive criterion of Small Groups—the formation of all possible pairs—does not appear, but instead one or a few leaders may interact with all members of the group, who cannot interact with each other. In Large Groups one, or a few, leaders may simply be *recognized* as such by all members of the group, but will not interact with them all individually.

This principle of asymmetry is of particular importance in Giant Groups of the type of professional armies or nation-states. So, for example, if one examines the ratios between the populations of modern states and the sizes of legislatures, one finds that the legislature is $2.75\sqrt{}-3\sqrt{}$ of the total population, so that a nation of 50 million would have a legislature of 630, so producing a Medium Group that is quite capable of being organized on appropriate Medium-Group principles. But, as we know, a Medium Group is itself incapable of effective deliberation without an inner council, of Small-Group size, to co-ordinate its activities, and this is provided in all states by a small ruler's council or cabinet.

Indeed, when time is limited and information loads are high, as in the case of ruling councils and similar bodies, the optimum number is likely to be much less than 20, and there is abundant evidence that committees in a wide variety of organizations tend to have a membership of about 6 (or 7 including a chairman as tie-breaker). An example is the survey shown in Table 24 (James 1951, cited by Caplow 1957: 496).

When ruling councils or similar bodies consist of twenty or more

---

[13] Caplow (1957) distinguishes between groups as follows:
Small Groups
   (*a*) Primary   2–20
   (*b*) Non-primary   3–100
Medium Groups   50–1,000
Large Groups   1,000–10,000(?)

Table 24

Organization	No. of groups	Range of group size	Mean group size
US Senate sub-committee of 11 committees	46	2–12	5.4
US House of Representatives sub-committees of 14 sub-committees	111	2–26	7.0
State of Oregon executive, judiciary, boards, depts., commissions	96	2–14	5.7
Eugene, Oregon executive, council members, committees, boards	19	3–11	4.7
Subgroups in offices and board-of-director organizations of 4 large corporations	29	3–9	5.3
		Average	5.78

members, it is well known that there is always a small inner group of about five or six with greater influence in decision-making. As societies increase in size, the ruling body, whose size must remain constant, will therefore constitute a progressively smaller percentage of the total society, and hence the principle of asymmetry will become of increasing importance as access to the ruling body diminishes. The social network becomes ranked in a series of 'zones', whose size diminishes as they approach the centre of power, and size and stratification mutually reinforce one another.

Increased organizational complexity also results in increasing homogeneity of structure, whether we are considering business corporations or centralized states:

Large organizations with different purposes seem to resemble each other more than small organizations with different purposes do. It is not too fanciful to think of a single organizational type toward which all giant organizations tend. An army, an industrial enterprise, a newspaper, a philanthropy, and a university all resemble each other, or, more exactly, they all approach a common type. Their small group prototypes, by contrast, do not resemble each other. (Caplow 1957: 504)

Some of the most important consequences of increasing size in co-ordinated networks are therefore as follows:

1. The numbers in the ruling group (monarch and advisers, a general and his staff, and so on) will remain the same, but the number of subjects may increase many hundreds or thousands of times. This gives the rulers an increasingly powerful monopoly of information, initiative, and co-ordination, while the subjects find it increasingly difficult to discover what is going on, other than what their rulers wish to tell them, or to co-ordinate resistance because of the enormous number of PRs in the network. This is evidently one of the most important factors in consolidating the power of all governments. Quite apart from the monopoly of information and initiative conferred on the rulers of large societies, there is no way in which the business of such groups can be conducted other than by a small minority. Naive ideas of the people 'owning' the means of production, when these are any more elaborate than, say, grazing rights on a village common, have as much chance of success as perpetual motion.

2. Once large networks can be held together politically, then tiny percentages of society can expand to large numbers in absolute terms. If, for example, a particular economy can support non-producing craftsmen and other full-time specialists in the proportion of, say, 1 per cent of the population, a population of 5,000 will support 50, but a population of 1,000,000 will support 10,000. It is clear that, especially if these people are brought together at the seat of government, or in urban centres as typically happens, then the chance of new discoveries, competitive emulation, and mutual assistance, and the growth of further specialization in crafts and knowledge will be greatly facilitated. 'A correlation between the level of civilization and the size of the society has been made on numerous occasions (see Kroeber 1948: 272 ff., 281; also Braidwood and Reed 1957; Steward 1955, Ch. 11), and it seems clear that civilized societies cannot be small societies' (Dumond 1965: 313).

3. The greater the size of the social network, the greater will be

the information load at the level of government, and hence the greater the need for record keeping, including writing, with all the consequences that entails. More generally, I shall argue (in Section 5 below) that major increases in the number and diversity of entities to be classified impose significant new demands on cognitive processes generally.

4. The larger the organization, the greater the tendency to homogeneity of organizational type.

5. The emergence of the state

The necessary conditions for state formation are a clear basis of legitimate authority, normally derived from the descent system and the religion, together with the various means of co-ordinating large social networks that we have discussed. But these may exist in societies that have never developed the state, and we must therefore consider a number of other specific factors that seem to be of great importance in concentrating and intensifying centralized authority. It seems that in fact two of these—urbanization and irrigation—have not been as significant as some have supposed.

(a) The principle of circumscription

When the political unit reaches a certain size, there is an inherent tendency for local leaders to take advantage of their authority and establish their autonomy from the original unit:

. . . chieftaincies are sufficiently different from states to warrant separate classification. The key diagnostic feature is fission. All political systems up to the time of the early state, have as part of their normal political and demographic processes, inherent tendencies to break up and form similar units across the landscape . . . The state is a system that overcomes such fissiparous tendencies. This capacity creates an entirely new kind of society. One that can expand and take in other ethnic groups, one that can become more populous and powerful without necessarily having any upper limit to its size or strength. Only the state among all known human political systems is capable of such growth in size and power. (R. Cohen 1978: 35)

It is this possibility of fission that, in the majority of societies, has prevented the emergence of the state: 'Whatever the specific reasons, the hierarchical, inegalitarian, tendencies inherent in the organization of local autonomies are held in check by the continuing fission of such polities which is their dominant response to land shortages and internal conflicts' (ibid., 53).

Chiefs of the Murle (neighbours of the Nuer and Dinka)

> avoid doing anything without first consulting the elders, lest they should be thought tyrannical or 'bitter', for a chief of this type would tend to lose to other villages people not closely related to him . . . This mobility of society is an essential part of their structure, which acts as a safeguard against oppression by the chiefs . . . (B. A. Lewis 1972: 60)

And Gluckman says of early Zulu society, 'A tribe was divided into sections under brothers of the chief and as a result of a quarrel a section might migrate and establish itself as an independent clan and tribe' (Gluckman 1940: 25). Chiefdoms themselves often split up at the death of a chief, because of disputes over the succession, or because of ambition for independent authority.

Mobility itself, quite apart from fission created by chiefly ambition, is of great importance in preventing the emergence of political authority, even that of a chiefdom. The option of moving away is often exercised for reasons of land shortage, or as a means of escaping from local friction. In the case of New Guinea it has often been noted that the power of Big Men is greatly limited by the freedom of their followers to transfer their residence as well as their allegiance.

Carneiro (1970*b*) has therefore quite rightly maintained that the prevention of fission, or 'circumscription', must be a factor of primary importance in the development of the state. Carneiro suggested that the location of the earliest known states—the Nile, Tigris–Euphrates, Indus, the Valley of Mexico, and the mountain and coastal valleys of Peru—possess the common property of being areas of circumscribed agricultural land. Population pressure on land in such circumstances cannot be solved by migration, and thus leads to wars of conquest, with the political subjugation of the losers. (This still requires an effective basis of political authority in the first place, however.) More generally, he also recognizes the concentration of resources, as on the coast of Peru, can have a circumscriptive effect, as can social impediments to migration, as among the villages in the centre of the Yanomamo country.

Service, moreover, has pointed out that the principle of

'government by benefit', which we have already discussed, has also acted in a circumscriptive manner, and is

a universal in the formation of all persevering power relationships. Redistribution and economic well-being in general, priestly intervention with the gods, protection, and so on are all helpful in political integration when it is apparent that they are superior benefits compared to the alternative of moving away . . . (Service 1975: 223)

There is thus, at least initially, a process of positive feedback whereby the benefits of centralized authority can act as an important restraint on fission, which in turn reinforces the process of centralization.

Once a powerful state has been established, however, it is in the position of being able to use circumscription as a conscious policy for enhancing its own power. We noted this in the case of the kingdom of Jimma, whose encircling defences and military patrols were clearly designed not only to keep enemies out, but potential fugitives in, and the same policy has been adopted by many states in all times and places. Gibbon pointed out that in Europe of the eighteenth century tyranny was mitigated by the large number of adjacent and mutually independent monarchies, all of which offered refuge to one another's discontented subjects.

But the empire of the Romans filled the world, and, when that empire fell into the hands of a single person, the world became a safe and dreary prison for his enemies. The slave of Imperial despotism, whether he was condemned to drag his gilded chain in Rome and the senate, or to wear out a life of exile on the barren rock of Seriphus, or the frozen banks of the Danube, expected his fate in silent despair. To resist was fatal, and it was impossible to fly. On every side he was encompassed with a vast extent of sea and land, which he could never hope to traverse without being discovered, seized, and restored to his irritated master. Beyond the frontiers his anxious view could discover nothing, except the ocean, inhospitable deserts, hostile tribes of barbarians, of fierce manners and unknown language, or dependent kings, who would gladly purchase the emperor's protection by the sacrifice of an obnoxious fugitive. 'Wherever you are', said Cicero to the exiled Marcellus, 'remember that you are equally within the power of the conqueror'. (Gibbon 1776: 84)

(b) Warfare

Pre-state societies not only have inherent tendencies to break up, but also face increasing difficulties in extending political authority to other groups which already have their own leadership. We noted in Chapter III that primitive warfare is typically concerned with glory, vengeance, and booty, not with political conquest, which requires higher levels of subordination, discipline, specialization, and hierarchical command structures. When communities are small and techniques of warfare primitive, the normal result must be political stalemate, with no one group being able to dominate the others. There seems no doubt that warfare is by far the commonest means by which political authority is extended to new communities, and warfare will operate in conjunction with circumscription to extend the range of existing authority and consolidate its power.

The ability to develop a military organization which is capable of political conquest is likely to be associated with increased political organization in general:

Another group of scholars (Bagehot 1872; [Andreski 1968]; Fried 1967; Vayda 1968; Service 1975) suggest that societal evolution comes first, and then provides a basis for the increased scale, frequency, and success of warfare. Citing specific cases they note that a more disciplined, more organized polity produces larger armies, better defence against warring neighbours, and it stimulates the use of warfare as a form of inter-societal relations. More specifically, warfare between raiding nomads and outside predators, as described in Lattimore's (1940) work (cited in Service 1975) on northwest China leads to the strengthening of defences and the emergence of a more centralized polity among the sedentary peoples being threatened. Finally, warfare among roughly equivalent neighbours gives people an appreciation for the protection that centralized leadership affords (Service 1975: 299). In effect, Service concludes that people accept more centralized polities because of the utility of such a system in the face of outside dangers. (R. Cohen 1978: 46)

Indeed, warfare can be regarded as a kind of large-scale public work, like building pyramids or digging canals; a life-giving enterprise of the highest value to society, the successful leadership of which is a sign of divine favour. It is not surprising then, as we noted earlier, that leadership in war is one of the more or less universal attributes of all rulers of states (Claessen 1978: 562).

Successful warfare also provides booty and land, and thus makes a very significant contribution to one of those other basic attributes of the ruler—generosity to his people (see Claessen 1978: 563–5). There are so many references to the use of the spoils of war by rulers to consolidate their authority that further emphasis of this point is unnecessary.

Finally, of course, as armies become increasingly professionalized and distinct from the traditional descent and residence groups, they can also be used for the repression of internal rebellion within the state, and for the enforcement of all forms of control by the central government.

Warfare, in short, gives the cutting edge to political authority, and is the basic means by which the local community can be extended. It also has many profound consequences for society which will be considered in Section b

(c) Trade and markets

Trade has often been an important intensifier of state power. It depends on the availability of surplus goods, which is a condition that exists long before the state develops. We have already noted the importance of systems of redistribution in the consolidation of chiefly authority, and trade, like warfare, can greatly increase the wealth available to an increasingly centralized authority, and thus intensify the process of state formation:

An expanding government apparatus, the need for some kind of military force (for offensive as well as defensive purposes), a developing state religion—all these developments demand increased production, and increased production in turn makes possible the further development of these institutions. This is also a most favourable situation for the stimulation and the promotion of (already existing) trade and markets . . . (Claessen and Skalnik 1978b: 627)

In the actual process of state formation trade, like warfare, clearly depends on the prior existence of some degree of political authority (Claessen and Skalnik 1978c: 644), but it seems to have had a major consolidating importance in many early states. According to Claessen, ' . . . trade played a definite role in all the [21] states. In thirteen cases it appeared to be of great importance, and in eight cases was found to be minor importance' (Claessen 1978: 542). Significantly, 'In 17 cases markets were found, and in all of these governmental influence on trade and markets was mentioned' (ibid., 542). Long-distance trade also occurred in 17 cases, and professional traders in 9 cases.

The importance of long-distance trade in the consolidation of the state will obviously depend on geography:

If a pre-state polity or a group of them lies on or at a nodal point in an increasing long distance trade, then this environmental feature exerts pressure on the local leadership to increase their power and stabilize control over the trade. To do this they need greater military capability and full time officials who can coordinate the increased managerial functions associated with the trade (cf. Wright & Johnson 1975: 277). The results of such increased organization are the well-known trading states and ports of trade in which commerce and government are intimately linked. Conversely, however, if the pre-state polity is not located at a crucial nodal point along a developing trade route, as with many of the states of the Western Sudan, long distance trade has little or no causal significance for the rise of states. (R. Cohen 1978: 44)

The development of trade and markets will not only lead to an increase in full-time specialist craftsmen (18 out of 21 cases, and 3 cases of insufficient data, Claessen 1978: 544), but also, later in the development of the state, to a professional merchant class. But this does not mean that such men would be free to operate and make profits independently of state control. As Service says, 'There are those who see any evidence of movements of goods as "commerce", from which it follows that private entrepreneurs had appeared to become a "merchant class". The famous economic historian Karl Polanyi (in Polanyi *et al.* 1957) tellingly disputes this simplistic, ethnocentric interpretation' (Service 1975: 220). It is quite possible for those engaged in long-distance trade to be government officials, or acting under government control. In the Early Dynastic period of Sumer, for example, 'The agents responsible for the exchanges were officials, not free entrepreneurs, and were organized in a hierarchy. This does not mean that those same persons could not have engaged in some private trade, but only that their power, whatever it was, arose from their bureaucratic position, not from their private wealth gained through trade' (Service 1975: 221, citing Adams 1966: 155).

We have seen that the roots of authority lie in genealogical and religious status, and as political authority becomes stronger and more centralized its control over wealth and economic activity in general must also increase. It is unequal access to political authority, therefore, that is the origin of economic inequality, not the other way about, as Marx and others have supposed:

The relation of a priest-chief-redistributor to the agricultural workers in a chiefdom is best seen as a *political* power relationship, not an economic relationship that grew out of the unequal acquisition of wealth in a market economy. At any rate, there is no need to posit a class relationship that necessarily must have been founded on economic ownership. It is the power relationship itself that we are investigating, and so far it looks as if it began with an unequal power to make redistributive exchanges (and unequal access to gods rather than goods). (Service 1975: 212)

Once the state's control over the means of production, distribution, and exchange has been consolidated, there is no reason why it should ever be relinquished. The state may allow merchants to make substantial private profits but their economic activities will be exercised at the discretion of the bureaucracy and in the interests of the state. (The only major exception to this almost inevitable tendency occurred in Western Europe in the early Middle Ages.) The principal effect of the growth of trade and markets was not, therefore, that it brought a class of merchant capitalists into being, but that it strengthened the redistributive power of the king, and hence the whole apparatus of government and its ability to wage war.

It was also the prime cause of the development of money: 'Directly connected with trade and markets is the use of currency' (Claessen 1978: 541). The social consequences of money obviously extend far beyond the market-place. As it becomes increasingly common and accepted, it permeates a wide range of individual transactions and facilitates contracts, the commutation of personal services into cash payments, the collection of taxes and all aspects of government accounting, and produces far greater flexibility in all types of social relations.

(d) Urbanization

For Childe, the city was a basic factor in the development of the state because it was the essential institution for organizing the food surplus produced by intensive agriculture. In his paper 'The urban revolution' (1950) he argues that in all the early states urban settlements with several thousand inhabitants were centres of concentration for the agricultural surplus. For this reason it was here that the governing class of religious, military, and civil rulers lived, together with the bureaucracy necessary for administering the state. The surplus also liberated a wide range of full-time craftsmen and artists from the necessity of agricultural labour and they, too, resided in the cities, where they could, for example, construct monumental public buildings. Cities were also bases for the importation of goods on a large scale, and hence for long-distance trade. The complex administrative system produced the need for writing; and written texts, in turn, were the basis of arithmetic, geometry, and astronomy, the last being of especial importance in relation to calendrical knowledge.

There is no doubt that cities have been associated with all these developments, in different times and places, and to this extent the city is another of these institutions with a very high developmental potential. But, like the state, large urban centres have been produced by a variety of factors, of which an agricultural surplus is only one. They may initially be merely the seat of royal government, as in many African states, or centres for defence, or trade, or ritual, or any combination of these. Moreover, it does not appear to be true that they are the inevitable concomitants of the early state:

Urbanization was not found to play a decisive role in the formation of the early state. Several early states came into being without towns or cities being present at all; in others the role of urban centres came to be of importance only long after the emergence of the state (cf. Service 1975: xii). (Claessen and Skalnik 1978c: 644)

While the city was basic to Sumerian and later Mesopotamian civilization, it does not seem to have had any such importance for Egypt:

Ancient Egypt carried on her life through dozens of moderate-sized towns and myriads of agricultural villages. It is legitimate to say that for nearly three thousand years, until the founding of Alexandria, ancient Egypt was a major civilization without a single major city. (Wilson 1960: 135)

Nor does the city in ancient China seem to have that fundamental evolutionary significance which Childe claims:

I have been unable to correlate the advent of the compact city with, for example, any change in political status such as the expansion from city-state to territorial empire, or with any mutation in the organization of government such as that from religious oligarchy to kingship. Nor does it seem invariably to be directed or clearly related to any specific methods of warfare, or somewhat surprisingly, to specific advances in transportation technology. Possibly it may in some instances reflect the emergence of a new mode of economic exchange, but this topic is at present so obscure that it requires a study to itself. (Wheatley 1971: 480)

Nor was the city important in the development of Mayan civilization:

. . . all through the Classic Period there (i.e. down to c. AD 900) the bulk of settlement was segmented into small hamlets including from five to a dozen or so houses. Occasionally within a hamlet of this kind there was a little mound or separate structure larger than the others suggesting a special building or shrine occupied by a local elder or priest. Up to a dozen hamlets occurred within an areas about a kilometer in diameter, which generally also included a minor ceremonial center consisting of two or three small plazas surrounded by ceremonial mounds. A number of these minor ceremonial centers in turn would be found grouped at a distance from a major center, where a monumental ball court, carved stelae, hieroglyphic writing, and evidences of the great arts point unequivocally to the definition offered by Childe for the city in civilization. Yet even the greatest of these centers was primarily ceremonial in character; they cannot be described as large dwelling clusters. In a sense the Maya offer a sequence of development toward civilization without cities. (Willey 1960: 44–5)

It seems, therefore, that the city can at most intensify those other factors in the development of the state which we have considered and that it is perfectly possible for states to emerge with very little in the form of urban concentrations.

(e) Irrigation

From the observation that large-scale projects for water use and control are evident in all the ancient states (China, the Indus Valley, Mesopotamia, Egypt, Meso-America, and Peru) Wittfogel developed the well-known hypothesis that such hydraulic systems were essential factors in the rise of despotic, bureaucratic centralized states because of the planning and social co-ordination required to construct and maintain such systems. Marvin Harris has more recently reduced this to a simpler causal hypothesis, that irrigation systems produce highly centralized and absolutist political systems and that, conversely, rainfall agriculture, as in Europe, produces feudalism and capitalism (Harris 1980: 104–5).

It is obvious a priori, however, that large hydraulic systems presuppose the existence of a directing authority. As Friedman says, 'If the bureaucracy is necessary for the functioning of the irrigation works, how do we explain the fact that the irrigation works must precede this bureaucracy?' (Friedman 1974: 462). Wittfogel was certainly no vulgar materialist:

Man never stops affecting his natural environment. He constantly *transforms* it; and he *actualizes* new forces whenever his efforts carry him to a new level of operation. Whether a new level can be attained at all, or once attained, where it will lead, depends first on the institutional order and second on the ultimate target of man's activity: the physical, chemical, and biological world accessible to him. Institutional conditions being equal, it is the difference in the material setting that suggests and permits—or precludes—the development of new forms of technology, subsistence, and social control. (Wittfogel 1957: 11)

He also concludes that

Strictly local tasks of digging, damming, and water distribution can be performed by a single husbandman, a single family, or a small group of neighbours, and in this case no far-reaching organizational steps are necessary. Hydroagriculture, farming based on small-scale irrigation, increases the food supply, but it does not involve the patterns of organization and social control that characterize hydraulic agriculture and Oriental despotism. (Ibid., 18)

By 'hydroagriculture' he presumably has in mind such systems as those of the Ifugao, Kalinga, and Bontoc of the Luzon mountains of the Philippines, where elaborate systems of irrigated terraces for wet rice cultivation have been built but where, despite high population densities, a very low level of social organization prevails. So far, so good. But when he considers the constraints of larger-scale irrigation on social organization he supposes that these are much narrower than in fact they are:

A large quantity of water can be channeled and kept within bounds only by the use of mass labour; and this mass labour must be coordinated, disciplined, and led. Thus a number of farmers eager to conquer arid lowlands and plains are forced to invoke the organizational devices which— on the basis of premachine technology—offer the one chance of success: they must work in cooperation with their fellows and subordinate themselves to a directing authority. (Ibid., 18)

In the first place, given the obvious fact that all irrigation systems have to begin on a small scale, it is impossible to determine at what point 'subordination to a directing authority' will occur—if at all. So Millon (1962) shows in a survey of seven different societies with irrigation systems that the degree of centralization has no correlation with the size of the system or the population operating it (Table 25). Of the El Shabana in the Middle Euphrates, whose

Table 25

	Population	Irrigated Acreage	Allocation System
Pul Eliya	146	135	Partly decentralized; strongly traditionalized
Sonjo (Kheri)	650	700–800	Centralized
Halild	2000	1000–1200	Decentralized
El Shabana	2500–4500	8300	Largely centralized
Bali (Blaju)	5500–7500	3000–4000	Decentralized; strongly traditionalized
Teotihuacán	15,000	9500	Largely centralized
Twelve Village	30,000–50,000	13,600	Decentralized; strongly traditionalized

Source: Millon 1962: 80.

irrigation system in the traditional society was under the overall protection of the *shaykh*, he says:

The primary responsibility of the *shaykh* seems to have been defence of the water supply and landholdings of the tribe rather than direction of any irrigation works. Important canals of impressive size 'were not dug in one season but [were] gradually extended [from year to year] following natural depressions' created by the water as it flowed away from the river, the bed of which is normally at a higher level than the lands surrounding it. (Ibid., 73, citing Fernea 1959)

And of the Sonjo of Tanzania,

In only one of the seven societies under examination—the Sonjo—is centralization of authority possibly derivable from the practice of irrigation. The other possibility is that centralized authority in Sonjo villages arose as a response to the problems posed by the constantly marauding Masai. Possibly the two conditions served to reinforce one another. But whatever may be the explanation for conditions among the Sonjo, it is clear that centralized authority and the practice of irrigation are not necessarily related, even in systems of irrigation of an intermediate size such as the Twelve Village system in Japan. (Ibid., 83)

Millon also emphasizes that while large-scale irrigation *should* have some form of central direction if it is to work at optimum efficiency, this does not necessarily mean that the requisite degree of central direction will actually arise: conflict and anarchy are equally possible, unless there is some pre-existing form of social control:

Such systems of irrigation involve, simultaneously, the imposition of the necessity for cooperation and the generation of fundamental sources of conflict. It is commonplace in studies of people practising irrigation to stress the fact that cooperation involving numbers of people or groups of people is enjoined upon the participants in all but the very simplest of systems, if the people involved are to actualize the benefits inherent in a system of irrigation agriculture. And of course it is for a good reason that this has been emphasized, for in this lies an important difference between the practice of most kinds of irrigation agriculture and the practice of many kinds of rainfall farming. But the corollary of this is less often stressed, namely, that the practice of irrigation agriculture carries with it a strong potential for antagonism and conflict and is a potentially disruptive force. (Ibid., 84)

Wittfogel also emphasized the condition of full aridity as a basic prerequisite for the rise of hydraulic systems:

In a landscape characterised by full aridity permanent agriculture becomes possible only if and when co-ordinated human action transfers a plentiful and accessible water supply from its original location to a potentially fertile soil. When this is done, government led hydraulic enterprise is identical with the creation of agricultural life. This first and crucial moment may therefore be designated as the 'administrative creation point'. (Wittfogel 1957: 109)

Thus, as Leach rightly says, Wittfogel's 'ideal type' system of hydraulic society

. . . grows up where cultivation calls for *large scale* irrigation; the initial hypothesis is that in such societies *all* water supplies must be brought from afar.

But what are the facts? Is it the case that the great hydraulic societies of the past have grown up in the 'fully arid' regions of this sort? Chronologically the earliest successful hydraulic societies seem to have been those of Southern Mesopotamia followed by Egypt and the Indus Valley. In each case the natural environment which faced the original inhabitants may be summarised thus: an alluvial and fertile soil, an arid climate, a terrain of flat swamp land subject to periodic flooding. In such a context urban development calls for formidable and resourceful engineering but the first essential requirement of the agriculturalist is *not* irrigation on a grand scale but simply a little modest conservation of local water resources.

'Irrigation' in Sumeria did not require a despotic monarch to build vast aqueducts and reservoirs; it simply called for elementary and quite localized drainage and construction and perhaps the diversion of river flood water into the flat lands on either side of the main stream. (Leach 1959: 7)

Leach then shows from the case of Ceylon that it is quite possible for extremely large irrigation projects to be built without the aid of a vast bureaucracy or even large numbers of labourers. For example,

Before silting reduced the area, the Kalawewa tank may have been nearly forty miles in circumference. It leads out into a complex feeder canal system about fifty-five miles long. For the first seventeen miles of its length this canal has a steady fall of six inches a mile. (Ibid., 9)

It all *looks* like a colossal and highly organized piece of bureaucratic planning, the work of one of Wittfogel's idealised Oriental Despots. But if so, the planning must have been done by a kind of Durkheimian group mind! The system took about 1,400 years to build. The original Tissawewa tank at the *bottom* end of the system was first constructed about 300 B.C. The Kalawewa tank at the top end of the system was first constructed about 800 years later and elaborations and modifications went on for at least another 600 years. (Ibid., 13)

No doubt the accumulated man-hours of labour over the centuries were gigantic, but this does not itself imply that very large numbers of labourers were ever employed at any one time, and while professional engineers existed, they were members of Buddhist monastic institutions, not direct servants of the Crown. Gunawardana concludes that:

The emergence of a political system which brought the petty regional polities under the sway of Anuradhapura was not the response to the organizational demands of irrigation society. The vital social functions of constructing and maintaining small-scale irrigation works continued to be performed by village communities after the formation of the state, as they had been in prestate polities, with little intervention by the ruler. In Sri Lanka, rulers began to construct large-scale irrigation works of supralocal significance several centuries after the campaigns of Dutthagamani [161– 137 BC] had undermined the independence of petty chiefdoms. (Gunawardana 1981: 148) . . . irrigation activity only intensified the development of trends which were equally common to societies not dependent on irrigation: the relationship between irrigation and state formation was not one which gave a totally different and specific form to the state in irrigation society. (Ibid., 150–1)

From a study of data from Mesopotamia, Egypt, Meso-America, and Peru, Adams reaches conclusions on the relation between hydraulic systems and the centralized state that are essentially similar to those of Leach and Gunawardana concerning Ceylon. Of Mesopotamia Adams says.

... there appears to have been little change in settlement pattern between the beginning of widespread agricultural occupation in the Ubaid period (ca. 4000 BC) and the end of the third millennium BC or even later. There is historical documentation of occasional large canals and irrigation works as early as the Proto-imperial period, but on the whole the settlements followed closely the shifting, braided channels of the major rivers.

In other words, for a long time irrigation seems to have been conducted principally on an *ad hoc* and small-scale basis, which would have involved periodic cleaning and perhaps straightening of clogged natural channels, adjusting the location of fields and settlements in the closest possible conformity with the existing hydraulic regime, and for the most part constructing and maintaining only relatively small-scale field and feeder canals that were wholly artificial. When the king explicitly claims credit for initiating dredging operations on either a canal or a natural watercourse (as in modern Iraq, the same word is used for both), it is noteworthy that the aspect of canals as providers of irrigation water is entirely unmentioned ... Moreover, whatever the rhetoric of the king's claimed responsibilities, the necessary labor forces for the maintenance work were apparently organized and directed by the individual temples ... [Each temple was also apparently responsible for water allocation] ... In short, there is nothing to suggest that the rise of dynastic authority in southern Mesopotamia was linked to the administrative requirements of a major canal system. (Adams 1960*b*: 281)

Again, with regard to the significance of large-scale hydraulic systems in the development of the Meso-American state, Adams concludes:

On present evidence, then, Wolf and Palerm [1955: 275] rightly tend to regard planned large-scale canal irrigation not as a primary cause of Mesoamerican civilization but merely as its culminating activity in the economic sphere. They recognize, to be sure, that political controls in turn probably were centralized and intensified by the introduction of major irrigation works. (Ibid., 286)

In the case of Egypt,

In short, considering the number of known records of royal building activity in the Old Kingdom, it seems only fair to regard their silence on the construction of irrigation works as strange if the demands of large-scale irrigation had indeed been responsible for the initial emergence of a pharaoh at the head of a unified state. On the assumption of a centrally administered irrigation system, the failure of officials with long and varied careers of public service to refer to administrative posts connected with canal maintenance or water distribution is equally puzzling. To the degree that an *argumentum ex silentio* ever carries conviction, the Egyptian case parallels that of Mesopotamia. (Ibid., 282)

[In highland Peru] as in North Coastal Peru, Egypt, and southern Mesopotamia, we seem to have evidence here of a very gradual evolution of irrigation practices beginning with local and small-scale terracing which emphatically did not require political organization embracing a large group of communities. Large-scale, integrated programs of canalization and terracing apparently were attempted only after the perfection of the Inca state as a political apparatus controlling the allocation of mass-labor resources. They are consequences, perhaps of the attainment of a certain level of social development; we repeat that they cannot be invoked to explain the processes by which that level was attained. (Ibid. 284)

The role of large-scale irrigation and hydraulic systems in the intensification of the authority of an *already* existing state is well illustrated by the case of China towards the end of the Warring States period, *c.*300 BC, when large-scale irrigation projects were of great importance in consolidating governmental power. (Needham 1954: 96–7).

While there is no doubt, therefore, that the construction of large hydraulic works may greatly enhance the power of the state, their effect is only to intensify an evolutionary process that is already well advanced. Indeed, river valleys have properties that are more closely linked than those of irrigation with the development of the state: circumscription, the ability to support large populations, and good communications. Wittfogel's central assumption—that large-scale hydraulic works can *only* be undertaken by a centralized bureaucracy—seems highly dubious, since in a number of instances we have seen that local administrations can achieve comparable results over a sufficiently long period of time.

(f) Conclusions

It has already been noted that, because states are far more tightly integrated and much larger than primitive societies, they tend to be far more similar to one another than primitive societies, just as large business organizations resemble one another more than do small ones. Freeman and Winch (1957) on the basis of a sample of 48 societies have shown that a number of characteristics of social organization related to state formation tend to follow one another in a characteristic sequence (Figure 14).

Type	Written Language	Government	Education	Religion	Punishment	Economy
6	+	+	+	+	+	+
5		+	+	+	+	+
4			+	+	+	+
3				+	+	+
2					+	+
1						+

1. *Economy*	(*a*)	symbolic medium of exchange (money) present.
	(*b*)	barter and exchange the sole economic mechanisms.
2. *Punishment*	(*a*)	crimes against person or property punished through government action.
	(*b*)	crimes avenged by the person wronged, his kin group, or the gods.
3. *Religion*	(*a*)	full-time specialized real priest (not diviner or healer) present.
	(*b*)	no full-time specialized priest present.
4. *Education*	(*a*)	formal, with full-time specialized teacher.
	(*b*)	informal, without full-time specialized teacher.
5. *Government*	(*a*)	full-time bureaucrats, unrelated to government head present.
	(*b*)	part-time bureaucrats, related to government head, or none.
6. *Written Language*	(*a*)	written language present.
	(*b*)	written language absent.

Figure 14

Taking 'presence of (*a*)' to indicate a complex trait, and using a sample of 48 societies, the 6 traits listed above formed a nearly perfect Guttman scale (coefficient of reproducibility = 0.97).

We must also explain why the state did not develop in the majority of cases, and it is now possible to do this. Those societies, such as many in New Guinea, which have no basis for political authority, whether genealogical, religious, or derived from an age-grouping system, will not be able to develop any form of stable political authority, even if they have sufficient quantities of people as the result of agriculture. When chiefly authority does develop, it naturally tends, for genealogical reasons in particular, to a process of fission, rather than consolidation, and it is also very difficult for the small communities so produced to conquer one another, especially in the circumstances of primitive warfare. These are all formidable obstacles to the emergence of the state, and it can therefore easily be understood why it should only have appeared in a minority of cases. The structural approach adopted here also explains how state formation can be extremely rapid, why it can occur in isolation (Egypt, Polynesia, Peru), and why there are many different routes to a single destination.

Finally, it must be emphasized again that nothing in the present analysis requires any functionalist assumptions whatever. The whole process can be explained in terms of the properties of institutions and beliefs, plus simple individual motivations and short-range purposes. The emergence of the state also has a number of very important structural consequences on social organization in general, and we shall examine these further in the next section.

6. The rationalization of society

The emergence of the state can be said to involve the steady rationalization of society. By this I mean, first of all, the growing subordination of the whole of society to a few clear and overriding purposes: the maintenance and extension (where possible) of the authority and power of the ruler over his subjects, together with military success and control over trade and public works that support and enhance that power. The change that this produces in the nature of society is very well illustrated by the differences between the structural features of the pre-state East Cushitic societies and those of the state of Jimma. The 'core principles' of East Cushitic societies such as the relative subordination of kinship, the absence of hereditary leadership, the *gada* system, and the strong emphasis on peace and individual wealth are not functionally necessary at all, nor do they exist because they are specially adaptive to the environment. Other pastoral and agricultural societies in East Africa are able to survive just as well with very different types of organization and values. It is surely clear by now that primitive societies have great latitude in organization, and that while there will be some consistency between institutions, values, and beliefs, it will normally be pointless to ask 'What is the function of this particular institution?' It was equally clear, however, that as the state of Jimma developed it acquired a genuinely functional organization. While, for example, there is no functional explanation for the *gada* system, or the relative unimportance of descent groups, or for the nine Konso clans, there are very good functional reasons for the division of Jimma into a large number of small provinces whose boundaries do not coincide with those of the earlier society; the refusal to allow hereditary office holders; and the clear separation of administrative, fiscal, and military duties. These features of organization were functional for the *state*, of course, not for 'society', and while they were the result of clear administrative thinking, they were only possible because of those earlier characteristics of East Cushitic society which it is implausible to attribute to the conscious purposes of any specifiable individuals. But once some form of centralized political authority has developed it presents its rulers with a number of problems in the arts of government, to which they can bring conscious thought, the consequences of which will affect the whole of society.

The second sense of rationalization involves the substitution of increasingly general rules and categories for those of a more particularistic and idiosyncratic type. In particular, this process involves the diminishing importance of the ascriptive principles of kinship and age, and their steady replacement by such principles as individual achievement and ability, social class, and changes in the significance of territorial boundaries. This aspect of rationalization will be considered in more detail in Subsection (*a*).

The third sense of rationalization, which is related to the second, may be described as a process of simplification, and I shall explain what I mean by this in Subsection (*b*).

(*a*) *The decline of ascription*

In Chapter I, I referred to Maine's generalization that social evolution has been marked by a development from Status to Contract. While he, like many others, was wrong to suppose that, in primitive society, '*all* relations of persons are summed up in the relations of Family', since residence, age, ritual status, and so on affect social relations in every society, there is a great deal of truth in his general point that, particularly as a result of the state and the influences of warfare and trade, kinship becomes a more subordinate principle of social relations. Of course, there are some societies, such as the East Cushitic and the Indo-European, where this process is well under way before the development of the state, and it would also be an absurd exaggeration to claim that the state destroys kin groups altogether.

There is no doubt that while the succession to kingship itself always (to my knowledge) retains an hereditary basis, the ties of kinship and the hereditary claims of descent groups to ministerial office become an increasing nuisance to rulers as the state increases in size and complexity. The growing number of administrative functions and heavier demands on their competence created by the problem of large states strain the resources of traditional descent systems, and rulers also discover that the elevation to high office of intelligent strangers, slaves, and others with no claims of birth provides them with able servants who are dependent on them alone. The progressive decline of the hereditary basis of office with the increase in political complexity has been clearly demonstrated by Tuden and Marshall (1972) on the basis of a cross-cultural study of 184 societies from Murdock's and White's (1969) standard world sample.

One of their most crucial variables defining 'political complexity' is that of 'levels of sovereignty', which must be discussed here:

> The symbols below indicate the level of effective sovereignty, defined as the highest level of indigenous political integration at which functionaries have and commonly exercise the power to enforce important decisions at subordinate levels in the political structure— notably to compel participation in warfare, to collect taxes or tribute, and/or to exact sanctions for major delicts. Unless at least one of these powers is found at a particular level, a lack of effective sovereignty is assumed for that level.

A   Absence of effective sovereignty at any level transcending that of the local community, i.e., a stateless society.

B   Effective sovereignty occurs at the first (but no higher) level of political integration above the local community, as in the case of a petty paramount chief ruling a district composed of a number of local communities.

C   Effective sovereignty occurs at the second (but no higher) level of political integration above the local community, as in the case of a small state comprising a number of administrative districts under subordinate functionaries.

D   Effective sovereignty is found at the third (or higher) level of political integration above the local community, as in the case of a large state divided into administrative provinces which are further subdivided into lesser administrative districts. (Tuden and Marshall 1972: 438)

The correlation between levels of sovereignty and the decline of the hereditary principle is shown in tables 26–8.

Table 26

Selection of Executives	Levels	
	B+C	D
Hereditary	20	10
Ruling family	13	11
Non-hereditary	9	18
	42	39

$\chi^2 = 10.86$ df = 2 $p = <.01$
Source: Tuden and Marshall 1972: 454.

Table 27

Selection of Subordinates	Levels		
	B	C	D
Hereditary	15	3	0
Lineage	2	2	8
Elected	3	2	5
Appointed	2	5	26
	22	12	39

$\chi^2 = 38.09$ df = 6 $p = <.001$
Source: Tuden and Marshall 1972: 456.

Furthermore, if we examine the relation between the basis for the selection of the executive and the selection of advisers, the correlation shown in Table 28 appears.

Table 28

Selection of Executive	Advisers	
	Relatives	Administrators
Hereditary	6	2
Ruling family	8	3
Non hereditary	0	15
	14	20

$\chi^2 = 18.8$ df = 2 $p = <.001$
Source: Tuden and Marshall 1972: 455.

Kinship is weakened by other processes in the emergence of the state, of which warfare is perhaps the most important. Probably the most significant effect of warfare is that the conquest of one society by another is likely to disrupt the relations between descent groups and their land. In Polynesia, for example, 'Victorious chiefs arbitrarily divided an island into divisions, placing over them loyal and friendly chiefs or warriors regardless of kinship affiliations' (Goldman 1970: 545). Warfare is also liable to produce large numbers of refugees, seeking asylum in neighbouring societies and so strengthening the power of the chief who protects them:

. . . in a Bantu or Hottentot tribe many and often most of the chief's subjects are of alien origin; and since those particular people (or their ancestors) had joined the group through conquest or immigration, they were from the beginning in a condition of special dependence upon him. We thus get the basis of a system in which his descent group may be not only politically dominant but may also constitute a separate class in the community. (Schapera 1956: 124)

Conversely, warfare even at the primitive level may lead to the taking of captives, and the number of these may rise to huge levels when warfare becomes an agency of state conquest: 'Throughout history, captivity in warfare has been one of the major means by which persons have been reduced to slavery' (Patterson 1982: 106), even though we should not assume that the fate of prisoners of war was automatic slavery: 'In many advanced pre-modern societies prisoners of war were incorporated into the victors' societies in a dependent status other than slavery' (ibid., 107). Whatever the status of prisoners of war, which has certainly varied, their influx into the society of the conquering state entailed their assimilation on the basis primarily of class rather than kinship. As armies become larger, recruitment must increasingly become separate from descent affiliation. In Southern and East Africa age was an important basis of military grouping before the emergence of the state, and as the state grows in size, this effect of military recruitment on descent groups can only become intensified. Victorious states may give land in conquered territory to their soldiers and this, too, disrupts the traditional, kin-based, system of land tenure.

Warfare organized for conquest is both socially more important and administratively more demanding than primitive warfare, and the selection of leaders on the basis of their ability therefore assumes major importance. The army is perhaps the earliest type of organization which can offer the chances of wealth and social importance to those of humble birth. The growing importance of war leaders may later be a challenge to the traditional type of leadership whose authority is genealogical and religious.

Conquest warfare, by its very nature, increases the probability that the victorious state will include among its subjects those of different cultural or ethnic origins. This may produce marked differences of status based on class, or help to produce a more generalized notion of 'citizenship', defined by birth or residence within a certain territory rather than by descent. The propensity for conquest to produce class differences of an ethnic nature is, of course, well known: the kingdom of Ankole in Uganda is a clear example of such a class society based upon the conquest of the agricultural Bairu by the pastoralist Nilo-Hamitic Bahima (Oberg 1940), as is Ruanda, where the three levels of society 'are formed by the pastoral Tusi, the agricultural Hutu, and the Twa, a people of pygmy type, who live by hunting and making pots' (Mair 1962: 135).

The south African data, especially for Bantu, provide several instances to support the view that conquest may result in the creation of social classes, one of which clearly dominates the rest. I have already referred to the special position of the Venda nobility. Their ancestors invaded the Transvaal from the north about three centuries ago, and subjugated the various more primitive peoples, mostly Sotho, whom they found already living there. The conquerors made themselves masters of the country and became an aristocracy, unassimilated to this day. Here lies the explanation of a notable feature of Venda social organization, namely the unique position of the ruling families and the exalted status of their chiefs. (Schapera 1956: 127–8)

Without major cultural or racial differences, however, this is much less likely to occur (Fortes and Evans-Pritchard 1940: 9–10; Schapera 1956: 132).

The general diminution in the importance of kinship and its relation to land is also closely related to the changing significance of territorial boundaries. Sir Henry Maine discerned that the rise of the state involved a major change in the importance of territory and kinship. For him, the basis of primitive society was the idea of common descent, and 'the idea that a number of persons should exercise political rights in common simply because they happened to live within the same topographical limits was utterly strange and monstrous to primitive antiquity' (Maine 1931: 108). Only with the emergence of the state, in his view, could membership of the same local area be the basis of social relations.

In fact, it is clear from many ethnographic sources that common residence involves distinct and specific rights and obligations at all levels of social evolution, and that all groups have some idea of a territory that belongs to them, and hence of geographic boundaries between their group and its neighbours. Despite these qualifications, however, Maine has nevertheless identified something very important about the way in which the significance of boundaries and territory changes when centralized government arises. In pre-state society, obligations and rights on the basis of kinship, marriage, age, exchange partnerships, and so on, transcend the local community and to this extent are independent of residence. Where one lives, and with whom, is therefore only one among a number of factors that govern one's ties and obligations. Group boundaries will be relevant in, say, the allocation of hunting or grazing rights, but in many other aspects of social relations such boundaries may have little importance. The rise of the state, however, involves a marked change in the significance of boundaries, and hence of territoriality in general, because the existence of a central government involves its ability to impose its authority on a specific range of individuals by coercive force, and corresponding obligations on a specific range of individuals to support the government by tribute, corvée labour, obedience to its officials, and so on. Viewed simply in terms of networks of relations, it is obvious that centralization of those relations around some focal point of authority necessarily implies that the network of relations must be sharply bounded, and in real terms this means geographically bounded. (A network of relations with no common focus need not, of course, be clearly bounded at all.) For these reasons, external boundaries become far more important than they are in pre-state societies.

Similarly, internal boundaries, too, change their significance when societies develop centralized government. From being defined simply by kinship or residence, they now become the expressions of an administrative hierarchy, and take on much more precise functions in relation to the purposes of the centralized bureaucracy. Fortes and Evans-Pritchard distinguish between the significance of territoriality in state societies (Group A, below) and in pre-state societies:

The difference is due to the dominance of an administrative and judicial apparatus in one type of system and its absence in the other. In the societies of Group A the administrative unit is a territorial unit; political rights and obligations are territorially delimited. A chief is the administrative and judicial head of a given territorial division, vested often with final economic and legal control over all the land within his boundaries. Everybody living within these boundaries is his subject, and the right to live in this area can be acquired only by accepting the obligations of a subject. The head of the state is a territorial ruler.

In the other group of societies there are no territorial units defined by an administrative system, but the territorial units are local communities the extent of which corresponds to the range of a particular set of lineage ties and the bonds of direct co-operation. Political office does not carry with it juridical rights over a particular, defined stretch of territory and its inhabitants. Membership of the local community, and the rights and duties that go with it, are acquired as a rule through genealogical ties, real or fictional. (Fortes and Evans-Pritchard 1940: 10–11)

Goldman draws similar conclusions from his study of the evolution of Polynesian society:

Strong central authority disturbs the segmentary order by imposing a territorial (district) organization that at first coexists with the segmented ordering of kindred, but then reduces the kindred organization to a smaller scale. Speaking more generally, we may describe political power as disruptive of kinship unity . . .

The substitution of a territorial system of subdivisions for one of kinship branching has long been regarded as a major divide in human history. Apart from introducing new structural arrangements of great importance, this change has introduced a parallel change in outlook—apart from the specific imagery implied by terminology—from that of a natural to a political order. Kin groups bud, branch, and unfold. Territorial groups are created by chiefs. They express human agency. In this expression they assert a radically new social idea. (Goldman 1970: 544–5)

As we have seen, the importance of age-grouping is even more severely reduced by the emergence of the state. While in some societies it seems that age-sets can be led by members of chiefly or royal lineages, age-grouping systems are more usually related to an egalitarian philosophy which is incompatible with hierarchical types of ranking based on bureaucratic principles or on social class. The basic grades of elder and warrior are also too general to be of much use in the allocation of tasks in an administrative hierarchy. The *category* of elderhood may indeed survive as a necessary qualification for high office, but the corporate functions of the elders must give way before the power and interests of centralized government, and can only survive in executive form at the level of local administration. Both age and kinship become steadily supplanted by social class, in fact.

While social inequality exists long before the state, it is well established that the emergence of the state always leads to very significant stratification.

Our data show that social stratification in early states was a fairly complex matter. Several social categories with differential access to material and other resources were generally to be found. We distinguished between two basic social strata, an upper and a lower one, and moreover discovered that in the majority of cases a middle stratum also existed. The upper stratum we took to comprise the sovereign's kin, holders of high offices and clan and lineage heads, and the priesthood. The middle stratum was composed of such categories as ministeriales and gentry. To the lower stratum belonged among others smallholders and tenants, and less frequently such categories as artisans, traders, servants and slaves. (Claessen 1978: 587–8)

Class stratification is obviously the result of many different factors: the development of genealogical and ritual inequality, differential access to centralized authority, warfare and conquest, the increase in trade and markets, and the growth of bureaucracy and the creation of many more administrative positions in the state. It is worth noting again, however, that at this stage of social evolution it is differential access to power that leads to differences in wealth, and not the other way round:

... in early states communal ownership [that is, by descent group] is still the most common form of control over land. We therefore believe that private ownership should not be regarded as the exclusive factor responsible for stratification ... The unequal access to resources therefore does not appear to be based on differences in the relation to control of the means of production but on different positions in the clan and lineage systems and in the socio-political organization of the early state. (Claessen 1978: 553–4)

And Claessen found 'no classes based on the control of the means of production—supposed to be a typical feature for societies with a mature state organization . . . A class struggle, or overt class antagonism, was not found to be characteristic of early states' (ibid., 588; see also R. Cohen 1978: 57).

Over time, the hierarchical ranking of social classes comes to replace the segmentary ordering of descent groups, but this change does not occur because it is functional for the society or even for the state. It is the result of a number of related tendencies in the emergence of the state, and must be explained in terms of the combined structural properties of institutions—of descent groups, of the nature of religious authority, warfare, trade, and increased societal size, not in terms of any adaptive or functional value. Indeed, far from being valuable for society, it can be argued that class stratification intensified oppression and social division. We have here, then, yet another instance of an institution which is extremely common, but which cannot be explained by its contribution to the efficiency or the survival of the societies in which it occurs. But a society ordered by a series of classes is obviously governed by a much more generalized type of classification than one based on kinship, and which can be extended to a social system of any size.

(b) Simplification

It is conventional to describe the evolutionary process as one from the simple to the complex, and while this usage is obviously justified, it can also be said that societies have only increased their regulative capacities, and the conceptual power of their collective representations, by successive and selective *simplifications*. This claim may appear paradoxical, so let us reflect for a moment on the connotations of 'simple', 'complex', and 'complicated'. 'Simple' has at least three distinct, if related, connotations: (1) 'consisting of one substance, ingredient or element, uncompounded'; (2) 'free from elaboration'; (3) 'easy to do or to understand'. The term 'complex' is defined as (1) 'comprehending various parts connected together', and equally (2) 'consisting of parts involved in various degrees of subordination'; and correspondingly we often find that it has a third connotation (3) 'difficult to do or understand'. 'Complex' is however sometimes used as if it were interchangeable with 'complicated', whose connotations are in fact rather different: (1) 'folded, wrapped or twisted together': (2) 'combined intimately with'; (3) 'mixed up with in an involved way'.

The conventional usage of 'simple' and 'complex' first of all overlooks the possibility that while societies with less elaboration of organizational structure than others may indeed be less *complex*, they may also be more *complicated*, in the sense that social relations may be less differentiated, categorized, and orderly and hence more 'mixed up' and 'involved'. Secondly, it overlooks the possibility that the need for order on the part of individuals is proportional to the *number, diversity, unfamiliarity*, and *rate of change* of the materials on which they have to impose order; and thirdly, that it is therefore possible to order small, stable, homogeneous groups in 'complicated' ways that are impossible in groups of significantly greater number, diversity, rate of change, and resulting unfamiliarity. Finally, it may be noted that the conscious imposition of order is very difficult to achieve, and also that when we do not have to communicate a system of classification at all widely it tends to be *ad hoc*, idiosyncratic, and unanalytic. So, if what we are ordering is familiar to us and small in scale—our desk, our library, our kitchen—we find it easy to devise some personal system of order, though a stranger is likely to have considerable difficulty in following it. And when a limited number of individuals are interacting on a long-term basis they, too, can develop forms of social and cultural order that are easy for *them* to understand, on the basis of familiarity. In such circumstances human beings take the easy way out and tend to develop idiosyncratic, *ad hoc*, and unsystematic orderings because these come readiest to mind, especially when those concerned are neither literate nor have any formal schooling.

But these forms of classification are inherently difficult for a stranger to understand, and are also inappropriate when large numbers of diverse and unfamiliar entities have to be classified; in such cases complicated classification is inadequate and there must be a search for some more overtly systematic and hence *generalizable* basis of classification. As we all know, however, this is a demanding intellectual task and difficult to accomplish.

The initial stages of all human endeavours are usually marked by idiosyncratic [complication], irregularity, and lack of system, while simplicity (in at least one important sense of so difficult a concept) is the product of art and conscious reflection, in which order and clarity of design are imposed only with great effort and deliberation after prolonged trial and error. In these respects it is primitive society that is [complicated] and industrial society that is simple, always striving to axiomatize its values and institutions more clearly and consistently. (Hallpike 1979: vi)

Yet, the reader might respond, it seems obviously absurd to claim that modern industrial societies are really 'simple' by comparison with primitive societies: is it actually simpler to have a house built in Canada than in the mountains of New Guinea, for example? I am not, of course, trying to deny such obvious truths. In terms of 'social clockwork' our type of society clearly has more elaborate procedures, institutional forms, and rules and regulations than do primitive societies. But what I am saying is that there are actually two complementary processes at work here and that the apparent paradox can be resolved by distinguishing between the complex and the complicated. In small-scale, face-to-face societies it is 'easier' to develop what are actually more complicated forms of association and classification, but with the growth of size of society, and range of technology and culture, it is necessary for individuals to develop more generalizable forms of order that can transcend local idiosyncracies and embrace larger numbers and more diverse types of people: that is, to 'simplify' in the classificatory sense. But this is difficult, or 'complex', and will also involve an increasing number of categories, and elaboration (again, 'complex').

'Simplification', in this basic sense, is therefore a cognitive activity that is common not only to science, religion, and philosophy, but to social organization as well, since all respond to an increase in the number, diversity, unfamiliarity, and rate of change of entities that are encountered. It is, in short, a regulative problem-solving activity, and the classification of people and social relations involves some of the same cognitive problems as any other form of conceptual ordering of reality.

These arguments are well illustrated by two contrasting societies, the Tauade and the Konso. In Tauade society there are permanent autonomous groups of about 200 persons living within well-defined boundaries which I call 'tribes' (though individual members display considerable inter-tribal mobility). The tribe is composed of a number of clans, each descended from different immigrant groups which came to live on the tribal land at varying dates. Actual residential groups are the hamlets, which are impermanent collections of dwellings with at most 40–50 inhabitants; the membership of these hamlets is constantly changing, and the hamlets themselves only last for a few years before abandonment. The membership of hamlets is not based on kinship except for that between fathers and sons or groups of two or three brothers. Cognates, affines, and friends are all to be found in the same hamlet, and people may have houses in more than one hamlet simultaneously. Kinship itself is not seen as a separate jural principle and the various terms for 'kinsman' also mean 'friend'. Relations of 'blood' include cognates as well as agnates and one can get no closer to the notion of 'we are members of one tribe' than 'we share pandanus trees';

The bonds which they recognize are those of blood; upbringing in the same family or hamlet; possession of rights of use of land and pandanus trees; co-operation in gardening; common residence and the mutual support in disputes which that implies; the bonds between men created in the men's house; and the inheritance of influence by sons from their fathers. (Hallpike 1977*b*: 84)

None of these bonds, however, is distinguished in any categorical manner and the result is a mass of individual relationships in terms of descent, friendship, garden co-operation, membership of the same men's house, gift exchange, and so on, producing an amorphous and extremely complicated society with no large or stable groupings, the tribes themselves having very little internal unity. Not surprisingly it was also extremely difficult to understand the working of this society from the ethnographer's point of view.

In the case of the Konso of Ethiopia we have a very different situation, which I shall briefly review again. In this society the basic residential group is the autonomous walled town, with 500–3,000 inhabitants, average 1,500. The towns are divided into wards, with clear boundaries and rules of behaviour and legal obligations for ward members. Descent is organized by patrilineage, with a lineage head, and lineage members again have clear duties and obligations to one another distinct from those of ward members. Work co-operation is organized by a further type of association, the working party, which is a voluntary association with an elected leader. This is a named group with a fairly permanent membership. Differences of age, or rather generational seniority, are organized into an elaborate system of grades and sets. Political authority is based on elected ward councils and town councils; in these, elders exercise conciliar and ritual authority, while armed force is the prerogative of the warrior grade, acting as a police force under the direction of the elders. Lineage heads act as priests and mediators with respect to their lineages, and as spokesmen for their lineage members in court cases, while certain regional priests act as mediators in warfare between towns. Within towns a body of priests act as mediators in disputes between wards. There is also a hereditary class of craftsmen.

This specialization of social relationships into residence, descent, work co-operation, crafts, armed force, conciliar authority, mediatory functions, and generational seniority represents an enormous simplification by comparison with the Tauade in which all these different functions are intermingled, and allows the Konso to construct an extremely orderly society that can co-ordinate the relations of very much larger groups than can the Tauade.

But again, in terms of political organization, precisely because it is acephalous, Konso society is very complicated. There are the regional priests who act as mediators in warfare between the towns, but whose authority is essentially ritual. Within the towns are the councils, ideally comprising the elders, who have both ritual status as the deputies of God, but who also take political decisions and decide court cases, with the executive functions being carried out by the warriors. But in the case of fighting between the wards it is the priests, rather than the elders, who act as mediators. Sacred authority is thus divided between regional priests, lineage priests, and elders, while secular authority is an ambiguous mixture of the functions of the elders and the warriors.

It is clear, then, that by isolating political authority from other social relations, and by centralizing it, a whole new range of organizational possibilities and problems is created, permitting an elaborate development which is impossible when political authority is mixed up with other social relations, such as kinship or generational seniority. Monarchical rule, by centralizing political authority in a single office, is in fact a drastic simplification by comparison with the complicated nature of political authority in acephalous societies.

The principle of simplification as the basis of elaboration is an exceedingly general one in social and cultural evolution. Thus, as Flannery (1972: 399) observes, the change from a hunter-gatherer economy, in which a large and diverse number of floral and faunal species are utilized, to agriculture or pastoralism involves a drastic ecological simplification, as does industrial mass production by contrast with hand craftsmanship. The emergence of money is another instance: the crucial point is not whether a society has an official coinage, but the extent to which goods and services are mutually convertible by reference to some single standard of value. Writing is evidently a major simplification of speech sounds: syllabaries are simplifications of logographic scripts, and alphabets, in turn, are simplifications of syllabaries, and the alphabet itself has served increasingly important classificatory functions in European culture. Measurement and standardization are the basis of quantification in a wide variety of fields and represent one of the major simplifications of culture, as does the movement from the complicated and qualitative to the quantitative and analytic which is characteristic of the natural sciences in general. Again, bureaucracy and centralized administration depend on simplification to master the ever increasing information load that results from the emergence of the state. The increasing complexity and heterogeneity of society, especially when accompanied by commercialism and private contracts generates new types of disputes, and this gives rise to jurisprudence and the codification of law.

The origin of natural law in Roman jurisprudence

. . . was the increasing residence at Rome of merchants and other foreigners, who were not citizens and therefore not subject to Roman law, and who wished to be judged by their own laws. The best that the Roman jurisconsults could do was to take a kind of lowest common denominator of the usages of all known peoples, and thus attempt to codify what would seem nearest to justice to the greatest number of people. (J. Needham 1956: 520)

And in the case of many religions we find that general ethical principles come to supplant the minutiae of ritual and that the presence of different religions in the same society is a stimulus to the credal formulation of belief.

7. The role of the environment and technology in evolution

We have seen that a number of structural properties of institutions and beliefs can, in the appropriate circumstances, work together to produce the centralization of political authority with the monopoly of armed force, and that this in turn has far-reaching consèquences for society as a whole.

The 'appropriate circumstances' include the ways in which people use their physical environment. Population density and therefore the potential size of societies, types of property, permanence of settlement, trade and markets, economic surplus, the division of labour, communications, weapons, and large-scale public works may, in different degrees, be important factors in the evolutionary process, and for this reason no account of social evolution can leave the various modes of production out of account.

One may agree with the Marxist[14] proposition that 'The necessary condition for any society is that men should associate to produce their material means of subsistence. Without this collective action of men on nature, there is no human life, it constitutes the very essential of the human mode of life' (Cornforth 1976: 18). But the conclusion which Cornforth draws is invalid: 'The process of social production is, therefore, *the primary process of all social life* [*my emphasis*]. It is "primary" in this precise sense: that social life begins with it, that it is present continuously throughout all social life, and that no other activity or social relation can occur unless this primary activity, this primary social relation, sustains it' (ibid., 18).

---

[14] It will have become clear in the course of this book that I do not regard the classical Marxist theory of social evolution (e.g. Engels 1884; Cornforth 1976; Kuusinen (ed.) 1961) as of any particular relevance today. While Marx has certainly had an important general influence on the social sciences, his predictions on the future of society have been comprehensively refuted by events, and *The Origin of the Family, Private Property and the State* is an entirely obsolete account of social evolution. This is not surprising, since Marx and Engels developed their ideas on the basis of European history alone, during an unprecedented epoch and when anthropological knowledge was meagre in the extreme. Indeed, many of the ideas in *The Origin of The Family* are of Greek and Roman origin and the anthropological material is derived from a single source—Morgan 1877. Marxism was not even

One source of Cornforth's mistake lies in the belief that in order to produce the necessities of life, men are obliged to co-operate in highly *specific* ways. Modern industrial production certainly requires far more specific types of social relations than does shifting agriculture, but it should not be necessary to labour the point, established at length in Chapter IV, that primitive technologies are compatible with a very wide range of social organization. In this sense the mode of production does not determine the social relations that are involved with any degree of precision.

The second source of his mistake is to ignore the fact that the modes of production themselves depend on the types of social organization, beliefs, and knowledge that are available. It is precisely because tools do not, like the sorcerer's broom, go to work by themselves but have to be used by people in a social context that this social context is just as important as the tools in the development of technology. Large-scale hydraulic projects may enhance the power of governments, but they can only do so on the basis of some pre-existing authority. Industrial modes of production have certainly had profound social consequences, but factories did not build themselves. They could only come into existence in the first place because British society had previously developed in certain ways. The effects of technology too, will depend on the social context in which it occurs. Until the seventeenth century, Chinese technology was in many respects hundreds of years in advance of that in Western Europe (see e.g. Singer 1956: 770–1), but it produced no capitalism: and printing, gunpowder, and the stirrup, for example, had very different results in China from those which they produced in Europe. Modes of production themselves express the totality of each society's history, and to believe that they have a privileged position in determining its development is as absurd as believing that the hands could have built the body of which they are part: clearly, the hands have themselves evolved as an integral part of the body, and are in no sense primary, even if they do provide it with the necessities of life.

intended to be an objective scientific enquiry but to provide intellectual encouragement for the revolutionary destruction of the capitalist system. The last hundred years have seen the greatest expansion of knowledge in human history, and to suppose that when all the other sciences have been changed out of recognition it was somehow possible for Marx alone to have been right about all essentials is mere superstition. Subsequent attempts to revise Marxism to fit the enormous mass of new historical and ethnographic facts have left it so confused and contradictory that any attempt to refute it would be pointless.

The very adoption of a particular mode of production will therefore depend on the nature of each society: 'Between the desires and needs of man and everything in nature that can be utilized by him, beliefs, ideas, and customs interpose' (Febvre 1925: 167). So, for example, many groups of Australian Aborigines could have adopted agriculture:

No less than eleven species used for food in Australia are domesticated to some degree in Southeast Asia, and of these, eight were used for food there also. These eight include a species of yam, another tuber, Polynesian arrowroot, and several important fruits. It is also untrue that Australian Aborigines were so isolated from the rest of the world that they were never brought into contact with neolithic societies . . . we cannot ignore the long history of juxtaposition of Aborigines with partly agricultural economies at Torres Strait and the implications of Papuan influences in the cultures of the Cape York tribes. Indeed there is a plant growing wild in rainforest regions in that area, traditionally used by local Aborigines for food, that may mark the intrusion, and rejection, of the neolithic in Australia. This is taro, *Colocasia esculenta*, an important crop in agricultural economies of New Guinea and the Pacific, which the botanical evidence suggests is indigenous to regions much further west, whence it must have been brought by man. Neither is it want of the requisite technology that has prevented Aborigines becoming neolithic. The tool kit of the most sophisticated New Guinea agriculturalists is very simple: axes and/or adzes, traditionally of ground stone, for clearing bush, fire for burning it and providing the fertilizing ash, digging sticks of various forms for working ground, planting, weeding and harvesting, and human hands. The Aborigines had all these, or their equivalents, and had done so for many thousands of years on the archaeological evidence. More importantly they possessed the kind of knowledge of the plant world underlying the very rationale of agriculture. It is well recorded that Arnhem Landers during harvesting of wild yams leave the top of the tuber still attached to its vine intact in the ground, saying in explanation that the yam will grow again, thus allowing another harvest. Rhys Jones has recently described how the discard of wild fruit seeds at camping sites in Arnhem Land is responsible for, and well known by the Aborigines to be responsible for, the spread of food plants. Aborigines just do not choose to apply this knowledge in the way specified by social evolutionary theory. (Golson 1977: 8–9)

Our knowledge of the history of technology and of the emergence of the state has grown enormously since the time of Marx and Engels and the other nineteenth-century evolutionists, and their belief that changes in the mode of production have always initiated major changes in social organization is not well supported by the facts:

There is no evidence that the formation of early state systems follows in any invariant way the development of improved technology. Although improved technologies emerge, or are often associated with centralized government, few of these if any consistently appear as predictors, enablers, or triggering devices for the onset of early statehood . . .

Basic tools, for production in agriculture and craft work, show no systematic improvement before and immediately after state formation. The plow and other forms of machinery do not universally either precede or necessarily follow state formation. On the other hand the specialization occasioned by state formation especially in the urban centres allows for concentrated use of tools for specific purposes. This concentration, in which not everyone uses a similar set of tools, produces the enabling social basis for technological development. Society first, however, has to be organized economically, and politically so that such specialists are encouraged and supported. (R. Cohen 1978: 61)

While it is undoubtedly true that some environments, such as river valleys, are more propitious for the formation of states than others, such as rain forests or small islands, and that this is one of the reasons why the state has appeared in some places before others, the environment is only *one* factor among many:

. . . if we map pre-colonial state development, as Beals and Kelso (1975: 572) have done, there is very little correlation with environmental features except a marked lack of state development in extreme climate zones, and for North America in general. The distribution seems to argue for six separate regions of state development: (1) a continuous band across Europe, North Africa and the Nile Valley, the Far East and South Asia including India, China, and Japan; (2) a middle American development including both Mexico and Yucatan; (3) a south American development in the high Andes; (4) a West African zone; (5) an East African zone in the lake region and the Ethiopian highlands; and (6) a Polynesian zone . . . It is hard to imagine what such widespread regions have in common geographically that could have stimulated state formation. (R. Cohen 1978: 38–9)

It is therefore obvious that not only can men accommodate to a particular environment in a number of possible ways but, much more fundamentally, this process of accommodation also involves the assimilation of the environment into each society in ways dependent on the prior social and cultural structure of that society, because what the environment *is* depends on how we define it, and on our social capacities for manipulating it. Modes of production, therefore, depend not only on the environment, but on the social organization, values, beliefs, and cognitive abilities of the particular groups of people who are interacting with it. This in no way denies the fundamental importance of man's uses of his environment in understanding social evolution, for once adopted, certain uses of the environment open up remarkable possibilities[15] for change in organization that are often irreversible. As a result, some societies learn to exploit these opportunities more effectively than others, but the very process of exploitation will itself produce further consequences within each society. So, many societies have exploited the possibilities of domesticating plants and animals; this, in turn, has allowed larger numbers of people to occupy a given area of land. Some societies have used these populations to produce more elaborate types of social organization, while others have not.

We should therefore regard the environment not so much as a set of obstacles or determinants, still less as the primary selective agency in the Darwinian manner, but as a set of opportunities to be exploited, the kinds of exploitation themselves depending on social organization and ideology.

---

[15] This view of man's relations with his environment (often referred to as 'possibilism') is, of course, by no means new and was lucidly defended by, among others, Febvre 1925 and Forde 1934. It has recently been criticized by R. F. Ellen who presents possibilism in essentially negative terms, e.g., 'The environment set limits but did not determine' (Ellen 1982: 21), and 'The notion of "limiting factor" is central to the possibilist conception of human ecological relations' (ibid., 32). With this conception of possibilism it is then easy to argue that it is not a true alternative to determinism at all since, where specific goals or priorities exist, the setting of limits by the environment also determines final outcomes (ibid., 50). So, for example, 'If we accept that pastoralist subsistence is a constant, then it makes perfect logical sense to say that the movement to drier zones is *determined* by tsetse distribution, under given conditions' (ibid., 50). All this means is that, having chosen an end, we are always constrained to some extent in our choice of means! Obviously, a society of pastoralists who wish to keep their cattle are no more likely to take them into tsetse-fly country than they are to drive them into the sea, and in this quite trivial sense constraints are indeed determinants. But we may also ask the more basic questions, 'Why did their ancestors take up pastoralism in the first place, and why do they continue the practice, and what can we predict about their society and religion?' Ellen has in fact mistaken the essential point of possibilism, which is *not* the notion of 'limiting factor' at all but rather, as the very name of 'possibilism' implies, the creative use of the various possibilities of nature, and of man as the active agent and chooser.

VI

Core Principles

1. The nature of core principles[1]

IN Chapter V we established that a number of very common institutions and beliefs have certain structural properties which reinforce one another. As a result, in suitable conditions, the state will develop, but these institutions and beliefs also have certain properties that lead to political fission rather than to the centralization of authority. The evolutionary process must therefore depend on the nature of each society, and on its particular blend of institutions and beliefs. It was for this reason that so much attention was given to the distinctive characteristics of the state of Jimma, which were shown to derive from certain basic or core principles of East Cushitic society. In one sense the distinction being made here resembles that between general and specific evolution, but it must be emphasized that Sahlins and Service discuss specific evolution in terms of the diversity created by adaptation to local conditions (Sahlins and Service 1960: 12–44). This is a very different approach from the one that will be developed in this chapter, which is concerned with the process by which the core principles of each society affect its evolutionary development.

There are many types of system in which certain levels of organization are more resistant to change or disruption than others, and exercise a general regulatory influence. In psychology it is well known that certain basic aspects of personality, such as introversion/extroversion, or patterns of behaviour acquired in

---

[1] Though Steward uses the expression 'cultural core', he does so in a very different sense from mine. In his theory the cultural core refers to ' . . . the constellation of features which are most closely related to subsistence activities and economic arrangements. The core includes such social, political, and religious patterns as are empirically determined to be closely connected with these arrangements' (Steward 1955: 37). The sort of features he has in mind are monarchy, priestly castes, conquest warfare, and so on. His definition of 'core' is therefore based on a materialist theory of society, and is also concerned with very specific social institutions, whereas mine is concerned with more general structural principles that are not assumed to have any functional dependence on the mode of subsistence.

early childhood, are highly persistent throughout life (see e.g. Keesing and Keesing 1971: 353–4). A society is not an organism, but in the case of language it is well established that the rules of grammar change less easily than the lexicon, and that basic grammatical rules change less easily than those of a superficial kind (R. D. King 1969: 142–3, 148). The same is true of explicit knowledge structures such as scientific theories or disciplines, in all of which there are certain fundamental assumptions that are highly resistant to change. A good example is the concept of natural selection in Darwinian theory, which has proved itself quite capable of surviving major changes in biological knowledge at lower levels of generality, such as the mechanisms of heredity and, indeed, of governing the interpretations of this new knowledge. Why should so many systems be like this?

In the first place, every kind of system has certain aspects or variables that are of more importance than others. In the previous chapter we saw that for all societies descent, relative age, the relations between the sexes, rules of residence, authority and leadership, ritual status, and property rights, for example, are matters on which *some* rules and categories are developed, even though for primitive society there is great latitude in those that are available and can be combined together. Secondly, there will be *some* consistency in the rules and categories as they apply to these different aspects of organization. It is unlikely, for example, that a society which adopts strict patrilineal descent as the basis of residence and property rights will entirely ignore this principle in its criteria of ritual status or authority. (On the other hand, we should not exaggerate the consistency of basic social principles: we should remember, for example, the conflict between egalitarian and inegalitarian aspects of East Cushitic society.) Thirdly, some rules and categories are incompatible with others—lineality versus cognation as constituent principles of the same descent system, for example, or status ranking with egalitarianism. Fourthly, some rules and categories are of great generality and can subsume many different areas of social life and values—premises of equality versus inequality, or an approval or rejection of competition as acceptable behaviour. Finally, in so far as evolution involves the progressive elucidation and abstraction of more and more principles of organization which are given specialized functions (see above, Chapter V), there also has to be some process of selection from among these principles, because only a certain number of structural options can be realized in any particular society (or any other system).

For these reasons we can expect to find that the organization of every society will be based on certain rules and categories of a general nature, and that these will display a fair degree of internal consistency. All this does not occur because it is mysteriously and wonderfully 'good for society', but merely because any group of people who associate together permanently will seek to establish certain rules, categories, and priorities as the basis of co-operation, and because the human mind is particularly adept at seeking pattern and form. If we could not order specific information in terms of general principles we could never acquire culture or language or any organized knowledge at all.

So far, I have been discussing the principles of social organization, but as we established in the previous chapter these cannot be clearly separated from the way in which we order our total environment, from our world-view as a whole. Societies are systems, and individuals are organisms in pursuit of life, and for both these reasons general cosmological categories are likely to have great relevance to society as well. Social as well as natural processes may by cyclical, or they may ebb and flow, or alternate, or build up to a climax, or grow and decay; the cosmos and society may both be conceived as an organic, harmonious unity, or as a number of discrete parts in perpetual strife; order and disorder, weakness and strength, activity and passivity, creation and destruction, are concepts of such general import that they are relevant to all aspects of experience, not just the social. The Chinese concepts of yin and yang are good examples of the unity of natural and social categories. A society's core principles are therefore part of a total world-view, and not purely confined to the forms of social organization. (For this reason the much debated question of whether beliefs determine social structure or vice versa seems to me an unreal issue, certainly as far as primitive societies and early states are concerned.)

The rules and categories that make up the core principles of a society will not, of course, be restricted to cosmological principles of this type, but will also be expressed in such institutional forms as divine kingship, schemes of social classes, legal systems, and types of kinship, and also in such cultural values as paternalism, the glorification of war and competition, and individualism.

We saw in Chapter II that any attempt to establish some social analogue of the genotype/phenotype distinction based on the idea that genotype = information, phenotype = social reality must be entirely on the wrong track. But there is one common attribute of organisms and societies that is highly significant and often overlooked in this connection: both have means of maintaining existing design features and of adapting to change, so that the phylogenies of species and the histories of particular cultural traditions both display remarkable continuities despite a multitude of local variations. It is here, in the core principles of society, if anywhere, that the true analogue of the genotype/phenotype distinction is really to be found. The core principles are also the closest we are likely to come to any satisfactory idea of an 'infrastructure'. Because there is a hierarchical gradation in social systems from the most conservative and general levels of order to the most flexible and localized, the result is a permanent process of interaction between the flexible, change-inducing aspects of social systems, and the conservative, structure-maintaining. The lower-level processes of society, at which people apply the core principles and test alternative solutions, will normally be the major potential area of change. The core will interact with this level in a regulative manner, 'trying' to assimilate such changes into the enduring social structure through, for example, ritual, law, and collective representations.

There may, for example, be lower-level shifts of definition to accommodate change. Thus, according to Adkins (1960), in Ancient Greek society a good (*agathos*) man was a successful man, and in Homeric times this meant being a redoubtable warrior, rich, generous, and a capable protector of dependants; while in the society of the city-state success was attained by social abilities of a very different sort. Thus a 'good' man in one era behaved differently from a 'good' man in another, but the basic criterion of 'good' remains the same, i.e. success, rather than, for example, obedience to the will of God, or concern for one's neighbour. But core principles themselves may contain ambiguities and inconsistencies, as we saw in the case of East Cushitic society, and these may provide the basis for much more fundamental change, especially when the state develops. Thus we find Christianity used as the justification for the divine right of kings at one extreme, and as the basis for opposition to all class distinctions in the name of equality at the other. Evidently, if we think in terms of God the Father and Creator, hierarchical forms of government are easily justifiable as the earthly expression of the heavenly order, but if we think in terms of God the Son, and of the teachings of Christ and the brotherhood of man, then egalitarianism is equally well justified. It is therefore quite possible for the core principles to change their emphasis at different levels, and for ambiguities within them to be developed in new ways. They are part of a dynamic process, and it would be quite wrong to think of them as rigidly established for all time.

These principles are not, of course, developed out of thin air but are the collective and creative interpretation of experience; nor are they autonomous causal agencies since they simply define natural and social reality for the efficient causal agencies—individuals. They are however a great deal more than the epiphenomena of economic and social organization, since it is as a result of the core principles that many aspects of economy and social organization develop in the first place. I should therefore like to make it absolutely clear that I do not claim that the core principles are the autonomous and omnipotent factors governing the development of each society. This would only replace an adaptationist exaggeration by one of a different kind. Each society will evolve, or not evolve, as the result of an *interaction* between the opportunities provided by the environment (both natural and social) as these are interpreted in accordance with the core principles. In this interactive process, some core principles will be highly favourable to evolutionary advance, and others will not. So, for example, it seems highly unlikely that most New Guinea societies could ever have developed centralized political authority because there is no conception of unilineal descent and no other basis either on which the institutions of political authority could develop. Most East Cushitic societies have tended to stop short of centralized authority because of their clear separation of sacred and secular authority and the lack of inherited authority, quite apart from the fact that they were not for the most part involved in prolonged conquest relations with other peoples. But when, as in the case of Jimma, a centralized state did evolve, many of its characteristics are attributable to the core principles of East Cushitic society.

Since the core principles of societies are so persistent, tracing their distant origins must be extremely difficult, the more so because primitive societies have a wide latitude of organization. Without lapsing into pseudo-historical speculation, however, it does seem reasonable to infer that any small-scale society is particularly liable to the idiosyncracies and peculiarities of a few individuals or events—the 'founder principle'. This is very noticeable in small organizations in our own society, such as colleges, university departments, and business firms, whose distinctive features can often be traced to specific events and people. Once these organizational features have been established, however, they may be perfectly viable and survive indefinitely, even in organizations of much larger scale.

The evidence that societies have core principles is very substantial. Cross-culturally, we constantly find that groups of societies with common origins (as shown particularly in membership of the same language family) share many basic features of organization and world-view that cannot be explained on adaptive or functional grounds. Lewis and I have shown this for East Cushitic society; I have also elucidated some core principles of New Guinea society by comparison with East Cushitic society (Hallpike 1974*b*, 1977*b*); Maybury-Lewis (1967, 1979) and his associates have shown it for the Gê-speaking peoples of Brazil; and Goldman (1970) has shown it for Polynesian society, and demonstrated how a few core principles directed Polynesian evolution over many centuries. We shall also see that Dumézil has done the same for certain aspects of Indo-European society. At a much more specific level, Murdock, Wilson, and Frederick (1978), in a cross-cultural study of theories of illness, for example, found that

. . . the prevalent theories of illness tend strongly to remain constant among the societies belonging to any particular linguistic family. This is notably true of some of the largest groupings of linguistically cognate peoples in the world: (1) the speakers of Malayo-Polynesian, who dominate the insular Pacific but also extend into continental southeast Asia; (2) the speakers of Indo-European, who predominate in Europe but extend eastward into India; and (3) the speakers of Afro-Asiatic or Hamito-Semitic, who dominate the Near East and North Africa but whose Chadic and Cushitic branches penetrate southward deep into Negro territory. (Murdock, Wilson and Frederick 1978: 459)

In the remainder of this chapter I propose to demonstrate the validity of the idea of core principles of society by taking two examples—Chinese and Indo-European—and showing that while on one hand their general evolutionary development conforms to the structural principles established in Chapter V, the specific characteristics of this process have been very different in each case, partly because it has been regulated to a considerable extent by different core principles, which have endured for several *thousand* years. I have chosen these two cases because we can trace their development through written records and archaeological evidence over a much longer period than is possible for, say, New Guinean, East Cushitic, or Polynesian society. It must be emphasized that I have myself no expert knowledge of either Chinese or Indo-European studies, and that I have simply tried to use the best available scholarship of those who are specialists in these fields.

2. Chinese society

This section will trace the general development of Chinese society and state from the Shang (or Yin) dynasty c.1800 BC to the establishment of the Han dynasty (206 BC). The Shang is the first period of Chinese history for whose social institutions and religious beliefs there is substantial evidence (from archaeology and from inscriptions on oracle bones and bronzes), while the Han dynasty is generally agreed to mark the firm establishment of Chinese government on those classical Confucian principles which survived without major change until the present century.

The survey of so long a period, and of a society whose copious written records are but one aspect of an extraordinarily rich and subtle culture, must necessarily be of a very general nature. I have nevertheless been struck by the clarity with which the basic features of the Chinese world-view and social institutions can be discerned, and the more or less unanimous agreement upon them by the leading authorities, and by their extraordinary persistence through major social change. We find in Chinese history many typical features of general evolution: the legitimation of the early kings by descent and religion; the gradual demotion of kinship to a secondary place in social organization, which accompanied the strengthening of centralized government and bureaucracy; the enormous importance of warfare, especially in the creation of the Empire; the emergence of trade, coinage, and merchants; the rise and decay of feudal government of a type comparable in some respects to medieval Europe; and, of course, the development of administration by a professional bureaucracy. (In a previous chapter we also noted the increasing importance of large-scale irrigation and hydraulic works, especially in the later part of our period, as a very important factor in the intensification of the power of the state.)

But these typical evolutionary developments have been given a unique direction by the enduring core principles, which produced by Han times a society with a non-theistic religion and with no organized priesthood distinct from the secular authorities; a highly moralistic, paternal conception of the ideal relationship between government and people; a civilian bureaucracy chosen by merit through examination (more than one and a half millennia before this appeared in Europe); a marked lack of esteem for warfare and military glory; a legal system in which administrative and penal law were greatly elaborated by comparison with civil law; and a merchant class which, despite its great wealth, enjoyed neither prestige nor any legal autonomy that might have led to the emergence of capitalism.

(a) The social and religious institutions of the Shang state

The Shang state, which seems to have extended over the northern half of modern Honan, the southern half of Hopei, western Shantung, northern Anhwei, and north-west Kiangsu (Chang 1980: 252), had a highly specialized economy that included the manufacture of bronze, and a sophisticated art and system of writing. The ruler was the king, and segmentary patrilineal descent groups were of fundamental importance at all levels of society. The royal clan was Tzu, mythologically descended from a divine black bird (Chang 1976: 53); inheritance of the royal office was not from father to son, but seems to have passed to members of other lineages of the royal clan of the same generation before descending to the next generation (Chang 1980: 178–83). There were other clans of high status with whom the royal clan exchanged women, and also 'clans that were the *de facto* rulers of settlements and tribes within the state that were not under the direct rule of the Tzu princes' (Chang 1976: 54).

The basic unit of administration was the walled town, *yi*, of which there were at least 1,000 (Chang 1980: 210), and these were built on the king's orders by a relative or official, who was given the land and the necessary people, and also a new name, *shih*, which was also that of the town as well. The people were organized into *tsu*, kin groups of a hundred households, which also had an essential military and agricultural function, since each household was required to supply one soldier. While the meanings of kin terms from this period are very obscure, it seems, as the words *tsu* and *shih* indicate, that political and military organization were to a considerable degree amalgamated with descent-group organization, and with residence, so that the cities and towns were the seats of kin groups at the local level:

As lineages were hierarchically organized across the state, so were the various cities, towns, and local settlements . . . Significantly, in the Shang oracle records we often see that identical names were used for a local settlement, a lineage that occupied it, and individual members of the lineage or of the settlement. (Chang 1976: 54)

The large patrilineal descent group, within which are many gradations of social status and wealth, has retained, together with ancestor worship and the ideal of filial piety, a position of great importance in the lives of the ordinary Chinese people until the present day. It has also had great influence on moral and legal ideas. As we shall see, lineal descent groups have been of much less importance in Indo-European society.

The ruler of a town also had religious responsibilities, and was given ritual paraphernalia and regalia befitting his new political status and that of his town (Chang 1980: 161). The royal capital was larger than the other cities, but organized in essentially the same way.

It seems, therefore, that while the relations between the king and subordinate rulers were primarily expressed in the idiom of kinship and affinity, it is not known to what extent officials (of whom there were many) were recruited on the basis of kinship. Many were granted titles to walled towns and land and may have had considerable local autonomy (ibid., 189).

On the basis of sheer probability, it must be admitted that it would undoubtedly have been difficult for the Shang King to have maintained close and constant supervision of areas distant from the capital, so that local officials must necessarily have had a considerable measure of discretion. But did this extend so far that they enjoyed limited sovereignty and may properly be called vassals? We simply cannot tell. (Creel 1970: 33–4)

What does seem clear is that *ministers had a very high status*, and

Creel notes that 'The degree to which achievements are not credited to the ruler alone but to his ministers' seems to be a political tradition detectable as early as the Shang. 'A document written only a few years after the end of the dynasty names six ministers who, it says, assisted Shang kings, "protecting and directing their rulers" ' (Creel 1970: 37). 'This afforded an important precedent for the position that came to be afforded to the scholar-official in later China. And this Shang tradition, known and discussed at the beginning of Chou, provided an unusual climate for the later development of political ideas and institutions in China' (ibid., 40).

There were many officials in the Shang state (Chang counts more than 20 titles), including ministers, generals, and archivists, whose actual division of functions is far from clear, but 'the most important categories of officials in so far as our available data are concerned are the diviner, *p'u*, and the inquirer' (Chang 1980: 192). To explain the status of the diviners, we must understand the nature of Shang religion:

Shang religion was inextricably involved in the genesis and legitimation of the Shang state. It was believed that Ti, the high god, conferred fruitful harvest and divine assistance in battle, that the king's ancestors were able to intercede with Ti, and that the king could communicate with his ancestors. Worship of the Shang ancestors, therefore, provided powerful psychological and ideological support for the political dominance of the Shang kings. The king's ability to determine through divination, and influence through prayer and sacrifice, the will of the ancestral spirits legitimized the concentration of political power in his person. All power emanated from the theocrat because he was the channel, 'the one man', who could appeal for the ancestral blessings, or dissipate the ancestral curses, which affected the commonality. It was the king who made fruitful harvest and victories possible by the sacrifices he offered, the rituals he performed, and the divinations he made. If, as seems likely, the divinations involved some degree of magic making, of spell casting, the king's ability to actually create a good harvest or a victory by divining about it rendered him still more potent politically. (Keightley 1978: 212–13)

The general character of religion and ritual under the Shang is of the greatest importance for an understanding of the subsequent evolution of Chinese society, and we must therefore consider it in more detail here. One of the most striking features of later Chinese thought is the lack of interest in theistic conceptions of the universe, which had profound consequences for Chinese philosophy and science in general (see J. Needham 1956: 580–3), although such conceptions existed at the popular level. The foundations for this development are clearly detectable in Shang religion, where Ti, the sky god, is already a remote and impersonal figure, whom men can only approach through a complex hierarchy of ancestral spirits. The elaborate techniques of divination, directed to the ancestors rather than to Ti, can only have diminished the human-like qualities of this remote god still further, until he became the impersonal Heaven of later Chinese thought. The Shang were also literate and employed their writing as an essential aspect of their divinatory techniques. This clearly gave an enormous impetus to the development of classification in relation to cosmology because it allowed extremely precise and detailed questions to be put to the oracles in a manner which Keightley compares to bureaucratic procedures:

The logic of the sacrificial offerings and divinations was itself frequently bureaucratic: the nature of the offering was inscribed on the oracular bone or shell . . . the success of the offering depended on the correct fulfillment of 'defined duties', that is, the right number of cattle, to the right ancestor, on the right day. The concern with ritual number and ratios manifested in the sacrificial divination—two sheep or three sheep? five human victims or ten? what ratio of male to female animals?—anticipated, as it may help explain, the commitment to numbers, both real (as in census figures) and idealized (as in the symmetries of Chou-li), of later bureaucrats and thinkers. The mind of the Shang diviner was a quantifying mind. (Keightley 1978: 215)

According to Creel (1970: 163–4) the positive and negative principles, yin and yang, the so-called 'five elements' and the way in which phenomena are catalogued in many different series of fives (five metals, five virtues, five punishments, etc.) and other numerological arrangements were only developed late in the Spring and Autumn period (722–463 BC), and did not become pervasive until the time of the Warring States (463–221 BC). But while these systematizations were doubtless only achieved after centuries of scholarly elaboration and reflection, there seems no good reason to deny the evident relationship between divinatory classification, which was clearly highly elaborate in Shang times, and the nature and importance of later classificatory schemes.

The general characteristics of ancestor worship, and the absence of any lively pantheon of deities like those of the Indo-Europeans, or a personal deity such as Jehovah, upon whom man's welfare depended, seems also to have been crucial in preventing the development of a distinct priesthood which could institutionalize a separation between sacred and secular authority, and be the basis of an organized religion:

> The dominance of this [ancestral] cult probably goes far to explain one of the most striking differences between early China and many other civilizations: the absence in the former of a universal church or a significant priesthood. For this there is a twofold explanation. In the first place, the ancestral sacrifices of each clan were necessarily offered only to its clan ancestors, not to those of any other clan. Secondly, these sacrifices, in order to be effective, had to be performed by the clan member in person, not by priestly proxies. As a result, the ancestor cult was inevitably divisive rather than unifying in its effects. It could not readily develop into a national religion with a powerful organized priesthood. (Bodde n.d.: 44)

A further aspect of the religious system was that it involved the copious use of human sacrifices, and the necessary victims were obtained by capturing prisoners of war, from the Ch'iang people in particular:

> Oracle records abound in mentions of military campaigns involving the use of three thousand, five thousand, or even thirteen thousand troops and the taking of prisoners of war, as many as thirty thousand at one time. Within their own society, overwhelming garrison force must have been necessary for the imprisonment and sacrificial use of war captives in such large numbers: oracle records mention the sacrifice of as many as three hundred Ch'iang for a ritual of ancestor worship, and archaeological finds show that as many or more than 600 human victims were put to death at Hsiao-t'un for the construction of a single house and 164 were sacrificed at Hsi-pei-kang for the inside of a single tomb. (Chang 1980: 194)

We have seen that the basic kin and residential unit, *tsu*, was also a military unit, and there can be no doubt that warfare was an essential aspect of the Shang state: 'From the oracle records we learned that there was an enormous machinery of war, at the centre of which was the horse-drawn chariot and its bronze-tipped spears, arrows, and *ko*-halberds' (Chang 1976: 57).

Theoretically, all land belonged to the king, and when he granted title to the ruler of a town and its land he was entitled to the lord's services and a share of the grain produced from his land. There is no evidence that land was privately owned at this time (Chang 1980: 220), and 'New land was cleared and opened for farming on the order of the king' (ibid., 223):

> we can visualize . . . a territorial unit in which the king was entitled to a

share of all its produce and all its labour force. The entitlement was achieved in no small part by virtue of the king's status as the head of the grand lineage from which all the branch lineages were split, but it was certainly ensured through the king's military force and his control of near and remote walled towns through the lords he appointed to all corners of his kingdom. (Ibid., 216)

The king thus received tribute of grain, principally millet, and valuables from his lords, such as turtle shells for divination, and cowrie shells, as well as cattle, horses, elephants, and war captives (ibid., 236). With regard to redistribution, the records only refer to the king's gifts to his lords, and huge burial deposits in tombs.

Boats and human porters were certainly used to carry grain, and presumably animals were used for the same purpose, but no transport vehicles have so far been identified. Cowries were used as a medium of exchange, and traders were certainly important in Shang country. Some of the *tsu* were professional traders, and to this day the word for merchant, *shang jen*, is the same as the word for the Shang people (ibid., 241).

It is interesting to note that agriculture did not itself receive any significant assistance from the bronze technology of which the Shang were masters; the industry provided chiefly weapons and ceremonial objects, while the farmers used implements of stone, antler, bone, and wood for their hoes and two-pronged digging sticks (Chang 1976: 56). While there is at present no archaeological evidence for the use of ploughs at this period, F. Bray (1984: 161) maintains that ox-drawn ploughs made entirely of wood must in fact have been used.

(b) The Chou dynasty

In approximately 1025[2] BC the Shang dynasty was overthrown by King Wu of the Chou, who were western neighbours of the Shang. Subsequent Chinese tradition (Creel 1970: 59) clearly refers to the Chou as 'barbarians', meaning that they were rustic and uncouth, not the full possessors of authentic Chinese (i.e. Shang) culture: 'A member of the Chou ruling house complained that, even after they had been conquered, the Shang still dared to look down on the Chou as being "rustic", without culture' (Creel 1970: 60). The extent of the differences between the Chou and the Shang is important because of its relevance to our central theme of the core

[2] The date in traditional Chinese chronology is 1122 BC.

principles of Chinese society, and we must therefore give it close attention here.

Accusations of 'barbarism' and 'uncouthness' are unreliable evidence of what the outside observer would take to be major differences of culture. At the present time, for example, some Europeans profess to regard Americans as barbarous and uncouth, but what substantial differences in levels of culture does such an accusation really reveal? The Chou seem to have had no difficulty in communicating with the Shang. Creel says, for example, 'It is quite remarkable that we do not find more mention of difficulties of communication, and of the use of interpreters, in the early literature' (ibid., 202), and it seems likely that the two peoples were linguistically separated, at most, by different dialects of the same language. The Chou also possessed writing, and claimed to have been part of the 'Hsia' group of peoples (to which the Shang also belonged) well before their conquest of the Shang. (Hsia is the name of the mythical dynasty preceding the Shang.) The ability of the Chou, whose technology was the same as that of the Shang, to conquer so well-organized a state also suggests that they possessed a comparable level of military organization, and the political system imposed by the Chou seems to have been essentially similar to that of the Shang, though involving a somewhat greater emphasis on professional administrators at the expense of kin ties. Nevertheless, King Wu certainly gave fiefs to a large number of his relatives, and to others who had been associated with him in his victory. 'The terms of address used by the king to his dukes and vice versa are those of the family. Dukes possessing the same surname as the royal house were addressed by the king as paternal uncles; dukes with other surnames were addressed as maternal uncles' (Hsu 1965: 3).

It seems likely, from Creel's account, that military control was strengthened: the king had fourteen standing armies which 'were stationed in garrisons and dispatched to any point at the King's pleasure. There were also royal guard posts and royal troops charged with patrolling and protecting principal roads' (Creel 1970: 54–5). This, of course, is quite understandable for a conquering power which initially needed to maintain its rule by force. Again, the administrative needs of a territory now covering an area 'considerably larger than the combined areas of France, Belgium and the Netherlands' (ibid., 101) would probably have required a table of administrative organization somewhat larger and more elaborate than that of the Shang, with greater scope for the professional administrator. While, on the one hand, 'royal officers were not professionals in the sense of getting their livings, wholly and directly, from payment for the performance of their duties. Instead, they derived their emoluments chiefly or wholly from fiefs . . . ' (ibid., 117), nevertheless, 'It is clear that some men at least were educated for official service and spent their whole lives in it. There is little indication that, as has often been supposed, men in Western Chou times commonly inherited offices simply because their fathers had occupied them' (ibid., 117). For further discussion of the selection of officials, see below, Section 2e(*iv*), note 7.

In these areas of political, military, and administrative organization, therefore, the Chou period seems only to have involved an intensification and refinement of institutions and procedures already established under the Shang. Creel maintains, however, that in one crucial area at least—the ideology by which rulers exercised authority, and lost it—the Chou made a revolutionary innovation in the form of the doctrine of the Mandate of Heaven:

> The cornerstone of the ideology of the Chinese state is the conception of the Mandate of Heaven: the idea that the ruler of China holds a sacred trust from the highest deity which permits him to rule, so long as he does so for the welfare of the people—but subject to the peril that if he fails in this trust, Heaven will appoint another to rebel and replace him. This was the keynote of the propaganda by which the Chou sought, ultimately with complete success, to reconcile those they had conquered to their rule; it became the basis of the constitution of the Chinese state. (Ibid., 44)

The Chou deity, Heaven, was T'ien, whereas the Shang sky god was Ti, or Shang Ti, and Creel maintains that the Shang had no knowledge of T'ien before the Chou conquest. (References to T'ien in the Shang oracle records are not, according to Creel, references to a deity at all: see his Appendix C on this point.) He quotes a modern Chinese authority, Ch'i Ssu-ho as saying, 'the doctrine of the Mandate of Heaven is the most distinctive aspect of Chou thought, a point of fundamental difference from that of the Shang' (ibid., 45), and maintains as we have seen, that the idea was a propaganda device to reconcile the Shang to the legitimacy of the Shang conquest.

At this point the anthropologist must respectfully beg to differ from the sinologists. No conquering people who wished to persuade their new subjects of the legitimacy of that conquest could conceivably do so on the basis of a new and contentious theory of royal authority. Such a procedure could only aggravate the problem of legitimacy, not resolve it. On such occasions new regimes will obviously search for the *common* ground uniting rulers and ruled, and if the Shang had not previously held beliefs very similar to the Mandate of Heaven they would certainly not have accepted the 'new' ideas as rapidly as they apparently did. Christian missionaries, for example, do not if they are wise tell their potential converts that all their previous beliefs are nonsense: on the contrary, they typically go out of their way to find elements of indigenous belief that can plausibly be represented as similar to Christian doctrine. (The difference in the names of the deities seems to me to prove nothing. Creel himself refers to the case of Jupiter and Zeus, which were correctly perceived by the Romans merely to be different names for the same deity.) We have noted in previous chapters that basic cosmological and religious beliefs are extremely stable and if, as seems probable, the Chou and the Shang had a common cultural origin, it is overwhelmingly likely that both societies would have had fairly similar beliefs on such fundamental issues as the relation of the king to the divine powers.

The Chou version of the Mandate of Heaven would, for obvious political reasons, have given special emphasis to its justification for *removing* a bad king, and to this extent may have been novel, but even here the matter is not free from doubt. According to Creel, the principal minister of the founding Shang king, T'ang, was I Yin. One of T'ang's successors on the throne, T'ai Chia, 'overturned the statutes of T'ang', and was banished by I Yin for three years. As Creel says, 'If I Yin was a usurper who sought to bring the Shang dynasty to an end, how can we explain the fact that he was highly honoured by later Shang kings, as the Shang inscriptions clearly show he was?' (ibid., 39).

From a more general anthropological point of view, one would also add that the belief that bad kings may be removed with supernatural approval is in no way unique to China, especially when the king is mystically responsible for good harvests and the physical well-being of his people. Chang (1980: 195) says that the king was required to possess physical strength; while this is no doubt useful to a military commander it is by no means essential, but it is a typical attribute of a 'Divine King' whose health and fitness are indissolubly linked with that of his people.

The Chou conquest does, however, seem to have produced one

important change in the religious legitimation of the royal authority. As so often happens in the development of the state, war and conquest are the disrupters of kinship and the ideologies related to it:

We must nevertheless remember that the Chou rulers belonged to a different kin group from that of the Shang rulers. Whatever cultural legacy the Chou inherited from the Shang, it could not have included the Shang conception of identifying Shang Ti with the ancestors of the Tzu clan. Two courses were apparently open to the Chou lords—namely, to sever the connection between Shang Ti and the Shang ancestors, and to identify Shang Ti with their own ancestors, or to sever that connection, period. The origin myth of the Chi clan testifies to the fact that the former course was not entirely untried, but the subsequent development in religious concepts of the Chou shows that the latter course had its way, and that the worlds of gods and ancestors became separated for the first time and, historically, for ever. (Chang 1976: 191)

A further point of ideology that had profound significance for subsequent Chinese history is the relative status of the Chou Kings Wen and Wu. Wen was the king of Chou before the conquest of Shang, and 'Undoubtedly it was Wen, more than any other single man, who prepared the downfall of the Shang. By the formation of alliances, and by victories over his enemies, he consolidated a power that, when the test ultimately came, proved invincible' (Creel 1970: 65). Yet he was not the actual conqueror of Shang and the founder of the Chou dynasty—these were the accomplishments of his son Wu, the man who actually obeyed Heaven's Mandate. It is therefore curious that the Western Chou sources themselves give far greater honour to Wen than to Wu. 'Why this strange preference for a King who was not a King, a founder who did not found, a conqueror who never conquered?' (ibid., 65). The two kings seem to have had very different characteristics as recorded by these Chou sources:

Concerning the character of King Wen we have many particulars. Least clear is the meaning of repeated references to his 'virtue'. More specific are the statements that he was pious and filial, obedient both toward the deities and spirits and toward his ancestors. Despite his great renown, he made no display of it. He was careful, cautious, boundlessly solicitous. He was accordant and accommodating to others and was able to bring those under him into harmony. He cared for the people, protected them, and sought to bring about tranquility. He did not dare to mistreat even the helpless and solitary. He was very careful about the use of punishments, and his practice in this regard was a model for his successors. (Ibid., 65–6)

King Wen and the institutions and forms of government associated with him, especially his ability to plan as displayed in the eventual conquest of Shang, became a model for subsequent generations. King Wu, however, seems to have been very different. While there are a few references to his building activities, and the tranquillity he established among the various subjugated states, the main emphasis is given to his 'martial bearing and achievements': ' "Terrifying and strong was King Wu!" He was said to be "very martial"; there are repeated references to his "ardor". "The cohorts of Yin-Shang were massed like a forest . . . Bright was King Wu, he killed and smote the great Shang." "King Wu conquered the Yin, he exterminated and killed them" ' (ibid., 67).

In subsequent Chinese history *wen* came to signify those accomplishments of the civilized man that distinguish him from the barbarian, and the whole tradition of the civilian rule by the scholar-official, whereas *wu* represents the military tradition. In the later part of this section we shall examine the opposition between these two aspects of Chinese society in more detail. For the time being we may simply note that this tradition is extremely ancient, and Creel points out that the accounts of King Wen and King Wu are not later Confucian reinterpretations of Chinese history:

It may well be that the portrait of King Wen found in even early Western Chou sources is an idealization. To whatever extent this may be true, however, it is a portrait of the kind of ruler most admired at that time. It will not have escaped notice that this ideal ruler is in many ways very similar to what we are accustomed to call the 'Confucian' ideal. But here there is no question of Confucian theories having been read backward; this is the temper, at least, of a significant segment of Western Chou thought. (Ibid., 68)

(c) *The Spring and Autumn Period*

The Western Chou came to an end in 722 BC when the bad King Yu was killed in a rebellion involving some of the barbarian states, and the new king removed his capital to the east, near modern Loyang. From this time begins the Eastern Chou, or Spring and Autumn Period, Ch'un Ch'iu. While the Chou dynasty itself continued until the Chi'in unification of China into the first Empire in 221 BC, and remained of undiminished religious importance, the bonds of centralized government disintegrated during this period to produce many effectively autonomous states, a process which intensified during the era of the Warring States, Chan Kuo (463–221BC). In particular, the kin group, in the form of noble clans, re-established itself at the expense of royal authority. In the Ch'un Ch'iu, 'Again and again we find the authority of nominal rulers usurped by ministers, rulers deposed by ministers in alliance with noble families, and even palace revolutions climaxed by the division of the state among the victors . . .' (Hsu 1965: 24). On the other hand, the religious and social importance of descent and ancestor worship remained strong: the king was still, therefore, pre-eminent by virtue of his descent and his unique relationship to the ancestors:

Since a noble owed his status to the charisma his clan had inherited from their ancestors, it was only reasonable that the ruler, who represented the maintenance of the clan, had inherited more of the holy nature than a lesser member. [*Note*] A ruler could erect a temple for the worship of remote ancestors, while a noble was allowed to worship fewer generations of ancestors and could expect to enjoy ancestral blessings and share the hereditary nature in lesser degree than the ruler. (Ibid., 21)

The king's authority was comparable to that of a parent over his children, or a shepherd over his sheep: 'It was said that "Heaven, in giving birth to the people, appointed rulers to act as their superintendents and shepherds" ' (ibid., 20). This doctrine was evidently incapable by itself of maintaining the authority of rulers over the large and complex states of the Chou period, and there was an ever increasing tendency for power to shift to ministers and away from the relatives of the king: 'It is clear . . . that fewer and fewer sons of rulers held important positions in government as time went on' (ibid., 31), and

At the end of the Ch'un Ch'iu period, no brother or son of a ruler held the chancellorship of any state but Ch'iu. The brother or son might have been given a small fief where he could live in comfort, but his importance in state affairs was far less than it would have been at the beginning of the Ch'un Ch'iu. The decline in his power marked the first step toward the time when the enfeoffment of royal relatives would be ended by the first emperor of Ch'in. (Ibid., 31)

The growth of the power of ministers seems to have allowed them to hand on their offices to their sons. Younger brothers, the *shih*, either accepted junior official posts, or sought employment by another clan. The frequent need for younger sons to find employment by non-kin had extremely important consequences, for these were literate gentlemen, trained in war and ritual and the polite arts, but who were available for employment by those who could use their talents:

A moral code developed among the *shih* which may have been the basic code of the entire feudal society. One of its tenets was loyalty to one's master; after a *shih* submitted himself to a master, neither father nor ruler could force him to renounce the relationship. A *shih* was proud of his status and derived strong self-respect from it. Improper favours to *shih* were not to be accepted even in matters of life and death. The code of the *shih* was adapted and given new moral content by Confucius and his disciples in the Chan Kuo period . . . (Ibid., 8)

For the time being, however, power in each state was concentrated in the hands of a few large and powerful clans:

Most of them were established by segmentation from ruling houses when sons of rulers established separate lineages . . . The richer or more powerful the lineage, the greater its ability to provide for its sub-lineages. Yet frequent polysegmentation may drain the resources even of a rich ruling house, to the point where the ruling house becomes 'skimmed' and the ministerial lineages become strong enough to take over the commanding position. (Ibid., 32)

These powerful families reached the climax of their power in the period 632–573 BC, but competition for power led them to fight one another to extinction. Warfare between states became the norm (see Hsu 1965: 62–5 for the statistics), and rulers and ministers of vanquished states could be reduced to the status of slaves. Large numbers of captives were taken, and

every defeat or conquest of a state caused the social degradation of some former citizens of the defeated state; a downward social mobility took place. The number of people who thus lost status is not even approximately known, but since several hundred battles took place, and one-hundred-odd states were extinguished during the Ch'un Ch'iu period the number must have been quite large. (Ibid., 62)

While some were degraded by the fortunes of war, others of talent and ability were given the chance to rise, especially by military employment, and it is clear that in this period there was extraordinary social disruption as the result of warfare.

(d) The Period of the Warring States

By the end of the Spring and Autumn period, in about 463 BC, the many small states into which China had fragmented after the collapse of the Western Chou had become amalgamated by war into only twenty-two, and the nature of administration had also changed because the class of feudal nobles had more or less destroyed itself in the struggle for power. 'A few decades after the beginning of the Chan Kuo period, not a single minister belonging to Ch'un Ch'iu ministerial families appears in the records' (Hsu 1965: 89), and rulers were able to regain the power they had lost in the previous period. They were no longer bound by the hereditary claims of relatives of feudal lords to offices of state, and could appoint magistrates of their own choice to govern the districts of a state:

Such a consolidated state demands that persons of the highest ability be selected as officials and be well controlled to avoid jeopardizing the position of the sovereign. In order to provide such officials, professional education became a necessity. During the Chan Kuo period the new type of state reached a high stage of development with an organized administrative staff of well trained career experts. (Ibid., 93)

Such men were readily available from the ranks of the *shih*, to whom we have already referred. This class of younger sons of the nobility was also open to the more able and talented commoners, whose potential usefulness to the state and to ministers outweighed any disadvantages of birth.

The reduction in the number of the states meant a corresponding increase in their size and the difficulties of administering them:

If a state were several times the size of a noble fief, the complexity of governing it was not merely proportionally multiplied. For instance, a steward who was competent to collect tribute from a few farms of several square miles could have felt completely at a loss in administering a state the size of a major European country. A chariot-warrior of the early Ch'un Ch'iu period, who was used to fighting game-like battles with thousands of his fellow knightly warriors, could have felt quite confused if he were asked to lead an army ten times larger in tricky, bloody and brutal infantry warfare. Statecraft had become so complicated and specialized that the former type of training was no longer useful. (Ibid., 99)

As a result, a new type of school emerged in late Ch'un Ch'iu times to produce the needed administrative experts and strategists. A Master taught his disciples his own ideas on various subjects, and they learned by living with him and by informal discussion.

Confucius (551–479 BC)[3] is the most outstanding example of this type of Master, and his teachings ultimately became the official political doctrine of the Han Empire towards the end of the second century BC. Social disruption and confusion frequently induce men to reflect on the basic principles which should govern their lives, if the society's intellectual level is high enough, and these were just the times to stimulate such an appraisal:

[Confucius] lived in an environment where generally chaos reigned. Between the feudal states there was constant war, the smaller ones serving as battlefields for the larger. There was little law and order save what each man could enforce by personal strength, armed followers, or intrigue. Aristocratic pastimes, hunting, war and extravagant living, laid crushing burdens on the common people, while at all levels human life was cheap. (J. Needham 1956: 6)

The social and moral philosophy of Confucius was one attempt to rethink the nature of Chinese society, and in many ways, as we might expect, his teachings were a distillation of those traditional values and beliefs that are evident from the Shang period onwards. (Confucius said of himself that he was a transmitter rather than an innovator.) But in other respects his teachings mark a definitive break with tradition. The traditional side of his teaching emphasized the paternal responsibility of the ruler for his people: ' . . . in early Confucianism there was no distinction between ethics and politics. Government was to be paternalistic. If the prince was virtuous the people would also be virtuous' (J. Needham 1956: 9). The importance of leadership by moral example rather than by the harsh imposition of repressive rule by the state led the Confucians to envisage the ideal state as founded on

the body of ancient custom, usage and ceremonial, which included all those practices, such as filial piety, which unnumbered generations of the Chinese people had instinctively felt to be right—this was *li*, and we may equate it with natural law. In other words, the *li* was the sum of the folkways whose ethical sanctions had risen into consciousness. Moreover, it was necessary that the 'right' behaviour be taught, rather than enforced, by paternalistic magistrates. Moral suasion was better than legal compulsion. Confucius had said that if the people were given laws [in the sense of detailed codes] and levelled by punishments, they would try to avoid the punishments but would have no sense of shame; while if they were 'led by virtue' they would spontaneously avoid disputes and crimes. (Ibid., 544)

[3] Though Confucius lived at the end of the Spring and Autumn period, his teachings are most relevant to the period of the Warring States.

In these respects Confucianism was conservative, but his teachings also, for the first time, unequivocally denied that birth was a relevant qualification for government office. Confucius himself accepted as a student anyone sufficiently capable and willing to learn, without regard to their family origins (although he was himself a *shih*), and said that, since good government required high intelligence and moral integrity, men with such qualifications must be sought from far afield. Since the right education was also essential for the production of officials who were fit to govern, it, too, should be available to all. Though the doctrine of the Mandate of Heaven was not discussed by Confucius, it was later developed as an article of Confucian doctrine by Mencius.

Seen against the background of social turmoil, oppression, war, and other kindred horrors in which Confucius lived, the nobility of his principles and personal example is especially impressive, and was also fully in the Chinese social tradition we have been considering, but despite the fact that many of his students gained high office it was another three centuries before Confucianism became the official political ideology of the state.

For his was not the only possible response to the problems of Chinese society. Some, such as the Taoists, considered society so corrupt as to be beyond saving, and therefore withdrew from the world altogether, until men could return to a more primitive condition of society in which class distinctions and the oppression of the state were abolished. Others, who became known as the Legalists and arose in the fourth century BC, prescribed more rigorous and drastic remedies:

The fundamental idea of the Legalists was that *li*, the complex of customs, usages, ceremonies and compromises, paternalistically administered according to Confucian ideals, was inadequate for forceful and authoritarian government. Their watchword, therefore, was *fa*, positive law, particularly *hsien ting fa*, 'laws fixed beforehand', to which everyone in the State, from the ruler himself down to the lowest public slaves, was bound to submit, subject to sanctions of the severest and cruellest kind. The lawgiving prince must surround himself with an aura of *wei* (majesty) and *shih*[4] (authority, power, influence). (J. Needham 1956: 205)

Accepted morality, venerated custom, and the good of the people themselves counted for nothing against the need to maintain the authority of the state and enforce the obedience of its subjects, and

---

[4] A different word from that denoting younger brothers.

it therefore seemed logical that the most trivial offences should be punished with extreme severity, so that they did not lead to the commission of graver crimes. The following are some examples of Legalist teaching:

> It should be made worse for the people to fall into the hands of the police of their own State than to fight the forces of an enemy State in battle. The timorous should be put to death in the manner they most hate. Strictness in the application of penalties should have no exceptions . . . There was an elaborate system of delation and denunciation; omission to denounce a culprit was punished by the friend being sawn in two, and other tortures were employed. The kind of thing of which the Legalists approved is shown in the story quoted by Han Fei Tzu of Prince Chao of the State of Han. The prince having got drunk and fallen asleep was exposed to cold, whereupon the crown-keeper put a coat over him. When he awoke he asked who had covered him, and on being informed, punished the coat-keeper but put the crown-keeper to death, on the principle that transgression of the duties of an office was worse than mere negligence. (Ibid., 207)

These unpleasant maxims were peculiarly agreeable to the rulers of the rigorously centralized and militarized State of Ch'in, where the Legalists became the dominant political theorists as the era of the Warring States drew to its close. Already reduced from twenty-two to seven, the remaining independent states were conquered by Ch'in, which achieved the first Unification of China in 221 BC, and had the chance of imposing these theories throughout the Empire. Rebellion soon followed, however, and the Han dynasty came to power in 206 BC. After attempting to rule under a modified version of Legalist principles, the Imperial government increasingly adopted Confucian policies as the official political philosophy, particularly towards the end of the second century BC. Despite later elaborations, it remained the basic ideology of Chinese society until the present century.

(e) Some themes in the evolution of Chinese society

In the course of our survey of Chinese history and its development from the early to the mature state, we have observed a number of changes, and the emergence of certain institutions, that are not unique to China: the progressive decline in the importance of kinship as the basis of state organization; the emergence of a feudal aristocracy, devoted to warfare and hunting, especially in the Spring and Autumn period; the use of professional armies to create a unified empire; the rise of a wealthy merchant class; the creation of a professional bureaucracy; a written legal system, and so on. Yet in all these and other cases, the core principles of traditional Chinese society gave to these changes and institutions a distinctive pattern and significance which are unique to China. These we may now explore in more detail.

(i) Chinese ideas of cosmic and social harmony

We observed earlier in this section that one of the distinctive features of early Chinese culture was the importance of divination, in a wide variety of forms, and that this was closely related to an increasingly elaborate system of classification and symbolic correlations involving all aspects of life. These correlations, in turn, were evidence of the whole cosmic order, Tao, by which Nature, Society, and the Individual were regulated:

> The key-word in Chinese thought is *Order*, and above all *Pattern* (and, if I may whisper it for the first time, *Organism*). The symbolic correlations or correspondences all formed part of one colossal pattern. Things behaved in particular ways not necessarily because of prior actions or impulses of other things, but because their position in the ever-moving cyclical universe was such that they were endowed with intrinsic natures which made that behaviour inevitable for them. If they did not behave in those particular ways they would lose their relational positions in the whole (which made them what they were), and turn into something other than themselves. They were thus parts in existential dependence upon the whole world-organism. And they reacted upon one another not so much by mechanical impulsion or causation as by a kind of mysterious resonance. (J. Needham 1956: 281)

All cultures, of course have developed to greater or lesser degree some scheme of the natural order which in turn is related to society, but the unusual feature of the Chinese scheme is that it regards cosmic order not only as inherently harmonious, but as independent of any divine regulation and control: 'This cosmic pattern is self-contained and self-operating. It unfolds itself because of its own inner necessity and not because it is ordered by any external volitional power' (Bodde 1981c: 286). Or, in the words of Needham, 'Universal harmony comes about not by the celestial fiat of some King of Kings, but by the spontaneous cooperation of all beings in the universe brought about by their following the *internal* necessity of their own nature' (J. Needham 1956: 562).

In Chinese thought, the social order is or ought to be a reflection of the cosmic order, and just as this is essentially a harmonious, organic whole, society too should be organized on harmonious principles that do not depend on external compulsion:

Chinese ideals involved neither God nor Law. The uncreated universal organism, whose every part, by a compulsion internal to itself and arising out of its own nature, willingly performed its functions in the cyclical recurrences of the whole, was mirrored in society by a universal ideal of mutual good understanding, a supple régime of interdependencies and solidarities which could never be based on unconditional ordinances, in other words, on laws . . . Thus the mechanical and the quantitive, the forced and the externally imposed, were all absent. The notion of Order excluded the notion of Law. (Bodde 1981c: 290)

As we shall see, Chinese attitudes to legal disputes and social conflict of all kinds were powerfully affected by this general world-view, which sought to 'merge seemingly conflicting elements into a unified harmony' (Bodde 1981c: 272). A good example are the opposing principles of yang and yin, respectively light/dark, active/ passive, hard/soft, male/female, ruler/subject, father/son, and so on. There is an evident inequality as well as an opposite nature in these two principles, but

Never, however, is the suggestion made . . . that the one could or should wholly displace the other. Hence there is no real analogy with the dualisms based on conflict (light vs. darkness etc.) so familiar to us in the West. On the contrary, the *yin* and *yang* form a cosmic hierarchy of balanced inequality in which, however, each complements the other and has its own necessary functions. (Ibid., 279)

Similarly, the Chinese were well aware of the differences between human beings in mental and physical abilities, and believed that class differences were expressions of these, but they did not accept the necessity of conflict between classes or individuals:

On the contrary, the welfare of the social organism as a whole depends upon harmonious co-operation among all of its units and of the individuals who comprise those units. This means that every individual, however high or low, has the obligation to perform to the best of his abilities those particular functions in which he is expert and which are expected of him by society. Thus the ruler should rule benevolently, his ministers should be loyal yet at the same time ready to offer if need be their frank criticism, the farmers should produce the maximum of food, the artisans should take pride in their manufactures, the merchants should be honest in their dealings, and no one should interfere needlessly in the tasks of others for which he is not well qualified. In other words, society should be like a *magnified family* [*my emphasis*], the members of which, though differing in their status and functions, all work in harmony for the common good. (Ibid , 264–5)

Indeed, the model of society as ideally patterned on relations of kinship seems to have been extremely pervasive in Chinese culture; filial piety was a basic principle of morality, and patrilineal descent groups have remained of the first importance in social life. In this respect China has been markedly different from Indo-European society where, as we shall see, relations of kinship seem always to have been more cognatic and more restricted in range and importance.

In Chinese thought, therefore, conflict is either an illusion, or a falling away from the ideal state of things, but here again we shall see that the Indo-European view was very different; while it, too, gave a central place to order, this was maintained by the volition and intervention of divine beings, and by conflict at all levels of the cosmos.

(*ii*) *'Church' and 'State' in China*

In the final part of this chapter we shall see that one of the most ancient and cardinal principles of Indo-European society was the distinction between the priest and the warrior, a distinction which was also quite compatible with Christ's injunction 'Render to Caesar the things that are Caesar's and to God the things that are God's'. As is well known, the relations between Church and State throughout European history have been highly complex, each at varying times claiming supremacy over the other; the status of the king, in particular, who was sacred but not a priest, remained ambiguous, since it was always possible for kings, as bearers of the sword, to offend against the laws of God in their actions and edicts. But this tension between Church and State was unknown in Chinese society, and the last words of Thomas More, Knight and Saint, on the scaffold, 'I die the King's good servant, but God's first', would have been quite meaningless in China.

In the European tradition the word 'religion' has always denoted man's relations with the divine, but the nearest Chinese equivalent, *chiao*, does not necessarily have any such connotation:

The Chinese word for 'religion' is *chiao* which means teaching or a system of teaching. To teach people to believe in a particular deity is a *chiao*; but to teach them how to behave toward other men is also a *chiao*. The ancients did say that 'the sages founded religions (*chiao*) on the ways of the gods'. But it is not always necessary to make use of supernatural expedients. And the Chinese people make no distinction between the theistic religions and the purely moral teachings of their sages. Therefore, the term *chiao* is applied to Buddhism, Taoism, Mohammedanism, Christianity, as well as to Confucianism. They are all systems of moral teaching. Teaching a moral life is the essential thing; and 'the ways of the gods' are merely one of the possible ways of sanctioning that teaching. That is in substance the Chinese conception of religion. (Bodde n.d.: 39, citing Hu Shih)

We have already noted (above, Section 2*a*) that the special features of Chinese ancestor worship, in which the king or emperor was the supreme officiant, were extremely important in preventing the emergence of a distinct priesthood under the Shang and Chou dynasties. Traditional Chinese religion, based on ancestor worship, the worship of heaven and minor naturalistic deities such as gods of the soil, various types of divination, especially geomancy, and sacrifice, was an integral part of the social order. Though a cult of Confucius developed, with temples and sacrifices, those who officiated at these rites were simply local scholars and officials, never a distinct priesthood.

Chinese diffused religion, by its very nature, could exert little power apart from the secular institutions in which it was diffused. Its main function was to provide supernatural support for the ethical values already present in these secular institutions, rather than to serve in itself as a source of such values. Thus its role in Chinese society was deeply conservative: that of peripherally supporting already well-established social institutions. The contrast is sharp with the institutional religions, which often required from their adherents a major break with the past and avowed commitment to radically new ways of life. (Bodde n.d.: 49–50)

The introduction of Buddhism and the development of religious Taoism in the first century AD did produce organized religion in China, which remained of considerable importance until the ninth century. Bodde says of Buddhism,

The commercial and industrial activities of some of its temples and monasteries included the operation of water-powered stone rolling mills and oil presses, as well as hostels, pawn-shops, and large landed estates. At the same time, Buddhist welfare activities included the maintenance of hospitals, feeding stations for the hungry, havens for the aged and decrepit, bathhouses, resthouses along the routes to famous shrines, road building, bridge construction, well digging, and tree planting. (Bodde n.d.: 46)

But at the height of its power, Buddhism probably had little more than half the proportion of clergy to population that the Church had in thirteenth-century England, and Buddhism itself had no centralized organization:

> . . . whatever centralization did exist in Chinese Buddhism was imposed upon it by the government rather than self-created. The history of Chinese Buddhism and, *pari passu*, of religious Taoism and the syncretic sects, is, to an important extent, the history of the efforts of the state to control and regularize them. In these efforts the state was almost invariably successful. (Bodde n.d.: 47)

In short, by the time institutional religion arose Chinese society was already formed in such a way that these religions could produce no effective challenge to the state's authority or to the traditional world-view, and no division between Church and State comparable to that in Europe was possible because the Emperor was still 'the one man' interceding between Man and Heaven. In the same way, as we shall see, the Confucian bureaucracy was able to stifle any attempt by the merchant class to establish its autonomy from state control.

(iii) *The status of the soldier*

Those who believe that ideology is simply a response to the practical necessities of social life would surely have predicted that by the time of the Han Empire the status of warfare and of generals in particular would have been very high, and perhaps even comparable to the prestige of the army under the Roman Empire. China had been more or less constantly at war for the past two thousand years or so; the Chou dynasty had been established by force of arms; the Chinese Empire itself had been produced by the military victories of the State of Ch'in; the doctrine of the Mandate of Heaven sanctioned armed rebellion against a wicked sovereign; during the Spring and Autumn period a chariot-driving military aristocracy had enjoyed great prestige; and, throughout the period we have been considering, the states that were Chinese in culture had relied on their armies to defend themselves against the attacks of those whom they considered barbarians. Despite all this, the Chinese[5] persisted in regarding the civilian arts of government, epitomized in the character of King Wen, as superior to those of war and the whole military tradition (*wu*).

With the exception of the Legalists, all ancient Chinese schools of thought were strongly opposed to war and violence. Even the Legalists in fact wanted a powerful army simply to build up a powerful state. Never, in Western fashion, did they glorify war as spiritually ennobling. Among classical Chinese thinkers, the most biting anti-war statements came from Mo Tzu, yet even he was criticised by the Confucians for basing his arguments heavily on utilitarian considerations: the economic wastefulness of war and armaments. On this matter as all others the Confucians were uncompromisingly moral. 'Those who are good at war should suffer the highest punishment . . .', said Mencius, and again: 'There are those who say "I am good at marshalling troops, I am good at conducting battle". These are great crimes. If the ruler of a state loves goodness (*jên*), in all-under-Heaven he will have no enemies'. (Bodde n.d.: 165)

Religion, in particular, played no part in Chinese reasons for going to war:

. . . holy wars are not easy to find in the Chinese imperial records, just as an avenging God and the wrath of Jehovah are far to seek. Moral values are not handed down from a deity who is on one's side, ready to smite the infidel. The whole view of the world is less anthropomorphic and less bellicose than that of the Old Testament, or of Islam. (Fairbank 1974: 1)

In response to the question of why soldiers and generals *themselves*[6]

---

[5] Here and elsewhere it should be remembered that the views represented as typical of Chinese society were predominately those of the scholar-officials, and were not necessarily those of the unlettered peasantry. So Bodde observes that ' . . . many of the most popular Chinese novels and dramas—from which, until recently, the ordinary man derived much of his knowledge of Chinese history—deal in most colorful fashion with famous wars and military figures of the past. This, no doubt, can largely be explained by fondness—widespread in China as elsewhere—for gallant deeds of derring-do, especially when sufficiently remote from the present as to become enshrouded in a haze of romantic glamour. Another factor of some sociological importance is that many of China's historical military heroes began their careers as bandits and have become identified in the popular mind as Robin Hood-like protagonists of the people against a corrupt social order. Even in these exciting novels and dramas however, it is noteworthy that chief applause is often reserved for the man who prefers guile to force for gaining the submission of his opponent' (Bodde 1981*c*: 272).

[6] Generals seldom if ever took the civil service examinations. In so far as they did take examinations at all, they were the less highly regarded examinations intended for the military.

should have conceded the superiority of the civilian officials Needham says:

What immediately came to my mind in replying was the imperial *charisma* carried by the bureaucracy; [Note: One should add the high moral standards of Confucianism which exerted great social pressure throughout the ages upon the members of the mandarinate]; the holiness of the written character (when I first went to China the stoves for giving honourable cremation to any piece of paper with words written on it were still to be seen in every temple), and the Chinese conviction that the sword might win but only the logos could keep. (J. Needham 1969: 199)

(iv) The rejection of competitive values

The traditional Chinese rejection of militarism and violence, except as unpleasant practical necessities, leads us in turn to ask what were their attitudes to competition in general. Europeans are the heirs to a tradition of competitive games and sports at least as old as Homer and the Vedas, but while a few physical games have existed in China, including some that involved body contact, the theme of competitive sports has been a very minor one in the Chinese tradition. While in the later Chou chariot driving was one of those 'six accomplishments' of the nobility previously mentioned, there is apparently little evidence that organized chariot racing ever occurred. The aristocracy hunted, but this was not competition; the only sport of feudal China that was certainly competitive was archery. The Western Chou kings maintained an archery academy, but contests seem to have been ritual in nature, to the accompaniment of music and the correct movements (see note 7 below on the moral significance of archery), and organized on the basis of teams (Bodde n.d.: 219). Competitive games before massed spectators were held at the Ch'in court in 208 BC, and probably included archery, charioteering, and wrestling (possibly of a ritual nature), but the games were abolished in 44 BC and thereafter forgotten. Football was popular among soldiers since at least the Warring States, as was wrestling, but when football was played at the T'ang court it did not involve body contact; a player from each team alternately tried to kick the ball through a hole in a suspended piece of cloth. The tug-of-war at the T'ang court was ritual in nature, although polo, imported from Persia, was played. In so far as competitive sports existed, they tended to involve teams rather than individuals: 'One is tempted to see in this an early example of a Chinese characteristic which is very prominent today, that is, an intense aversion to subjecting any individual to public humiliation . . . what is commonly called the desire to preserve 'face', for others as well as for oneself' (Creel 1936: 322).

Indeed, intellectual competition, especially in the form of personal argument, was also discouraged, and despite the contending schools of philosophy that grew up in the fifth century BC and later, argument was not generally considered a reliable method of reaching the truth:

> Throughout its history, Confucianism has deprecated the use of debate as a means of advancing knowledge. So glorious is the Tao, the Confucians would say, that its validity should be self-evident without the need for argument. If, nonetheless, it has today become obscured by a welter of controversy, this is simply sad evidence of the degenerate world in which we live.
>
> This viewpoint, as we shall see shortly, was widespread among other classical schools of thought as well, even though the Tao for them might be quite different from the Confucian Tao. Herein lies a significant difference between ancient China and ancient Greece. In ancient Chinese philosophy—indeed probably in all Chinese literature—there is hardly anything comparable to the Socratic dialogue. Dialogues, when they occur, are rarely more than three or four interchanges long, and usually consist of respectful questions (not probing objections) addressed by the disciple to the master in order to facilitate his exposition. In the rare cases in which sharp debate between the master and an outsider is recorded—perhaps the most famous is that between Mencius and Kao Tzu on human nature—the outcome is predetermined in the sense that after a very few exchanges, the master always has the last triumphant word while his opponent is reduced to silence. (Bodde n.d.: 75)

> The word *pien*, 'argument or disputation', was used pejoratively not only by Confucians but by Taoists, as for example in the *Chuang Tzu*, where members of the School of Names (the Logicians) are more than once referred to as *pien-che*, 'arguers'. The criticisms directed against 'the arguers' by a variety of thinkers are all remarkably similar in tone. They accuse them, among other things, of 'deceiving and confusing the ignorant masses' (Hsün), 'causing subtle divisions and disorder' (Pan Ku quoting Liu Hsin), 'throwing a deceiving glamour over men's minds' (Chuang Tzu), and 'specialising in the definition of names but losing sight of human feelings (Ssu-ma T'an). (Bodde n.d.: 78)

It is certainly true that the civil service examination[7] was highly competitive, since there were vastly more applicants than were needed to fill the small number of vacancies. The few successful candidates brought renown to their birthplace as well as to themselves, and it would therefore be a considerable exaggeration to say that the competitive spirit was absent in Chinese society. Rather, in the case of the examination system, it was intellectual rather than physical in type and in any case was simply the necessary result of the search for excellence.

[7] It might be supposed that the selection of civil servants by written examination which was established under the Han dynasty (the earliest certain date is 165 BC) was a practical response to an obvious need in a literate, politically centralized society. But the same 'need' existed for many centuries in Europe, for example, to say nothing of other areas, yet did not produce a similar response until 1693, when the first written civil service examinations were administered in Berlin, as the result of direct Chinese influence (Creel 1970: 26). Recruitment to the British civil service by written examination was not established until 1855. Nor were written examinations used for the selection of officials under the Roman Empire, despite the enormous size and complexity of its bureaucratic organization. It cannot therefore be maintained that literate, centralized states of any size *need* to select their officials by examination, and in order to explain the very early appearance of this practice in China we must have recourse, yet again, to some of the distinctive features of Chinese culture. In our culture we naturally think of written examinations simply as tests of intellectual ability, whereas for the Chinese they seem to have been even more important as evidence of virtue. Chinese emphasis on the necessity of virtue in rulers was, as we have seen, a very ancient aspect of their culture, and this requirement applied also to officials, who seem to have been selected from among the people even before the Spring and Autumn Period. Initially, military prowess seems to have been emphasized and, indeed, the Chinese character which later came to mean scholar or civil servant originally meant a chariot-borne commander. But by 650 BC we find a prince of Ch'i giving primary emphasis to moral qualities, when he directs: 'In your district there should be some men who are tranquil and love study, pious towards their parents, humane and faithful. Get information about them in all the villages of your district.' Only then does the prince go on to discuss physical and military prowess. For many centuries the basic qualifications for officials in selection and promotion were knowledge of archery, charioteering, music, and ritual, and while charioteering was strictly physical (and was later treated with contempt by Confucius for this reason), archery was, like music and writing, traditionally regarded in China as requiring composure and serenity of mind. So Confucius wrote: 'How difficult it is to shoot. How difficult it is to listen (to the music)! To shoot exactly in harmony with the note (given) by the music, and to shoot without missing the bull's-eye on the target; it is only the archer of superior virtue who can do this! How shall a man of inferior character be able to hit the mark?' It is this aspect of archery which explains its survival (in desultory fashion) until at least 6 BC in the Imperial examinations for the civil service: applicants for examination first shot at small wooden targets on the back of which were written different examination questions. Those who did not hit the target were disqualified. Music, too, was regarded as closely associated with government from early times; according to Pan Ku's vivid reconstruction of the past, even before 700 BC commissioners travelled the countryside collecting songs of protest from the peasants, which were brought to the

(v) *Ideas of law*

One might expect the Chinese conception of law to be affected by such attitudes to competition and argument, as well as by their whole world view. We recall ' . . . the Chinese conviction, already repeatedly referred to, that the universe is a harmony, the basic principle of which is therefore one of goodness; that the human world is an integral part of this harmony; and that man's nature is the vital link between the two' (Bodde 1981*c*: 257). We have also seen that the relationship between ruler and subject was from the earliest times seen as analogous to that between father and children or the shepherd and his sheep. It is scarcely surprising that this world view should have deeply affected Chinese concepts of law:

Fa is the usual generic term for positive or written law as an abstraction ('law' or '*the* law'), but it may also be used in the plural to mean separate 'laws'. The word was already in common use before its appearance in legal contexts. Its root meaning is that of a model, pattern or standard; hence of a method or procedure to be followed. From this root meaning comes the notion, basic in Chinese legal thinking, that *fa* is a model or standard imposed from above, to which the people must conform. (Bodde 1981*b*: 175)

As we have seen, this was the conception of law favoured by the Legalists, whereas the Confucians emphasized the concept of *li*. In the narrowest (and probably original sense) *li* meant the performance of all kinds of religious ritual (sacrifice and divination). More broadly, it meant all ceremonial or polite

Grand Master of Music who assessed their genuineness by means of humming tubes. Intellectual ability and virtue were also closely associated in knowledge of the rites, and when these were recorded in writing these books could be studied, and proficiency in this knowledge tested by examination. As Confucius wrote, 'Let man first be incited by the *Songs*, then given a firm footing by the study of ritual, and finally perfected by music', and the literary basis of virtue received increasing emphasis from the time of Confucius onwards. It seems, then, that while Chinese officials were obviously expected to be intelligent and capable, the system of written examinations was developed primarily as a test of virtue, whereas in Europe it was regarded merely as a test of intellectual competence. The Chinese emphasis on virtue, and their belief that there were objective methods of discovering this quality in human beings clearly gave a unique impetus to the development of competitive written examinations for the selection of officials. It must not be forgotten, of course, that the selection of officials for their ability rather than their birth was a necessary part of this development as well, but such a policy does not in and of itself require written examinations. (I owe this information to an unpublished paper written in 1981, which Mr Kenneth Robinson has very kindly made available to me and which is now in the holdings of the East Asian History of Science Library. I alone, of course, am responsible for the conclusions drawn from it.)

behaviour. In the broadest sense of all, it refers to all institutions and relationships, political or social, which promote harmonious living in Confucian society.

These views both of *li* and of law (*fa*) share at least one important premiss, that social harmony is the primary goal, and both are fundamentally opposed to the idea of litigation as either good or moral. (The maxim *fiat justitia, ruat coelum* would have been utterly incomprehensible.) Hence civil law as it is understood in the Western tradition never really developed:

The written law of pre-modern China was overwhelmingly penal in emphasis, . . . it was limited in scope to being primarily a legal codification of the ethical norms long dominant in Chinese society, and . . . it was nevertheless rarely invoked to uphold these norms except where other less punitive measures had failed. Chinese traditional society, in short, was by no means a legally oriented society and this despite the fact that, as we shall see, it produced a large and intellectually impressive body of codified law.

The penal emphasis of such law, for example, meant that matters of a civil nature were either ignored by it entirely (e.g. contracts), or were given only limited treatment within its penal format (e.g. property rights, inheritance, marriage). The law was only secondarily interested in defending the rights—especially the economic rights—of one individual or group against another individual or group, and not at all in defending such rights against the state. What really concerned it—though this is to be surmised rather than explicitly discovered in the Chinese legal literature—were all acts of moral or ritual impropriety or of criminal violence which seemed in Chinese eyes to be violations or disruptions of the total social order. The mere existence of the law was intended to deter the commission of such acts, but once they occurred, the restoration of social harmony required that the law be used to exact retribution from their doer. In the final analysis, a violation of the social order really meant, in Chinese thinking, a violation of the total cosmic order, since, according to the Chinese world-view, the spheres of man and nature were inextricably interwoven to form an unbroken continuum.

For these reasons, the official law always operated in a vertical direction from the state upon the individual rather than in a horizontal plane directly between two individuals. If a dispute involved two individuals, individual A did not bring a suit directly against individual B. Rather, he lodged his complaint with the authorities, who then decided whether or not to prosecute individual B. No private legal profession existed to help individuals plead their cases . . . On the lowest level, that of the *hsien* or county, which was the level where governmental law impinged most directly upon the people, its administration was conducted by the *hsien* magistrate as merely one of several administrative functions. This meant that, though usually devoid of any formal legal training, he was obliged to act as detective, prosecutor, judge and jury rolled into one. (Bodde 1981*b*: 171–172)

The magistrate was assisted by a professional legal secretary, who could prepare cases for trial, suggest appropriate sentences, and write legal reports for cases that were appealed to higher levels of government, but this secretary was the employee of the magistrate, and not part of the official legal system itself. Thus,

. . . the ordinary man's awareness and acceptance of such [ethical] norms was shaped far more by the pervasive influence of custom than by any formally enacted system of law. The clan into which he was born, the guild of which he might become a member, the group of gentry elders holding informal sway in his rural community—these and other extra-legal bodies helped to smooth the inevitable friction in Chinese society by inculcating moral precepts upon their members, mediating disputes, or, if need arose, imposing disciplinary sanctions and penalties. (Bodde 1981*b*: 172)

Creel (1970: 164) maintains that, in the time of the Western Chou, litigation between private citizens was far more acceptable than it later became, and cites Bodde and Morris (1967: 48 n. 95) concerning a series of Western Chou bronze inscriptions involving legal contests: 'The give-and-take spirit apparent in these disputes distinguishes them sharply from the vertically oriented court procedures of imperial times, and suggests a society closer in spirit to Western society than was later possible when Chinese government became bureaucratized.' It also seems that, certainly in the Spring and Autumn period, and even earlier under the Western Chou, it was permitted for advocates to present cases in court on behalf of the principals. In the one case that Creel cites, however, where two royal ministers sued one another, the advocates were retainers of the principals, and it is not clear on what basis advocates were chosen in other cases.

Neither is there any indication that a special class of advocates developed, as it did in Rome, where Cicero was no doubt the most famous of such men. This early practice never eventuated in China, as it did in the West, in the development of the professional legal advocate or 'barrister', who regularly appears in court for and with the parties involved in cases. In later times such persons have normally been excluded from Chinese courts. (Creel 1970: 178)

There are many instances of amateur advocacy in the ethnographic literature (indeed, it is simply one aspect of spokesmanship), and one may readily believe that for a time such an institution was normal in China, too. But it is clear that the basic tendency of Chinese culture, especially as refined by the Confucians and applied by the scholar-officials, was fundamentally hostile to the idea:

There have never been advocates. They have always been looked upon with disfavour. Above all, for all the reasons that one can deduce from the special conception that the Chinese have of the law. To admit that its ɒꞅꞏꞁɩꞇɒꞇɩꞁꞇ ɒꞁꝺ ɩꞇꞇꞁꞅꝑꞅꞇꞇꞇɩꞁꞇ ꞇꞁꞇꞁꝺ ꝺꞁ ꞇꞁꞁ ꞇꞁꞇꞁꞇꞇ ꞁꝺ ꝺɩꞁ ꞇꞇꞁꝺꞁꞁꞁ, ꞁꞇ ꞇꞁꞇꞇ ꞇꞁꞁ judge could be differed with, would indicate an intolerable confusion. The fact is that there is no place for an advocate in the traditional Chinese judicial organization. (Escarra 1936: 255, cited in Creel 1970: 178)

Here again, a common institution and possible line of development that appeared for a time in Chinese society was ultimately repressed by the general developmental tendency of the society as a whole.

(vi) The repression of capitalist development

We can now understand from these basic characteristics of Chinese society and ideology why capitalism, in the sense of powerful associations of entrepreneurs free to make profitable investments where they choose, with the protection of elaborate laws of property and contract, could not have developed. In Chapter IV we noted the extremely high level reached by Chinese technology by the time of the Han dynasty, and there was also a wealthy merchant class, with ample opportunity to make profits. In an earlier epoch, it seems that the idea of some kind of contract between rulers and merchants was not unknown:

The famous statesman Tzu-ch'an, of the state of Cheng, is quoted as saying that the first ruler of the state, Duke Huan (806–771 BC), had sworn a covenant with certain merchants. In this covenant the Duke said: 'If you do not revolt from me, I will not interfere with your trade. I will neither ask for nor seize anything from you. You may have your profitable markets and precious goods, without my taking any cognizance of them'. On the basis of this covenant, Tzu-ch'an says, the rulers and the merchants 'have been able to rely upon each other down to the present day', over a period of two and one-half centuries. (Creel 1970: 139)

This germ of capitalist autonomy, however, was unable to develop; those who control the apparatus of the state control the means of production, distribution, and exchange, and the characteristics of the Chinese state, under the influence of basic Chinese values, were opposed to individualism and competitiveness. Moreover, in the society at large, wealth itself was not the object of real admiration:

Wealth as such was not valued. It had no spiritual power. It could give comfort but not wisdom, and in China affluence carried comparatively little prestige. The one idea of every merchant's son was to become a scholar, to enter the imperial examination and to rise high in the bureaucracy. (J. Needham 1969: 202)

By this time, too, the law and the bureaucracy had developed in such a way that

Claims, titles, privileges, immunities, deeds, charters were never granted. Any sign of initiative in the other [merchant] camp was usually strangled at birth, or if it had reached a stage when it could no longer be suppressed, the state laid hands on it, took it under control, and appropriated the resultant profit. As seen from below, there was, in these relations, no legal way of obtaining an immunity, a franchise, since the state and its representatives, the officials, were almighty. (Balazs 1964: 41)

Balazs goes on to comment in terms similar to Needham's on the way in which the merchants, like the military, accepted the superiority of the scholar official: 'The outstanding feature in these relations is the absence of pluck, the complete lack of a fighting spirit . . . they had no real desire to be different, to oppose their own way of life to that of the ruling class . . . ' (ibid., 41–2). He concludes that, apart from the abundance of labour,

What was chiefly lacking in China for the further development of capitalism was not merchant skill or scientific aptitude, nor a sufficient accumulation of wealth, but scope for individual enterprise. There was no individual freedom and no security for private enterprise, no legal foundation for rights other than those of the state, no alternative investment other than landed property, no guarantee against being penalized by arbitrary exactions from officials or against intervention by the state. But perhaps the supreme inhibiting factor was the overwhelming prestige of the state bureaucracy, which maimed from the start any attempt of the bourgeoisie to be different, to become aware of themselves as a class and fight for an autonomous position in society. Free enterprise, ready and proud to take risks, is therefore quite exceptional in Chinese economic history. (Ibid., 53)

(vii) The development of a scheme of social classes

The first recognized social classes in explicit Chinese thought seem to have been based on occupation, which was broadly defined. In the Western Chou the term *shih*, later applied to the scholar-gentry of the Empire, was used to refer to 'officials', who were doubtless well-born, 'But by the Spring and Autumn period (722–484 BC) a definite social stratum seems to be intended, consisting of the younger sons and peripheral branches of ministerial and official families, who thus stood at the bottom of the aristocratic ladder' (Bodde n.d.: 106); *nung*, 'farmer' denoted all who worked the land themselves, whether as proprietor, tenants, or hired labour. The term *kung*, 'artisans', included not only skilled craftsmen and experts such as architects and engineers, but those of any level of skill who lived by the practice of some craft. The term *shang*, 'merchants', similarly denoted all those who earned their living by trade, of whatever kind. Later, as we shall see, these categories became more precisely defined, but at this stage it does not seem that there was any explicit idea of society as being ideally and essentially composed of these particular classes or 'functions'. (The point of this observation will become clear when we consider early Indo-European institutions.) The only social classification even vaguely comparable to such a notion is the hierarchical distinction between the elite and the masses.

. . . between the small groups of 'superiors' (*shang*) and the much larger mass of 'inferiors' (*hsia*); that is, in modern parlance, between the 'haves' and the 'have-nots'. The two basic terms used in the early texts to express this dichotomy are *chün tzu*, 'lord's son', and *hsiao jên*, 'small (or petty) man'. Other parallel terms serving to designate the 'superiors' are *pai hsing* or 'the hundred surnames', and *ta jên*, 'great man'; for designating the 'inferiors' the most common word is *min*, 'the people', either used alone or prefixed by descriptive epithets in terms like *shu min*, 'the multitudinous people', *chung min*, 'the numerous people', or *li min*, 'the black-haired people'. (Bodde n.d.: 107)

So far, there is nothing in these types of social classification that cannot be found in many other centralized states. The explicit idea of some kind of 'organic', mutually dependent relationship between different classes seems first to have arisen with Confucianism. In the words of Mencius,

Some labour with their brains and some labour with their brawn. Those who labour with their brains govern others; those who labour with their brawn are governed by others. Those governed by others, feed them. Those who govern others, are fed by them. This is a universal principle in the world. (Mencius IIIa, 4)

If there were no men of superior quality (*chün tzu*), there would be no one to rule the country folk. If there were no country folk, there would be no one to support the men of superior quality. (Mencius IIIa, 3; cited in Bodde n.d.: 113)

These reflections on the mutual relationship between those who use their mental powers to rule and those who use their labour to provide food to the rulers are evidently part of those general reflections of the Confucians on the nature of the well-ordered state, and it seems that the Legalists, in particular, were responsible for developing the theory of the Four Classes of society (*shih, nung, kung*, and *shang*) more systematically:

These men wanted to reduce the vagaries of personalised government by creating an impersonal machinery of institutions. Thus they laid the foundations for what became the bureaucratic way of government in imperial times. They also wanted to build up the state's wealth and power through a planned economy that would involve the total population and utilise quantitative techniques. Thus it is natural that they, more than any other thinkers, should be interested in classifying the population along socio-economic lines. (Bodde n.d.: 113–14)

The Legalist work known as *Kuan Tzu*, composed during a period from the Warring States to the middle of the third century BC, and whose text was finally stabilized in the first century, referred to the Four Classes in the following terms:

Farmers (*nung*) should begin cultivating soil as soon as the snow melts away . . . Scholars (*shih*) should listen and pay heed to those who are broadly learned . . . Merchants (*ku*) should be aware of the rise and fall of prices and should daily go to the market place . . . Artisans (*kung*) should devote themselves to the appearance and capability of whatever goods they produce. (*Kuan Tzu*, Chapter 5, 1b)

Scholars (*shih*), farmers (*nung*), artisans (*kung*), and merchants (*shang*): these four categories of people (*ssu min*) are the pillars (*lit.* 'stones') of the state. (*Kuan Tzu*, Chapter 20, 2)

Let the scholars (i.e. officials) be incorrupt, the farmers single-minded, and the merchants and artisans honest. (*Kuan Tzu*, Chapter 30, 3; cited in Bodde n.d.: 116–17)

It seems that the major social changes of the late Chou period, the growth of private land ownership, luxury and extravagance, trade, and social mobility in general, were seen as dangerous to the state, leading to the neglect of farming in particular:

> If the sovereign does not hold dear the basic occupation (agriculture), the secondary activities (those of artisans and merchants) will then not be kept in check. If these secondary activities are left unchecked, the people will then become lackadaisical in their seasonal (agricultural) activities and indifferent to the profits of the land . . . If merchants stand in the court, material wealth will flow upward (in the form of bribes). (*Kuan Tzu*, Chapter 3, 10a; cited in Bodde n.d.: 117)

The basic concern of those administrators of the Former Han who tended to be Legalists thus seems to have had the essentially pragmatic goal of defining the mutual relations of those classes seen as essential for the well-ordered state. The Confucians, however, were more interested in ranking the classes in a hierarchy of moral value and were much more hostile to the very idea of profits than were the Legalists, who regarded mercantile activity with favour, as long as it was closely controlled by the state. With the final establishment of the Confucians as the orthodox philosophers of the Empire, the Four Classes became an ideal hierarchy of social merit—scholar-officials at the top, followed by farmers, artisans, and merchants in the lowest category.

Four groups of major significance in other civilizations are notably lacking from this scheme: priests, nobles, soldiers, and slaves. We have already noted that the lack of an organized priesthood is one of the major differences between China and most other states. 'The omission of an hereditary nobility is not surprising because, though all-important in pre-imperial China, these men (aside from the emperor himself) were rarely allowed, under the empire, to hold much political power; their once dominant role was replaced by that of the scholar-gentry known as *shih*' (Bodde n.d.: 104). The omission of the class of soldiers, however, is more striking. While the bulk of the Imperial armies were peasant conscripts, there was still a nucleus of professional soldiers, and we seem here to encounter another instance of the Confucian antipathy to warfare, and the belief that 'a military class does not properly belong to a truly well-ordered state' (ibid., 105). Finally, while public and private slavery certainly existed, the institution had nothing like the importance which it assumed in the Graeco-Roman world (see Wilbur 1943, Keightley n.d.). It may therefore be that 'the real reason for their exclusion from the traditional social ranking is the conviction that they, like the military, are anomalies in the well-ordered state; hence that they should not be recognized as a distinct social group' (Bodde n.d.: 105).

The striking feature of the Chinese scheme of the social classes is how late it was in developing as a formal ideology; that it was essentially pragmatic and moralistic in its inspiration; that it was capable of ignoring the military function altogether; and that it had no cosmological or religious significance. We shall see that in medieval Europe too, when men were faced with the problem of social anarchy and the collapse of political authority, they developed a theory of the Three Estates, but, unlike the Chinese, they were drawing upon a far older scheme of the tripartite nature of society that long antedated the development of the state. The political problems of the Chinese and the Europeans were somewhat similar, but their solutions drew upon their radically different cultural traditions.

3. Indo-European society

It is the purpose of this section to show that a number of those basic institutional and ideological forms which we regard as characteristic of Western European (and especially English) society, such as competitive individualism, the importance of civil law, the pursuit of wealth, the admiration of war, and representative government, are not simply responses to particular geographical challenges, or the product of fairly recent technological and economic change, but can be traced to a much more remote Indo-European origin. This ancient institutional and ideological complex seems to have comprised at least the following elements: (1) an idea of society as based on three distinct functions, all of which were essential for the well-being of society as a whole—priests, warriors, and food producers (who were emphatically not just plebeians, but *freemen*, with full social status); (2) a king who was the embodiment or representative of the whole society, not of one section alone, with sacred status, elected from among the members of a royal descent group and ratified by the assembly of all free men; (3) an idea of society as ruled by holy law, which under the control of the gods governed both the natural events of the physical world and the relations between men; (4) the basic importance of the assembly which had sacred status, where debates were held, the decisions of the leaders ratified, and judicial cases tried; (5) a close association between the priesthood and the law; (6) a high regard for war, which produced plunder and booty, and was thus sacred, like the activity of the food producers; (7) an equally striking acceptance of competition, both verbal (as in oratory and litigation) and physical (as in a variety of games and sports); (8) the fundamental importance of loyalty by followers to their leader in war, and the corresponding obligations of generosity and protection on the part of the leader; and (9) the absence of large corporate lineal descent groups.

Individually, perhaps, none of these traits is unique to the Indo-Europeans, but the combination certainly is, and we shall also discover that they had an extraordinary persistence and longevity quite comparable to those core principles of Chinese society which we examined in the previous section. On the other hand, of course, it is obvious that Chinese society has had a far greater geographical and political unity over the last four millennia than the societies in the Indo-European tradition, which have become dispersed over a vast area, and which have encountered in the process conditions of much greater diversity than existed in China. One thinks here, in particular, of the Indo-European societies that migrated to the Mediterranean region and produced the city-states of Greece and Italy, or those which invaded India with an ancient civilization of its own, or the Iranians, who encountered the great Semitic empires, by contrast with the Germanic, Scandinavian, and Celtic peoples who experienced very different conditions.[8] It would obviously be quite impossible to trace here, even in outline, the histories of all the societies in the Indo-European tradition (the case of India, in particular, would require a long section to itself), and I shall therefore concentrate on those of Northern Europe, although some reference will be made to Greek and Roman society as well as to the Indo-Iranians. Unlike the previous section, it will not be possible to follow a chronological account, and we shall instead consider a number of basic institutions and beliefs and their development.

The account of Indo-European institutions that follows is therefore only intended as a brief survey, a general sketch, of a number of essential institutions and beliefs, but even this very limited survey will show clearly that the subsequent development of

---

[8] It must be remembered that when the Indo-Europeans expanded into the different regions of Europe these lands were already occupied by peoples of other languages and cultures, with whom the Indo-Europeans intermingled.

European society and government was vitally affected by its ancient Indo-European ancestry, which had evolved its distinctive characteristics long before the emergence of the state.

(a) Place of origin and mode of life

Comparative linguists have been aware for more than a century and a half that many languages of Europe, Western Asia, and India share a common origin, but the location of the original speakers of this Proto-Indo-European (PIE) has until recently been much debated. From a comparison of literary sources with archaeological evidence and features of the natural environment mentioned in these sources, it now seems that this homeland was in the steppes of the Kazakh-Kirghiz region[9] (Gimbutas 1970; Littleton 1973: 25–31), and the combination of this evidence allows us to form a fairly clear impression of the basic features of the society and its economy at this period, which extends back to the fifth millennium BC. Archaeologically it is known as the Kurgan Culture, from the *kurgans*, or round barrows in which the cremated bones of leaders were deposited, and which are characteristic of the area.

Early Kurgan society (to the end of the fourth millennium BC) north of the Black Sea, before expansion into Danubian Europe and the Near East (Gimbutas 1970: 177), was technologically at the Chalcolithic stage (use of copper and stone). The economy was mainly pastoral, based on horses, cattle, sheep, goats, and pigs; fishing was significant, but hunting seems to have been relatively unimportant. Agriculture, however, was certainly practised. Wheeled vehicles, with two or four wheels of solid oak, presumably harnessed to oxen, seem to have been known at this period, and certainly by the beginning of the third millennium BC.

Typically, the Kurgan people settled in flat grasslands, in a landscape favorable to horse and cattle grazing. When they expanded it can be seen that they were searching for pasture lands, such as the steppe area north and west of the Black Sea, Dobrudja, the Danube Plain, the East Hungarian puszta, the Kuro-Araxes Valley in Transcaucasia, and the prairie lands of Syro-Palestine. (Gimbutas 1970: 161)

The Middle Kurgan (third millennium BC–c.2200 BC) is the period in which continuous waves of expansion occurred into central Europe and Iran, overrunning the agricultural peoples in these

[9] A conclusion disputed by Goodenough 1970.

areas. The Late Kurgan was a Bronze-Age culture with chariots, and expanded into the Aegean and Western Europe, and into Syria and Palestine. The high level of technology allowed the upper classes to amass huge quantities of wealth objects (ibid., 168).

(b) *Indo-European kinship*

We can infer relatively little about early Indo-European kinship: to be sure, most pastoral societies are patrilineal, and almost all are patrilocal (see above, Chapter IV, Section 2), so it is fairly safe to attribute these characteristics to Indo-European society, but what does this imply about actual organization? Friedrich (1966) claims that they had an 'Omaha' type of kinship system: this involves a rigid division into patrilineal descent groups, and the rules that one may not marry a woman of one's own clan, one's mother's clan, or one's father's mother's clan. In fact, the only PIE kin terms that can be reliably established are those for 'father', 'mother', 'brother', 'sister', and 'daughter' (Benveniste 1973: 167), and even that for 'son' shows considerable variability. But this evidence is quite inadequate to establish the existence of *any* specific type of kinship system, even patrilineality itself. To establish the existence of an Omaha or any other type of system we need to know the terms for father's sister, father's brother, mother's brother, mother's sister, and the cross- and parallel-cousins, and this evidence is entirely lacking, as even Friedrich admits (1966: 33).

From the Rig-Veda we know that Vedic society was divided into five 'tribes', but even if these were patrilineal in composition this tells us little about the extent to which lineality as such was the basis of actual co-operation. Again, there seem to have been four 'organizational levels' in Indo-European society, which are clearest in ancient Iran: *dam* (family, house); *vis* ('clan', or group of several families); *zantu* ('tribe', the whole of those of the same birth); and *dahyu* ('country', presumably a confederation of tribes) (Benveniste 1973: 240). This evidence, too, tells us little or nothing about the actual importance of lineal descent as the basis of corporate rights and duties.

Property inheritance, however, does not seem to have been strictly patrilineal, to judge from a passage in the Rig-Veda (3. 31. 1, 2) which refers to the case of a man dying without a son, who is allowed to leave his property to his *daughter's* son, rather than to his nearest agnate. Similarly, RV 10. 27. 12 seems clearly to refer to the institution of the dowry, and to suitors wishing to marry a girl who will bring them great riches. The dowry is a distinctively Indo-European institution (Fox 1967: 238; and see Table 3 Goody and Tambiah 1973: 22), which is closely associated with an emphasis on monogamy and cognatic descent rather than on lineality (Goody and Tambiah 1973: 50, Table 5). The Rig-Veda also refers in several places to the ritual importance of the householder, especially as the person responsible for employing a priest to conduct religious ceremonies. These indications, slender as they are, point to the family, or joint family, together with its immediate cognates and affines, as the locus of co-operation, rather than to any large corporate lineal descent group comparable to that of Chinese society.

We also know that the war band was a very early Indo-European institution and, especially with the introduction of the chariot at the beginning of the second millennium BC, these bands would have been composed of wealthy young men, quite possibly of the same age as well, but there is no indication that common descent was the basis of such bands.

The basic importance of assemblies for the debate of public affairs, and the judging of legal cases, again, does not suggest that unilineal descent was the *major* organizing principle of Indo-European society. This impression is strengthened by the account which Tacitus[10] gives of Germanic society:

What the *Germania* appears to describe is a society in which bilateral relationship is a central feature of the kinship system. Unilineal categories or groups are given no special functions and, outside the house community, the kindred defines those prerequisites and obligations based on kinship. This is true not just of less tangible benefits, but also of significant legal or political processes such as inheritance and feud. (Murray 1983: 57)

At *Germania* 6. 5, Tacitus says that military units of 100 men are recruited on a residential basis, for which he uses the Roman term *pagus*, and explains that 'the strongest incentive to courage lies in this, that neither chance nor casual grouping makes the squadron or the wedge, but family and kinship' (7. 3), literally, 'families and relatives', *familiae et propinquitates*.

---

[10] I agree with the arguments of Murray (1983: 42–50) for disregarding the evidence of Caesar's *Gallic War* on lineal descent groups among the ancient Germans.

While this description *could* apply to a society organized on the basis of patrilineal clans, it is also compatible with the view that the German residential unit comprised affines, cognates, and friends, as well as agnates. The statements that 'Sisters' sons mean as much to their uncles [*avunculus*, MB] as to their fathers' (20. 4), and that 'some tribes regard this blood tie as even closer and more sacred than that between son and father, and in taking hostages make it the basis of their demand, as though they thus secure loyalty more surely and have a wider hold on the family', give rather stronger support to the belief that cognatic ties were very important in Germanic society. To be sure, it is well known that in patrilineal society the mother's brother often has close ties, especially of a ritual nature, with his sister's son; but the clearest evidence for a basically cognatic system comes in the next paragraph: 'However . . . so far as heirship and succession are concerned, each man's children (*liberi*) are his heirs, and there is no will; if there be no children, the nearest degree of relationship for the holding of property are brothers, paternal uncles, and uncles *maternal* [*my emphasis*]' (20. 5). There seems no reason for Tacitus to have used the term *liberi*, 'children', here instead of *filii*, 'sons', unless he had had good reason for believing that the German law of inheritance allowed daughters as well as sons to inherit, even if, as Murray suggests (ibid., 58), he meant that male heirs take precedence over female. The reference to maternal uncles is also highly significant in relation to the inheritance of property. The passage in question also makes it clear that the ownership of moveable property was individual, and not corporate. This individualism is also stressed at 25. 1 'Each freeman remains master of his own house and home.' With these passages in mind, we can interpret the statement 'It is incumbent to take up a father's feuds or a kinsman's not less than his friendships' (2. 1) as implying that the feud was conducted on the basis of the kindred and not on any patrilineal principle.

The institution of the dowry is clearly decribed in Chapter 18, where the legal procedures for payment are stated in some detail, and where the autonomy of the married man and his household is also emphasized again, as is monogamy and the strength of the marriage bond (although a few men of high birth are said to have more than one wife). None of this evidence suggests the existence of strong lineal descent groups.

It is well established, of course, that in Anglo-Saxon society there were no lineal descent groups but only cognatic kindreds (e.g.

Seebohm 1911), nor do we find evidence of lineal descent groups among the Scandinavian peoples. There is no space here to discuss the origin of the Roman patrilineal *gens*, but the development of the Roman state drastically reduced its social importance, and by the fall of the Empire it can be said that kinship, beyond the range of close relatives, was an insignificant aspect of social organization, especially in Western and Northern Europe. Just as among the East Cushitic peoples, the importance of this development (which I am suggesting was probably of great antiquity in Indo-European society) was the opportunity which it gave the alternative modes of organization, especially in the society of the early Middle Ages:

. . . to the individual, threatened by the numerous dangers bred by an atmosphere of violence, the kinship group did not seem to offer adequate protection, even in the first feudal age. In the form in which it then existed, it was too vague and too variable in its outlines, too deeply undermined by the duality of descent by male and female lines. That is why men were obliged to seek or accept other ties. (Marc Bloch 1961: 142)

The relative weakness of kinship by comparison with China, and also with many pre-state societies, was therefore a very important aspect of Indo-European society that had a significant effect on its subsequent development.

(c) *The three functions*

One of the most distinctive features of Indo-European culture is its division into the celebrated 'three functions', so brilliantly elucidated by the work of Dumézil ' . . . the central motif of Indo-European ideology [is] the conception according to which the world and society can live only through the harmonious collaboration of the three stratified functions of sovereignty, force, and fecundity' (Dumézil 1970: 4). These are associated respectively with the priests (who are the guardians of the law, as well as of ritual); the warriors and especially the warrior bands, the *Männerbund*; and the farmers and herdsmen, the food producers; and between these classes there is both complementarity and tension. But the three functions are not merely social categories or classes, nor are they merely an ideological reflection of such classes:

I recognized toward 1950 that the 'tripartite ideology' was not necessarily accompanied, in the life of a society, by a *real* tripartite division of that society according to the Indian mode; on the contrary, I recognized that, wherever one can establish its presence, the tripartite ideology is nothing (or is no longer, or perhaps never was) but an ideal and, at the same time, a method of analysis, a method of interpreting the forces which assure the course of the world and the lives of men. (Dumézil 1971: 15 trans. Littleton)

Dumézil explains the three functions as follows:

We must certainly understand [by these] the three basic activities by which groups of men—priests, warriors, and producers—can be assured of their collective subsistence and prosperity. But the domain of the 'functions' is not limited to this social perspective. They had already supplied Indo-European philosophy, as in the abstract substantives *brahman, ksatra, vis* which are the principles of the three classes in vedic and post-vedic Indian thought, with what can be considered a means of exploring material and moral reality or, a means of ordering the general stock of ideas accepted by society . . .

It is now easy to label the first and second functions in a way that covers all their shades of meaning. The sacred comprises both the relations between men and the sacred (cult, magic) and the relations of men with one another, under the regard and guarantee of the gods (law, administration), and also the sovereign power exercised by the king or his delegates in conformity with the will and favour of the gods; and, finally, more generally, knowledge and understanding, inseparable from meditation and from the ritual use of sacred objects. The second function is that of brute force, and the customs associated with it, which are chiefly but not exclusively those of warrior-hood. It is less easy to comprehend the essence of the third function in a few words. It extends over numerous domains, between which many obvious links appear, but which do not unite around any precise focus: fecundity, to be sure—human, animal, and vegetable—but also food and riches, health and peace—with all its satisfactions and benefits—and often sensuality and beauty as well. There is also the important idea of the 'large number', applied not only to goods (abundance), but also to the men who make up the mass of the people. These are not *a priori* definitions, but convergences that result from many applications of the tripartite ideology. (Dumézil 1958: 18–19)

While, as R. Needham (1981) rightly says, the opposition between sacred and secular authority is found in many other social traditions, and there is also a universal quest for life, usually linking religion with the means of production, there are many different ways in which these relationships can be represented, so that the tri-functional ideology does appear to be a distinctive articulation of these ideas. As Dumézil says, 'it is one thing for a society to feel and to satisfy its basic needs, but to represent these consciously, and to reflect on them in making an intellectual structure and a cast of thought is quite another matter: in the ancient world, only the Indo-European made this philosophical step [of the three functions]' (Dumézil 1958: 23), and we certainly find no such parallel tripartition among the Finno-Ugrians, Siberians, Chinese, Hebrews, Phoenicians, Mesopotamians, or any other neighbours of the Indo-Europeans (ibid., 16).

This ideology has many significant consequences: it renders the status of the king, who is not clearly identified with any of the functions, ambiguous; it gives warfare a necessary place in the scheme of social life (quite unlike Chinese ideology); law and justice are sacred, and allocated to the priests and to the assembly; and it considers that the social functions of political authority, war leadership, the adjudication of disputes, and the priestly task of sacrifice must be distributed among different sections of society rather than being combined in a single office, such as the Egyptian Pharaoh, the kings and emperors of China, the Bantu chief and king, or the Islamic caliph.

Early Indo-European society seems clearly to have been divided into three classes; priests, warriors, and farmers/herdsmen, but these were not the rigid castes that later developed in India. The generic terms for these classes, Vedic *varna*, Avestan *pistra*, both have the basic meaning of 'colour',[11] and in ancient Iran priests wore white, warriors red, and farmers blue (Benveniste 1973: 27). The function of the priests (Vedic *brahman*, Avestan *athravan*) was to ensure the performance of the rites in the prescribed form, the rites being in particular the preparation of the sacred drink *soma* (from an unidentified plant) which was offered to all the gods but especially to Indra, god of war; the kindling of the sacred fire; and animal sacrifice. The ceremonies were held in assemblies of the people, which were sacred gatherings, and priests also performed the rites for individual householders. Priesthood seems to have been an inherited function, and certainly involved the learning of a large body of oral texts, hymns, which were essential to the invocation of the gods at religious ceremonies. The warrior class in India was *ksattriya* or *rajanya*, 'who had martial power', Iranian *rathaesta*, 'one who stands in the chariot' (ibid., 233). By the beginning of the second millennium BC and the use of bronze, the warriors were clearly a chariot-driving aristocracy and specialists in

[11] For Roman, Celtic, Norse, and Hittite parallels, see Littleton 1982: 113–14 and references to Dumézil cited there.

warfare, but it is not altogether clear how far the herdsmen/farmers were also involved in warfare. Stock raiding was an essential feature of warfare which could not have been achieved by chariots alone, and it therefore seems obvious that the ordinary freemen must have been involved in war, both in stock raiding and probably as an infantry complement to the charioteers in battle. The widespread custom of the freemen going armed to the assembly provides additional support for the belief that warfare was a general social obligation, and not restricted to a single class. Presumably, therefore, the warrior class were the *leaders* in war, chariot specialists drawn from the wealthier families, and the herdsmen/farmers made up the bulk of the ordinary fighting men.

The third class of herdsmen/farmers, Vedic *vaisya* ('man of the *vis*, "clan", man of the people'), Iranian *vastryo*, *fsuyant* (*vastar* = 'herdsmen', *fsuyant* a present participle from the root *fsu-* 'to rear stock') (Benveniste 1973: 234), were definitely not a proletarian or plebeian mass, and were clearly distinguished from a fourth class of slaves. In Hindu society the *varna* of priests, warriors, and farmers are all 'twice-born', in opposition to the fourth caste, the *shudra*. 'Each of the Indo-European societies is pervaded by a distinction founded on free or servile condition' (ibid., 262), and the concept of 'freedom' is closely associated with two PIE terms, **leudh*, 'to grow, develop', and **priyos*, Skt. *priya*, Av. *frya*, 'dear'. 'The first sense is not, as one would be tempted to imagine, "to be free of, rid of something", it is that of belonging to an ethnic stock designated by a metaphor taken from vegetable growth. Such membership confers a privilege which a stranger and a slave will never possess' (ibid., 264). The second sense refers to the bonds between the free men, illustrated in the Roman idea of *civis*. The word *civis*, citizen, designates properly the quality of a citizen and, collectively, the totality of the citizens, the city itself.

The authentic sense of *civis* is not 'citizen', as it is traditionally translated, but 'fellow-citizen'. A number of ancient uses show the sense of reciprocity which is inherent in *civis*, and which alone accounts for *civitas* as the designation by which the members of a group, who enjoy indigenous rights, originally addressed each other, as contrasted with the different varieties of 'strangers', *hostes*, *peregrini*, *advenae*. (Ibid., 274–5)

As we shall see, the assembly itself, and the central importance of law in Indo-European society, depend on the existence of the freemen.

The trifunctional ideology has proved remarkably enduring, and I shall here refer in particular to English and French society. While the Germanic societies seem to have lost the *corporate* groups of priests, such as the Druids of the Celts, or the Brahmans and Athravans of Vedic and Iranian society, they clearly had priests. Tacitus describes the priests of the Germans as having very clear social functions relating to law and punishment as well as their purely ritual responsibilities. Bede, too, provides clear evidence for the ritual opposition between priestly and warrior functions in his description of the conversion to Christianity of the High Priest Coifi of the Kingdom of Northumberland:

And incontinently casting away vain superstition [Coifi] besought the king to grant him harness and a stallion war horse whereon he might mount and destroy the idols. For it was not before lawful for a priest of the sacrifices either to wear harness or to ride on other than a mare. Girded therefore with a sword about his loins he took a spear in his hand, and mounting the king's war horse set forth against the idols. (Bede, II. 13)

He hurled the spear into the temple, which he then ordered to be burned.

In 897–8 (Dubuisson 1975: 37), King Alfred of Wessex had translated Boethius's *De Consolatione Philosophiae*, and in Book II, chapter 17, which discusses the nature and value of temporal power, the translation interpolates the following passage:

You know of course that no one can make known any skill, nor direct and guide any authority, without tools and resources; a man cannot work on any enterprise without resources. In the case of the king, the resources and tools with which to rule are that he have his land fully manned: he must have praying men, fighting men, and working men. You know also that without these tools no king may make his ability known. (Asser, 1983 edn., 132)

At the end of the tenth century and the beginning of the eleventh, Aelfric refers to the three functions in three passages, of which I shall quote one here:

It is necessary to realise that there are in this world three classes, who are working men (*laboratores*), praying men (*oratores*), and fighting men (*bellatores*). The *laboratores* are those who, by their labour, provide our sustenance; the *oratores* are those who intercede for us with God; the *bellatores* are those who protect our land against the army of the invader. In truth the labourer must work to feed us, the soldier must fight against our enemies, and the servant of God must pray for us and fight spiritually against invisible enemies. (Dubuisson 1975: 38)

In about 1010, Wulfstan wrote:

Every legitimate throne which keeps itself perfectly straight rests on three columns: the first is the *oratores*, the second is the *laboratores*, and the third the *bellatores*. (Ibid., 39)

In France, Gerard Bishop of Cambrai, between 1023 and 1025, is described as saying 'From the beginning, mankind has been divided into three parts, among men of prayer, farmers, and men of war', and between 1027 and 1031,[12] in a poem dedicated to King Robert the Pious, Adalbero Bishop of Laon wrote

The ecclesiastical order forms a single body, but the division of society comprises three orders . . . The city of God, which one thinks of as one, is divided into three orders: some pray, others fight, and others work. These three orders live together and cannot be separated. The services of one permit the services of the other two. Each in turn lends its support to all. (Ibid., 36–7)

These expressions of the tripartite nature of society elaborated by men of learning were not drawn out of thin air, nor were they mere 'reflections' of contemporary social life. Their derivation from ancient Indo-European tradition is quite obvious. But there were good reasons why this folk-model of society was given such emphasis at this period in European history. Just as Confucius drew upon the ancient tradition of the Chinese world view when his society was in a state of anarchy and collapse, in an effort to provide a clear ideology for the guidance of the rulers of his day, so the Anglo-Saxon and French scholars and priests were responding to the anarchy and turmoil of their society:

At the time that Alfred and his friends were writing the trifunctional theme into the margins of Boethius' text, God was subjecting Wessex to cruel tribulation. To extirpate this mortal danger, the sovereign had to call on all his powers. Both armed force and the law would be needed. In his entourage a bitter meditation on sovereignty was being pursued . . . I think it worthy of note that as was to be the case again in France one hundred and twenty-five years later, reflective men should have employed an image of society in which the subjects of the realm were seen as performing three functions just when the throne seemed tottering on the verge of collapse, and that they should have done so in order to consolidate the monarchy's power. (Duby 1980: 100)

In the time of Aelfric and Wulfstan, renewed Danish invasions led

[12] I follow the dating of Duby (1980) here, rather than that of Dubuisson.

to monks taking up the sword to defend the kingdom and to irresponsible military violence in general, a confusion in social functions to which the tripartite ideology was highly relevant. The problems of peace and civil order were also uppermost in French society of the eleventh century, and in Christendom generally. Royal authority was weak, armed force was being used (even by royal castellans) against the people rather than against foreign invaders or wrongdoers, and the very necessity of a priestly order was being questioned. Gerard was also strongly opposed to the scheme whereby all men would take an oath to keep the peace and refrain from violence, on the ground that the oath was too sacred to be made a universal obligation, and because a general oath-taking would utterly confuse the distinct functions of bishop and king: the tasks of the priest were to admonish kings 'so that they may fight manfully for the salvation of the fatherland', and to pray, 'so that they might vanquish.' ' "It is the task of kings to repress sedition by their *virtus*" (that energy with which their blood was fraught, that strength with which they were endowed, the quality, according to Georges Dumézil, specific to the second function), to put an end to wars, to encourage peaceful commerce' (Duby 1980: 29). Heretics of the time were also advancing views that seem to Gerard to threaten the whole fabric of society. This heresy ' . . . did not consist in criticism of priests, or denunciations of their impurity. It lay rather in the wish to forgo their services, in the desire to deny the clergy's usefulness. Why should certain men, setting themselves apart from the rest, claim custody of the extraordinary privilege of administering the sacred?' (Duby 1980: 31). Gerard answered these arguments by maintaining ' . . . that within human society there existed an inviolable boundary marking off a particular category of men, an 'order' (*ordo*) whose members alone were designated to perform certain acts for the benefit of all' (ibid., 31). He also maintained the essential importance of celibacy for the clergy, as it separated them from the world in the same way as their freedom from physical labour.

Adalbero's poem is concerned in particular with the nature of royal authority, with sovereignty, the first function:

. . . the king was a sacred personage, like a bishop, and at the same time the man who each spring rallied the warriors about his person. He thus stood at the point where the visible arms of the cross that underlay the architecture of all creation intersected the invisible arm. Thus he bore responsibility for peace, that projection onto our imperfect world of law, of the order regnant on high. *Rex, lex, pax*—three words whose consonant echo reverberates throughout the work—are the keys to the whole poem, the nails which hold the entire framework together. (Ibid., 46)

As royal authority became stronger in England and France, the ideology of the Three Estates became an essential constitutional principle, whose institutional forms survived in France until the Revolution, and survives in certain aspects of the British constitution until the present day.

There is, however, a more general implication of the trifunctional model of society that remains a vital part of Western political culture. This is the idea that society is inherently composed of different functions, which *must not* be performed by the same people. A precise expression of this idea is found, for example, in the separation of powers laid down in the American Constitution, and by law or convention in the whole of the English-speaking world, and in other societies of Western Europe. While this separation of powers is now justified by pragmatic arguments about the liberty of the individual (quite reasonably), the roots of the idea are of far greater antiquity than the state. Similarly, the whole history of the relations between Church and State in Europe has been profoundly affected by this ideology, which is diametrically opposed to that of China and many other societies, which operate on the basis that all the functions can and should be performed by the sovereign. Both models of society, however, are perfectly viable under the conditions of the state, and are excellent examples of institutions arising under ascriptive conditions that can exercise a profound effect on subsequent evolution. It will also be noted that whereas the Chinese scheme of social classes seems to have been a late development, that of the Indo-European was far more ancient and fundamental.

(d) The concepts of order and law

The concept of law (Iranian *arta*, Avestan *asa*, Sanskrit *rta*), as regulating the course of nature and the social relations of man, was absolutely fundamental to the Indo-European world-view, and refers to the cosmic and social order maintained by the gods:

This term, it is now generally accepted, represents a concept which cannot be precisely rendered by any single word in another tongue. It stands, it seems, for 'order' in the widest sense: cosmic order, by which night gives place to day and the seasons change; the order of sacrifice, by which this natural rhythm is strengthened and maintained; social order, by which men can live together in harmony and prosperity; and moral order or 'truth'. In both India and Iran to possess *rta* or *asa*, to be *rtavan* or *asavan*, was to be a just and upright being . . . (Boyce 1975: 27)

(See also Benveniste 1973: 379.) The association of the concept with 'order' has been explored by Benveniste, according to whom the Latin *ars*, natural disposition, *artus*, joint, *ritus*, rite, and the Greek *ararisko*, to fit, adapt, harmonize, again express the basic idea, 'order, arrangement, the close mutual adaptation of the parts of a whole to one another' (ibid., 380), even though the derivations have undergone different semantic specializations in different languages. 'We thus have for Indo-European a general concept which embraces, by numerous lexical variants, the religious, legal, and technological aspects of "order" ' (ibid., 380).

The concept of law was part of the ancient Indo-European conception of sovereignty, the first function. This had two aspects, represented by the gods Mitra and Varuna. Varuna was the creator god, manipulator of the forces of the cosmos, maintainer of the correct ritual relations between man and the divine, and the general enforcer of the moral order, and his awesome and terrible aspect has elements of the irrational and magical (Littleton 1982: 65–7). Mitra, however, was essentially concerned with the contract or covenant which was of central importance in Indo-European law. Meillet (1907) first identified this essential function of Mitra:

As he pointed out, in past times 'the contract was in principle a religious act, encircled by prescribed ceremonies, made with certain rites; and the words which accompanied it were not those of simple individual undertakings; they were those of formulas [i.e. *mathras*], endowed with a force of their own, which would, by virtue of this inner potency, turn back against any man who should transgress them. The Indo-Iranian *Mitra* is at the same time "contract" and the power immanent in the contract.' (Boyce 1975: 25) [According to Boyce, the word 'covenant' more exactly conveys to English readers what Meillet translated as '*contrat*'.]

To know who is *asavan*, Mithra must assess the actions of men, and see who keep the many covenants, *mithras*, that hold society together, who betray them. The wide range of these covenants is indicated in his *yast*, where the list includes agreements between friends and fellow-citizens, the contracts of trading partners, and the marriage bond joining husband and wife, as well as treaties entered into between states. (Boyce 1975: 28)

The oath and the ordeal were closely related to this central concept of the covenant, and Boyce notes that in ancient India and Iran it was customary to swear to covenants in the presence of fire; and the various ordeals by fire were used to discover the guilt or innocence of the man accused of swearing falsely (ibid., 29, 35–6). Ordeal by battle was also part of the same complex of ideas, discussed further in section (*e*) below.

Thus both the Indo-Europeans and the Chinese gave the concept of cosmic order a fundamental place in their world-views, but for the Indo-Europeans this order was enforced by active agencies whereas the Chinese regarded the maintenance of order as a spontaneous process:

> Later on we shall have occasion to quote that famous sentence of Heracleitus: 'the Sun will not transgress his measures, otherwise the Erinyes, the bailiffs of Dike, will find him out'. Here a phenomenon of Nature could rebel, and could be forced into submission by the executive branch of a cosmic constitution. With great acuity, Misch found the complementary passage to this in a text and its commentary from the *I Ching* (Book of Changes). Speaking of the top line in the first hexagram, *Chhien*, the text says 'The dragon exceeds its proper bounds; there will be occasion for repentance.' Then the Wen Yen commentary explains: 'This phrase "exceeds its proper bounds" means that it knows how to advance but not to retire, how to survive but not how to be dissolved, how to obtain but not how to let go. He alone is the sage who, knowing progression and retrogression, coming into being and passing away, never loses his true nature. Truly he alone is the sage.' But the sage is only finding out what all natural bodies, celestial and terrestrial, spontaneously know and perform. Misch rightly maintained that Chinese thinkers in all the descriptions which they gave of the regularity of natural processes had in mind, not government by law, but the mutual adaptations of community life. (J. Needham 1956: 283)

Among the Germans, Scandinavians, and Celts it is clear that law and punishment were closely associated with the gods and with the priests. We have already noted the observations of Tacitus on the priestly functions with regard to law and punishment. Among the Celts:

> The task of 'finding', interpreting [law] and applying this devolved first on the Druids (again like the Brahmins in India), later on the *filid*, lit. 'seers', a learned caste who preserved and transmitted all the native lore in verse, later still on a more specialized caste (doubtless an offshoot from the *filid*) of professional jurists, the *'brehons'* (Ir. *brithemoin*, lit. 'makers of judgements'). In the period with which we are concerned here, these are the custodians and interpreters of the law, which, once it has been 'found', is

regarded as the permanent and immutable formulation of ancestral wisdom. As arbitrators in litigation between members of different kindreds they apply its rules, and in their professional schools they expound and interpret it. (Binchy 1970: 16. See also Powell 1958: 78)

While the Icelandic *godi* (pl. *godar*) is usually translated 'chieftain', the *godi* originally meant a man who conducted sacrificial ceremonies. In the time of the Commonwealth (930–1264) the *godar* were the owners of temples, men of rank and wealth who were also the founders of the district assemblies, but it would be more accurate to regard them as a kind of priest. Temples, sacrifice, *godar*, courts, litigation and oaths were thus closely bound up together, e.g.:

A temple-ring weighing two ounces or more . . . should be kept upon the altar of every major temple . . . Every chieftain (or: temple priest) should wear the temple-ring on his arm in attendance at any of the regular assemblies which were convened under his leadership. First, however, he should immerse the ring in the blood of the bull offered as sacrifice by the chieftain himself. Anyone transacting legal business before a court should first take an oath on the temple-ring [etc.]. (Johannesson 1974: 56)

All men had to declare allegiance to a specific *godi*, but this was a private contract between *godi* and each follower; a man could change his *godi* no more than once a year, and no kin ties were involved. So essential was the law, both in Iceland and in Norway, that it was the common possession of a body of law which was seen as defining the body politic; Iceland of the Commonwealth period had no executive, and the state was referred to as '*var log*', 'our laws' (ibid., 40).

We shall have more to say about the fundamental importance of law in Indo-European society, especially in the section on the assembly, and it is perhaps unnecessary to do more here than emphasize the extraordinary importance that the development of civil law has had in European society. The Romans provide the supreme example, but in Greek, Celtic, Germanic, and Scandinavian society civil law was also quite fundamental.

(e) *The relation between order and competition in Indo-European society*

The fundamental significance of conflict in the Indo-European world-view is clearly illustrated in Vedic mythology by the account of Indra's combat with the dragon Vrtra:

Indra slays with his *vájra* [a *mana*-like quality] the power of resistance (*vrtrá-*) of the inert Chaos, which power is conceived as residing on the primordial hill that floats on the surface of the cosmic Waters. Indra, while slaying this *vrtra*, at the same time splits the hill, which is now riveted to the bottom of the Waters, and Fire and Water (*Agni-Súrya* and *Ápah-Sóma*) are forced to leave the undifferentiated world of inertia and to join the ranks of the heavenly Gods (RS X. 124. 2, 6). Indra further separates by the same Vrtra-slaying Heaven from Earth, by which act a cosmic dualism of upper world and nether world . . . is constituted. To Varuna, the ancient god of the Waters of Chaos, a new function is now assigned as guardian of the cosmic law (*rtá-*), which remains hidden in the nether world (e.g. RS. V. 62.1). (Kuiper 1960: 218–19)

Thus it is by an act of violence, of combat, that a higher level of order is created, and the goods of life, symbolized by Fire and Water, are released for the benefit of man. Indra is frequently referred to as 'winner of the sun', 'lord of the sun', etc., and ritual chariot races were run with a symbol of the sun as the prize, in imitation of Indra's primordial act (ibid., 220).

Usas, Goddess of the Dawn, was also released by Indra from the nether world, and Kuiper presents convincing evidence that she was worshipped in particular at the festival of the winter solstice: 'The appearance of Usas represents the victory of Light over Darkness, of Life over Death. Her victory, like Indra's and Agni's, releases the goods of Life from the bonds of the nether world' (ibid., 227). But these goods are won by men not only through sacrifice and ritual, but through competition: 'She bestows wealth, but this wealth is also won in strife, in contests which are fought with the traditional weapons of the Aryans, viz. with races and word duels' (ibid., 236).

These word duels were conducted in assemblies (Skr. *sabha*, Av. *vyaxman*), and the chief aim of the contestants was to win applause and assent by their quick wit and eloquence. In the words of an Avestan text, 'All friends rejoice when their companion famous Returns from the assembly hall a victor, He drives away reproach and wins them nurture: he is sent out as fitted for the contest' (ibid., 250). Such verbal powers were regarded as divine in origin: ' . . . inspiration was to the Vedic poet an "opening of the doors of the mind" which was on a level with the "Opening of the doors of the primordial hill" ' (ibid., 249) and ' . . . the Vedic texts leave no doubt that the verbal contest was also a reiteration of the primordial fight with the cosmic forces of resistance (*vrtráni*); this is, indeed, true of all sorts of combat: "He verily slays Vrtra who is a victor in the battle" ' (ibid., 251).

On the importance of eloquence in general, as distinct from quick-wittedness, Kuiper cites Kristensen:

> Eloquence had not quite the same meaning for the ancient peoples which it has for us. They did not associate the word[13] with verbal art only, or with an artistic skill. The main thing to them was the authority of the spoken word, its wisdom and power, the success it was attended with. The eloquent word of the popular leader gave his audience the impression of absolute validity; it was authoritative, because one felt that it revealed a law of life. It was as irresistible and valid as the law of life itself. It was no mere beautiful sound, which existed for a moment. Once pronounced it maintained itself, it created a new situation, it turned itself into reality. Eloquence, therefore, was nothing short of a creative force, a vital energy. Its essence was the mystery of Creation and Life. (Ibid., 254)

So the Germanic kings spoke first in the assembly: 'It must be recalled, moreover, that the priest-kings of the *Germania* ruled in the assembly by *auctoritate suadendi*; if the source of their inspired word was the god from whom late Germanic kings traced their descent, Woden, so the god who gave magic words was "the beginning of every speech", as in turn the sacral king's speech was the first in the assembly' (Chaney 1970: 23).

Indra was also known as *maghavan*, giver of presents, and this was a title given to liberal patrons as well, and especially to those who rewarded the poets who represented them in the word duels. Kuiper suggests that the giving of presents in a competitive spirit may well have been an aspect of ritual, especially at the winter solstice, when 'these patrons had the same function on the social level as Indra had on the religious one, viz. that of distributing the goods of life, the *maghas*' (Kuiper 1960: 238).

More generally, men were supposed to have *vajra*, an inner power perhaps somewhat similar to the Polynesian *mana*, 'which manifested itself through wealth and which was won through the acquirement of this wealth' (ibid., 239), especially through racing,

---

[13] According to Dumézil (1981), there was an important Indo-European tradition that religious and legal texts should not be written because written characters were seen as dead, and also as deceitful.

verbal duels, and gambling, which was also an important aspect of ancient Indo-European social life.

Competition in every aspect was therefore a vital feature of Indo-European culture. Warfare and fighting were considered glorious, and one of the essential foundations of society. The Rig-Veda and Homer, in their different ways, harp endlessly on bloodshed, slaughter, the vanquishing of enemies, and the pillage of vast quantities of booty. A variety of athletic contests, especially chariot racing, seem also to have been an integral part of social life from the earliest times, and have retained great importance throughout subsequent European history. Oratory and competitive speeches were essential features in the conduct of assemblies, and the vital importance of law necessarily gave litigious competition a central place in society. Argument in general was therefore normal and admired in Indo-European society, most of all perhaps in ancient Greece, where it had extremely important cognitive and philosophical consequences (Lloyd 1979: 65). Lloyd notes that one of the most striking characteristics of Greek philosophy is 'an argumentative, competitive, even combative quality' (ibid., 234), of which the Platonic dialogue was the obvious product, just as the arts of rhetoric were developed in the assembly and the law courts: ' . . . even such, as we might suppose, specialised or technical topics as the ultimate constituents of man were the subject of public debates between contending speakers in front of a lay audience in the late fifth or early fourth century BC' (ibid., 93). With the revival of classical learning in the Middle Ages, rhetoric and dialectic again became of central importance in European thought.

These different aspects of competition were not, of course, mere belligerence, and there was an equally strong conviction that conflict must be regulated. Litigation and debate, athletic contests and warfare, were ideally governed by rules to which all the competitors gave their ultimate allegiance. Indeed, battle itself was seen as inherently judicial. So, according to Dumézil, *Tiwaz-Mars was not only a war god, but a juridical god as well:

These two conceptions (god of battle, god of law) are not contradictory. War in fact is not just a bloody clash of arms, it is a *decision*, obtained between the contesting parties, and guaranteed by precise rules of law. When one reads in the histories how the Germans in Roman times arranged the time and place of battles beforehand one realises that this was an activity which must be carried out according to strict juridical principles . . . The symbolic gestures associated with battle are the incontestable proof of this:

the declaration of war of the Latins by the *hasta ferrata aut praeusta sanguinea* is directly comparable to the ritual by which the Germans of the North hurled a spear into the enemy host; and this spear has the same essential meaning as that which was set up in the middle of the place of the *Ding*: if the Scandinavian Tyr . . . carried a spear, this was less of a weapon than a sign of his juridical authority. (Dumézil 1948: 99)

Trial by battle, which seems to us an entirely irrational and contradictory procedure, is an expression of these ideas. So in Iceland, 'the place where the official sword-duel, the *hólmganga*, was fought was close beside the site of the Chief Assembly of Iceland, where the important law cases were held' (Davidson 1964: 58). While subsequent European history has seen the disappearance of this particular institution (for an illuminating discussion of medieval Christian thought on the subject see Radding 1979), there is no doubt that the general belief in competition as leading to truth and virtue of all kinds is as lively as ever: scholarly and scientific debate, the lawcourts, the forces of the market-place, and the struggles of political parties under constitutional rules being some of the most obvious examples.

(f) Kingship

According to Benveniste the term *rex* and its cognates (Irish *ri*, Gaulish *rix*, Skt. *raj-* (*an*)) are found only in Italic, Indic, and Celtic culture, and belong to a very ancient group of terms relating to religion and law, though, as we shall see, the idea expressed by *rex* also appears among the Germans and Scandinavians. *Rex*, *rix*, *ri*, and *raj* all derive from an ancient stem **reg-*, as do *regio*, *rectus*, and German *recht*:

The important word *regio* did not originally mean 'region' but 'the point reached in a straight line' . . . In the language of augury *regio* indicates 'the point reached by a straight line traced out on the ground or in the sky' and 'the space enclosed between such straight lines drawn in different directions'.

The adjective *rectus* can be interpreted in a similar way 'straight as this line which one draws'. This is a concept at once concrete and moral: the 'straight line' represents the norm, while the *regula* is 'the instrument used to trace the straight line', which fixes the 'rule'. Opposed to the 'straight' in the moral order is what is *twisted*, *bent*. Hence 'straight' is equivalent to 'just', 'honest', while its contrary 'twisted' 'bent' is identified with 'perfidious', 'mendacious', etc . . . .

In order to understand the formation of *rex* and the verb *regere* we must start with this notion, which was wholly material to begin with but was susceptible of development in a moral sense. This dual notion is present in the important expression *regere fines*, a religious act which was a preliminary to building. *Regere fines* means literally 'trace out the limits by straight lines'. This is the operation carried out by the high priest before a temple or a town is built and it consists in the delimitation on a given terrain of a sacred plot of ground. The magical character of this operation is evident: what is involved is the delimitation of the interior and the exterior, the realm of the sacred and realm of profane, the national territory and foreign territory. The tracing of these limits is carried out by the person invested with the highest powers, the *rex*.

Thus in *rex* we must see not so much the 'sovereign' as the one who traces out the line, the way which must be followed, which also represents what is right . . . The Indo-European *rex* was much more a religious than a political figure. His mission was not to command, to exercise power but to draw up rules, to determine what was in the proper sense 'right' ('straight'). It follows that the *rex*, as thus defined, was more akin to a priest than a sovereign. It is this type of kingship which was preserved by the Celts and Italic peoples on the one hand, and the Indic on the other. (Benveniste 1973: 311)

Dumézil (1958: 32) notes that the relation of the king to the three functions varies considerably: sometimes he is outside and above them altogether, 'when the first function is then centred on the pure administration of the sacred, on the priest, rather than on power, on the sovereign and his agents'. Sometimes, however, the king's attributes are a mixture of all three functions, especially the second, the warrior function, with which kings become increasingly identified. The king also has important relations to the third function, typically being supposed to bring fertility, rain, and bountiful crops. This variability in royal function must be examined in more detail here.

It seems that the king had an essential religious function in relation to war in a number of Indo-European societies. In ancient Ireland, Binchy describes the king as having the traditional function of leader in battle (emphasized by all the laws, annals, and sagas), but in what sense was he a real war leader on whom depended the effective conduct of the battle? Or, how real was the warfare?

There is even a remarkable convention, doubtless of great antiquity, that when the king has been slain the battle is lost, no matter how advantageous the position in which he has left his army—exactly as in a game of chess. Indeed, the whole pattern of tribal warfare is rather like a ritual game, and in later times the utter disregard of its rules by the Norse invaders, who insisted on continuing the battle after their leader had perished, shocked and dismayed the native chroniclers. Valour in battle was the supreme test of rightful kingship. A law tract compiled about AD 700 lays down that if a king is wounded in the back of the head while fleeing from the battlefield, he sinks to the level of a 'churl' . . . (Binchy 1970: 17)

According to Chaney, the Germanic (and Anglo-Saxon) king 'is above all the intermediary between his people and the gods, the charismatic embodiment of the "luck" of the folk' (Chaney 1970: 12), and the 'luck' of the king was supposed to bring not only good crops but victory in battle. Bede's account of King Sigbert the Learned of East Anglia, who had resigned the throne to a kinsman and retired to a monastery, but was forcibly taken to the battlefield by the warriors in the hope that his presence would win the day even though he refused to fight (Bede III. 18), seems to provide an example of this belief.

Warfare was not, for the Indo-Europeans, merely a profane activity but also life-giving, and it was therefore quite appropriate that the king should be at least the nominal leader in battle, even if the real decisions were taken by specialist warriors. In Western Europe kings became increasingly significant as war leaders after the fall of the Roman Empire, and we shall consider this function in more detail in our discussion of war leadership and vassalage.

But to the extent that the king became closely identified with the warrior element he would have become increasingly distinct from the priests, the special representatives of the first function. In the Indian tradition, kingly office is clearly derived from the second function and thus ' . . . the king depends on the priests for the religious function, he cannot himself operate the sacrifice on behalf of the kingdom, he cannot be his own sacrificer, instead he "puts in front" of himself a priest, the *purohita*, and then he loses the hierarchical pre-eminence in favour of the priests, retaining for himself power only' (Dumont 1962: 54). A similar development seems to have taken place in Christian Europe in the relations between the king and the Church.

The king also had important associations with the third function. Dumont refers to the persistent association in India of the righteous king with the earth, even as being married to the earth, and with rain, and with plenty (ibid., 60–1).

In the Homeric conception of kingship there survive certain ideas which recur in some guise in other Indo-European societies. Of especial importance is the idea of the king as the author and guarantor of the prosperity of his people, if he follows the rules of justice and divine commandments. We read in the Odyssey (19, 110 ff.) the following eulogy of the king: 'a good king (*basileús*) who respects the gods, who lives according to justice, who reigns (*anásson*) over numerous and valiant men, for him the black earth bears wheat and barley, the trees are laden with fruit, the flocks increase unceasingly, the sea yields fish, thanks to his good government; the people prosper beneath his rule.' (Benveniste 1973: 321)

In the case of Ireland, Binchy describes the various blessings that *fír flathemon*, literally 'the prince's truth', the just rule of a righteous king, was supposed to confer on his people:

Through *fír flathemon* come prosperity for man, beast and crops; the seasons are temperate, the corn grows strong and heavy, mast and fruit are abundant on the trees, cattle give milk in plenty, rivers and estuaries teem with fish; plagues, famines, and natural calamities are warded off, internal peace and victory over external enemies are guaranteed. (Binchy 1970: 10)

Chaney (1970) also provides convincing evidence for a similar conception of the king in Germanic, Anglo-Saxon, and Scandinavian society.

It seems most likely, therefore, that the king was traditionally associated most closely with the first function, but also had essential links with the other two and, in a sense, was the personification of all three at a general level, especially in the role as intermediary between his people and the gods. Thus each people seems to have been defined by its allegiance to a particular king, and Binchy (1970: 6) shows that the term for 'people' is cognate in the Germanic, Scandinavian, Celtic, Greek, and Italic languages.

How were the principles of hereditary right and of election combined in the succession to kingship, especially among the peoples of Western Europe? To be of royal blood was a necessary although not sufficient qualification for kingship. In ancient Irish society ' . . . it was the royal blood as a whole, the royal kindred, that counted, not the claim of a particular member. The mere fact that a man was the son of the reigning king did not give him an automatic right to succeed . . . ' (Binchy 1970: 25). This combination of hereditary qualification together with an element of choice or election may well have been general to the Indo-Europeans as a whole. So Tacitus says of the Germans: 'They take their kings on the ground of birth, their generals on the basis of courage: (*reges ex nobilitate, duces ex virtute sumunt*). The authority (*potestas*) of their kings is not unlimited or arbitrary (7. 1).'

According to Benveniste, the German *könig* ultimately derives from the root **gen-* to be born, which belongs to the same group as the Latin *gens*, and the Greek *genos* (Benveniste 1973: 368). The basic association of the term with 'birth' does seem to give clear evidence for the belief that his office was seen as having an essential hereditary element.

In the opinion of Chaney, the idea of a royal line, a *stirps regia*, descended from a god (Woden in particular) is clearly found in Scandinavian, Germanic, and Anglo-Saxon concepts of monarchy, but this was not incompatible with an elective principle:

> In this light, the tribal election of the sacral ruler was not so much a 'democratic' institution, as nineteenth-century constitutional historians, obsessed with the antecedents of parliamentary government, loved to portray it; rather it was the right to assure itself of the *mana*-filled, god-sprung king, selected from the royal race for his obvious 'luck'. The election was thus the tribal right to choose the one who was the 'incarnation of the mystical powers of the whole community of the folk' and whose divinely inspired word gives the *auctoritas suadendi*, by which he rules that assembled folk. This tribal selection of the ruler dominates Anglo-Saxon elevations into kingship from our earliest sources for it down to its close when 'all the people chose Edward (the Confessor) as King'.[14] (Chaney 1970: 16–17)

The early Frankish kings may well have been derived from the leaders of the war bands, the *duces* of Tacitus (Wallace-Hadrill 1962: 153), and the same may have been true of the Anglo-Saxon kings as well. But success in battle, wealth, and power of leadership would have been convincing evidence of the sacral luck which was essential for a king. It is also important to remember that armed force has a dual aspect in the trifunctional scheme. It can be armed force, the war band, and nothing more, and it can also be the instrument of the sovereign power, used to maintain order, punish wrongdoing, and defend society from foreign enemies.

In conclusion, it can be said that the kings of the early Middle Ages in northern Europe were legitimated by birth and by sacred status, but that they were by no means absolute, even in theory. The doctrine of their legitimacy contained an elective element. They were restrained by customary law, and by the requirement of consulting with the chief men of the realm, and the Christian

---

[14] On the association between hereditary and elective principles of monarchy among some East Germanic peoples see Grierson 1941, who considers that the evidence for a *stirps regia* is thin for these societies.

Church had substantially reinforced the position of the priesthood. The status of the king was therefore very different from that in many other early states, where religious, military, and judicial functions are united in the same person.

(g) *The war band and the origins of vassalage*

The warriors and, more particularly, the warrior bands, were of great importance in Indo European society.

> More than any single military implement, the I-E warrior band, or *Männerbund*, organized around the person of a fearless leader . . . seems to have been the 'secret weapon' that facilitated the I-E expansion. The warrior was thus the prop and, in many respects, the pivot of the social system. Yet the very separateness of the warrior class, the extent to which the warrior role was clearly distinct from that of priest or cultivator, seems to have led inevitably to a structural opposition between this class and the others; especially does this appear to have been true of the sovereign priest class. (Littleton 1982: 127–8)

Indra (Woden, Mars), god of war, might seem to be indistinguishable from Varuna, but as Dumézil shows, particularly in his *The Destiny of the Warrior* (1970), there is in fact an essential difference: whereas Mitra and Varuna are inherently sinless, Indra can and does sin:

> How could Mitra, Varuna, and the other Aditya sin? They form one body with the *rtá*, the moral as well as cosmic and ritual order which they created, which they uphold and which they enforce. Milder, more evenly shaded, more comforting in connection with Mitra, more rigorous, even terrible in connection with Varuna, it is always the *rtá* that is the principle of action for these gods and, in the case of Varuna, one can almost say his 'passion' . . .
>
> Indra and his warriors have been given a very different cosmic and social position. They cannot ignore order, since their function is to guard it against the thousand and one demonic or hostile endeavours that oppose it. But in order to assume their office they must first possess and entertain qualities of their own which bear a strong resemblance to the blemishes of their adversaries . . . And so they are transfigured, made strangers in the society they protect . . . The revolts of generals and military coups d'état, the massacres and pillages by the undisciplined soldiery and by its leaders, all these are older than history. And that is why Indra . . . is 'the sinner among the gods'. (Dumézil 1970: 105–7)

The first adequate description of the war band comes from Tacitus and, according to him, a young man received the spear and shield of warrior status from a chief or his father in the assembly, when he was considered capable of using them, after which he tried to attach himself to the retinue of a chief:

Conspicuously high birth, or signal services on the part of parents win the chieftain's approbation even for very young men: they mingle with the others, men of maturer strength and tested by long years, and have no shame to be seen among his retinue. In the retinue itself degrees are observed, depending on the judgement of him whom they follow: and so there is great rivalry among the retainers to decide who shall have the first place with his chief, and among the chieftains as to who shall have the largest and keenest retinue. This means rank and strength, to be surrounded always with a large band of chosen youths—glory in peace, in war protection . . .

When the battlefield is reached it is a reproach for a chief to be surpassed in prowess; a reproach for his retinue not to equal the prowess of its chief; but to have left the field and survived one's chief, this means lifelong infamy and shame: to defend and protect him, to devote one's own feats even to his glorification, this is the gist of their allegiance: the chief fights for victory, but the retainers for the chief. (13. 2–14. 2)

Warfare was essential for the maintenance of this institution: '. . . you cannot keep up a great retinue except by war and violence, for it is from their leader's bounty that they demand that glorious warhorse, and that murderous and masterful spear: banquetings and a certain rude but lavish outfit are equivalent to salary. The material for this free-handedness comes through war and foray' (14. 3). In Homeric society, 'The *laoi* form part of the retinue of the chief; they are often under his orders; they owe him fidelity and obedience; they would not be *laoi* unless they were attached to him by mutual consent. They may be engaged in his cause in battle' (Benveniste 1973: 372).

As Marc Bloch says (1961: 154), the followers (Latin *comes*, Old German *gisind*) of the Germanic war chief, loyal to the death in battle, and generously rewarded by him in turn, provided an institution whose basic form and values persisted for centuries in Anglo-Saxon, Germanic, and Scandinavian society. In Celtic society, too, 'Before the coming of the legions there was no Gaulish chieftain who was not surrounded by a group of retainers, either peasants or warriors' (ibid., 149). After the collapse of the Roman Empire, moreover, and the consequent disappearance of professional infantry,

In Frankish Gaul, everything conspired to make it more and more necessary to recruit professional warriors, men who had been trained by a group tradition and who were, first and foremost, horsemen. Although service on horseback for the king had continued almost to the end of the ninth century to be exacted in theory of all free men rich enough to be subject to it, the nucleus of these trained and well equipped mounted troops—the only ones of whom a high standard of efficiency was expected—was naturally provided by the armed followers which had long been included in the retinue of kings and great personages. (Ibid., 154)

The term *gasindus* was still used in Merovingian Gaul and the whole of the barbarian world to mean the private fighting man or retainer (ibid., 155), but was progressively displaced by the term, of Celtic origin, *vassus*, *vassallus*, 'vassal', whose original meaning was 'servant', and indicates that for a time the armed retainers were of lower social origins than the traditional *gasindi*. But the basic ideal of the old war band was not dead:

Modest as was the original social status of many of the 'thugs' maintained by the magnates and even by the king, from now on it grew steadily in prestige. The ties which bound these war companions to their chief represented one of the contracts of fidelity freely entered into which were compatible with the most respectable social position. The term which designates the royal guard is extremely significant: *trustis*, that is to say fealty. The new recruit enrolled in this body swore to be faithful; the king in turn undertook to 'bear him succour'. These were the principles of all 'commendation'. Doubtless the powerful men and their *gasindi* or vassals exchanged similar promises. To be protected by a person of rank offered, moreover, a guarantee not only of security but also of social standing. As the disintegration of the state proceeded, every person in power was obliged to look for support more and more to those directly attached to him; and, as the old form of military service decayed, the recruitment of professional fighting men became daily more necessary and the role of whoever bore arms more respected. In these conditions, there was a growing conviction that of all forms of personal service the highest consisted in serving on horseback with sword and lance a master of whom one had solemnly declared oneself a faithful follower. (Ibid., 156)

In Anglo-Saxon England, however, the relations between the lord and his retainers were of unbroken continuity from pagan Germanic society:

Everywhere in the Germanic world the ruler, whether king or chief, was attended by a body-guard of well-born companions. No Germanic institution has a longer history. The phrases in which Tacitus describes the retinue of a first-century chief can be applied to the companions of King

Cynewulf of Wessex in the eighth century and to those of Earl Byrhtnoth of Essex in the tenth. Much that is characteristic of the oldest Germanic literature turns on the relationship between the companions and their lord. The sanctity of the bond between lord and man, the duty of defending and avenging a lord, the disgrace of surviving him, gave rise to situations in which English listeners were always interested until new literary fashions of Romance origin had displaced the ancient stories. There is no doubt that this literature represented real life. It was the personal reputation of a king which attracted retainers to his court, and it was the king's military household around which all early fighting centred . . . The migration to Britain produced no change in the relation of the king to his retinue. There is no essential difference between the king's companions of the heathen age and the nobles who attest the earliest English royal charters. (Stenton 1971: 302)

As we read in Tacitus, chiefs were expected to reward their followers with generous gifts, and this tradition was maintained by the English kings:

The most admired virtue of an early king was generosity to his followers. It was probably accepted throughout the north that every member of a king's household might expect to receive an endowment in land from his lord [probably for his lifetime only]. In England, in the very earliest times, the endowment may often have consisted of a stretch of newly conquered land, on which the recipient and his household could be maintained by the food-rents and services of subject Britons and dependent Englishmen. (Ibid., 306)

This military vassalage also had the potential of forming the basis of a hierarchical political structure in Europe generally:

The [Carolingian] monarchy had at its disposal only a small number of officials: but these were in any case not very reliable men and—apart from a few churchmen—they lacked professional tradition and culture. Moreover, economic conditions precluded the institution of a vast system of salaried officials. Communications were slow, inconvenient and uncertain. The principal difficulty, therefore, which faced the central government was to reach individual subjects, in order to exact services and impose the necessary sanctions. There thus arose the idea of utilizing for government the firmly established network of protective relationships. The lord, at every level of the hierarchy, would be answerable for his 'man' and would be responsible for holding him to his duty. This idea was not peculiar to the Carolingians. It had already been the subject of legislation in Visigothic Spain . . . and the very lively mistrust of the 'lordless man' which is reflected later in the Anglo-Saxon laws reflects a similar attitude. (Marc Bloch 1961: 157)

(h) The assembly

One of the distinctive features of Indo-European society is the assembly, which had a number of functions: a place of debate and word duelling, a war council, a court of law and of the punishment of criminals, and a ritual centre, among others.[15]

The most important type of assembly in Vedic society was the *sabha*, and its equivalent in Iranian society was *vyaxman* (Kuiper 1960: 255). Rau rejects the interpretation of *sabha* as 'village assembly and meeting house', and provides evidence that it had the more specific meaning of the homestead of a wealthy man, with cattle stalls and threshing floor, a hearth and gambling area, where feasts and debates took place. It was forbidden to women, and here distinguished men gave official audience, nobles and *brahman* assessors decided legal cases, and criminals were punished (Rau 1957: 75–81). *Samiti* seems to have been more restricted in meaning, denoting a tribal council and war council in which the king took part, though here, too, glory was much sought after in debate.

We have already noted the religious significance of all kinds of contests in Indo-European society, and especially of the verbal duel and eloquence and of gambling, and it therefore seems clear that the *sabha* and *vyaxman* were not simply places for feasting and settling disputes but had a very important religious significance, in which debates and word duels were essential elements. While according to Rau (1957: 83) the Brahmana texts are silent on the extent to which the ordinary freemen participated in the *sabha* and *samiti*, the fact that, as we shall see, the freemen were essential to the assembly of the Greeks, Romans, Germans, Celts, and Scandinavians strongly suggests that they also participated in the assemblies of ancient Indian and Iranian society as well. Indeed, the enormous emphasis on success in debate and in word duels in Indo-Iranian society seems hard to explain unless there was a substantial audience before whom the speakers could compete, and whose assent and applause would be the prize for the victor.

The assembly of the freemen of the tribe, as distinct from the council of the chief or king which seems to have existed in Indo-European society as elsewhere, is also known to have been a feature of early Greek society:

The great questions that concerned them all, of peace or war, were settled

[15] Unfortunately, I only became acquainted with the rich materials collected by Gomme (1880), in his *Primitive Folk-Moots*, after the final draft of the MS of this book had gone to press.

by the muster of all the warriors of the tribes, who gathered together and shouted 'Yes' or 'No' to what was proposed to them. The chiefs had their council of wise men, elders and men of especial renown and valour, and these formed with the chiefs the executive that carried out the policy approved by the warriors as a whole. (Michell 1964: 93)

The close association of the assembly with justice and competition is brought out very clearly in the following anecdote from the *Iliad*:

. . . the folk were gathered in the place of assembly; for there a strife had arisen, and two men were striving about the blood-price of a man slain; the one avowed that he had paid all, declaring his cause to the people, but the other refused to accept aught; and each was fain to win the issue on the word of a daysman [mediator]. Moreover, the folk were cheering both, showing favour to this side and to that. And heralds held back the folk, and the elders were sitting upon polished stones in the sacred circle, holding in their hands the staves of the loud-voiced heralds. Therewith then would they spring up and give judgement, each in turn. And in the midst lay two talents of gold, to be given to him whoso among them should utter the most righteous judgement. (*Iliad* XVIII. 497—508)

In early Rome, it is also clear that the council of chiefs and the general assembly of freemen were the basis of government:

On the one hand the senate appears as a representative council of chiefs, with inalienable prerogatives of its own, and claiming to be the ultimate depositary of the supreme authority and of the *sacra* connected with it. The senators are the *patres*; they are taken from the leading *gentes*; they hold their seats for life; to them the *auspicia* revert on the death of a king; they appoint the *interrex* from their own body, are consulted in the choice of the new king, and their sanction is necessary to ratify the vote of the assembled freemen.

The popular assembly of United Rome in its earliest days was that in which the freemen met and voted by their *curiae* (*comitia curiata*). The place of assembly was in the Comitium at the north-east end of the Forum, at the summons of and under the presidency of the king, or failing him, of the *interrex*. By the *rex* or the *interrex* the question was put, and the voting took place *curiatim*, the *curiae* being called up in turn . . . Assemblies of the people were also, and probably more frequently, convened for other purposes. Not only did they meet to hear from the king the announcements of the high days and holidays for each month, and to witness such solemn religious rites as the inauguration of a priest, but their presence (and sometimes their vote) was further required to authorize and attest certain acts, which in a later age assumed a more private character [wills, adoptions, etc.]. (Pelham and Conway 1911: 617)

Tacitus makes it clear that the assembly in ancient Germanic society was of central social importance, and that there was also a council of chiefs:

On small matters the chiefs (*principes*) consult; on larger questions the community; but with this limitation, that even the subjects, the decision of which rests with the people, are first handled by the chiefs. They meet, unless there be some unforeseen and sudden emergency, on days set apart—when the moon, that is, is new or at the full: they regard this as the most auspicious herald for the transaction of business . . .

It is a foible of their freedom that they do not meet at once and as it commanded, but a second and a third day is wasted by dilatoriness in assembling: when the mob is pleased to begin, they take their seats carrying arms. Silence is called for by the priests, who thenceforward have power also to coerce: then a king or chief is listened to, in order of age, birth, glory in war, or eloquence, with the prestige which belongs to their counsel rather than with any prescriptive right to command. If the advice tendered be displeasing, they reject it with groans; if it please them, they clash their spears: the most complimentary expression of assent is this martial approbation. At this assembly it is also permissible to lay accusations and to bring capital charges . . . (*Germania*, 11–12)

Similarly, among the Celtic people the king met the people in the assembly, *óenach*. These 'were held at certain festivals each year, and if need be at other times. In addition to their legal function, they fulfilled important ritual and economic needs, and were held, if not at the king's residence, at a sacred site which was often associated with the burial place of the dynasty' (Powell 1958: 78).

In the old Commonwealth of Iceland, the Althing, or assembly of freemen, was held annually at a sacred site around the Lögberg, and hallowed by the chieftain[16] who held hereditary authority (*godord*) of Thorsteinn Ingóllfson and his descendants. This man bore the title of *allsherjargodi* (supreme chieftain). The supreme chieftain determined the precincts of the Althing, and declared the area within them a sanctuary. (This area is often referred to as *thinghelgi*, the sanctuary of the assembly). It is likely that the supreme chieftain also formally prorogued the assembly at the conclusion of business, and made announcements on the calendar. In typically Germanic fashion, men came to the *thing* fully armed, and would indicate agreement with the wapentake (*vapnatak*), the clashing of weapons. The supreme chieftain was essentially more of a religious than a secular official, and the actual conduct of business in the

---

[16] The essentially religious nature of Icelandic chieftains was discussed above, Section *d*.

assembly was in the hands of the Lawspeaker, the only paid public servant of the Commonwealth. The chiefs' council also met at this time, as the Council of the Legislature (Johannesson 1974: 44–6).

The history of popular assemblies in Anglo-Saxon England is obscure, but certain inferences on their nature and function can be drawn with a reasonable degree of confidence. Our approach to an understanding of this matter must be through the territorial organization on which they were based.

English historians of the eighth century seem to have known only one kind of territorial unit less than an entire kingdom. They refer continually to districts vaguely described as *regiones* or *provinciae*, which clearly formed the fundamental divisions of the several English peoples. Neither *regio* nor *provincia* was in any sense a technical term, and there is little evidence to show what English word lay behind them. An archaic '*ge*' 'district', cognate with the German *gau*, forms the second element of the names Surrey and Ely, each of which is called a *regio* by Bede . . . [etc] . . . But it had passed out of common use at an early date, and no single equivalent was ever found for either *regio* or *provincia* when Latin histories came to be translated into English. Among the various words by which these terms were rendered the most significant is *meagh*, a word originally meaning kindred, which had early developed the wider sense of tribe or people. It would be unwise to infer from this translation that the primitive English *regio* had been the territory of a particular group of kinsmen, but it brings out the important fact that these divisions originated in tribal settlements, and not in any deliberate division of land for administrative purposes. (Stenton 1971: 293)

There is evidence for these *regiones* in every English kingdom (ibid., 294), and Stenton says 'For a long time, perhaps for a century, after the occupation of a tract of country, the men of each *regio* may have been able to deal with their own affairs in assemblies at which all were present' (ibid., 299), and 'From the earliest phase of permanent settlement the need must have arisen for local assemblies where, as in the later hundred courts, men might 'defend' their holdings against the king's ministers seeking the king's dues' (ibid., 297—8). The well-known term for such assemblies, 'folkmoot', *folcgemot*, 'does not appear in the laws before the time of Alfred, when the meetings covered by the term, at which it is assumed that a royal minister will be present, suggest the shire courts of late time rather than the moots of primitive *regiones*' (ibid., 298), but it seems clear from Stenton's account that popular assemblies had existed from the time of the earliest settlements. Some of the basic functions of the *regio* were payment of the king's food rents, regulating the use of common woods, and the administration of customary law (ibid., 294). It seems, however, that with increasing societal complexity, the assemblies or moots of the *regiones* became subdivided into what became the hundred courts:

But as the law of their country became more elaborate, and as the original arrangements by which they maintained their king were complicated by the taking of new land into cultivation, there must have arisen an urgent necessity for some form of assembly intermediate between the meeting of the whole folk and the meeting of a village community. It cannot have been easy for a folkmoot of perhaps seven hundred farmers to administer the intricate and technical West Saxon law of Ine's reign, or to determine the contribution of each local community to public charges such as the king's *feorm*. (Ibid., 299–300)

By the last century before the Conquest the hundred court, as well as the shire court, was well developed, and

administered customary law in private pleas, did justice on thieves and on those who had been slack in their pursuit, and moderated discussion between the king's financial officers and the individual taxpayer. The Old English hundred court had all the features of an ancient popular assembly. It met in the open air, and at regular intervals of four weeks, so that no summons was necessary to compel the attendance of its suitors. The judgements which it gave represented the deliberations of peasants learned in the law, who might be guided but could never be controlled by the intervention of the king's reeve, their president. (Ibid., 299)

The growth in size of the Anglo-Saxon kingdoms effectively eliminated the possibility of a popular assembly at the national level as the result of the great distances and the large numbers of people involved, as E. A. Freeman long ago pointed out (1877: 100–2), and a national parliament did not develop until representative[17] institutions were devised in the course of the thirteenth century in particular (see for example Holt 1981 and the discussion there of the

---

[17] In Iceland, with no executive body, national participation was of great importance and representation therefore developed very early. 'While in attendance at a district assembly, each chieftain was at liberty to make the request from the assembly hill that every ninth farmer of those within his jurisdiction on whom the thing-tax was levied should accompany him to the annual meeting of the Althing . . . The farmers themselves decided which representatives should accompany the chieftain, and the representatives provided their own horse and their own food for the journey' (Johannesson 1974: 61).

processes involved).[18]

This development of representative assemblies occurred also in Spain, France, Germany, and Scandinavia. The historian who denies that there can be any connection between these assemblies and those of the ancient Indo-Europeans must therefore regard their medieval development either as a functional necessity, or as a strange coincidence. But comparative studies of state formation in other parts of the world (e.g. Claessen and Skalnik 1978*a*, 1981) show that while royal councils (of varying composition) are the norm in early states, as in Europe, there is apparently no trace of popular assemblies above the level of the village or its equivalent. It is, in functional terms, perfectly possible to operate a judicial system, to collect taxes, and to ensure the military security of the state without any recourse to an institution such as a representative assembly, and historians who suppose that the development of such institutions in Europe was *nothing more than* a response to the needs of administering a state must therefore explain how these needs generated such an unusual form of the state in Europe.

It may seem that the Indo-European assembly of freemen must at least have been a normal feature of *pre*-state government, and indeed the basic idea of a meeting of all adult males of the local community for deliberation and settling disputes is presumably universal in primitive society. But assemblies above the village or hamlet level become very much rarer, primarily because they are inefficient ways of deciding political and judicial matters, which can be settled far more quickly by small councils of leaders such as elders and heads of descent groups (as we noted in the section on social size, in Chapter V). A typical example of this in a politically uncentralized society is described by Buxton (1958: 80–1). A Tswana chief could call a tribal assembly, *kgotla*, but it is clear from Schapera's account (1955) that it was summoned by the chief when it was to his advantage to do so; it had no sacred functions, and it

---

[18] The freemen (freeholders, yeomen) continued to play an essential part in the political scheme of things: 'There are traces amply sufficient to prove their importance from the reign of Henry II onwards, but the recognition of their political right grows more distinct as the middle ages advance and the election act of 1430, whatever its other characteristics may have been, establishes the point that the freeholders possessing land to the annual value of forty shillings were the true constituents of the 'communitas comitatus', the men who elected the knights of the shire. They were the men who served on juries, who chose the coroner and the verderer, who attended the markets and the three-weeks court of the sheriff, who constitute the manorial courts, and who assembled, with the arms for which they were responsible, in the muster of the forces of the shires' (Stubbs 1880: III. 596).

could not try cases or make laws. General assemblies of the Israelites described in the Book of Numbers were organized on the basis of the twelve tribes, and each tribe was represented by its prince. There is little or no resemblance either in importance or function to the Indo-European assembly. At the level of towns and 'cities' we encounter that more or less universal phenomenon, the local council of senior and influential men, but even here family status seems to have been of great importance (see Bodorman 1926: 30, 36–7). Service (1975: 209) refers to the possibility that in the Proto-literate period of Sumeria the cities each had an assembly of adult male citizens guided by a council of elders, but this institution, if it ever existed, seems not to have survived as it did, however, in Greece and Rome. The only clear parallel to the Indo-European assembly that I have been able to find in the ethnographic literature is the Gumi Gayo of the Borana Galla (Legesse 1973: 93–7), and doubtless among other Galla groups, e.g. Knutsson 1967. But because this type of assembly was so closely related to the *gada* system, it does not seem able to have survived the development of monarchy, as in the case of Jimma. We are therefore entitled to conclude that the Indo-European assembly, far from being just a 'response' to the demands of practical necessity, (which to some extent, of course it was) also expressed a distinctive world-view.

(i) The origins of the merchant guilds

My object here is to show that we can find ancient institutional forms[19] of voluntary association (not based on kinship) in Germanic (including Frankish and Anglo-Saxon) society and in Scandinavia that very easily lent themselves to a process of development at the end of which emerged the merchant guilds of early medieval Europe. This idea was proposed in various forms by a number of nineteenth-century scholars: Stubbs, for example, said

> The origin of the guilds . . . runs back to remote antiquity [to the *convivia* described by Tacitus]. The simple idea of a confraternity united for the discharge of common or mutual good offices, supported by contributions of money from each member and celebrating its meetings by a periodical festival, may find parallels in any civilised nation at any age of the world. (Stubbs 1880: I. 469)

---

[19] Whether the institutions that will be examined here were common to a wider range of societies seems to be unknown, as is their Indo-European antiquity.

Stubbs was, of course, quite right in thinking that some kinds of voluntary association, such as secret societies and men's clubs, are to be found in many societies, but they are certainly not universal, and it will be shown that the ancestral forms of the guilds had a number of features that made them especially apt for subsequent commercial development.

Tacitus refers to the *convivia* of the ancient Germans in the following terms:

To make day and night run into one in drinking is a reproach to no man: brawls are frequent, naturally, among heavy drinkers: they are seldom settled with abuse, more often with wounds and bloodshed; nevertheless the mutual reconciliation of enemies, the forming of family alliances, the appointment of chiefs, the question even of war and peace, are usually debated at these banquets; as though at no other time were the mind more open to obvious, or better warmed to larger, thoughts. (22. 2–3)

On the following day, when the participants were more sober, the decisions of the banquet were ratified.

What at first sight seems nothing more than the drunken carousing of our 'rude forefathers' had a much deeper significance. Not only is it clear from Tacitus that these banquets were the occasion of very important social decisions (see also Benveniste 1973: 60), but we know that beer-drinking had an important religious significance for the ancient Germans and Scandinavians, among whom beer had replaced mead, the old sacred Indo-European drink. While beer could be used on profane occasions (Cahen 1921: 107–9), when ritually prepared and blessed it became, in the libation, as essential a feature of ritual as *soma* had been for the early Indo-Europeans. Nor was the drunkenness morally reprehensible (ibid., 136).

Our information on the religious and social significance of beer and the libation is particularly detailed for Scandinavia. The basic religious act was sacrifice, in which not only the consecrated flesh of the animal victim but also the consecrated beer were offered to the gods. The sacred beer, in a horn, was blessed by the officiant who made over it the sign of the hammer of Thor, and prayed for a good harvest, peace, or victory, after which is was passed round the circle of worshippers. In domestic rites the animal sacrifice might be dispensed with, but not the libation, over which the master of the house officiated, and the libation was an essential element of all public and private rites (ibid., 5–9).

Indeed, the circle around which the libation must pass was also a fundamental ritual element. *Hvirfingr*, 'circle', in its most primitive sense, could apparently denote important associations of individuals who wished to obtain a particular objective: 'All those who, at any particular time, had a strong reason for uniting together by the power of the communal rite, formed a *hvirfingr*, or as we would say "formed a circle" for the libation' (ibid., 58). These *hvirfingr* might meet only once for some special purpose, or maintain a more permanent existence; they were composed of individuals unrelated by ties of blood; and the libation was the central religious act which maintained their solidarity. In early Scandinavia and Germany kinship could also be created by the sacred oath sworn between two men: *fostbroedr*, or milk brothers, *eidbroedr*, *svarbroedr*, *fratres conjurati*, sworn brothers, who also undertook the obligation of blood vengeance. According to Gross, 'The foster-brotherhood seems to have been unknown to the Franks and Anglo-Saxons, the nations in which medieval gilds first appear . . .' (Gross 1890: 14). But the idea of the sworn covenant was certainly fundamental, in Anglo-Saxon England and in Frankish society.

The libation also existed in Anglo-Saxon England: Coornaert refers to the *convivia religiosa* at the time of Augustine, and Alcuin (between 793 and 804) denounced 'Those conventicles, in which the people are deceived, forsaking the churches and seeking out mountainous regions, worshipping there not by prayers but by drunkenness', and it is clear from the Anglo-Saxon material that drinking was central to guild activities, while on the Continent Archbishop Hincmar, in the text already mentioned, warns his priests against the excesses of food and drink at guild meetings (Coornaert 1948: 34, 35). In England, 'From all the evidence, drinking is the very centre of the life of the guilds, which it sustains everywhere, constantly, before the Norman Conquest. Afterwards, it still remains, for contemporaries, their essential feature' (ibid., 40). Violence was so normal a feature of the drinking at guild feasts that the guilds themselves made special provision to police such occasions.

Christianity, indeed, imposed its forms on the guild, and European and Anglo-Saxon guilds placed themselves under the patronage of a particular saint, as later occurred in Scandinavia, whose feast was celebrated by the guild. In particular, it was the solemn obligation of guild members to pray for the souls of deceased brothers, to sing psalms, to pay for masses for the dead, and to distribute alms to the poor. While all these religious obligations were at one level the obvious result of Christianity, the basic religious nature of the guilds can be traced to pagan origins. The direct ancestors of the medieval guilds did not appear in Scandinavia, but among the Franks and Anglo-Saxons. A capitulary of Charlemagne in 779 denounces the swearing of oaths in the '*gildonia*': 'Concerning the mutual swearing of oaths in guilds, that no one shall presume to do so. In whatever other ways they may make agreements concerning alms, fire, or shipwreck, no one shall presume to swear an oath in these matters.' In this passage the guilds (gilds) (a term whose meaning I shall discuss presently) appear as societies whose members were bound by a sacred oath— it was to this that Charlemagne was objecting as conspiratorial and subversive; who gave alms, and who insured one another against fire and shipwreck. For the first time we have clear evidence of that special combination of religious and economic motives together with the oath which was distinctive of the guilds, and we have seen that the libation was also basic to the guilds.

It is also worth noting that local groups whose members insured one another against loss by fire and murrain (*hreppar*) developed early in Iceland (Johannesson 1974: 85), and it seems very likely that insurance, in the sense of contributions or assistance by the members of the guilds to one of their number in distress, was the earliest economic activity of the guilds in Europe.

There is very little direct evidence in Anglo-Saxon guild regulations before the Conquest concerning economic functions, but some indications of this appear. Thus the guild regulations cited by Whitelock (1970: 603–7) not only refer in all cases to the payment of contributions of members for religious purposes and guild feasts, but also to oaths of mutual assistance in secular as well as religious matters, and in one case, the Bedwyn guild (ibid., 605–6), the members are to provide building materials if a member's house is burned down. There is also some evidence of financial profit in the regulations of the remarkable 'peace-gild' of London, established under Athelstan, which according to Stenton (1971: 355) 'certainly included all Middlesex, and may also have comprised Surrey and part of Hertfordshire'. The guild was organized on elaborate hierarchical principles, and its primary function was the killing of thieves and the restoration of stolen property. Apart from being an instrument of public order organized on voluntary principles, the guild was also organised to make a profit. For it is prescribed in the guild regulations that the thief is to be killed, and after the value of the stolen goods has been deducted from his possessions (clearly to be returned to the victim of theft), *all* his possessions are to be confiscated and divided into three parts—one for the wife, if she is innocent of the crime, one for the king, and one part for the guild (Whitelock 1970: 423).

The feasts of the guilds, together with the expenses incurred by the mutual obligations of the brothers, naturally required that each member should pay an entrance fee, and make regular contributions to the common chest, and it is from this fee or contribution that the term 'guild', 'gild', derives. In Gothic, *gild* was used to translate the concept of 'tribute'; in Old Icelandic *gjald* is 'recompense, punishment, payment'; Old English *gield* is 'substitute, indemnity, sacrifice'; in Old High German *gelt* is 'payment, sacrifice' (Benveniste 1973: 58, 60). The person who paid (*geldan*) was in Low French-Latin *gildo*, Old English (*ge*)*gilda*, Scandinavian *gildi* (Cahen 1921: 62). It was this sense of members contributing their dues which became of increasing relevance as the economic potential of this type of association began to be realized in the changing economic circumstances of Frankish, Anglo-Saxon, and Frisian society. It was as a primarily mercantile institution that the guild was introduced by Frisian and Saxon merchants into Scandinavia in the tenth century, or perhaps even earlier (Cahen 1921: 59, 223 n. 41 and 42). The Scandinavians used their own, cognate, word *gildi* to refer to the new institution.

In conclusion, it is clear as Coornaert says (1948: 55) that the economic functions of the guilds involved no radical transformation of their identity. From the beginning, in early Germanic and Scandinavian society there had been the institutions of the libation and the oath by which non-kin could join together in a powerful union of mutual assistance under religious auspices, and this type of association was clearly appropriate in a society where the bonds of kinship were weak. Increasing social disorder only augmented the advantage of belonging to such groups, which were also ideally suited to town life where many unrelated individuals congregated together (cf. Cahen 1921: 15). The principle of contributions by members, initially only to defray the costs of feasts, could readily be applied to more purely economic ends, such as insurance against fire, theft, and shipwreck, and become the basis of substantial investment. Most significant of all, the later guilds were the basis of corporate, independent groups of merchants, bound by ties of mutual assistance in a confraternity, and this seems to have been of great significance in establishing the social influence of the merchant class. Under the Roman Empire, for example, capitalist enterprise seems to have been essentially individualistic, and such guilds as existed were established for the administrative convenience of the government, rather than being the expression of any corporate solidarity among the merchants themselves (Rostovtzeff 1957: 178). Precisely the same seems also to have been true of the Chinese merchant guilds.

The *marbara* and *parga* of the Konso (Hallpike 1972: 78–80) are very similar to the early guilds, and the importance of voluntary, non-kin, associations 'with disciplined membership, leadership, and a treasury maintained by dues assessment' (Hamer 1967a: 73) for economic enterprise in the Third World has been attested by many anthropological studies of modernization. So Hamer, for example, writes of such associations among the Sidamo of Ethiopia:

I wish to show how developing associations among the Sidamo of Southwestern Ethiopia are providing the structures for adaptation to a cash crop economy and a centralized Ethiopian state system. These associations not only duplicate traditional work patterns and values about the importance of wealth, but also combine them with modern concepts of labor efficiency, marketing principles, and political action, in structures which are adaptable to the government and economy of a nation state. (Ibid., 73)

The European guilds are thus an excellent example of voluntary associations of a type quite familiar to the anthropologist, and which have great economic potential.

4. Conclusions

At the beginning of this chapter I emphasized that the core principles of societies must not be treated as autonomous causal factors that drive each society in a certain direction willy-nilly, independently of all other circumstances. The fact that the Indo-Europeans were predominantly pastoral and migratory for a long period in their history, whereas the Chinese seem always to have been sedentary agriculturalists, was no doubt very important in explaining why large and powerful states developed much earlier among the Chinese. We have also seen that in the later part of our period the opportunity for large-scale hydraulic works in China allowed a significant intensification of the power of the various states and the Empire, an opportunity that was lacking in Europe. In Europe, on the other hand, there were greater opportunities for long-range, coastal seafaring trade that were largely absent in China. F. Bray (1983) has shown that wet rice cultivation leads to very different ways of organizing labour and land use than does the dry-grain farming of Europe dependent on wheat, barley, and rye. It would be a gross distortion to leave these and many other such factors (e.g. the relations between the Roman Empire and other European societies) out of account, and to suppose that the core principles of a society are all that is necessary to explain its evolution. This would only replace one kind of exaggeration by another, equally mistaken. My purpose in this chapter has been to redress an imbalance in sociological explanation, by showing that societies are not simply bundles of adaptations to the here-and-now. The facts of Chinese and Indo-European history clearly demonstrate that societies can inherit certain basic institutional and ideological principles from a remote and primitive antiquity, and that these principles are often of vital significance both in the definition of the various challenges societies encounter, and in their response to these challenges. The same circumstances may permit a variety of responses, and those that are actually made will depend, among other things, on the particular cultural traditions that have been inherited.

It is, of course, quite true that men are constantly faced with new historical situations which they must define, interpret, and resolve, and in doing so they may well hit upon novel institutional forms. History is full of such innovations, and it would indeed be absurd to depict all societies as permanently confined within a restricted set of institutions and beliefs from which they can never escape. On the other hand, the ethnographic record shows again and again that we can often predict more about social institutions and culture generally from knowing what language family a society belongs to than from knowing what its environment is like. It is all too easy to suppose that the nature of every challenge is self-evident, and is alone sufficient to explain the nature of the response.

So, we noted many features of Chinese social evolution that conform to those general principles of social evolution discussed in Chapter V, but, also, that the Chinese assimilated the problems of warfare, mercantile enterprise, the organization of state bureaucracy, the administration of law and justice, and the relations between ruler and people into their own distinctive world-view. Similarly, the Indo-Europeans of Western Europe can be shown to have developed a set of institutions and ideas that vitally affected the kind of state that they developed, and it seems clear that capitalism, in particular, is not a universal stage of social evolution at all, but an oddity that owes its existence to the special character of Indo-European society as this developed in Western Europe.

The core principles ascribed to Chinese and Indo-European society undoubtedly have a heterogeneous quality: some are predominantly institutional in nature, such as the assembly, while others are more cosmological, such as notions of competition and harmony. I have not attempted a more abstract analysis because anthropology has not yet at its disposal sufficient comparative, cross-cultural studies of world-views on which a more refined and sophisticated typology of core principles can be based. In addition, a detailed ethnographic description of the institutions and beliefs in which the core principles are most clearly manifested is likely to carry more conviction than a generalized discussion.

CONCLUSIONS

The most fruitful approach to the problem of social evolution is to begin at the beginning and investigate the early forms of organization and belief. A very little reflection will tell us that the early forms of anything are likely to be those that are the easiest to produce and, by the same token, these early forms are likely to be relatively crude and inefficient. They survive because in the circumstances of primitive society, small in scale and rudimentary in technology, where the demands on efficiency are low, where there are few, if any, variant forms to choose from, and where the level of competition is weak, even crude and inefficient forms will work, or seem to after a fashion, and will to some degree satisfy the desires of those who introduce or maintain them. The significance of early forms is that they are the easy pathways to new developments and discoveries, for all institutions and beliefs have a multiplicity of properties, many of which may be unsuspected by the people concerned, and some of these properties may have great developmental potential. This is especially true of religion, magic, divination, ritual, and the whole range of symbolic representations. These have encouraged man to engage in enterprises whose logical justification is often small and whose adaptive value in terms of energy yields, security, or procreation may be non-existent, but which have nevertheless been the foundation of vast evolutionary developments. The same is true of warfare, which although largely pointless at the level of primitive society, has been an essential component of the evolutionary process in the long run. If man's logical and critical faculties had surpassed his imagination and creativity, and if he had been content to govern his life by criteria acceptable to rational materialists, it does not seem that very much would ever have occurred at all in the way of evolution.

Primitive societies are not, therefore, beautifully adapted little organisms put together like watches, in which every component functions for the well-being and survival of the whole. The frequency of traits often had nothing to do with adaptive advantage, and functional efficiency is an emergent property of evolution, which only begins to dominate societies with the advent of the state and which leads to a wide range of institutions having the clear purpose of maintaining the power and authority of the government. To explain this process, however, we do not rely on the notions of adaptation and function, but on the multiple properties of institutions, and the fact that the same institutions may be adopted for a variety of different reasons. As a result, agriculture, lineal descent, primogeniture, ritual authority, and war leadership, for example, can be expected to develop in many different societies, and this in itself gives a direction to evolution. These institutions will also mutually reinforce one another in such a way that their latent potential for producing centralized authority, the co-ordination of large numbers of people, and simplification, can be realized in the development of chiefly authority and in some cases the state, when circumstances are appropriate.

This combinatorial approach to innovation, by which new forms are explained in terms of the combination of *existing* (but often latent) properties of institutions and ideas, is fundamentally different from the mutational view of innovation, and is an essential basis of the directional nature of social evolution.

This process is certainly not purposeful, in so far as no one ever sat down and planned the state, but it is not usefully explained in terms of random variation either. Cultural selectionists use the notion of randomness as a kind of conjuror's hat from which they think they can pull anything they like. But the only properties of randomness that are relevant to social evolution are its extreme slowness and its utter incoherence. The extremely rapid pace of the evolution of societies, the independent appearance of the state in many different areas of the world, and the shortage of time demonstrate conclusively that any explanation of social evolution must be based on the structural properties of institutions and beliefs. To be sure, the people involved do not always clearly understand these, and there is also a very obvious contingent element in the history of all societies. But the contingent and the accidental are quite compatible with the development of structures, and the activities of individuals are, of course, the efficient causes by which the potential of structure is realized.

In primitive society, especially, many ways of doing things and many ways of representing the world are all equally viable, and while some types of institution and belief are either demoted in importance by evolutionary development or destroyed altogether, others are capable of surviving indefinitely across major evolutionary change and of giving a unique quality to the evolution of each society. We saw in the case of China that a non-theistic, organic conception of the universe, a moralistic view of society, a paternalistic relationship between ruler and subjects, and the devaluation of military force, for example, are principles that could not only survive major change in Chinese society, but also guide its development. In the same way, the Indo-European principles of the creative nature of conflict and competition, the glorification of war, the division of functions, the assembly, voluntary associations, and the relations between war leaders and their retinue were also capable of surviving from a remote antiquity and of exercising a profound influence on the nature of European state and society as these developed in the Middle Ages.

This explanation of social evolution is not as parsimonious as, for example, selectionism or materialism. Nor do I regard this as a defect, since I can see no reason why so vast and elaborate a process as the evolution of society should be explicable by one or two simple assumptions. As Bertrand Russell has observed,

It is customary to add to the postulate that there are natural laws the explicit or tacit proviso that they must be *simple*. This, however, is both vague and teleological. It is not clear what is meant by 'simplicity', and there can be no *a priori* reason for expecting laws to be simple except benevolence on the part of Providence towards men of science. (Russell 1948: 497)

We have only reached this understanding of the evolutionary process by discarding a number of assumptions dear to the hearts of many biologists, psychologists, and anthropologists. Arthur Koestler has described the 'four pillars of unwisdom' of the life sciences in this century as the doctrines

(a) that biological evolution is the result of random mutations preserved by natural selection;

(b) that mental evolution is the result of random tries preserved by 'reinforcements' (rewards);

(c) that all organisms, including man, are essentially passive automata controlled by the environment, whose sole purpose in life is the reduction of tensions by adaptive responses;

(d) That the only scientific method worth that name is quantitative measurement; and, consequently, that complex phenomena must be reduced to simple elements accessible to such treatment, without undue worry whether the specific characteristics of a complex phenomenon, for instance man, may be lost in the process. (Koestler 1967: 17)

All these assumptions, in one form or another, underlie the various selectionist and adaptationist theories of social evolution which have been the major intellectual casualties of our enquiry. While I have not denied, of course, that adaptation, competition, selection, variation, and trial-and-error learning have a place in social evolution, it should now be obvious that these are at best ancillary processes in the generation and transformation of structures.

On the other hand, while this is a thoroughly endogenist theory of social evolution, it is emphatically not an organic theory because it denies that social systems have any necessary conditions of existence that are not trivial, and that every institution exists because of its functional necessity for the society as a whole. While the theory also justifies the belief that evolution is a directional process that realizes the latent potential of societies, this orthogenetic property can be explained in a way that is entirely free of any mysterious connotations such as vitalism or teleology in biology.

The idea of evolution as a directional process raises the problem of stages. The stage concept is most appropriate to the life cycle of the individual organism, and it is essential to note that two aspects of this ontogenetic process emphatically do not apply to social evolution. The first is the inevitable progression of the normal individual through the various stages of life: it is clear that social evolution is quite unlike the development of the organism in this respect, since societies need not undergo any of these major changes of the kind we describe as evolutionary. And, secondly, while the life cycle of the organism ends in death, social evolution in principle seems to be open-ended, with no obvious conclusion (unless, of course, we simply blow ourselves up).

But there seems little doubt that specific aspects of social organization and of culture in general can be shown to have stage-like properties: technology (Mumford 1934), writing (Gelb 1963), the graphic arts (Gablik 1977, Gowans 1979), colour terms (Berlin and Kay 1969), money (Einzig 1966), thought (Hallpike 1979), and, more specifically relevant to our central theme here, the stages of political evolution, e.g. Service 1971, Claessen and Skalnik 1978*a*. When we are considering specific aspects of society such as these, where a limited number of closely related variables or factors are involved, one may reasonably expect to find stage-like properties of development. Problems arise, however, when we try to combine sequences of stages from widely different areas of social organization and culture in general. What correlation is there, for example, between the stages of writing, graphic representations, money, political organization, and cognitive development? There is certainly *some* connection between them, but the proposition that all aspects of social evolution can be subsumed in a single sequence of stages does not appear to be either feasible or useful, at least in our present state of knowledge.

Here, I think, we need to use the notion of the developmental potential of specific institutions (using this term in the broadest sense to include technological and cognitive discoveries) and their interaction. Huxley (1956: 23) proposed a somewhat similar idea when he suggested the classification of organic types in terms of some 'advance' such as temperature regulation, walking limbs, and the protection of the embryo by amniotic fluid. On this kind of basis it would therefore be possible to treat social evolution as a set of pathways between significant innovations, some of which, such as agriculture or the state, would be of considerably greater potential than others, such as alphabetic writing or perspective drawing. In rather crude fashion, of course, we already do something like this when we distinguish between societies as literate/pre-literate, industrial/pre-industrial, or state/stateless. In our present understanding of social evolution it is probably wisest to use stage concepts to refer to the major dimensions of evolution, especially the political, and to leave the question of any overall stages of evolution as a whole to future research.

The principles of social evolution developed in this book can certainly be applied to many aspects of the evolution of technology and science. The natural world, like society, is structured, and there are various routes into an understanding of this structure, some of which are easier or more productive than others. The various technological examples we have considered illustrate the need for a theory of invention that escapes from the dilemma of pure randomness, on one hand, and total determinism on the other. It is surely obvious that some societies are more likely than others to develop particular inventions, and that the existence of a certain invention in any society is likely to be related to the appearance of others.

I have said little about diffusion, but anthropologists should make a comparative study of cultural traits in order to determine which traits diffuse more easily than others, the extent of independent invention, and the ways in which novel traits are assimilated into alien cultures. As indicated in the previous chapter, we also need a far more extensive cross-cultural study of world-views, in order to develop a more refined typology. It seems likely that, as in some other areas of culture, a limited number of structural forms and relations will emerge of which the world-views of all societies will be variant combinations. R. Needham (1978: 17–18) has remarked on the very limited number of symbolic motifs and relationships, and with social organization, too,

In spite of much variation in the discrimination of jural statuses, relationship terminologies everywhere can readily be analysed and compared by reference to certain common principles. Instead of making up an endless range of forms of classification (as one might find for example in the classification of objects), these terminologies tend to cohere into a very limited number of forms composed by the combination of a similarly restricted set of principles. Similarly, descent systems can be compared universally by reference to only six elementary modes, and of these six only four are socially feasible. Even rules of marriage can be assorted into a very small number of formal possibilities.[1] (Ibid., 19)

The hypothesis that linguistic affiliation is a reliable predictor of many aspects of social organization and culture generally should also be tested on a world-wide basis. We now have a very large body of ethnographic and linguistic data at our disposal which should be quite sufficient to make this a feasible project in the immediate future.

In conclusion, it seems clear that the major theoretical issues of sociology, such as functionalism, the relation of modes of production to social organization, and the significance of ideology, require not only cross-cultural comparison but also an evolutionary perspective. For only in the process of development can the different aspects of society and culture be observed at work, in their mutual interaction upon one another. And if it is true that functional efficiency is an emergent property of evolution we shall

---

[1] Even when many cultural options seem theoretically possible, it is striking that man commonly utilises only a small fraction of them. Thus the 11 basic colour terms (black, white, red, green, yellow, blue, brown, pink, purple, orange and grey) are either present or absent in any culture, and this theoretically would yield 2^{11} or 2048 possible combinations of colour terms. That is, one culture might only have red, blue, and white, another blue, black, purple, green, and so on. We find, however, that colour terminologies tend to evolve cross-culturally in a fairly strict sequence, such that only about 22 systems of colour terminologies are actually used, approximately 1% of the total possible (Berlin and Kay, 1969: 3–4).

gain little insight into the nature of primitive societies by attempting to apply to them the theories developed through knowledge of modern industrial states. The study of social evolution, moreover, is not only concerned with the dimension of time, since it is also inherently comparative, and it is this comparative awareness that should be regarded as essential for the historian, for without it there can be no sure means of distinguishing the accidental peculiarities of each society's history from developmental features of much wider significance.

References

Abercrombie, M., Hickman, C. J., and Johnson, M. L. (1973) *The Penguin Dictionary of Biology*, 6th edn. London: Penguin

Aberle, D. F., *et al.* (1950) 'The functional prerequisites of a society', *Ethics*, 60. 100–11.

Adams, R. M. (1956) 'Some hypotheses on the development of early civilizations', *American Antiquity*, 21. 227–32.

—— (1960*a*) 'The background for the expansion of society in the ancient Near East', in *City Invincible: A symposium on urbanization and cultural development in the ancient Near East*, eds. C. H. Kraeling and R. M. Adams, 23–34. Chicago: University of Chicago Press.

—— (1960*b*) 'Early civilization, subsistence, and environment', in *City Invincible*, eds. C. H. Kraeling and R. M. Adams, 269–95. Chicago: University of Chicago Press.

—— (1966) *The Evolution of Urban Society: Early Mesopotamia and Prehispanic Mexico*. Chicago: Aldine.

Adams, R. N. (1975) *Energy and Structure, A theory of social power*. Austin: University of Texas Press.

—— (1981) 'Natural selection, energetics, and "cultural materialism" ', *Current Anthropology*, 22. 603–24.

Adkins, A. W. H. (1960) *Merit and Responsibility. A study in Greek values*. Oxford: Clarendon Press.

Agassi, J. (1960) 'Methodological individualism', *British Journal of Sociology*, 11(3). 244–70.

Alexander, R. D. (1979) *Darwinism and Human Affairs*. Seattle and London: University of Washington Press.

Alland, A. (1972) 'Cultural evolution: the Darwinian model', *Social Biology*, 19. 227–39.

—— and McCay, B. (1973) 'The concept of adaptation in biological and cultural evolution', in *Handbook of Social and Cultural Anthropology*, ed. J. J. Honigmann, 143–78.

Andreski, S. (1968) *Military Organization and Society*, 2nd edn. London: Routledge and Kegan Paul.

Asser *Alfred The Great*, trans. S. Keynes and M. Lapidge (1983). London: Penguin.

Bagehot, W. (1872) *Physics and Politics. Thoughts on the application of the principles of 'natural selection' and 'inheritance' to political society*. London: H. S. King.

Balazs, E. (1964) *Chinese Civilization and Bureaucracy. Variations on a theme*, trans. H. M. Wright, ed. A. F. Wright. New Haven: Yale University Press.

Barkow, J. H. (1978) 'Culture and sociobiology', *American Anthropologist*, 80. 5–20.

Barnes, J. A. (1983) Foreword to *Structural Models in Anthropology*, P. Hage and F. Harary, ix–xi. Cambridge: Cambridge University Press.

Barry, H. (1968) 'Regional and worldwide variations in culture', *Ethnology*, 7. 207–17.

Baxter, P. T. W. (n. d.) The Social Organisation of the Galla of Northern Kenya. D. Phil. Thesis (1954), Oxford University.

—— (1966) 'Stock management and the diffusion of property rights among the Boran', in *Proceedings of the Third International Conference of Ethiopian Studies*, 116–27. Addis Ababa.

—— (1975) 'Some consequences of sedentarization for social relationships', in *Pastoralism in Tropical Africa*, ed. T. Monod, 206–28. London: International African Institute.

Beals, K. L. and Kelso, A. J. (1975) 'Genetic variation and cultural evolution', *American Anthropologist*, 77. 566–79.

Beattie, J. (1964) *Other Cultures*. London: Cohen and West.

Bede, *Ecclesiastical History of England*, trans. J. E. King (1930). Loeb Classical Library, London: Heinemann.

Beidelman, T. O. (1981) Review of C. R. Hallpike 'The Foundations of Primitive Thought', *American Ethnologist*, 8. 812–13.

Bender, M. (1971) 'The languages of Ethiopia', *Anthropological Linguistics*, 13. 165–288.

Benveniste, E. (1973) *Indo-European Language and Society*, trans. E. Palmer. Florida: University of Miami Press (Miami Linguistics Series No. 12).

Berlin, B. (1974) 'Folk systematics in relation to biological classification and nomenclature', *Annual Review of Ecology and Systematics*, 4. 259–71.

——, Breedlove, D. E., and Raven, P. H. (1973) 'General principles of classification and nomenclature in folk biology', *American Anthropologist*, 75. 214–42.

—— and Kay, P. (1969) *Basic Color Terms. Their universality and evolution*. Berkeley: University of California Press.

Bernardi, B. (1954) 'The age-system of the Masai', *Annali Lateranensi*, 18. 257–318.

Berndt, R. M. and C. H. (1964) *The World of the First Australians. An introduction to the traditional life of the Australian Aborigines*. London: Angus & Robertson.

Berringer, H. R., Blanksten, G. I., and Mack, R. W. (eds.) (1965) *Social Change in Developing Areas*. Cambridge, Mass.: Shenkman.

von Bertalanffy, L. (1968) *General System Theory*. London: Allen Lane.

—— (1969) 'Chance or law', in *Beyond Reductionism*, eds. A. Koestler and J. R. Smythies, 59–76. London: Hutchinson.

Binchy, D. A. (1970) *Celtic and Anglo-Saxon Kingship*, O'Donnell Lectures for 1967–8. Oxford: Clarendon Press.

Black, P. (1973) 'Some linguistic evidence on the origins of the Konsoid peoples', *First U.S. Conference on Ethiopian Studies*, Michigan State University (Mimeograph).

Black-Michaud, J. (1975) *Cohesive Force. Feud in the Mediterranean and the Middle East*. Oxford: Blackwell.

Blackwood, B. (1978) *The Kukukuku of the Upper Watut*, ed. C. R. Hallpike. Oxford: Pitt Rivers Museum Monograph Series No. 2.

Bloch, Marc (1961) *Feudal Society*, trans. L. A. Manyon. London: Routledge & Kegan Paul.

Bloch, Maurice (1975) *Marxist Analyses and Social Anthroplogy*, ASA Studies No. 2. London: Mallaby.

—— (1983) *Marxism and Anthropology*. Oxford: Clarendon Press.

Blum, H. F. (1963) 'On the origin and evolution of human culture', *American Scientist*, 51. 32–47.

Blute, M. (1979) 'Sociocultural evolutionism: an untried theory', *Behavioral Science*, 24. 46–59.

Bodde, D. (n.d.) Unpublished monograph, dealing with the intellectual and social factors that may have encouraged or discouraged the development of science in pre-modern China.

—— (1981*a*) 'Authority and law in ancient China', in *Essays on Chinese Civilization*, eds. C. LeBlanc and D. Borei, 161–70. Princeton University Press.

—— (1981*b*) 'Basic concepts of Chinese law: the genesis and evolution of legal thought in Chinese philosophy', in *Essays on Chinese Civilization*, eds. C. LeBlanc and D. Borei, 171–94. Princeton University Press.

—— (1981*c*) 'Harmony and conflict in Chinese philosophy', in *Essays on Chinese Civilization*, eds. C. LeBlanc and D. Borei, 237–98. Princeton University Press.

—— and Morris, C. (1967) *Law in Imperial China*. Cambridge, Mass.: Harvard University Press.

Bossard, J. H. S. (1945) 'The law of family interaction', *American Journal of Sociology*, 50. 292–4.

Boulding, K. E. (1970) *A Primer on Social Dynamics. History as dialectics and development*. New York: Free Press.

—— (1978) *Ecodynamics. A new theory of societal evolution*. Beverly Hills & London: Sage.

—— (1983) 'The evolution of riches', *Science Digest*, 91(6).

Bowen, R. and Albright, F. P. (1958)*Archaeological Discoveries in South Arabia*. Baltimore: The Johns Hopkins Press.

Bowler, P. J. (1975) 'The changing meaning of "evolution" ', *Journal of History of Ideas*, 36. 95–114.

Boyce, M. (1975) *A History of Zoroastrianism* (Vol. I). Leiden: Brill.

Boyd, R. and Richerson, P. J. (1982) 'Cultural transmission and the evolution of cooperative behaviour', *Human Ecology*, 10. 325–51.

Braidwood, R. S. and Reed, C. A. (1957) 'The achievement and early consequences of food-production', *Cold Springs Harbor Symposia on Quantitative Biology*, 22. 19–31.

Bray, F. (1983) 'Patterns of evolution in rice-growing societies', *Journal of Peasant Studies*, 11. 3–33.

—— (1984) *Science and Civilisation in China*, Vol. VI, Part 2: Agriculture, Cambridge: Cambridge University Press.

Bray, W. (1973) 'The biological basis of culture', in *The Explanation of Culture Change. Models in prehistory*, ed. C. Renfrew, 73–91. London: Duckworth.

Brown, P. (1978) *Highland Peoples of New Guinea*. Cambridge: Cambridge University Press.

Buckley, W. (1967) *Sociology and Modern Systems Theory*. Englewood Cliffs: Prentice Hall.

Burnham, P. (1973) 'The explanatory value of the concept of adaptation in studies of culture change', in *The Explanation of Culture Change. Models in prehistory*, ed. C. Renfrew, 93–102, London: Duckworth.

Burrow, J. W. (1966) *Evolution and Society. A study in Victorian social theory*. London: Cambridge University Press.

Buxton, J. (1958) 'The Mandari of the southern Sudan', in *Tribes Without Rulers. Studies in African segmentary systems*, eds. J. Middleton and D. Tait, 67–96. London: Routledge & Kegan Paul.

Caesar, *The Gallic War*, trans. H. J. Edwards (1979). Loeb Classical Library, London: Heinemann.

Cahen, M. (1921) *Études sur le Vocabulaire Religieux du Vieux-Scandinave: La Libation*. Paris: La Société de Linguistique de Paris.

Campbell, D. T. (1956) 'Adaptive behavior from random response', *Behavioral Science*, 1. 105–10.

—— (1965) 'Variation and selective retention in sociocultural evolution', in *Social Change in Developing Areas*, eds. H. R. Berringer, G. I. Blanksten, and R. W. Mack, 19–48. Cambridge, Mass.: Schenkman.

—— (1974) 'Evolutionary epistemology', in *The Philosophy of Karl Popper* (Vol. I), ed. P. Schilpp, 413—63. Lasalle, Illinois: Open Court.

Campbell, J. K. (1964) *Honour, Family, and Patronage*. Oxford: Clarendon Press.

Cancian, G. M. (1968) 'Varieties of functional analysis', *International Encyclopaedia of the Social Sciences*, 6. 29–43.

Caplan, A. L. (1979) 'Darwinian and deductivist models of social structures', *Studies in History and Philosophy of Science*, 10. 341–53.

Caplow, T. (1957) 'Organizational size', *Administrative Science Quarterly*, 1. 484—505.

Carneiro, R. L. (1967) 'On the relationship between size of population and complexity of social organization', *Southwestern Journal of Anthropology*, 23. 234–43.

—— (1970a) Foreword to K. Otterbein, *The Evolution of War*. New Haven: HRAF Press.

—— (1970b) 'A theory of the origin of the state', *Science*, 169, 733–38.

—— (1973) 'The four faces of evolution', in *Handbook of Social and Cultural Anthropology*, ed. J. J. Honigmann, 89–110.

Cavalli-Sforza, L. L. (1971) 'Similarities and dissimilarities of sociocultural and biological evolution', in *Mathematics in the Archaeological Sciences*, ed. F. R. Hodson *et al.*, 535–41. Edinburgh: Edinburgh University Press.

—— and Feldman, M. W. (1979) 'Towards a theory of cultural evolution', *Interdisciplinary Science Review*, 3. 99–107.

—— and Feldman, M. W. (1981) *Cultural Transmission and Evolution. A quantitative approach*. Princeton: Princeton University Press.

Chagnon, N. (1977) *Yanomamö. The fierce people*. 2nd edn. New York: Holt Rinehart, Winston.

Chaney, W. A. (1970) *The Cult of Kingship in Anglo-Saxon England. The transition from paganism to Christianity*. Manchester University Press.

Chang, K. C. (1976) *Early Chinese Civilization. Anthropological perspectives*. Cambridge, Mass.: Harvard University Press.

—— (1980) *Shang Civilization*. Yale University Press.

Childe, V. G. (1950) 'The urban revolution', *Town Planning Review*, 21. 3–17.

—— (1951) *Social Evolution*. London: Watts and Co.

Chomsky, N. (1980) *Rules and Representations*. New York: Columbia University Press.

Chü, T'ung-tsu (1961) *Law and Society in Traditional China*. Paris & The Hague: Mouton.

Claessen, H. J. M. (1978) 'The early state: a structural approach', in *The Early State*, eds. H. J. M. Claessen and P. Skalnik, 535–96. The Hague: Mouton.

—— and Skalnik, P., eds. (1978a) *The Early State*. The Hague: Mouton.

—— and —— 1978b 'Limits: beginning and end of the early state', in *The Early State*, eds. H. J. M. Claessen and P. Skalnik, 619–35. The Hague: Mouton.

—— and —— (1978c) 'The early state: models and reality', in *The Early State*, eds. H. J. M. Claessen and P. Skalnik, 637–50. The Hague: Mouton.

—— and —— (1981) *The Study of the State*. The Hague: Mouton.

Cloak, F. T. (1975) 'Is a cultural ethology possible?', *Human Ecology*, 3. 161–82.

Cohen, M. N. (1977) *The Food Crisis in Prehistory. Overpopulation and the origins of agriculture*. New Haven & London: Yale University Press.

Cohen, R. (1978) 'State origins: a reappraisal', in *The Early State*, eds. H. J. M. Claessen and P. Skalnik, 31–75. The Hague: Mouton.

Coornaert, E. (1948) 'Les ghildes médiévales (V–XIV siècles). Definition—evolution', *Revue Historique*, 199. 22–55; 200. 208–43.

Cornforth, M. (1976) *Historical Materialism*, 3rd edn. London: Lawrence & Wishart.

Creel, H. G. (1936) *The Birth of China*. London:
—— (1970) *The Origins of Statecraft in China*. Chicago University Press.

Crick, F, (1981) *Life Itself. Its origin and nature*. New York. Simon & Schuster (Touchstone).

Dahl, G. (1979) 'Ecology and equality: the Boran case', in *Pastoral Production and Society*. Proceedings of the International meeting on nomadic pastoralism, Paris 1–3 December 1976, 261–81. Cambridge: Cambridge University Press.

Dahrendorf, R. (1959) *Class and Class Conflict in Industrial Society*. London: Routledge & Kegan Paul.

Damas, D. (1969) 'Environment, history, and Central Eskimo society', *National Museums of Canada Bulletin*, 230. Contributions to Anthropology: Ecological Essays.

Darwin, C. (1902) *The Origin of Species by Means of Natural Selection*, 6th edn. London: John Murray.

Davidson, H. R. E. (1964) *Gods and Myths of Northern Europe*. London: Penguin.

Davie, M. R. (1929) *The Evolution of War. A study of its rôle in early societies*. New Haven: Yale University Press.

Dawkins, R. (1978) *The Selfish Gene*. London: Paladin Books (first published 1976, Oxford University Press).

Denton, M. (1984) *Evolution: A Theory in Crisis*. London: Barnett Books.

Diener, P. *et al.* (1980) 'Ecology and evolution in cultural anthropology', *Man* (NS), 15. 1–31.

Divale, W. T. and Harris, M. (1976) 'Population, warfare and the male supremacist complex', *American Anthropologist*, 78. 521–38.

Dole, G. E. (1973) 'Foundations of contemporary evolutionism', in *Main Currents in Contemporary Anthropology*, eds. R. and F. Narroll, 247–80. Englewood Cliffs: Prentice-Hall.

Douglas, M. (1966) *Purity and Danger. An analysis of concepts of pollution*. London: Routledge & Kegan Paul.

Drummond, H. (1897) *The Ascent of Man*. London: Hodder & Stoughton.

Dubuisson, D. (1975) 'L'Irlande et la théorie des "trois ordres" ', *Revue de l'histoire des religions*, 188. 35–63.

Duby, G. (1980) *The Three Orders. Feudal society imagined*, trans. A. Goldhammer. Chicago: University of Chicago Press.

Dumézil, G. (1948) *Mitra-Varuna. Essai sur deux représentations indo-européennes de la souveraineté*, 2nd edn. Paris: Leroux.
—— (1958) *L'Idéologie Tripartie des Indo-Européens*. Brussels: Latomus.

—— (1970) *The Destiny of the Warrior*, trans. A. Hiltebeitel. Chicago: University of Chicago Press.

—— (1971) *Mythe et Épopée* I. 2nd edn. Paris: Gallimard.

—— (1973) *Gods of the Ancient Northmen*. Berkeley: University of California Press.

—— (1981) 'La tradition druidique et l'écriture: le vivant et le mort', in *Cahier pour un Temps: Georges Dumézil*, 325–38. Paris: Centre Georges Pompidou/Pandora Editions.

—— (1983) *The Stakes of the Warrior*, trans. D. Weeks. Berkeley: University of California Press.

Dumond, D. E. (1965) 'Population growth and cultural change', *Southwestern Journal of Anthropology*, 21. 302–23.

Dumont, L. (1957) 'For a sociology of India', *Contributions to Indian Sociology*, 1. 7–22.

—— (1962) 'Kingship in ancient India', *Contributions to Indian Sociology*, 6. 48–77.

—— (1970) *Homo Hierarchicus*. London: Weidenfeld & Nicolson.

Durham, W. H. (1976*a*) 'The adaptive significance of cultural behavior', *Human Ecology*, 4. 89–121.

—— (1976*b*) 'Resource competition and human aggression. Part 1: a review of primitive war', *Quarterly Review of Biology*, 51. 385–415.

Durkheim, E. (1947) *The Elementary forms of the Religious Life*, trans. J. W. Swain. New York: Collier Books.

—— (1964*a*) *The Division of Labor in Society*. New York: Free Press.

—— (1964*b*) *The Rules of Sociological Method*, 8th edn, trans. S. A. Solovay and J. H. Mueller. New York: Free Press.

—— and Mauss, M. (1963) *Primitive Classification*, trans. R. Needham. London: Cohen & West.

Dyson-Hudson, N. (1966) *Karimojong Politics*. Oxford: Clarendon Press.

Eibl-Eibesfeldt, I. (1979) *The Biology of Peace and War*, trans. E. Mosbacher. London: Thames & Hudson.

Einzig, P. (1966) *Primitive Money*, 2nd edn. Oxford: Pergamon Press.

Eisenstadt, S. N. (1956) *From Generation to Generation. Age groups and social structure*. Glencoe: Free Press.

—— (1963) *The Political Systems of Empires*. New York: Free Press.

Ellen, R. (1982) *Environment, Subsistence and System. The ecology of small-scale social formations*. Cambridge: Cambridge University Press.

Ember, M. (1963) 'The relationship between economic and political development in nonindustrialized societies', *Ethnology*, 2. 228–48.

—— (1982) 'Statistical evidence for an ecological explanation of warfare', *American Anthropologist*, 84. 645–9.

Engels, F. (1884) 'The Origin of the Family, Private Property and the State'. Republished 1968, in *Karl Marx and Frederick Engels. Selected Works*. London: Lawrence & Wishart.

Escarra, J. (1936) *Le Droit Chinois*. Peking: Éditions Henri Vetch.

386 *References*

Evans-Pritchard, E. E. (1937) *Witchcraft, Oracles, and Magic among the Azande*. Oxford: Clarendon Press.

—— (1940) *The Nuer. A description of the modes of livelihood and political institutions of a Nilotic people*. Oxford: Clarendon Press.

—— (1956) *Nuer Religion*. Oxford: Clarendon Press.

—— (1961) *Anthropology and History*. Simon Fund Lecture. Manchester: Manchester University Press.

—— (1963) *The Comparative Method in Social Anthropology*. L. T. Hobhouse Memorial Lecture, No. 33. London: School of Economics and Political Science. University of London: Athlone Press.

—— (1981) *A History of Anthropological Thought*, ed. A. Singer. London: Faber & Faber.

Fairbank, J. K. (1974) 'Introduction. Varieties of the Chinese military experience', in *Chinese Ways in Warfare*, eds. F. A. Kierman and J. K. Fairbank. Harvard University Press.

Febvre, L. (1925) *A Geographical Introduction to History*. London: Kegan Paul, Trench, Trubner.

Feldman, M. W. and Cavalli-Sforza, L. L. (1976) 'Cultural and biological evolutionary processes: selection for a trait under complex transmission' *Journal of Theoretical Population Biology*, 9. 238–59.

Ferguson, R. B. (1984) 'Introduction: studying war', in *Warfare, Culture, and Environment*, ed. R. B. Ferguson, 1–81. Orlando: Academic Press.

Fernea, R. A. (n.d.) 'Irrigation and Social Organization among the El Shabana: a Group of Tribal Cultivators in Southern Iraq', Ph.D. dissertation (1959), University of Chicago.

Fisher, R. A. (1930) *The Genetical Theory of Natural Selection*. New York: Dover.

Flannery, K. V. (1972) 'The cultural evolution of civilizations', *Annual Review of Ecology and Systematics*, 3. 399–426.

Fleck, L. (1979) *The Genesis and Development of a Scientific Fact*, eds. T. J. Trenn and R. K. Merton. Chicago: University of Chicago Press.

Forde, C. D. (1934) *Habitat, Economy and Society. A geographical introduction to ethnology*. London: Methuen.

Forge, A. (1972) 'Normative factors in the settlement size of Neolithic cultivators (New Guinea)', in *Man, Settlement, and Urbanism*, eds. P. J. Ucko, R. Tringham, and G. W. Dimbleby, 363–76. London: Duckworth.

Fortes, M. (1940) 'The political system of the Tallensi of the Northern Territories of the Gold Coast', in *African Political Systems*, eds. M. Fortes and E. E. Evans-Pritchard, 239–71. London: Oxford University Press.

—— (1959) *Oedipus and Job in West African Religion*. Cambridge University Press.

—— and Evans-Pritchard, E. E. (1940) Introduction to *African Political Systems*, eds. M. Fortes and E. E. Evans-Pritchard, 1–23. London:

Oxford University Press.

Fosbrooke, H. A. (1948) 'An administrative survey of the Masai social system', *Tanganyika Notes and Records*, 26. 2–50.

Fox, R. (1967) *Kinship and Marriage. An anthropological perspective.* London: Penguin Books.

Freeman, D. (1974) 'The evolutionary theories of Charles Darwin and Herbert Spencer', *Current Anthropology*, 15. 211–37.

Freeman, E. A. (1877) *The History of the Norman Conquest of England. Its causes and its results*, 3rd edn. Oxford: Clarendon Press.

Freeman, L. C. (1968) 'Conflict and congruence in anthropological theory', in *Theory in Anthropology. A source book*, eds. R. A. Manners and D. Kaplan, 193–5. London: Routledge & Kegan Paul.

—— and Winch, R. F. (1957) 'Societal complexity: an empirical test of a typology of societies', *American Journal of Sociology*, 62. 461–6.

Freud, S. (1938) *Totem and Taboo*, trans. A. A. Brill. (Originally published 1913.). London: Pelican Books.

Fried, M. H. (1960) 'On the evolution of social stratification and the state', in S. Diamond, ed., *Culture in History: Essays in Honour of Paul Radin*, 713–31. New York: Columbia University Press.

—— (1961) 'Warfare, military organization and the evolution of society', *Anthropologica* (NS), 3. 134–47.

—— (1967) *The Evolution of Political Society. An essay in political anthropology.* New York: Random House.

Friedman, J. 'Marxism, structuralism, and vulgar materialism', *Man* (NS), 9. 444–69.

—— and Rowlands, M. J. (eds.) (1977a) *The Evolution of Social Systems.* London: Duckworth.

—— and —— (1977b) 'Notes towards an epigenetic model of the evolution of "civilisation" ' in *The Evolution of Social Systems*, 201–76.

Friedrich, P. (1966) 'Proto-Indo-European kinship', *Ethnology*, 5. 1–36.

Gablik, S. (1977) *Progress in Art.* New York: Rizzoli.

Gelb, I. J. (1963) *A Study of Writing.* 2nd edn. Chicago: Chicago University Press.

Gerard, R. W., and Kluckhohn, C., and Rapoport, A. (1956) 'Biological and cultural evolution. Some analogies and explorations', *Behavioral Science*, 1. 6–34.

Geschwind, N. (1979) 'Specialization of the human brain', *Scientific American*, 241(3). 164–79.

Gibbon, E. (1776) *The History of the Decline and Fall of the Roman Empire*, London.

Gimbutas, M. (1970) 'Proto-Indo-European culture: the Kurgan culture during the fifth, fourth, and third millennia B.C.', in *Indo-European and Indo-Europeans*, eds. G. Cardona, H. M. Hoenigswald, and A. Senn, 155–97. Philadelphia: University of Pennsylvania Press.

Ginsberg, M. (1956) 'The concept of evolution in sociology', reprinted in

On the Diversity of Morals. 180–99 (M. Ginsberg collected papers). London: Heinemann.

Gluckman, M. (1940) 'The kingdom of the Zulu of South Africa', in *African Political Systems*, eds. M. Fortes and E. E. Evans-Pritchard, 25–55. London: International African Institute.

—— (1954) 'Political institutions', in *The Institutions of Primitive Society*, 66–80. Oxford: Blackwell.

—— (1963) *Custom and Conflict in Africa*. Oxford: Blackwell.

—— (1967) *Politics, Law, and Ritual in Tribal Society*. Oxford: Blackwell.

—— (1973) *The Judicial Process among the Barotse of Northern Rhodesia*, revised 2nd edn. Manchester: Manchester University Press.

Goddard, D. (1965) 'The concept of primitive society', *Social Research*, 32. 256–76.

Godelier, M. (ed.) (1977) *Perspectives in Marxist Anthropology*. Cambridge Studies in Social Anthropology No. 18. Cambridge: Cambridge University Press.

Goldman, I. (1970) *Ancient Polynesian Society*. Chicago: University of Chicago Press.

Goldschmidt, W. (1979) 'A general model of pastoral social systems', in *Pastoral Production and Society*. Proceedings of the international meeting on nomadic pastoralism, Paris, 1–3. December 1976, 15–27. Cambridge: Cambridge University Press.

Golson, J. (1977) *The Ladder of Social Evolution. Archaeology and the bottom rungs*. Australian Academy of the Humanities Annual Lecture. Sydney: Sydney University Press.

Gombrich, E. H. (1963) *Meditations on a Hobby Horse and Other Essays on the Theory of Art*. London: Phaidon.

—— (1982) *The Image and the Eye*. Oxford: Phaidon.

Gomme, G. L. (1880) *Primitive Folk-Moots*; *or open air assemblies in Britain*. London: Sampson Low, Marston, Searle, and Rivington.

Goodenough, W. H. (1970) 'The evolution of pastoralism and Indo-European origins', in *Indo-European and Indo-Europeans*, ed. G. Cardona, H. Hoenigswald, and A. Senn, 256–66. Philadelphia: University of Pennsylvania Press.

Goody, J. (1971) *Technology, Tradition, and the State in Africa*. Oxford University Press, for International African Institute.

—— (1977) 'Population and polity in the Voltaic region', in *The Evolution of Social Systems*, eds. J. Friedman and M. Rowlands, 535–45. London: Tavistock Press.

—— and Tambiah, S. J. (1973) *Bridewealth and Dowry*. Cambridge Papers in Social Anthropology 7. Cambridge University Press.

Gould, S. J. and Vrba, E. (1982) 'Exaptation: a missing term in the science of form', *Paleobiology*, 8. 4–15.

Gowans, A. (1979) 'Child art as an instrument for studying history. The case for an "ontogeny repeats phylogeny" paradigm in universal history', *Art History*, 2. 247–74.

Graicunas, V. A. (1937) 'Relationship in organization', in *Papers on the Science of Administration*, eds. L. Gulick and L. Urwick, 183–7, New York Institute of Public Administration. (First published in Bulletin of the International Management Institute, 1933.)

Grierson, P. (1941) 'Election and inheritance in early Germanic kingship' *Cambridge Historical Journal*, 7. 1–22.

Gross, C. (1890) *The Gild Merchant: A contribution to British municipal history*. Oxford: Clarendon Press.

Guilford, J. P. (1970) 'Traits of creativity', in *Creativity*, ed. P. E. Vernon, 167–88. London: Penguin.

Gunawardana, R. A. L. H. (1981) 'Social function and political power', in *The Study of the State*, eds. H. J. M. Claessen and P. Skalnik, 133–54. The Hague: Mouton.

Haas, J. (1982) *The Evolution of the Prehistoric State*. New York: Columbia University Press.

Haberland, E. (1963) *Galla Süd-Athiopiens*. Stuttgart: Kohlhammer.

Hacking, I. (1975) *The Emergence of Probability. A philosophical study of early ideas about probability, induction and statistical inference*. Cambridge: Cambridge University Press.

Hage, P., and Harary, F. (1983) *Structural Models in Anthropology*. Cambridge Studies in Anthropology 46. Cambridge University Press.

Haldane, J. B. S. (1932) *The Causes of Evolution*. London: Longmans, Green, & Co.

—— (1955) 'Population genetics', *New Biology*, 18. 34–51.

Hall, R. H., Haas, J. and Johnson (1967) 'Organizational size, complexity, and formalization', *American Sociological Review*, 32. 903–12.

Hallowell, A. L. (1955) *Culture and Experience*. Philadelphia: University of Pennsylvania Press.

Hallpike, C. R. (1968) 'The status of craftsmen among the Konso of southwest Ethiopia', *Africa*, 38. 258–69.

—— (1970*a*) 'Konso agriculture', *Journal of Ethiopian Studies*, 8. 31–43.

—— (1970*b*) 'The principles of alliance formation between Konso towns', *Man* (NS), 5. 258–80.

—— (1971) 'Some problems in cross-cultural comparison', in *The Translation of Culture: Essays to E. E. Evans-Pritchard*, ed. T. O. Beidelman, 123–40. London: Tavistock.

—— (1972) *The Konso of Ethiopia. A study of the values of a Cushitic society*. Oxford: Clarendon Press.

—— (1973) 'Functionalist interpretations of primitive warfare', *Man* (NS), 8. 451–70.

—— (1974*a*) Letter 'Functions of war', *Man* (NS), 9. 488–9.

—— (1974*b*) 'Aristotelian and Heraclitean societies', *Ethos*, 2. 69–76.

—— (1976*a*) 'The origins of the Borana *gada* system', *Africa*, 46. 48–56.

—— (1976*b*) 'Is there a primitive mentality?', *Man* (NS), 11. 253–70.

—— (1977*a*) Review of A. P. Vayda 'War in Ecological Perspective', *Man* (NS), 12. 556–7.

—— (1977*b*) *Bloodshed and Vengeance in the Papuan Mountains. The generation of conflict in Tauade society.* Oxford: Clarendon Press.

—— (1978) Introduction to B. Blackwood, *The Kukukuku of the Upper Watut*. Oxford: Pitt Rivers Museum Monograph Series No. 2.

—— (1979) *The Foundations of Primitive Thought.* Oxford: Clarendon Press.

—— (1981) 'The culturgen: science or science fiction?', *The Behavioral and Brain Sciences*, 5. 12–13.

—— (1984*a*) 'The relevance of the theory of inclusive fitness to human society', *Journal of Social and Biological Structures*, 7. 131–44.

—— (1984*b*) 'Fitting culture into a Skinner box', *The Behavioral and Brain Sciences*, 7. 504–5.

—— (1985*a*) 'Social and biological evolution I: Darwinism and social evolution', *Journal of Social and Biological Structures*, 8. 129–46.

—— (1985*b*) Review of R. B. Ferguson (ed.) 'Warfare, Culture, and Environment', *Man* (NS), 20. 756–7.

—— (1986) 'Social and biological evolution II: some basic principles of social evolution', *Journal of Social and Biological Structures*, 9. 5–31

Hamer, J. H. (1967*a*) 'Voluntary associations as structures of change among Sidamo of south-western Ethiopia', *Anthropological Quarterly*, 40. 73–91.

—— (1967*b*) 'Myth, ritual, and the authority of elders in an Ethiopian society', *Africa*, 46. 327–39.

—— (1970) 'Sidamo generational class cycles. A political gerontocracy', *Africa*, 49. 50–70.

—— and Hamer, I. (1966) 'Spirit possession and its socio-psychological implications among the Sidamo of southwest Ethiopia', *Ethnology*, 5. 392–408.

Hamilton, W. D. (1963) 'The evolution of altruistic behaviour', *American Naturalist*, 97. 354–6.

—— (1964*a,b*) 'The genetical evolution of social behaviour', I and II, *Journal of Theoretical Biology*, 7. 1–16, 17–52.

Harner, M. (1970) 'Population pressure and the social evolution of agriculturalists', *Southwestern Journal of Anthropology*, 26. 67–86.

Harré, R. (1981) 'The evolutionary analogy in social explanation', in *The Philosophy of Evolution*, eds. U. J. Jensen and R. Harré, 161–75. Brighton: Harvester.

Harris, M. (1960) 'Adaptation in biological and cultural science', *Transactions of the New York Academy of Science*, 23. 59–65.

—— (1969) *The Rise of Anthropological Theory. A history of theories of culture*. London: Routledge & Kegan Paul.

—— (1971) *Culture, Man, and Nature; an introduction to general anthropology*. New York: Crowell.

—— (1975) *Cows, Pigs, Wars, and Witches. The riddles of culture*. New York: Vintage Books.

—— (1978) *Cannibals and Kings. The origins of cultures*. London: Collins.

—— (1980) *Cultural Materialism. The struggle for a science of culture*. New York: Vintage Books.

—— (1984) 'A cultural materialist theory of band and village warfare: the Yanomamo test', in *Warfare, Culture, and Environment*, ed. R. B. Ferguson, 111–40. Orlando: Academic Press.

Henry, J. (1955) 'Homeostasis, society, and evolution: a critique', *Scientific Monthly*, 81. 300–9.

Hill, J. (1978) 'The origin of sociocultural evolution', *Journal of Social and Biological Structures*, I. 377–86.

Ho, M.-W., and Saunders, P. T. (1984) *Beyond Neo-Darwinism. An introduction to the new evolutionary paradigm*. London: Academic Press.

Hocart, A. M. (1970) *Kings and Councillors. An essay on the comparative anatomy of human society*, ed. with Introduction by R. Needham. (First published 1936.) Chicago: Chicago University Press.

Holt, J. C. (1981) 'The prehistory of Parliament', in *The English Parliament in the Middle Ages*, eds. R. G. Davies and J. H. Denton, 1–28. Manchester: Manchester University Press.

Homer, *The Iliad*, trans. A. T. Murray (1924). Loeb Classical Library, London: Heinemann.

Hsu, Cho-yun (1965) *Ancient China in Transition. An analysis of social mobility, 722–222 B.C.* Stanford University Press.

Huizinga, J. (1955) *Homo Ludens. A study of the play element in culture*. Boston: Beacon Press.

Hull, D. (1981) 'Units of evolution: a metaphysical essay', in *The Philosophy of Evolution*, eds. U. J. Jensen and R. Harré, 23–44. Brighton: Harvester.

Hultkrantz, A. (1966) 'An ecological approach to religion', *Ethnos*, 31. 131–50.

—— (1974) 'Ecology of religions: its scope and methodology', *Review of Ethnology*, 4. 1–12.

Hume, D. (1888) *A Treatise of Human Nature*, ed. Selby Bigge. London: Oxford University Press.

Huntingford, G. W. B. (1969) *The Galla of Ethiopia. The Kingdoms of Kaffa and Janjero*, 2nd edn. Ethnographic Survey of Africa: North Eastern Africa Part II. London: International African Institute.

Huxley, J. S. (1956) 'Evolution, cultural and biological', in *Current*

Anthropology, ed. W. L. Thomas, Jr., 3–25. Chicago: University of Chicago Press.

—— (1974) *Evolution. The modern synthesis*, 3rd edn. London: Allen & Unwin.

Huxley T. H. (1894) *Evolution and Ethics*. London: Macmillan.

James, J. A. (1951) 'A preliminary study of the size determinant in small group interaction', *American Sociology Review*, 16. 474–7.

Jensen, U. J. and Harré, R. (eds.) (1981) *The Philosophy of Evolution*. Brighton: Harvester.

Johannesson, J. *A History of the Old Icelandic Commonwealth*, trans. H. Bessason. University of Manitoba Press.

Jorgensen, J. (1980) *Western Indians*. San Francisco: W. H. Freeman & Co.

Kearney, M. (1984) *World View*. California: Chandler & Sharp.

Keesing, F. M. and Keesing, R. (1971) *New Perspectives in Cultural Anthropology*. New York: Holt, Rinehart & Co.

Keightley, D. N. (1978) 'The religious commitment: Shang theology and the genesis of Chinese political culture', *History of Religions*, 17. 211–25.

—— (n.d.) 'Public Work in Ancient China: a study of forced labor in the Shang and Western Chou', Ph.D. Thesis (1969), Columbia University.

Keith, A. B. (1925) *The Religion of a Darwinist*. Conway Memorial Lecture, London: Watts.

Keller, A. G. (1915) *Societal Evolution*. New Haven: Yale University Press.

Kephart, W. M. (1950) 'A quantitative analysis of intragroup relationships', *American Journal of Sociology*, 55. 544–9.

Kidd, B. (1894) *Social Evolution*. London: Macmillan.

King, R. D. (1969) *Historical Linguistics and Generative Grammar*. New Jersey: Prentice Hall.

King, V. T. (1976) 'Migration, warfare and culture contact in Borneo; a critique of ecological analysis', *Oceania*, 46. 302–27.

Kluckhohn, C. (1967) *Navaho Witchcraft*. Boston: Beacon Press.

Knutsson, K. E. (1967) *Authority and Change. A study of the Kallu institution among the Macha Galla of Ethiopia*. Göteborg: Etnografiska Museet.

Koch, K-F. (1974) *War and Peace in Jalémo. The management of conflict in Highland New Guinea*. Cambridge, Mass.: Harvard University Press.

Koestler, A. (1967) *The Ghost in the Machine*. London: Hutchinson.

Kroeber, A. L. (1948) *Anthropology*. New York: Harcourt, Brace, and World.

Kuhn, T. S. (1970) *The Structure of Scientific Revolutions*, 2nd edn. Chicago: University of Chicago Press.

Kuiper, F. B. J. (1960) 'The ancient Aryan verbal contest', *Indo-Iranian Journal*, 4. 217–81.

Kuper, A. (1983) *Anthropologists and Anthropology. The British School 1922–1972*, 2nd edn. London: Routledge & Kegan Paul.

Kuusinen, O. (ed.) (1961) *Fundamentals of Marxism-Leninism*. London: Lawrence & Wishart.

Leach, E. R. (1959) 'Hydraulic society in Ceylon', *Past and Present*, 15, 2–26.

—— (1964) *Political Systems of Highland Burma. A study of Kachin social structure*. 2nd edn. London: Bell.

—— (1982) *Social Anthropology*. Oxford: University Press.

Legesse, A. (1973) *Gada*. New York: Free Press.

Lévi-Strauss, C. (1963) *Structural Anthropology*, trans. C. Jacobson and B. G. Schoepf. New York: Basic Books.

—— (1969) *The Elementary Structures of Kinship*, trans. J. H. Bell and J. R. von Sturmer, ed. R. Needham. Boston: Beacon Press.

Lewis, B. A. (1972) *The Murle. Red chiefs and black commoners*. Oxford: Clarendon Press.

Lewis, H. S. (1965) *A Galla Monarchy*. Madison & Milwaukee: University of Wisconsin Press.

—— (1974) 'Neighbours, friends, and kinsmen: principles of social organization among the Cushitic-speaking peoples of Ethiopia', *Ethnology*, 13. 145–57.

Lewis, I. M. (1976) *Social Anthropology in Perspective. The relevance of social anthropology*. London: Penguin Books.

Lewontin, R. C. (1957) 'The adaptation of population to varying environments', *Cold Springs Harbor Symposia in Quantitative Biology*, 22. 395–408.

—— (1979) 'Sociobiology as an adaptationist program' *Behavioral Science*, 24. 5—14.

Lienhardt, G. (1958) 'The Western Dinka', in *Tribes Without Rulers. Studies in African Segmentary systems*, eds. J. Middleton and D. Tait, 97–135. London: Routledge & Kegan Paul.

—— (1961) *Divinity and Experience. The religion of the Dinka*. Oxford: Clarendon Press.

Lincoln, B. (1981) *Priests, Warriors, and Cattle. A study in the ecology of religions*. Berkeley: University of California Press.

Linton, R. (1936) *The Study of Man. An introduction*. New York: Appleton-Century.

Littleton, C. S. (1982) *The New Comparative Mythology. An anthropological assessment of the theories of Georges Dumézil*. 3rd edn. Berkeley: University of California Press.

Lizot, J. (1977) 'Population, resources and warfare among the Yanomamö', *Man* (NS), 12. 497–517.

Lloyd, G. E. R. (1966) *Polarity and Analogy. Two types of argumentation in early Greek thought*. Cambridge: Cambridge University Press.

—— (1979) *Magic, Reason and Experience. Studies in the origins and development of Greek science.* Cambridge: Cambridge University Press.

Lowie, R. H. (1921) *Primitive Society.* London: Routledge & Kegan Paul.

—— (1927) *The Origins of the State.* New York: Harcourt, Brace, & Co.

—— (1937) *The History of Ethnological Theory.* New York: Holt, Rinehart, & Winston.

Lucretius, *De Rerum Natura,* trans. W. H. D. Rouse, revised M. F. Smith (1975), Loeb Classical Library. London: Heinemann.

Lumsden, C. J. and Wilson, E. O. (1981) *Genes, Mind, and Culture.* Cambridge, Mass.: Harvard University Press.

Maine, H. S. (1931) *Ancient Law.* (First published 1861.) London: Oxford University Press.

Mair, L. (1962) *Primitive Government.* London: Penguin Books.

Maitland, A. (1980) 'Cathedral Towns of England: Coventry. A story of courage and controversy', *This England,* 13(4). 46–51.

Malinowski, B. (1926) 'Anthropology', *Encyclopaedia Britannica,* 13th edn. (Supp. Vol. I), 131–40.

Marr, D. (1981) *Vision.* San Francisco: Freeman.

Marx, K. (1967) *Capital: A critique of political economy,* ed. F. Engels (3 vols.). New York: International Publishers.

Maybury-Lewis, D. (1967) *Akwe-Shavante Society.* Oxford: Clarendon Press.

—— (ed.) (1979) *Dialectical Societies. The Gê and Bororo of Central Brazil.* Cambridge, Mass.: Harvard University Press.

Mayr, E. (1980) 'Prologue: some thoughts on the history of the evolutionary synthesis', in *The Evolutionary Synthesis. Perspectives on the unification of biology,* eds. E. Mayr and W. B. Provine, 1–48. Harvard University Press.

McAdam, J. L. (1821) *Remarks on the Present System of Road Making,* 4th edn. London: Longman and other booksellers.

McArthur, A. M. (n.d.) 'The Kunimaipa. The Social Structure of a Papuan People', Ph.D. Thesis (1961), Australian National University.

McFarlane, A. (1978) *The Origins of English Individualism.* Oxford: Blackwell.

McLennan, J. F. (1865) *Primitive Marriage. An inquiry into the origins of the form of capture in marriage ceremonies.* London: Bernard & Quaritch.

Mead, M. (1940) *The Mountain Arapesh II. Supernaturalism.* American Museum of Natural History, Anthropological Papers, 37.

Meillet, A. (1907) 'Le dieu indo-iranien Mitra', *Journal Asiatique,* (Series 10), 9. 143–59.

Merton, R. K. (1957) *Social Theory and Social Structure,* 2nd edn. New York: Free Press.

—— (1967) *On Theoretical Sociology.* New York: Free Press.

Michell, H. (1964) *Sparta*. 2nd edn. Cambridge: Cambridge University Press.

Michels, R. (1915) *Political Parties. A sociological study of the oligarchical tendencies of modern democracy*. London: Jarrold & Sons.

Middleton, J. (1960) *Lugbara Religion. Ritual and authority among an East African People*. International African Institute. London: Oxford University Press.

Millon, R. (1962) 'Variations in social responses to the practice of irrigation agriculture', in *Civilizations in Desert Lands*, ed. R. B. Woodbury, Anthropological Papers No. 62, Dept. of Anthropology, University of Utah, 56–88. Salt Lake City: University of Utah Press.

Moore, O. K. (1957) 'Divination—a new perspective', *American Anthropologist*, 59. 69–74.

Moorhead, P. S. and Kaplan, M. M. (eds.) (1967) *Mathematical Challenges to the Neo-Darwinian Interpretation of Evolution*. Monograph No. 5. Philadelphia: Wistar Institute Press.

Morgan, L. H. (1877) *Ancient Society*. Chicago: Kerr & Co.

Morren, G. E. B. (1984) 'Warfare on the highland fringe of New Guinea: the case of the Mountain Ok', in *Warfare, Culture, and Environment*, ed. R. B. Ferguson, 169–207. Orlando: Academic Press.

Mumford, L. (1934) *Technics and Civilisation*. London: Routledge.

Murdock, G. P. (1949) *Social Structure*. Glencoe: Free Press.

—— (1959) *Africa: Its Peoples and Their Culture History*. New York: McGraw Hill.

—— (1960) 'How cultures change', in *Man, Culture, and Society*, ed. H. L. Shapiro. New York: Oxford University Press (first publsihed 1956).

—— *et al.* (1961) *Outline of Culture Materials*. 4th edn. New Haven: HRAF Press.

—— (1967) 'Ethnographic Atlas: a summary', *Ethnology*, 6. 305–26.

—— (1970) 'Kin term patterns and their distribution', *Ethnology*, 9. 165–207.

—— and Morrow, D. O. (1970) 'Subsistence economy and supportive practices: cross-cultural codes', *Ethnology*, 9. 302–30.

—— and White, D. R. (1969) 'Standard cross-cultural sample', *Ethnology*, 8. 329–69.

—— and Wilson, S. F. (1972) 'Settlement patterns and community organization: cross-cultural codes 3', *Ethnology*, 11. 254–295.

—— and —— and Frederick, V. (1978) 'World distribution of theories of illness', *Ethnology*, 17. 449–70.

Murphy, R. F. (1957) 'Intergroup hostility and social cohesion', *American Anthropologist*, 59. 1018–35.

Murray, A. C. (1983) *Germanic Kinship Structure. Studies in law and society in Antiquity and the early Middle Ages*. Toronto: Pontifical

Institute of Medieval Studies.

Nadel, S. F. (1951) *Foundations of Social Anthropology*. London: Cohen & West.

Nader, L. (1968) 'Conflict: anthropological aspects', *International Encyclopaedia of the Social Sciences*, 3. 236–42.

Naroll, R. (1956) 'A preliminary index of social development', *American Anthropologist*, 58. 687–715.

—— and Divale, W. T. (1976) 'Natural selection in cultural evolution: warfare versus peaceful diffusion', *American Ethnologist*, 3. 97–129.

Needham, J. (1954) *Science and Civilisation in China*: Vol. *1, Introductory Orientation*. Cambridge: Cambridge University Press.

—— (1956) *Science and Civilisation in China*: Vol. *2, History of Scientific Thought*. Cambridge University Press.

—— (1959) *Science and Civilisation in China*: Vol. *3, Mathematics and the Science of the Heavens and the Earth*. Cambridge University Press.

—— (1962) *Science and Civilisation in China*: Vol. *4, Physics and Physical Technology, Part I*: *Physics*. Cambridge University Press.

—— (1965) *Science and Civilisation in China*: Vol. *4, Physics and Physical Technology, Part II*: *Mechanical Engineering*. Cambridge University Press.

—— (1969) *The Grand Titration. Science and society in China and the West*. London: Allen & Unwin.

—— (1980) 'The guns of Kaifêng-fu', *Times Literary Supplement*. 11 January, 39–42.

Needham, R. (1974) *Remarks and Inventions. Skeptical essays about kinship*. London: Tavistock.

—— (1978) *Essential Perplexities*. Oxford: Clarendon Press.

—— (1980) *Reconnaissances*. University of Toronto Press.

—— (1981) 'Dumézil et le domaine du comparativisme', in *Cahiers pour un Temps*: *Georges Dumézil*, 283–91. Paris: Centre Georges Pompidou/ Pandora Editions.

Netting, R. McC. (1973) 'Fighting, forest, and the fly: some demographic regulators among the Kofyar', *Journal of Anthropological Research*, 29. 164–79.

—— (1974*a*) 'Kofyar armed conflict: social causes and consequences', *Journal of Anthropological Research*, 30. 139–63.

—— (1974*b*) Letter on 'Functions of war', *Man* (NS), 9. 485–7.

Newcomb, W. W. (1958) 'A re-examination of the causes of Plains warfare', *American Anthropologist*, 52. 317–30.

Oberg, K. (1940) 'The kingdom of Ankole in Uganda', in *African Political Systems*, eds. M. Fortes and E. E. Evans-Pritchard, 121–62. London: Oxford University Press.

Oppenheimer, F. (1914) *The State*: *Its History and Development Viewed Sociologically*, trans. J. M. Gitterman. London: Allen & Unwin.

Osgood, C. E. (1960) 'The cross-cultural generality of visual-verbal synesthetic tendencies', *Behavioral Science*, 5. 146–69.

——, May, W. H., and Miron, M. S. (1975) *Cross-Cultural Universals of Affective Meaning*. University of Illinois Press.

Otterbein, K. (1968) 'Internal war A cross-cultural study', *American Anthropologist*, 70. 277–89.

—— (1970) *The Evolution of War*. New Haven: HRAF Press.

Parsons, T. (1977) *The Evolution of Societies*, Englewood Cliffs: Prentice-Hall.

Patterson, O. (1982) *Slavery and Social Death*. Harvard University Press.

Pedersen, J. (1926) *Israel. Its life and culture*. Oxford University Press.

Pelham, H. F., and Conway, R. S. (1911) 'The beginning of Rome and the monarchy', *Encyclopaedia Britannica*, 11th edn., 23. 615–19.

Peoples, J. G. (1982) 'Individual or group advantage? A reinterpretation of Maring ritual cycle', *Current Anthropology*, 23. 291–310.

Peters, S. (1980) 'Comments on the analogy between biological and social evolution', *American Antiquity*, 45. 596–601.

Phillips, D. C. (1977) *Holistic Thought in Social Science*. London: Macmillan.

Piaget, J. (1971) *Structuralism*. London: Routledge & Kegan Paul.

Polanyi, K. *et al.* (eds.) (1957) *Trade and Markets in the Early Empires*. Glencoe: Free Press.

Polomé, E. (1982) 'Indo-European culture, with special attention to religion', in *The Indo-Europeans in the Fourth and Third Millennia*, ed. E. Polomé, 156–72. Ann Arbor: Karoma.

Powell, T. G. E. (1958) *The Celts*. London: Thames & Hudson.

Pulliam, H. R. and Dunford, C. (1980) *Programmed to Learn. An essay on the evolution of culture*. New York: Columbia University Press.

Radcliffe-Brown, A. R. (1940) Preface to *African Political Systems*, eds. M. Fortes and E. E. Evans-Pritchard, ix–xxiii. London: Oxford University Press.

—— (1948) *A Natural Science of Society*. Glencoe: Free Press.

—— (1952) *Structure and Function in Primitive Society*. London: Cohen & West.

Radding, C. M. (1979) 'Superstition to science: nature, fortune and the passing of the medieval ordeal'. *American Historical Review*, 84. 945–69.

Rappaport, R. A. (1968) *Pigs for the Ancestors. Ritual in the ecology of a New Guinea people*. Yale University Press.

—— (1977) 'Maladaptation in social systems', in *The Evolution of Social Systems*, eds. J. Friedman and M. J. Rowlands, 49–71. London: Duckworth.

—— (1978) 'Adaptation and the structure of ritual', in *Human Behaviour and Adaptation*, eds. N. Blurton-Jones and V. Reynolds, 77–102. London: Taylor & Francis.

Rau, W. (1957) *Staat und Gesellschaft im Alten Indien nach den Brahmana Texten Dargestellt*. Wiesbaden: Harrassowitz.

Renfrew, C. (ed.) (1973) *The Explanation of Culture Change. Models in prehistory*. London: Duckworth.

—— and Cooke, K. L. (eds.) (1979) *Transformations. Mathematical approaches to culture change*. London: Academic Press.

Rex, J. (1961) *Key Problems of Sociological Theory*, London: Routledge & Kegan Paul.

Rindos, R. (1984) *The Origins of Agriculture. An evolutionary perspective.* Orlando, Florida: Academic Press.

Rogers, C. R. (1970) 'Towards a theory of creativity', in *Creativity*, ed. P. E. Vernon, 137–51. London: Penguin.

Rosch, E. (1977) 'Human categorization', in *Studies in Cross-Cultural Psychology* (Vol. I), ed. N. Warren. London: Academic Press.

Ross, J. B. (1984) 'Effects of contact on revenge hostilities among the Achuara Jivaro', in *Warfare, Culture, and Environment*, ed. R. B. Ferguson. Orlando: Academic Press.

Ross, M. (1983) 'Political decision making and conflict: additional cross-cultural codes and scales', *Ethnology*, 22, 169–92.

Rostovtzeff, M. (1957) *The Social and Economic History of the Roman Empire*, 2nd edn. ed. P. M. Fraser. Oxford: Clarendon Press.

Rushton, J. P. *et al.* (1984) 'Genetic similarity theory: beyond kin selection', *Behavior Genetics*, 14. 179–93.

Russell, B. (1946) *History of Western Philosophy and its connection with political and social circumstances from the earliest times to the present day*. London: Allen & Unwin.

—— (1948) *Human Knowledge: Its Scope and Limits*. London: Allen and Unwin.

—— (1960) *Power. A new social analysis*. London: Unwin.

Russell, Lord John (1823) *An Essay on the History of the English Government and Constitution from the Reign of Henry VIII to the Present Time*, 2nd edn. London: Longman, Hurst.

Ruyle, E. E. (1973) 'Genetic and cultural pools: some suggestions for a unified theory of biocultural evolution', *Human Ecology*, 1. 201–15.

Sahlins, M. (1958) *Social Stratification in Polynesia*. Monograph of the American Ethnological Society. University of Washington.

—— (1961) 'The segmentary lineage: an organization of predatory expansion', *American Anthropologist*, 63. 322–45.

—— (1968) *Tribesmen*. Englewood Cliffs, NJ: Prentice Hall.

—— (1974) *Stone Age Economics*. London: Tavistock.

—— and Service, E. R. (eds.) (1960) *Evolution and Culture*. University of Michigan Press.

Schapera, I. (1955) *A Handbook of Tswana Law and Custom*, 2nd edn.

London: Oxford University Press.

—— (1956) *Government and Politics in Tribal Society*. London: Oxford University Press.

Schneider, D. and Gough, K. (eds.) (1961) *Matrilineal Kinship*. University of California Press.

Seddon, D. (ed.) (1978) *Relations of Production*. *Marxist approaches to economic anthropology*, trans. H. Luckner. London: Frank Cass.

Seebohm, F. (1911) *Tribal Custom in Anglo-Saxon England*. London: Longmans, Green.

Service, E. R. (1971) *Primitive Social Organization*. *An evolutionary perspective*. 2nd edn. New York: Random House.

—— (1975) *Origins of the State and Civilization*. *The process of cultural evolution*. New York: Norton.

Shack, W. A. (1966) *The Gurage*. *A people of the ensete culture*. Oxford University Press.

Sillitoe, P. (1977) 'Land shortage and war in New Guinea', *Ethnology*, 16. 71–81.

Simmel, G. (1902–3) 'The number of members as determining the sociological form of groups', *American Journal of Sociology*, 8. 1–46; 158–96.

Simon, H. A. (1965) 'The architecture of complexity', *General Systems*, 10. 63–76.

Simpson, G. G. (1953) *The Major Features of Evolution*. New York: Columbia University Press.

Simri, U. (n.d.) 'The Religious and Magical Function of Ball Games in Various Cultures', Ed. D. Thesis (1966), West Virginia University.

Singer, C. (1943) *A Short History of Science to the Nineteenth Century*, 2nd edn. Oxford: Clarendon Press.

—— (1956) 'East and West in retrospect', in *A History of Technology* (Vol. II), 753–6. Oxford: Clarendon Press.

Skinner, B. F. (1974) *About Behaviourism*. London: Cape.

—— (1981) 'Selection by consequences', *Science*, 213. 501–4.

—— (1984) 'Some consequences of selection', *The Behavioral and Brain Sciences*, 7. 502–23.

Smeds, H. (1955) 'The ensete planting culture of Eastern Sidamo, Ethiopia', *Acta Geographica* (Helsinki), 13. 1–35.

Smith, A. D. (1973) *The Concept of Social Change*. *A critique of the functionalist theory of social change*. London: Routledge & Kegan Paul.

Southall, A. W. (1953) *Alur Society*. Cambridge: Cambridge University Press.

Speck, F. G. (1935) *Naskapi*. Norman: University of Oklahoma Press.

Spencer, H. (1891) *Essays: Scientific, Political, and Speculative* (3 vols). London: Williams & Norgate.

—— (1893) *The Principles of Sociology* (3 vols), 3rd edn. London: Williams & Norgate.

—— (1898) *First Principles*, 5th edn. London: Williams & Norgate.

Stanley, S. and Karsten, D. (1968) 'The Luwa system of the Garbicco subtribe of the Sidama (Southern Ethiopia)', *Paideuma*, 14. 93–102.

Stanley, S. M. (1981) *The New Evolutionary Timetable. Fossils, genes, and the origin of species*. New York: Basic Books.

Stent, G. S. (1981) 'Cerebral hermeneutics', *Journal of Social and Biological Structures*, 4, 107–24

Stenton, F. M. (1971) *Anglo-Saxon England*, 3rd edn. Oxford: Clarendon Press.

Stevenson, R. F. (1968) *Population and political Systems in Tropical Africa*. New York: Columbia University Press.

Steward, J. H. (1955) *Theory of Culture Change. The methodology of multilinear evolution*. University of Illinois Press.

Stewart, F. H. (1977) *Fundamentals of Age-Grouping Systems*. New York: Academic Press.

Stocking, G. W. (1968) *Race, Culture, and Evolution. Essays in the history of anthropology*. New York: Free Press.

—— (1974) 'Some problems in the understanding of nineteenth century evolution in *Readings in the History of Anthropology*, ed. R. Darnell, 407–25. New York: Harper & Row.

Strathern, A. (1983) 'Research in Papua New Guinea. Cross-currents of conflict', *Royal Anthrop. Inst. News*, 58. 4–10.

Strauss, G. *et al.* (eds.) (1974) *Organizational Behavior. Research and issues*, Industrial Relations Research Association Series. University of Wisconsin Press.

Stubbs, W. (1880) *The Constitutional History of England in its Origin and Development* (3 vols). Oxford: Clarendon Press.

Sztompka, P. (1974) *System and Function. Toward a theory of society*. New York: Academic Press.

Tacitus, *Germania*, trans. M. Hutton, revised E. H. Warmington (1970). Loeb Classical Library, London: Heinemann.

Terray, E. (1972) *Marxism and 'Primitive' Societies*, trans. M. Klopper. New York: Monthly Review Press.

Terrien, F. W. and Mills, D. L. (1955) 'The effect of changing size upon the internal structure of organizations', *American Sociological Review*, 20. 11–13.

Thomas, H. L. (1970) 'New evidence for dating the Indo-European dispersal in Europe', in *Indo-European and Indo-Europeans*, eds. G. Cardona, H. M. Hoenigswald, and A. Senn, 199–214. Philadelphia: University of Pennsylvania Press.

Thompson, D'A. W. (1917) *On Growth and Form*, abridged edn. (1961), ed. J. T. Bonner. Cambridge University Press.

Tönnies, F. (1957) *Community and Society*, trans. and ed. C. P. Loomis. (First published 1887.) New York: Harper.

Toulmin, S. E. (1967) 'The evolutionary development of natural science', *American Scientist*, 55. 456–71.

—— (1981) 'Human adaptation', in *The Philosophy of Evolution*, eds. U. J. Jensen and R. Harré, 176–95. Brighton: Harvester Press.

Trivers, R. L. (1971) 'The evolution of reciprocal altruism', *Quarterly Review of Biology*, 46. 35–57.

Tucker, A. N. (1967) 'Fringe Cushitic', *Bulletin of the School of African and Oriental Studies*, 30. 655–80.

—— and Bryan, M. A. (1956) *The Non-Bantu Languages of North-Eastern Africa*. International African Institute: Handbook of African Languages Pt. III. London: Oxford University Press.

—— and —— (1966) *Linguistic Analyses: The non-Bantu languages of North-Eastern Africa*. Oxford University Press.

Tuden, A. and Marshall, C. (1972) 'Political organization: cross-cultural codes 4', *Ethnology*, 11. 436–64.

Turney-High, H. H. (1971) *Primitive War. Its practice and concepts*. 2nd edn. University of South Carolina Press.

Tylor, E. B. (1871) *Primitive Culture. Researches into the development of mythology, philosophy, religion, art, and custom* (2 vols). London: Murray.

Vayda, A. P. (1968) 'Hypotheses about functions of war', in *War: The Anthropology of Armed Conflict*, eds. M. Fried, M. Harris, and R. Murphy, 85–91. New York: Natural History Press.

—— (1971) 'Phases of the process of war and peace among the Marings of New Guinea', *Oceania*, 42. 1–24.

—— (1974) Letter on 'Functions of war', *Man* (NS), 9. 141.

—— (1976) *War in Ecological Perspective*. New York: Plenum.

—— (1979) Review of C. R. Hallpike 'Bloodshed and Vengeance in the Papuan Mountains', *American Anthropologist*, 81. 424–5.

—— and McKay, B. J. (1978) 'New directions in ecology and ecological anthropology', in *Human Behavior and Adaptation*, eds. N. Blurton and V. Reynolds, 33–51. Symposia of the Society for the Study of Human Biology, 18.

Waddington, C. H. (1967) Comments in *Mathematical Challenges to the Neo-Darwinian Interpretation of Evolution*, eds. P. S. Moorhead and M. M. Kaplan, 12–13. Philadelphia: Wistar Institute Press.

—— (1975) *The Evolution of an Evolutionist*. New York: Cornell University Press.

Wallace-Hadrill, J. M. (1961) *The Long-Haired Kings and Other Studies in Frankish History*. New York: Barnes & Noble.

Warner, L. (1937) *A Black Civilization*. New York: Harper.

Webster, G. and Goodwin, B. C. (1982) 'The origin of species: a structuralist approach', *Journal of Social and Biological Structures*, 5. 15–47.

Wedgwood, C. H. (1930) 'Some aspects of warfare in Melanesia', *Oceania*, 1. 5–33.

Wheatley, P. (1971) *The Pivot of the Four Quarters. A preliminary enquiry into the origin and character of the ancient Chinese city*. Chicago: Aldine.

White, (1959) *The Evolution of Culture. The development of civilization to the fall of Rome*. New York: McGraw Hill.

Whitelock, D. (ed.) (1970) *English Historical Documents*. Vol. 1 c.*500–1042*. London: Eyre Methuen.

Wilbur, C. M. (1943) *Slavery in China During the Former Han Dynasty*. Field Museum of Natural History.

Willey, G. R. (1960) Comments during symposium session, in *City Invincible*: *A symposium on urbanization and cultural development in the Ancient Near East*, eds. C. H. Kraeling and R. M. Adams, 44–5. Chicago University Press.

Williams, G. C. (1966) *Adaptation and Natural Selection. A critique of some current evolutionary thought*. Princeton University Press.

Williams, M. (1973) 'The logical status of the theory of natural selection and other evolutionary controversies', in *The Methodological Unity of Science*, ed. M. Bunge, 84–102. Dordrecht: Reidel.

Wilson, J. A. (1960) 'Egypt through the New Kingdom: civilization without cities', in *City Invincible*: *A symposium on urbanization and cultural development in the Ancient Near East*, eds. C. H. Kraeling and R. M. Adams, 124–64. Chicago University Press.

Wittfogel, K. A. (1957) *Oriental Despotism. A comparative study of total power*. Yale University Press.

Wolf, E., and Palerm, A. (1955) 'Irrigation in the old Acolhua domain, Mexico', *Southwestern Journal of Anthropology*, 11. 265–81.

Wright, H. T. and Johnson, G. (1975) 'Population, exchange, and early state formation in southwestern Iran', *American Anthropologist*, 77. 267–89.

Wynne-Edwards, V. C. (1962) *Animal Dispersion in Relation to Social Behaviour*. Edinburgh: Oliver & Boyd.

Young, R. M. (1969) 'Malthus and the evolutionists: the common context of biological and social theory', *Past and Present*, 43. 109–41.

INDEX